Introducing
Revit® Architecture 2008

Introducing
Revit® Architecture 2008

BIM FOR BEGINNERS W/ CD

EDDY KRYGIEL | GREG DEMCHAK | TATJANA DZAMBAZOVA

WILEY PUBLISHING, INC.

Acquisitions Editor: Willem Knibbe
Development Editor: Laurene Sorensen
Production Editor: Eric Charbonneau
Copy Editor: Tiffany Taylor
Production Manager: Tim Tate
Vice President and Executive Group Publisher: Richard Swadley
Vice President and Executive Publisher: Joseph B. Wikert
Vice President and Publisher: Neil Edde
Permissions Editor: Laura Atkinson
Media Development Specialist: Laura Atkinson
Book Designer: Caryl Gorska
Compositor: Chris Gillespie, Happenstance Type-O-Rama
Proofreaders: Heather Dweller, Ian Golder
Indexer: Jack Lewis
Anniversary Logo Design: Richard Pacifico
Cover Designer: Ryan Sneed
Cover Image: SPBR Architects

Dear Reader

Thank you for choosing *Introducing Revit® Architecture 2008*. This book is part of a family of premium-quality Sybex books, all written by outstanding authors who combine practical experience with a gift for teaching.

Sybex was founded in 1976. More than 30 years later, we're still committed to producing consistently exceptional books. With each of our titles we're working hard to set a new standard for the industry. From the paper we print on to the authors we work with, our goal is to bring you the best books available.

I hope you see all that reflected in these pages. I'd be very interested to hear your comments and get your feedback on how we're doing. Feel free to let me know what you think about this or any other Sybex book by sending me an email at nedde@wiley.com, or if you think you've found an error in this book, please visit http://wiley.custhelp.com. Customer feedback is critical to our efforts at Sybex.

Best regards,

Neil Edde
Vice President and Publisher
Sybex, an Imprint of Wiley

Dedication

For my two girls, Zoë and Maya. And a special thanks to my co-authors, for all the voodoo that you do so well.

— Eddy

To my many mentors and lifelong companions.

— Greg

To you Mom, wherever you might be.

— Your Tanjicka

Acknowledgments

Hats off to the innovators who conceptualized, designed, and made Revit happen. You have changed the world! ■ Huge thanks to all the faithful followers! Without you, Revit wouldn't be what it is today. ■ Personal thanks to the grand masters Philippe Drouant and Phil Read for their heroic dedication and help; to Simone Cappochin and Kubik & Nemeth, who keep on doing beautiful stuff with Revit and are willing to share it with us; and to our friends, Martin Taurer and Paul Woddy. ■ To Matt Jezyk, for being one of the tireless and ever-dedicated pioneers of Revit. To Erik Egbertson for his support, comments, and help; and Emmanuel Di Giacommo, who relentlessly shared his help and knowledge. ■ To all our friends who have contributed to this book and to the development of Revit, we wish to extend our sincerest gratitude. ■ And finally, thanks are due our excellent support team at Sybex: Laurene Sorensen, who helped us develop and focus the content; Tiffany Taylor, for making us look good in print; Eric Charbonneau for keeping things on track; and Willem Knibbe for his continuous support and upbeat attitude in the face of deadlines.

About the Authors

Eddy Krygiel is a registered architect, a LEED Accredited Professional, and an Autodesk Authorized Author at BNIM Architects. He has been using Revit since version 5.1 to complete projects ranging from single-family residences and historic remodels to 1.12-million-square-foot office buildings. Eddy is responsible for implementing BIM at his firm and consults for other architecture and contracting firms looking to implement BIM. For the last three years, he has been teaching Revit to practicing architects and architectural students in the Kansas City area and has lectured around the nation on the use of BIM in the construction industry. Eddy also coauthored a paper on sustainability and BIM that was presented at the 2006 AIA Technology in Architectural Practice conference.

Greg Demchak is a designer, a technology advocate, and an urban explorer. He holds architectural degrees from the University of Oregon and Massachusetts Institute of Technology. He is a product designer for Revit Architecture, and has been working on the development of Revit since the year 2000. He has been teaching Revit at the Boston Architectural College since 2003. He currently lives in Massachusetts.

Tatjana Dzambazova is a Product Manager for Revit Architecture. Before joining Autodesk, she practiced architecture for 12 years in Vienna and London. In the last 6 years she has focused on evangelizing technology and established herself as an internationally renowned speaker who has fostered relationships with architects and industry leaders around the globe. In her spare time, she lives with lions in Africa, goes to the theater, and enjoys reading books about destitute souls and existential crisis. She currently lives in the United States.

CONTENTS AT A GLANCE

Contents

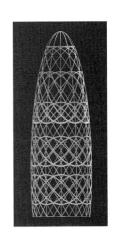

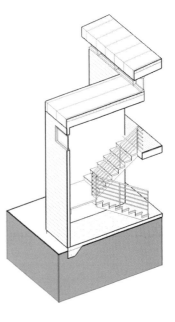

Introduction

Welcome to the first edition of *Introducing Revit Architecture*, which was written based on the 2008 release.

It was great fun writing the book. We enjoyed the synergy of three friends, three architects, three authors collaborating to bring this project into reality. But mostly, we were all driven by the feeling that we're doing something great: introducing Revit to those who have not been acquainted with its incredible power and its ability to put some fun back into using software and designing architecture.

This book is written for beginners who have never seen or may have just about heard about Revit. It's for architects of any generation—you don't need to be a high-tech wizard to get into Revit. Toward that end, we wanted to make a book that is as much about architecture as it is about software. We think we've succeeded, because the book is full of real-world examples that show how to use Revit practically and creatively.

This book is also for the seasoned user, who may have already received some training and is looking to discover useful tips and tricks that many users aren't aware of. We've added many time-saving and inspiring concepts to the book to get you motivated and to help you on your journey into the new era of Building Information Modeling.

This book will help you learn Revit and BIM basics easily and efficiently via straightforward explanations, real-world examples, and practical tutorials that focus squarely on accomplishing vital Revit tasks.

Our book begins with an overview of BIM concepts before introducing the Revit interface. You'll start working with basic modeling features, learning how to create walls, floors, roofs, and stairs. The book then explains how to use components and provides descriptions and examples of Revit's suite of editing tools.

The book continues by looking deeper into the capabilities of core modeling elements. We explain how Revit works with other applications, show you how to document the model for construction, and explore how you can integrate annotations into the model.

After we discuss printing to paper and files, we thoroughly explain the Family Editor. We explore worksets and team collaboration, followed by a look at some of Revit's more advanced options. The book concludes with a chapter on troubleshooting and best practices; that's where we try to share our practical experience with you so you can avoid common beginner pitfalls (and enjoy beginner's luck). Also featured is an Appendix containing inspirational Revit projects.

The CD included with this volume features all the tutorial files necessary to complete the book's exercises, plus sample families and a trial version of the Revit software.

Enjoy! Revit has changed our lives. Maybe it will change yours as well.

We welcome your feedback! Please feel free to email us at `IntroducingRevit2008@gmail.com`.

Eddy Krygiel
Greg Demchak
Tatjana Dzambazova

CHAPTER 1

Understanding BIM

> *"A great building must begin with the unmeasurable, must go through measurable means when it is being designed and in the end must be unmeasurable."*—LOUIS KAHN

Building Information Modeling is an emerging approach to the design, analysis, and documentation of buildings. At its core, BIM is about the management of information throughout the entire lifecycle of a design process, from early conceptual design through construction administration, and even into facilities management. By information we are referring to all the inputs that go into a building design: the number of windows, the cost of materials, the size of heating and cooling equipment, the total energy footprint of the building, and so on. This information is captured in a digital model that can then be outputted as coordinated documents, be shared across discipline, and serve as centralized design management tool. With a tool like Revit, you will reap the benefits of fully coordinated documents, but this represents just the tip of the BIM iceberg.

Implementing BIM requires careful planning if you are to achieve successful and predictable results. In this chapter, we'll present the basics of BIM and summarize how BIM differs from traditional drafting–based methodologies. We will explain the key characteristics of Revit, and how Revit is truly designed to deliver the benefits of Building Information Modeling.

Topics we'll cover include:

- **A brief history of architectural documentation**
- **Advantages of a BIM approach**
- **How BIM is different from CAD**
- **Why Revit?**
- **Revit Concepts**
- **Types of elements in Revit**
- **Tips for getting started in Revit**

A Brief History of Architectural Documentation

The production of design documents has traditionally been an exercise in drawing lines to represent a building. These documents become instruction sets: an annotated booklet that describes how the building is to be built.   The Plan, Section, and Elevation: all skillfully drafted, line by line, drawing by drawing.   Whether physical or digital, these traditional drawing sets are composed of graphics—where each line is part of a larger abstraction meant to convey design intent so that a building can eventually be constructed.   When Filippo Brunelleschi drew the plans for Santa Maria del Fiore (Figure 1.1) in Renaissance Italy, the drawings represented ideas of what the building would look like. They were simplified representations of a completed project, used to convey ideas to the patron. In those days, the architect also played the role of builder, so there was no risk of losing information between the documentation of the building and actually building it. This was the age of the master builder, where architect and builder shared the same responsibility and roles. Even so, Brunelleschi still needed to communicate his vision to his patrons and his workers, and produced not only beautiful drawings, but also built elaborate scale models so that others could easily visualize the project.

Figure 1.1

Santa Maria del Fiore; *image courtesy of Laura Lesniewski*

As buildings became more and more complex, specialization in the design and construction process emerged. In turn, this led to the need for more elaborate forms of information exchange. One person was no longer responsible for both the design and construction phases, so it became necessary for designers to convey design intent with richer amounts of information and instructions.

Jump ahead in time to the twentieth century. The use of steel had been fully embraced, allowed buildings to reach higher than ever before; the age of the skyscraper and modern construction was in full force. Kansas City, Missouri, 1931. The Power and Light Building (Figure 1.2) was erected in only 19 months. An art deco testament to the boldness of the times, the building was built without the use of modern earth-moving machinery or other heavy equipment. The drawing set for a building of this size in the 1930s would have been about 30 pages long. The Power and Light Building was more complex than its predecessors but far simpler than today's large commercial projects. There were no data or telecom systems, no air conditioning other than operable windows, and no security systems other than locks on the doors.

Figure 1.2

Power and Light Building, Kansas City, MO

Fast-forward to the present day. Buildings are more complex than ever before. Documentation sets span all disciplines, and are hundreds of pages long. The number of people that will touch a set of drawings—to produce them, evaluate them, or use them to build the building—has become huge. Integrated building systems continue to expand with the growth of technology. Today, we have more security, electrical, data, telecom, HVAC, and energy requirement than ever before. (see Figure 1.4). The amount of information that goes into a documentation set can no longer be thought of as abstract approximations. The cost of error is too high, and the production of coordinated drawings has become the staple of the profession. The use of computer-based technology has replaced the use of pen and paper, yet remains a largely a 2 D representational system. Drawing and editing lines has become faster and more efficient, but in the end, they are still collections of manually created, non-intelligent lines and text.

Figure 1.3

The founders and some original members of Revit technology, having a tug-of-war at a release party, circa 2000.

Figure 1.4
Layers of design

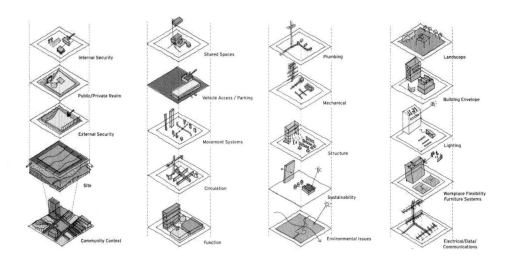

1998—dawn of the Internet boom. Technology companies are flourishing, and start-ups are a dime a dozen. In the suburbs of Boston, a new approach to architectural documentation is about to be launched. The premise is simple: Model the building once, and let architects view, edit, and annotate the model from any point of view, at any time. A change to the model from any view simultaneously updates all other views. Drawings cease to be separate, uncoordinated collections of lines, and become by-products of a model-based design approach. Revit is born, and with it the foundation for a new approach to how buildings are designed, evaluated, represented, and documented. Welcome to the world of Building Information Modeling.

Advantages of a BIM Approach

The ultimate benefits of BIM are still emerging in the market, and will radically change the way buildings are designed and built. A shift in process and expectation is happening in the construction market, and architects are stepping up to the challenge. The focus is shifting from traditional 2D abstractions to on-demand simulations of building performance, usage, and cost. This is no longer a futuristic fantasy, but a practical reality. In the age of information-rich digital models we can now have all disciplines involved with a project sharing a single database. Architecture, structure, mechanical, infrastructure, and construction are tied together and able to coordinate in ways never before possible. Models can now be sent directly to fabrication machines, bypassing the need for traditional shop drawings. Energy analysis can be done at the very outset of design, and construction costs are becoming more and more predictable. These are just a few of the exciting opportunities that a BIM approach offers.

BIM has shifted how designers and contractors look at the entire building process, from preliminary design through construction documentation, into actual construction, and even into post-construction building management. With BIM, a parametric 3D model is used to autogenerate traditional building abstractions such as plans, sections, elevations, details, and schedules. Drawings produced using BIM are not just discrete collections of manually coordinated lines, but interactive representations of a model.

Working in a model-based framework guarantees that a change in one view will propagate to all other views of the model. As you shift elements in plan, they change in elevation and section. If you remove a door from your model, it simultaneously gets removed from all views, and your door schedule is updated. This enhanced document-delivery system allows unprecedented control over the quality and coordination of the document set.

With the advent of BIM, designers and builders have a better way to control and display information, with some added benefits. Some of the advantages that first-time users can expect to realize are as follows:

- 3D design visualization of the building and its spaces improves understanding of the building and its spaces and gives users the ability to show a variety of design options to both the team and the client.
- Integrated design documents minimize errors in cross-referencing and keynoting, allowing clearer, more precise documents.
- Interference checking permits the user to immediately see conflicts among architectural, structural, and mechanical elements in 3D, and avoids costly errors on site.
- Automated schedules of building components (like door and room-area schedules) are generated, improving visibility of costs and quantities.
- Material quantity take-offs allow better predictability and planning.
- Sustainable strategies enable you to design better buildings and make a better world.

How BIM Is Different from CAD

The key difference between BIM and CAD is that a traditional CAD system uses many separate (usually 2D) documents to explain a building. These documents are created separately and have no intelligent connection between them. A wall in plan is represented with two parallel lines, with no understanding that those lines represent the same wall in section. The possibility of uncoordinated data is very high. The change management created by CAD is a tedious and error-prone process. BIM takes the opposite approach: It assembles all information into one location and cross-links that data among associated objects. (See Figures 1.5 and 1.6.)

By and large, CAD is strictly a 2D technology with a specific need to output a collection of lines and text on a page. These lines have no inherent meaning, whether inside the computer or on the printed sheet. CAD drafting has its efficiencies and advantages over pen and paper, but is really just a simulation of the act of drafting. This form of drawing is how architects and other designers have worked for the last couple of hundred years.

Historically, the designer drew a set of plans and then used those plans to manually derive sections, elevations, and details. During the development of a project, if any of those items changed, the designer had to modify each of the other drawings that were affected to take the change into account. For a long time, this meant getting out an erasure and an erasure shield, and spending days picking up changes. Today, you can use the Delete key, but the goal is fundamentally the same. This is where BIM makes a significant departure from legacy CAD platforms.

Figure 1.5
Typical CAD outputs

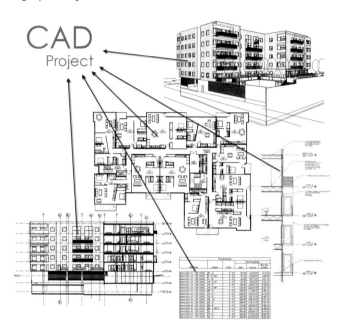

Figure 1.6
Typical BIM outputs

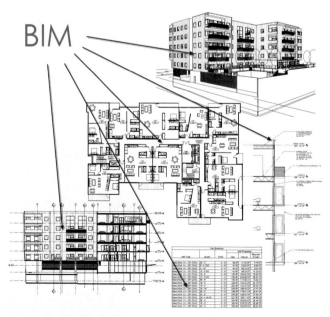

The beauty of BIM is that it manages change for you. Unlike CAD, the intent of BIM is to let the computer take responsibility for redundant interactions and calculations, providing you, the designer, with more time to design and evaluate your decisions. A core feature of BIM is that it allows you to create and modify everything in one design context. The system will propagate changes to all relevant views in the project. As you model in plan, the elevations, sections, and details are also being generated. Where you make the change is up to you, and the system will take care of the rest. With a BIM tool such as Revit, if you change the size of a window opening in elevation, this change is made throughout the entire model.

Here are a few other big differences between BIM and CAD:

BIM adopts a task-oriented rather than an object-oriented methodology. In CAD, you draw two lines (objects) to represent a wall. In BIM, the task of creating a wall is presented in the form of an interactive tool named `create wall`. This wall has properties like width, height, bearing or nonbearing, demolished or new, interior or exterior, fire rating, and materials (such as boards or brick). The wall interacts with other walls to join geometries and clean up connections, showing how the walls will be built. Similarly, if you add a door, it's more than four lines and an arc; it's a door in plan and elevation. Adding it to the wall automatically creates an opening in the wall in all views where the door is visible. As we will discover, the tools available for walls are specific to walls, allowing you to attach walls to roofs and floors, punch openings, and change the layered construction of the wall. Again, all of these interactions are not just properties, but focused on specific tasks associated with a wall component.

BIM keeps you honest. An additional advantage of a BIM methodology is that you can't cheat your design. Because the elements have properties based on real-life properties, you'll find it difficult to fake elements within the design. If you have a door in plan, it automatically appears in the other associated views. In a CAD-based system, this can be easy to overlook, because the door has to be manually transcribed from plan to section and elevation. Because BIM is based on actual assemblies it's very difficult to misrepresent dimensions or objects within the model.

BIM is more than a modeler. Other software packages, like SketchUp, Rhino, and 3ds Max, are excellent modeling applications. However, these modeling applications don't have the ability to document your design for construction, nor be leveraged downstream. This is not to say these tools don't play a part in a BIM workflow. Many architects use these tools to generate concept models, which can then be brought into a BIM application and progress through design, analysis, and documentation.

BIM is a data-driven design tool. BIM lets you create custom content and libraries throughout the course of your project. It's much more than a drafting application.

BIM is based on an architectural classification system—not "layers." Because a building model is an assembly of meaningful, to-be-built objects, you control visibility and graphics of objects using a rational list of well-understood categories. This is different from CAD, where every line belongs to a layer, and it is up the user to manage all these layers. For example, in Revit there is no way to accidentally place a window into the "wall" layer. In a BIM world, layers become obsolete—after all, in the real world buildings are not made of abstract color-coded layers.

Potential Hazards

One of the powers of Revit is the ability to work in a single-file environment where the design and documentation of the building happens on a holistic model.. This can also be a disadvantage if not taken seriously and given full consideration. Users who may be quick to make changes without thinking how such a change will ripple through the model can cause unintended problems if not careful. Revit is a parametric modeler—it creates relationships between building elements in order to streamline the design process. For example, if you delete a Level from your model, then all the walls, doors, and furniture on that level will also be deleted. Likewise, if you delete a wall, all the doors and windows in that wall will be deleted. If you underlay the roof in your second floor so that you can see the extents of the roof overhang, deleting the lines that represent the roof overhang actually means deleting the roof! These are some basic mistakes that new users might encounter as they re-adjust their mental model, and come to see the model as much more than lines, but actual building elements. A nice consequence of this is that Revit will not let you leave elements floating around in an abstract 3D vacuum. You will not have views cluttered with fragmented geometry from some other file, exploded blocks, or mysterious lines. At the same time, you must take care when making large-scale changes to a model, especially the further along in the design process you go.

Anticipate that tasks will take different amounts of time when compared to a CAD production environment. It isn't an apples-to-apples equation. You'll perform tasks in Revit that you never had in CAD; conversely, some of the CAD tasks that took weeks (chamfering and trimming thousands of lines to draw walls properly or making a door schedule) take almost no time using Revit.

If you've never worked in a 3D model–based environment, it can be frustrating at first to move from a strictly 2D world to a 3D one. At the same time, it's really quite nice to have immediate access to perspective views at any time! The Revit world is one with a white screen, no layers, and no x-references. This often leads to generic comparisons and some growing pains, but just stick with it, be patient, and you'll be hooked in no time at all. With any transition there is a learning curve; as you begin to use Revit you'll quickly see the benefits.

Why Revit?

Revit is the newest and most technologically advanced BIM application. Currently, a number of BIM applications are on the market, provided by a host of different software vendors. Although most other products in today's market are based on technology that is 20+ years old, Revit was designed from the ground up as a BIM tool to specifically address problem areas of the architecture, engineering, and construction (AEC) industry: communication, coordination, and change management. As you complete more projects with Revit, you'll begin to understand some of its advanced functionality. Being able to go direct to fabrication with your designs, provide digital shop drawing submittals, and execute 4D construction planning are just a few of the possibilities.

Revit is a technological platform that supports architectural, structural, and mechanical disciplines. It's supported by a patented parametric change engine that is unmatched in sophistication. It's also the leading software package in the international market. It's not the only package out there, but it offers the most holistic approach.

Revit Concepts

Revit comes from *Revise Instantly* and is built for managing change, something that we have to do in our practice all the time.

Parametric Objects and Parametric Relationships

We all hear about *parametric objects*, but what makes an object parametric? A parametric object is a smart object that can change its size, materials, and graphic look but is consistently the same object. For example, think of a door. A single flush door can be 32″, 34″, or 36″ (70, 75, 80, 85, or 90cm). It can also be painted or solid wood. All of these sizes and colors can be part of the same door family, with different parametric values applied.

Or consider a table—it can be the same shape but made out of wood or metal, with a glass or wood top, and with the top extending over the legs or flush with them. Again, they're all in the same table family; only the parametric values are different. The parameters are meaningful ways to create variations of an element. And most importantly, this information is always accessible, reversible, editable, and schedulable.

In most CAD systems, to accommodate all these doors, you need to make not only a separate block for each representation (thus, plan, elevation, and section typically comprise 7 or 8 blocks) but also as many blocks as sizes you need. If you then wish to make a table that is 4′-0″ square (50/50) to 5′-0″ square (70/70), you use the scale command that unfortunately makes the table legs bigger than needed because they resize along the table top! A parametric object allows you to affect a change on each parameter without affecting the others unless desired. So, you can change the size of the table legs independent from the table top, and so on.

Bidirectional Associativity

Objects with parameters that can be edited are nothing new in the world of software. But what makes Revit unique is its ability to create relationships *between* objects. This ability has been referred to as the *Parametric Change Engine*, and is a core technological advantage built into Revit. Walls, for example, can be attached to roofs. If the roof changes to a new shape or size, all walls attached to the roof automatically adapt to the roof shape. Walls, Floors, Roofs, and Components all have explicit relationships to Levels. If a Level changes height, all elements associated with that level will update automatically. When you change the size of a room by moving walls, you are changing not only the wall, but everything that wall effects in the model: the size of the room, color-fill diagrams, ceilings, floors, and the doors and windows in the wall, and any dimensions to that wall.

The parametrics are extended to annotations and sheet management as well. Tags are not simple graphics with a text notation: They are interactive graphical parameters of the element being tagged. To edit a tag is to edit the element, and vice versa. When you're laying out sheets and a section view is placed onto a sheet, the section key automatically references the sheet number and detail number on the sheet. Change the sheet number, and the section tag updates instantly. *This* is what a real parametric engine is and what ensures total coordination of your documentation. This parametric engine guarantees that a "change anywhere is a change everywhere."

You'll learn a lot about this concept and the value of it by doing the exercises in this book, but let's start with a simple example. If you draw a wall in CAD and place a dimension, the dimension reads the length of the wall. If you change the length of the wall to 6′-0″ (2.4m), the width dimension, because it's associative, also changes to 6′-0″ (2.4m). But Revit goes even further: When you change the dimension to 4′-0″ (1.5m), the wall length changes to 4'-0" (1.5m). As you can see, dimensions in Revit not only report information, but also drive the design and size of objects.

Embedded Relationships

Revit has embedded intelligent relationships among elements that are in logical relationship so that when one is affected, all related objects follow the change. To illustrate this, let's try a *smart move*. Look at Figures 1.7 and 1.8. To make one of the rooms smaller and move the south wall 3′-0″ (1m), you pick the wall and drag it. The four walls perpendicular to and intersecting this wall extend themselves, and the room area automatically updates. All you do is move the one wall. There is no need to create complex window selections, no need to use trim and extend tools, and no need to re-compute room areas. Revit does all of this for you with a few simple mouse clicks.

Now, what if your client doesn't want those other walls to lengthen or move? Making this change is also easily done. To move just that one wall and not affect the contiguous walls or areas, select the wall, and then select **Options → Disallow Join**.

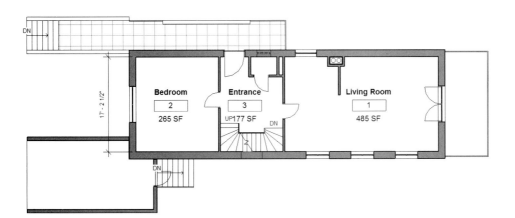

Figure 1.7

The floor plan before the change

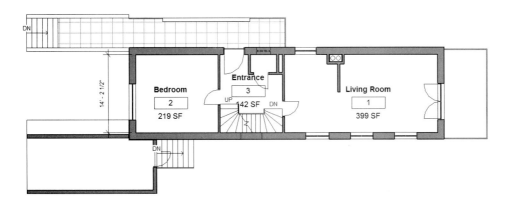

Figure 1.8

The same floor plan after moving the wall

If for some reason this automatic behavior is not to your liking—perhaps you are dealing with a renovation, and do not want to have existing conditions be affected by new construction—this is not a problem. Revit allows you to break the "smart" relationships if needed. You can also lock elements into place to prevent unintended consequences. However, for the most part, you'll find the default embedded behaviors make sense, and you'll even start to take them for granted once you get into the swing of things.

User-Defined Rules

During the design phase, you may want to maintain some dimensional rules and make sure these are not violated. Things like keeping the structural gridlines fixed or keeping a hallway a fixed width are some typical examples. You want to lock this rule down, and keep it persistent as the design evolves. These design rules are used all the time, but not many software applications let you capture this design intent and apply it in the model. For instance, you want your door jamb positioned always at 4″ (25cm) from the wall corner; you want the three windows in a room to be always positioned at equal distances;

you want the sill height for your windows to always be 4′-0″ (1.20m) above the floor. You want the rules/relationship to be remembered regardless of how many changes occur in the design process. Revit allows you to define and *lock* these relationships with *constraints*: explicit dimensional rules that keep elements locked to one another.

Types of Elements in Revit

Every parametric object in Revit is considered a *family*. In this section, we'll discuss how Revit organizes data. Then we'll explain the available types of families, the principles of their behavior, how to create them, and where to find them. The categories are divided into two primary buckets: Model categories and Annotation categories.

How Revit Organizes Data

Revit uses a building-industry-specific classification to organize all the data in the model. This system of organization manages relationships among classes of elements as well as their graphical display. At the top of this organization is a fixed list of categories into which all elements are grouped.

Model Categories

Model categories include all representations of physical object types that are typically found in buildings. This includes 2D elements that are used to add more detail to the model, such as floor patterns and ceiling hatch. For elements that don't fit into Revit's categorization system, the Generic Model category can be used.

Annotation Categories

Annotation categories are all the annotations, symbols, and 2D data added to a view to describe how the building is to be constructed. For example, all walls in a project are members of the model category Walls, and all wall tags are members of the annotation category Wall Tags. Annotation categories also include 2D graphics that are overlaid on the model in order to convey additional information about the model. These annotations are view-specific and appear only in the view they were created in. The one exception to this rule is entities created in dependent views. Examples include dimensions, tags, callouts, section marks, and text notes.

To view all the model and annotation categories, go to **Settings → Object Styles**. The table of categories is shown in Figure 1.9

Annotation categories don't appear in 3D views.

Below each category can be many subcategories. If Door is the main category, the elevation swing, frame/mullion, glass, opening, panel swing, and any other user-defined elements that can be made when creating the door are listed. The beauty of this system is that you can control the visibility of each subcategory independently. So, in our door example, you can turn off the door leaf and still see the frame, mullions, and glass. As Figures 1.10 through 1.12 show how different sub-components of a door can be turned on and off in a view.

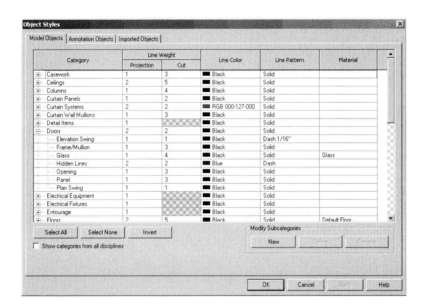

Figure 1.9

The Object Styles dialog sets the graphics for all categories and subcategories in the project

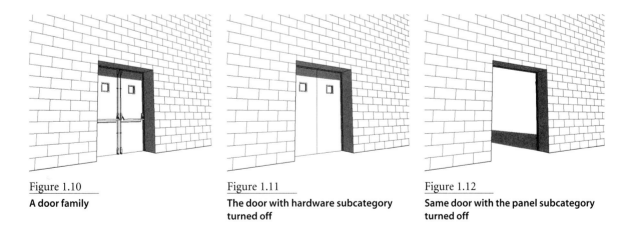

Figure 1.10

A door family

Figure 1.11

The door with hardware subcategory turned off

Figure 1.12

Same door with the panel subcategory turned off

Controlling the Visibility of Elements in Revit

As you learned earlier in this chapter, there are no layers in Revit. You may be asking yourself, "Just a second! How will I live without layers?"

Let's look at the origin of layers. In the predigital era (and still, in some offices) projects were drawn manually on translucent paper called *trace*. Multiple layers of paper were stacked and shuffled to create different representations of the same plan. Furniture might go on one sheet, mechanical systems on another, and so forth. In a paper-based workflow, to make a change, you erased something on one sheet and redrew it on another.

CAD applications employ a digital version of trace to control the visibility of elements. Their digital layers allow you to move an element from one layer to another.

Instead of using layers, Revit uses object categories. For example, instead of putting door handles on their own layer so they show only in certain views, Revit has commands to control the visibility of elements. If you don't want to show the glass in windows, doors, or curtain walls, you can turn them off in the view.

Families in Revit

Independently of whether it's a model or annotation category, a Revit family can be a system family, a standard family, or an in-place family.

System Families

Examples of system families are walls, roofs, stairs, railings, ramps, and mullions. To create such a family, you need to duplicate an existing family of the same type and modify it. So to create a new wall type, you must duplicate an existing wall. To reuse system families from one project to another, select **File → Transfer Project Standards**.

Figure 1.13

The Visibility/ Graphic Overrides dialog controls visibility of categories on a view-by-view basis

Examples of system families include walls, roofs, stairs, railings, and ramps. To create new types of System Families with unique properties, you duplicate an existing type, and then modify its properties. This method of duplicating a type to create new types is used frequently in Revit, so get use to this concept. While you cannot save a system family to a shared library as a standalone component, it is possible to transfer these families between projects. We'll go into more detail about creating and using system families later in this book.

We'll go into more detail about creating and using system families later in this book.

Standard Families

Standard families are created outside of the project environment—still in Revit, but in a specific environment called the Family Editor, designed for creating library objects. System families have their own file format extension (.rfa) and can be stored or edited as separate files outside of a model and loaded at any time into the project.

To see how Revit organizes family objects, choose **File → Load Library → Load Family**. You'll see the folders in which these families are stored.

To create a new standard family, you can either duplicate an existing one and modify it in the Family Editor or create a new one, using the family templates included with each copy of Revit. Revit doesn't require you to know any programming or scripting language in order to create new smart, parametric families. This is an important advantage of Revit.

To open a template, choose **File → New → Family**. Embedded in each template are smart behavior characteristics of the family you're creating. Doors, windows, balusters, casework, columns, curtain wall panels, entourage, furniture, massing elements, generic objects, and plantings are all examples of standard Revit families.

In-Place Families

In-place families are custom objects that are specific to a certain context within the model. A complex sweep as a railing fence on a site is an example of an in-place family.

Tips for Getting Started in Revit

Knowing how and where to begin your journey can be a challenge, and we want ot give you a few pointers. Although this list isn't complete by any means, it should help steer you in the right direction:

Begin with the end in your mind. When you begin any project, planning is always a good way to start. You can set yourself up for a successful implementation from the beginning by using a bit of forethought about your process, workflow, and desired outcome.

Get your project and office standards in place early. As design professionals, we have a tendency to develop unique graphic conventions and styles for our documents. This is a specific area where good planning leads to a good project. If possible, get your standards in place before you begin a project. Revit does an excellent job of getting you started with a good template of graphic standards to work with. However, if you're like most architects, an application right out of the box is never quite nice enough. Revit provides a good starting point for customization, and with some up-front time, you soon can have your project and office standards up and running.

Remember that the first project you do in Revit is a change in methodology. You're leveraging technology to help you change the way you approach design and documentation. Don't expect the process to have the same workflow as it did in a CAD-based system. Try to stay flexible in your expectations and schedule, and allow yourself time to adapt to the change.

Don't try to conquer the world on the first project. There are many advantages to using BIM as a design and documentation methodology. As this process becomes more mainstream within the industry, those benefits will only increase. All of these things and more are possible with the use of Revit, but it will take a couple of projects to get there. Tailor the use of BIM to the project, and use the features that will maximize the benefits of using BIM. Choose your goals realistically based on the expertise of your project team, and plan in advance so those can be successful.

One of the most important rules to follow as you begin your project is to model the building as it will be built, and keep in mind that you do not need to model every condition three-dimensionally.

Model correctly from the beginning. We can't stress this enough. As you refine your design, it's critical to begin modeling correctly from the beginning so you don't have to fix things later. What does this mean? As an example, think of your wall. Does it sit on the floor, or does the floor attach to the wall? If you can begin to think about how your project will be assembled, it will save you a lot of time at the end. It's good practice to plan ahead, but remember that Revit will allow you to make major changes at any stage in the process, and maintain coordination.

Get information into the project as soon as it becomes known. A key advantage of using Revit is the ability to change your project schedule. In a traditional design process, most of the effort on a project is realized during the construction-document phase. At that time, a typical project has the most staff working on the project, and it can be fairly difficult to implement major changes to the project design. This is due to the complexity of the documents by this time and the amount of effort for the team to redraw all the changed information. You'll find that with Revit, design change is largely managed by the software itself. This gives you a great deal of flexibility in both your design and documentation. Take advantage of this shift in the process, and add information to your model early. It can be in the form of more detailed content or show the material construction of your wall system. Remember that you can change all this information much more quickly and easily than you ever could in CAD, so don't assume you're locked into the information you displayed early in the design process.

Plan for better communication among team members early in the process.
Communication within a team is critical for understanding a project and documenting it successfully. One of the downfalls inherent in a CAD-based system is that there
is no connection between the different files that make up the drawing set. This phe-
nomenon carries through to the project team and is a function of project workflow
and project management. In CAD, it's possible for team members to work in some
degree of isolation. They aren't forced to immediately reconcile their changes with
changes made by their teammates. Revit's single-file environment forces a much
higher degree of team communication between not only the architects, but also your
structural and mechanical engineers.

Don't try to model everything. Most of us have drafted in a 2D environment until
now. Moving to a 3D world is a significant change. Do you have to model every single
screw? every mullion? every stud? That's a good question. The simple answer is no,
you don't have to, and in fact you should not attempt to do so. Like any BIM system, Revit isn't 100 percent 3D information. Typical workstations aren't capable of
handling all the data of a building in model form. Additionally, few projects have the
time in their schedule to model the screws in a sheet of gypsum board or the sealant
around all the windows; some of that information is best presented in 2D or in the
specifications. This still leaves you with a wide range of options for modeling. In the
beginning, err on the side of simplicity. It's far easier to add complexity to your
model later on as you gain experience and confidence than it is to troubleshoot
over-constrained parameters early in the process. Start with the big ideas: walls,
openings, roofs, and so forth. Work your way down to a comfortable level of detail
for both you and your computer.

Organize your team. A BIM project team includes three basic technical roles. These
roles are interchangeable, especially on smaller projects with fewer team members.
However small the team, it's useful to make sure all these roles are filled:

- *Content/Family Creator*—The Family Creator's primary role is to create the
  parametric content in the Revit model. This is typically someone with 3D experience who also has a firm understanding of Revit and Revit families. The families,
  as you'll see later, have parameters that can control visibility, size, color, proportion, and a number of other things.

- *Designer*—This is the person or team whose primary responsibility is to figure
  out what the project will look like and how it will be made. They create walls,
  floors, and roofs, and locate windows, doors, and other building elements.

- *Documenter*—This role supplies the bulk of the documentation. It consists of
  drafting some of the 2D linework over portions of the 3D model to show detail,
  adding annotations and keynotes and creating details.

Ask for help. If you get stuck along the way, don't assume you're alone. There are myriad resources to help you find a specific solution to your problem. Chances are, someone has tried the same thing before. In our digital age, a wealth of information is available online, so before you spend hours trying to work through a particular problem, try tapping some of the existing resources:

- *Revit Help menu*—Your first stop, if or when you get stuck, should be the Revit Help menu. It's one of the easier and more robust Help menus out there, and it can give you a lot of useful information very quickly. It's also the most accessible help source. As with most applications, it's at the far right of the menu bar.

- *Subscription Support*—If you have bought Revit on subscription, Revit Subscription Support offers an exemplary web-based support system. Their responses are speedy, and their advice is top-notch. If you need information more quickly, Revit also has an online knowledge base of FAQs that is available without a subscription. Both of these resources can be accessed at www.autodesk.com/revit.

- *AUGI*—Autodesk User Group International (AUGI) is also an excellent source for tips and tricks. It's an online service managed by Autodesk and is free after you register on the site. It has a host of information and forums populated by others in the industry. Because it's a forum, you can post and answer questions or engage in discussions surrounding an array of topics. The address is www.augi.com.

- *Revit City*—Looking for content and families? Revit City, another free online service, has a growing database of free families posted by other users. Its address is www.revitcity.com.

- *Autodesk Discussion Groups*—These pages offer insightful discussions and some great Q&A threads: http://discussion.autodesk.com/

- *Revit OpEd*—A blog with some great information, useful links, and helpful tips and tricks. Put together by a longtime Revit guru, and fellow author, Steve Stafford: http://revitoped.blogspot.com/

- *AECbytes*—A website dedicated to following and reporting on the trends in the the AEC industry, with a strong focus on BIM, technology, and the direction of the industry. Put together by Lachmi Khemlani: http://www.aecbytes.com/

CHAPTER 2

Getting Acquainted with the Revit Interface and File Types

In this chapter you'll get acquainted with the graphical user interface of Revit Architecture. We'll explain terminology, menu arrangements, tools, views, common commands, and the basics to get you up and running. This chapter covers:

- **The Revit user interface**
- **Modifying and personalizing the interface**
- **Selecting and manipulating content**
- **Setting up your project environment**
- **Revit file formats**

The Revit User Interface

In this section we'll look at how Revit appears when first opened out of the box, and get you familiar with how the interface is organized. We'll explore the use of some standard-looking toolbars and menus, as well as some features that are unique to Revit. One of the things you'll notice from the beginning is that Revit is tailored for the architectural design community. The tools, commands, and objects that you use in Revit are based on tasks and requirements taken directly from the practice of architecture.

> Throughout this book, when we say *Revit* we're referring to Revit Architecture. It's simpler this way!

Starting Revit

There are several ways to start Revit: by double-clicking the Revit icon that was automatically created on your desktop during installation, by going to C:\Program Files\Revit Architecture 2008\Program and double-clicking Revit.exe, or by double-clicking on any file with the .rvt extension.

The Basic Screen

When you open Revit for the first time, the window shown in Figure 2.1 is the first image that you'll see. (There may be slight differences depending on which language version you have installed.) You'll notice that the toolbars along the top are similar to those in other Windows-based applications.

Figure 2.1

The Revit GUI

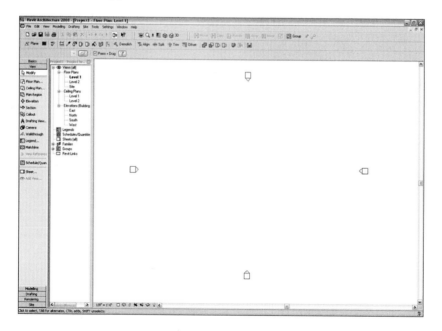

The Revit interface is composed of multiple components, each of which is described below:

Title bar This is displayed at the top of the entire Revit application frame, like in other Windows applications. In the Title bar (Figure 2.2), you see the version of Revit that you're running as well as the name of the project that is currently active. If a single view is open in the main view window, the name of that view will be displayed after the file name. If more than one view is open in the View window, the name of the current view is not shown.

The title bar in Figure 2.2 indicates that Revit Architecture 2008 is running, the name of the open file is Botta, and the name of the active view is Floor Plan: 0 Ground.

Menu bar The menu bar (Figure 2.3) contains pull-down menus for all features and settings available in Revit. Many of the commonly used commands located in the menus are also accessible via toolbars and the Design bar (described shortly). However, in some cases, tools are accessible only from the drop-down menus.

File Edit View Modelling Drafting Site Tools Settings Window Help

Toolbars Revit provides toolbars with standard Windows tools (save, delete, new, copy, etc), as well a host of Revit-specific tools. The default toolbar settings used at startup (Figure 2.4) do not display all available tools. To hide/unhide tools, right-click an empty area in the toolbar. A pop-up menu will allow you toggle tools on and off.

Type Selector The Type Selector (Figure 2.5) is a drop-down list of element types available in the project. The content of the list changes depending on the type of element that is selected or being created. For example, if you select a wall, the Type Selector will show you what you have selected, and also show you a list of other types of walls in your project. Choosing a different wall type from the list will change the wall on the fly. This works with just about any element you can select in Revit, and is an extremely powerful way to make changes to the model. This Type Selector is also used when creating new elements is the current type determines what will be created.

Figure 2.2
The title bar

Figure 2.3
The menu bar

Figure 2.4
Default toolbar settings

Figure 2.5
The Type Selector

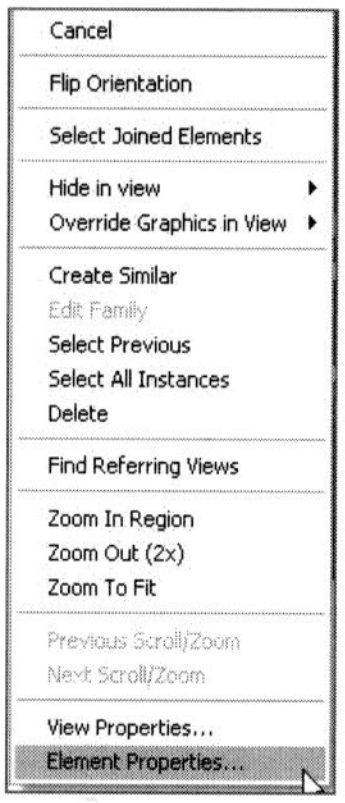

Figure 2.6
Context menu that appears when you right-click elements

Properties button The Properties button ( ) is located next to the Type Selector and becomes active when an element is selected. Clicking this opens the Element Properties dialog, where all instance and type parameters of selected elements are displayed and can be edited. The Element Properties dialog can also be accessed from the right-click menu (Figure 2.6) when elements are selected.

Options bar The Options bar displays context-sensitive options that vary depending on the type of element being created or selected. This menu changes dynamically depending on the active tool. It also changes as you select different types of elements. In Figure 2.7, you can see several manifestations of the Options bar.

Status bar The Status bar is located at the very bottom of the application window. Here you see the names of elements when you mouse over them or select them. The Status bar also provides information about how to use a tool when activated and offers helpful indicators of what to do next. Whenever you aren't sure what the next step should be, look at the Status bar. See Figure 2.8 for a sample of the Status bar in action.

Design bar The Design bar (Figure 2.9) is a set of tabs that contain tools related to common tasks that occur in a project. Some tools are repeated on multiple tabs because they're used in various tasks. The Dimension tool is an example: Dimensions are used when modeling, drafting, and laying out structures. When you start Revit, by default only the Basics, View, Modeling, and Room and Area tabs are visible. To activate other tabs, click an empty space on the Design bar, and then right-click to bring up options for more tabs. On some smaller monitor resolutions (less than 1280×1024), it's possible you won't see all the tools available in a design tab. To access these tools, click on the More Tools flyout at the bottom of the tab.

Project Browser This is the heart and soul of the Revit user interface. From the Project Browser, you can navigate to all your views, create new views, access element properties, and place all forms of content in your project ranging from linked Revit files to rendered images. Let's take a moment to explain the different parts of the Project Browser.

Figure 2.7
The Options bar changes for (top) walls, (center) doors, and (bottom) rooms.

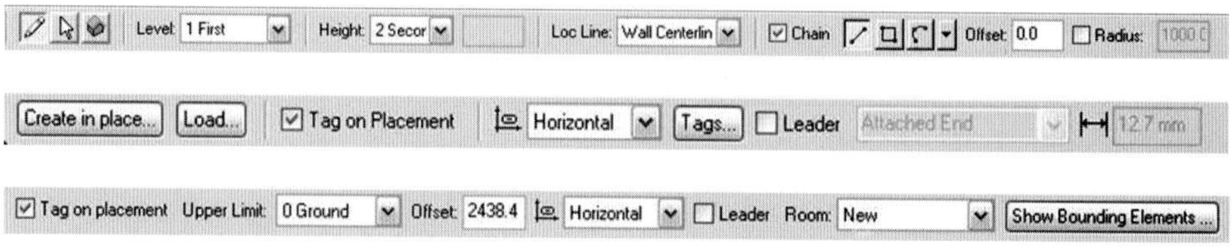

Figure 2.8
The Status bar when (top) selecting or hovering over a wall, (center) drawing a wall, and (bottom) using the Rotate command

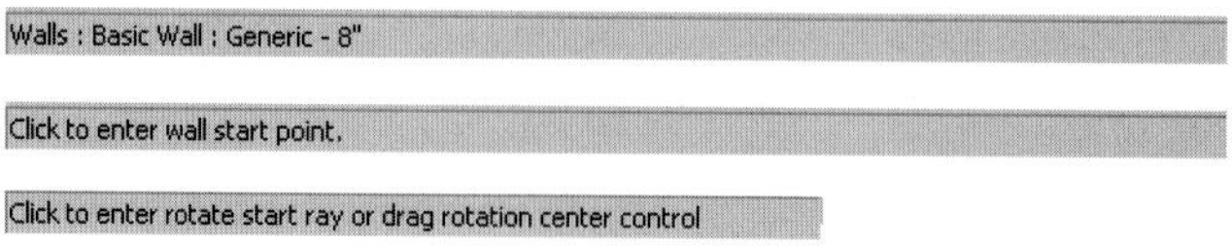

Views There are many types of views in which building information can be represented in Revit. These views are listed and organized in the Project Browser using a collapsible tree navigation framework. Types of views include plans, ceiling plans, sections, elevations, 3D views, animations, schedules, tables, legends, and sheets. Once a view has been created, it can be duplicated to create a similar view and then modified to fit the requirements of different design deliverables. Every view has properties that determine information such as scale, name, and visibility/graphics settings. These properties can be accessed by right-clicking on the view name in the Project Browser (Figure 2.10), and opening Properties.

Families In the Project Browser, you can also see all the loaded elements (families) in your project. From here, you can drag and drop elements into the drawing area, query element properties, create new types of elements, and even select all instances of a given element in the model in order to perform wholesale changes. The right-click menu for families (Figure 2.11) is different from that for views.

Revit Links Starting from 2008 release, Revit links (other Revit projects that can be linked into your project) are also listed in the Project Browser. From here you can reload, unload, open, copy, and visually identify the links in your project. This improves the workflow when using Revit links (as pictured in Figure 2.12).

Figure 2.9
Design bar

Using the Select All Instances command from the Families menu of the Project Browser is a great way to instantly change all instances of a particular element from one type to another. For example, if you have placed a series of 2′ × 2′ windows and need to change them to another size, you can choose Select All Instances and choose a new size from the Type Selector. Doing so changes all the instances throughout the entire model.

Figure 2.10
Context menu for a view

Figure 2.11
Context menu for a family

Figure 2.12
Links appear in the Project Browser.

Navigating through a Project

Figure 2.13

Use of the Type Selector

To open views listed in the Project Browser, double-click on the desired view name. The current active view name will be displayed in bold letters in the Project Browser. The Project Browser makes navigating through a project easy—all views are at your fingertips and organized into familiar categories. We'll discuss views in more detail in Chapter 3.

Organization of the Project Browser

The Project Browser (🗔) displays information about views in an organization structure that is predefined. The default behavior shows views organized by view type (plan views, ceiling plans, sections, and so on). Several other predefined organization methods are provided, and these can be customized to suit your specific needs. When you click the Project Browser title, the Type Selector shows a list of organizational types (Figure 2.13). Try them, and you'll notice the difference. To explore how these are set up and to make your own, press the Properties button and check out the rules used to structure views.

View Window

The View window is the area where the model is generated. It's where all the action takes place. The View window can show just one view, or it can be tiled to arrange as many views as you need when working on a project. One of the functionalities unique to Revit is that whenever you modify or create an element in one view, all other views instantly update, reflecting the change. If you have multiple views open, you can see the change reflected concurrently in all the windows. All of this happens without any need to refresh the views as you'd need to do in other applications.

GETTING ACQUAINTED WITH THE VIEW WINDOW

In this simple exercise, we are going to open a project file, open some common views, and then tile the views. When you select something, note how it gets selected in all views. This is a core concept when working in an integrated 3D model.

1. Open the file residence taurer 1.rvt.

2. Open the plan view (ground floor), section view, and 3D axonometric view.

3. Use the Window menu, choose Tile, or use the keyboard shortcut WT.

4. Select a wall—notice how it turns red (indicating selection) in all open views.

The View window shows three different views: plan view (ground floor), section view, and a 3D axonometric view. Revit allows you to open and work in as many views as needed for clarity of the task. You can also simultaneously view changes taking place as the model is edited.

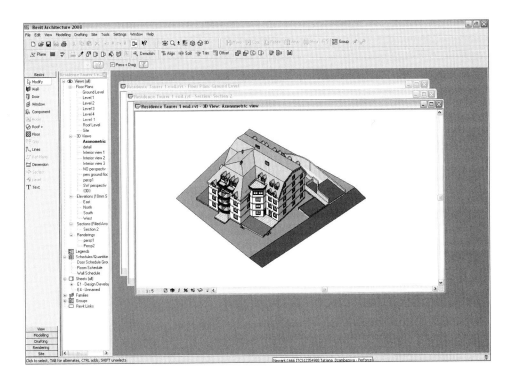

Figure 2.14

Cascaded views

project: courtesy of
Architect Martin Taurer

Figure 2.14 shows three open views that have been cascaded, stacking one view behind another. The Cascade Views functionality is available under the Window menu or via the keyboard shortcut by typing WC.

> It's quite easy to open many views when working. This will make the tile and cascade options essentially useless. To reduce the number of open views, choose one primary view, and maximize it. Then use the option in the Window menu: Close Hidden Windows. This will close all views but your active one, and is a great way to clear the clutter.

Notice that one of the title bars of the tiled views is blue. This denotes this view as the active one. Any activity that you do (such as draw, modify, or delete) takes place in the active view. The name of the active view is displayed in the Project Browser in bold letters.

Another way to arrange the open views is Tiling, as demonstrated in the previous exercise. When selecting this method of arrangement, your views will be neatly arranged within the view area.

> While Revit allows you to open and work in as many views as you wish, you will need to pay attention to how many you open. Having too many open views can affect Revit's overall performance (speed). The number of views you can open and your performance also depends upon the speed of your computer and the amount of RAM it has.

Figure 2.15

Tiled views

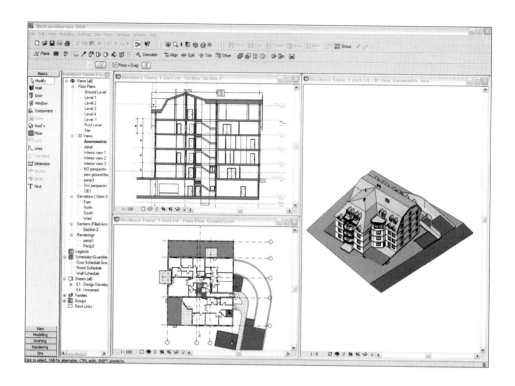

Communication Center

You'll be familiar with the Communication Center (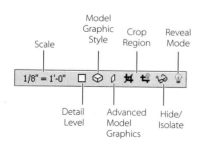) if you've used applications such as AutoCAD. When connected to the Internet, the Communication Center delivers information and announcements about new software updates, product support information, tips and tricks, and industry news. You can access and activate the Communication Center by clicking the satellite-dish icon at the bottom right of the Revit UI.

View Control Bar

A view in Revit can be represented in many different scales, levels of detail, and model graphic styles. Shadows can be turned on and off; crop regions can be used to limit what is visible, and the view can also hide elements and categories of elements. The View Control bar (Figure 2.16) contains shortcuts to many of the tools you'll use most often; the following sections look at some of these tools.

Figure 2.16

The View Control bar

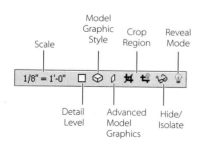

SCALE

The first tool indicates the scale in which the drawing will be printed. Clicking on the Scale will give you a standard set of scales to choose from. The scale of the view will determine how big your drawing will be when printed, and also creates a visual relationship between annotations and the model. Annotations are always shown in paper size, and the model will adjust its graphics according to the view scale. Put simply, a plan view at ¼″ = 1′-0″ (1:50) will be twice as large as a plan view at ⅛″ = 1′-0″ (1:100) when printed, but in each view the text notes will be the same size.

THIN LINE MODE

If lineweight makes it difficult to read the model, the Thin Line mode tool (🖿) allows you to see all lines drawn a single pixel wide.

This feature controls the way lines are displayed in all views. As Figure 2.17 demonstrates, when selected, Thin Line mode displays all lines as being a single pixel wide, regardless of view scale. When this tool is deselected, the line thickness corresponds to the thickness you have assigned to the elements and shows how the drawings will look when printed.

Note that this command affects only how Revit appears in the screen views and not how Revit prints. Thin Line mode is located in the View toolbar because it affects all views, not just the active view (Figure 2.18).

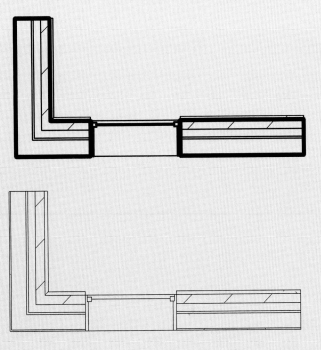

Figure 2.17

(top) standard view; (bottom) Thin Line view.

Figure 2.18

Thin Line toggle

DETAIL LEVEL

This icon indicates the level of detail assigned to the view. There are three levels of detail, illustrated in Figure 2.19, which can be used to show more or less information in a view: Coarse, Medium, and Fine.

Figure 2.19

Detail Level in the View Control bar

Depending on the type of drawing and where in the process your project is, you can use the level-of-detail options to expose more or less information. At $1'' = 50'$ (1:200) scale, for example, you may represent a wall as a solid fill, regardless of the number of layers in the wall construction. At $\frac{1}{4}'' = 1'\text{-}0''$ (1:50), you'll probably want to show the different layers of the wall assembly. The same applies to a door or window. A door is represented with different levels of abstraction depending on the scale. Figure 2.20 illustrates a standard door shown at each of the detail levels available in Revit.

When using a CAD system, you use separate blocks for each of these symbolic representations. In the case of a door, you would have to create three different symbols that are drawn in different levels of detail. In Revit, the door can be designed to show itself in meaningful representations for different scales as well as view types. The trick is that it's always the same object—it's just showing different levels of information about itself.

Figure 2.20

Detail Level options

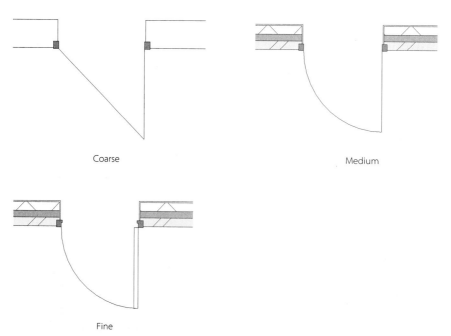

Coarse

Medium

Fine

MODEL GRAPHIC STYLE

You may already be acquainted with this type of graphic display from using other design applications. The options shown in Figure 2.21 allow you to display the model in one of four modes: Wireframe, Hidden line, Shaded, and Shaded with edges. These are demonstrated in Figure 2.22.

ADVANCED MODEL GRAPHICS

Advanced Model Graphics is a set of view options available from this menu that let you fine-tune the sun angles, time of day, intensity, and other variables. The settings shown in Figure 2.23 let you add additional graphic embellishments, such as shadows and bold silhouette outlines.

Figure 2.21

Model Graphic Style in the View Control bar

Figure 2.22

Model Graphic Style

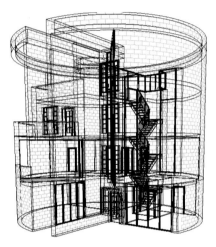

Wireframe

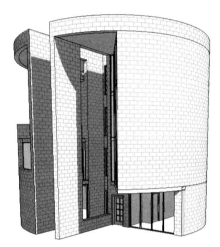

Hidden Line

Shaded

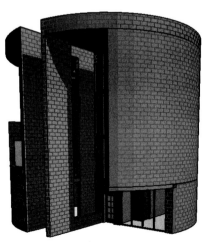

Shaded with Edges

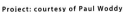

Project: courtesy of Paul Woddy

Figure 2.23

Advanced Model Graphics in the View Control bar

Shadows and sun Shadows can be turned on or off using the buttons from the View bar. The location of the sun relative to your model can be relative to the view; controlled directly; or use specific time, date, and place data. Using the Sun and Shadows settings in the Advanced Model Graphics dialog box shown in Figure 2.24, it's possible to create accurate sun-angle studies by locating the model on the earth and dialing in various times and dates. The controls become available from the Advanced Model Graphics dialog whenever the Cast Shadows option is selected. You'll learn how to create sun studies at the end of this book. Some examples of sun studies are shown in Figure 2.25.

Figure 2.24

Advanced Model Graphics dialog box

Figure 2.25

Sun studies

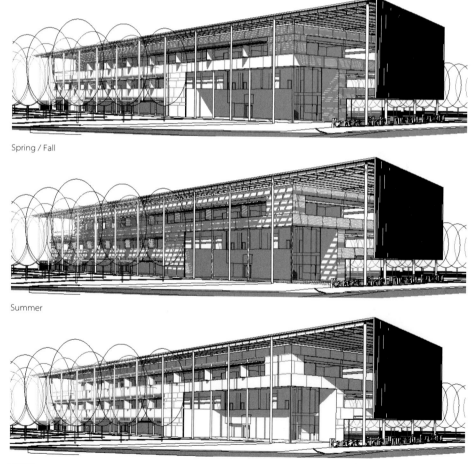

Spring / Fall

Summer

Winter

images courtesy of BNIM Architects

USE CAUTION WITH SHADOWS

When you're working on bigger projects, shadows can affect performance in a particular view significantly. Try to keep this feature turned off while you work, and activate it only when you need to print.

Silhouette edges Creating silhouette effects can give a nice artistic touch to your perspective or axonometric views, as shown in Figure 2.26. Silhouette edges can be applied only to the Hidden Line and Shaded with Edges Graphic styles.

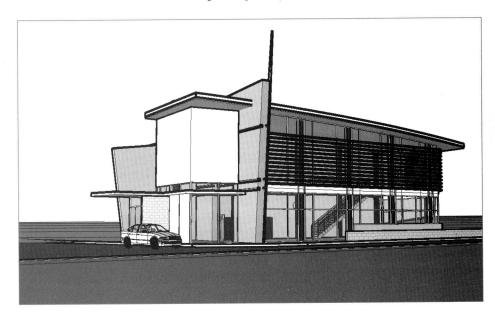

Figure 2.26

Shadow view with silhouette edges

You can use any linestyle as a silhouette edge style—those offered by Revit as well as custom-created lines. Should you wish to emphasize some corners more then others, you can use a linework tool and override different lines with stronger or weaker line types.

CROP REGION

The Crop Region tool allows you to limit what part of the model is visible within a rectangle. All interactive views have a crop region. The region will be visible or invisible depending on how the view was generated. For example, when making sections and callout views, a crop region is automatically generated and is visible by default in those views. Plan views, on the other hand, do not show their crop regions by default. The Crop Region tool is accessible from the View Control bar, as shown in Figure 2.27.

Figure 2.27

Crop Region option in the View Control bar

Figure 2.28

Crop region examples

Crop region active but not used

Crop region used to show less of the floor plan

The Crop view toggle makes the Crop region active and it crops the view, Do Not Crop View keeps the crop boundary but it does NOT crop anything. (This is very useful for the newly introduced Dependent views that we will cover later).

You can toggle the visibility of the crop region using the "Show/Don't show" Crop button. You'll notice a border show up around your model when the region is visible. You can change the size of this border by selecting it and dragging it with the blue arrows. The crop region can also be activated through **View → Properties** and is applicable in both 2D and 3D views. (See Figure 2.29.)

TOOLS FOR CONTROLLING THE EXTENT OF A VIEW: 2D VIEWS

Note the difference between the two dialog boxes in Figure 2.29. The first one is the View Properties dialog box of a 2D view; the second is for a 3D view. Some tools are specific only to certain type of views. Let's review them.

Figure 2.29

Extended View Properties

Parameter	Value
Title on Sheet	
Referencing Sheet	
Referencing Detail	
Default View Template	None
Extents	
Crop View	
Crop Region Visible	
Annotation Crop	
View Range	Edit...
Associated Level	Level 1
Scope Box	None
Phasing	
Phase Filter	Show All
Phase	New Construction

Parameter	Value
Identity Data	
View Name	{3D}
Dependency	Independent
Title on Sheet	
Default View Template	None
Documentation Category	Construction Documentation
Extents	
Crop View	
Crop Region Visible	
Annotation Crop	
Far Clip Active	
Section Box	
Camera	
Render Scene	None
Render Image Size	Edit...

continues

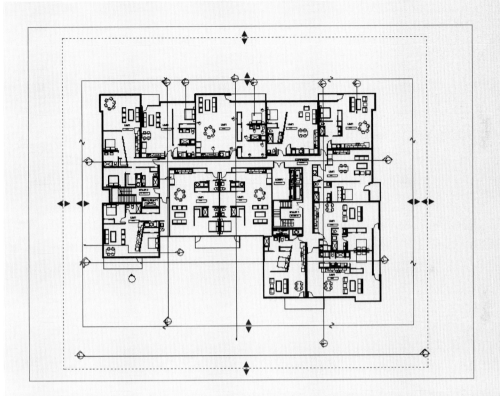

Figure 2.30
**Annotation
crop visible**

Annotation Crop

This is new functionality in the 2008 version and by default it is turned OFF. You'll need to go to View Properties and enable it. If you need to crop a floor plan with text, dimensions, and keynotes on it and want to show just half of the plan, the Crop tool crops model elements but not the annotations. Selecting the Annotation Crop option (shown in Figure 2.29) makes the crop region aware of annotations as well and lets you crop them with a second crop region. The model and annotation crop are separately controlled, and you can change their extents using the blue arrows when the border of the crop is activated. This is shown in Figure 2.30 and demonstrated by the outer dashed box. The annotation crop can never be smaller than the model crop. The offset between the annotation crop and model crop can be preset by selecting the crop region and in the Options bar, click on the Size button. This will open the Crop region size dialog where you can present the offset for the Annotation crop.

HIDE—ISOLATE

Temporary hide / isolate The hide and isolate mode in the View Control bar allows you to temporarily change the visibility of elements in a view. It's useful in visually cluttered situations when you want to isolate an object in order to work freely with it without the disturbance of other objects, or where you need to overview a portion of the model without the presence of certain elements. This feature allows you to change the visibility of a view independent of object types.

To hide or isolate an element or an entire category, first you need to select the element(s) and choose among the options under the eyeglasses icon () . Figure 2.31 shows the different options available with the Hide / Isolate tool. Please note the following:

- Isolating an element isolates only the selected element in that view.

- Hiding an element hides only the selected element in that view.

- Isolate Category isolates the entire category in that view.

- Hide Category hides the entire category in that view.

Once you've hidden an element, the eyeglasses icon turns cyan and a cyan border is drawn around the view to indicate that something is temporarily hidden in this view. To reset the view to the normal state, select Reset Temporary Hide/Isolate. The temporary hide/isolate state is applied to *one* view only and is instantly lost when you press Esc, change a view, or reopen a project. The state isn't saved and is not printable.

The Apply Hide/Isolate to View option allows you to convert a temporary hidden or isolated element into a permanently hidden element in the active view.

Permanent hide/isolate Up until version 2008, Hide/Isolate mode was only temporary, so although you could turn objects on and off, you couldn't save the state or print a view as it was shown on the screen. In 2008, a new permanent Hide/Isolate state has been introduced. This allows elements to be hidden in a view that can be saved and printed.

There are two ways to permanently hide/isolate elements.

1. Create a temporary hide/isolate in a view, and then convert it to a permanent state using the Apply Hide/Isolate button.

2. Select an element in the drawing area, right-click, select Hide in View from the context menu, and choose Element or Category from the menu (shown in Figure 2.32).

Both the temporary and the permanent hide and isolate tools are applied in the current view only.

Figure 2.31

Hide/Isolate options in the View Control bar

Figure 2.32

Hide/Isolate context menu options

REVEAL MODE

When you're working in a team, some members of a team may hide certain elements in a view and leave them hidden when they leave the view. Reveal mode, introduced in 2008, is a special way to display the view: The model is represented as halftone, and hidden elements/categories are shown in a bold magenta color, so it's clear what has been hidden.

In this mode, the temporary hidden elements/categories (if any) are represented with cyan and the permanent hidden elements with magenta, as shown in Figure 2.33. To indicate that you're in a reveal mode, the drawing window has a purple line around the drawing area. The light bulb icon ()is purple as well.

Figure 2.34 shows a sample plan and the same plan with Reveal mode turned on. Unlike using temporarily hidden elements, Reveal mode allows you to add elements/categories to or remove them from the permanent hidden mode. To do this, select any element (regardless of its state), right-click, and select Hide or Unhide from the context menu. You can also use the Options bar to unhide elements or categories.

Figure 2.33

Reveal Mode options in the View Control bar

Figure 2.34

Floor plan

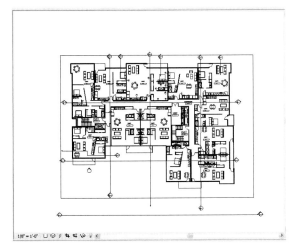

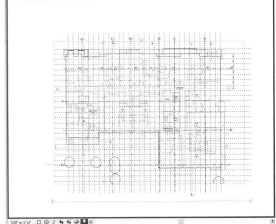

Floor plan with Reveal mode turned on

CONTROLLING THE EXTENT OF A 3D VIEW: SECTION BOX

For 3D views, an additional cropping feature is available that allows you to crop the model with a 3D clipping box. This option, named Section Box, cuts through your model like a cake, vertically and horizontally, and is available in both axonometric and perspective (Camera) views. This tool is effective for creating perspective sections that are highly informative, creative, and appealing (Figure 2.35 provides an example) and show what's going on in your model. To enable Section Box, use the check-box option in View Properties. If you orient the 3D view to another view (Menu: View → Orient → To other View…) a section box will be turned on and automatically initialized.

continues on next page

Figure 2.35

A rendered view using the Section Box tool

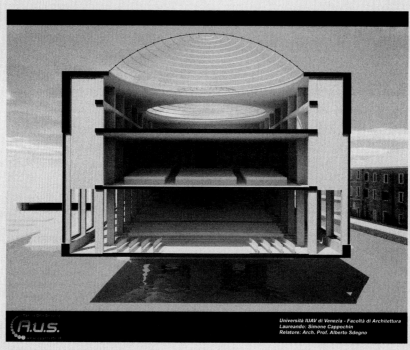

IMAGE COURTESY OF UNIVERSITY IUAV OF VENICE – FACULTY OF ARCHITECTURE; GRADUATE: SIMONE CAPPOCHIN; PROFESSOR: ARCH. PROF. ALBERTO SDEGNO

Tooltips

When you hover over an element in the view, Revit helps you identify that object with a tooltip. (See Figure 2.36.) You can read the name of the object and the type of family to which it belongs. The same information is also displayed in the Status bar.

Figure 2.36

Tooltip

Modifying and Personalizing the Interface

If you expected to be able to modify the interface and move around or create your own toolbars in Revit, you may be disappointed. Revit doesn't allow you to customize the interface *ad infinitum*. Here are some of the allowed modifications available today:

Button display   Right-clicking any of the toolbar icons drops down a list where you can choose to turn text labels on or off. When turned on, some of the toolbar icons display an image and text; when off, only an icon with image is displayed. See Figure 2.37 for clarification.

Figure 2.37

Button display with text turned on and off

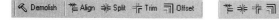

Project Browser The Project Browser can be undocked and moved around on the screen (Figure 2.38). To do this, grab it by left-clicking in the title bar of the Project Browser and dragging it to the desired place. After its position is modified, if you close and then reopen Revit, the Project Browser defaults back to its standard position. If for some reason you don't see the Project Browser, this is because it has been turned off. To turn on the Project Browser, use the icon in the Standard toolbar.

You can also minimize the Project Browser by clicking the X in the upper-right corner. To maximize it again, click the Browser icon in the toolbar (Figure 2.39); the Project Browser will reappear at its standard position at the right of the Design toolbar.

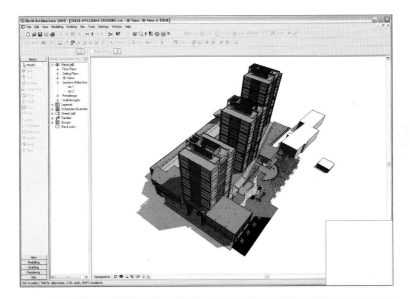

Figure 2.38

Undocking the Project Browser

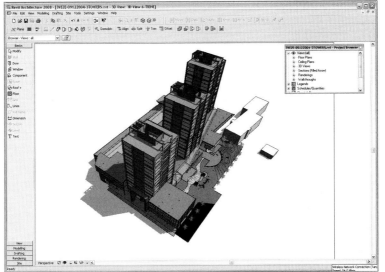

Figure 2.39

Project Browser undocked

project courtesy of Kubik&Nemeth Architects

EXERCISE: THE PROJECT BROWSER

To get a feel for how to use the Project Browser, follow these few simple steps:

1. Open Botta.rvt.

    You'll see a 3D axonometric view of the project you're viewing, as in the one pictured in the following graphic.

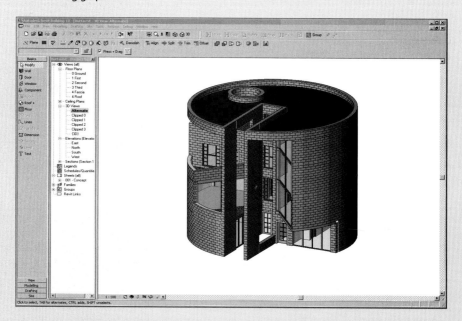

2. To see the plan views, double-click *0-Ground Floor* in the Project Browser. The 0-Ground Floor name is now displayed in bold, indicating that it is the active view in the project.

3. Following the same logic, double-click *First Floor* and *4 Roof Floor* or any of the 3D views or elevations. Double-click the wall schedule to open a Schedule view of all walls in the project. Or double-click the Sheet List to view the sheet prepared to be printed and sent out to the owner.

    In Revit, all the documents you just opened are called views, and they show different representations of information from the underlying database of this building. You'll learn how to create and manage different views, and many other things about the Project Browser, in Chapter 3.

4. Close the file without saving.

Keyboard shortcuts (accelerators) Computer users like using keyboard shortcuts to speed up common commands and minimize the need to interrupt workflow. When you open any of the menus in the menu bar, the keyboard shortcut is indicated to the right of the tool name (Figure 2.40). Revit contains preset keyboard shortcuts when installed, but you can modify the default shortcuts by editing the `keyboard.txt` file located in the `C:\Program Files\Revit Architecture 2008\Program` folder. Be aware that Revit's shortcuts are two-key shortcuts and are available only for commands that already exist in the GUI. As you change the shortcuts in the `Keyboard.txt` file, Revit also changes the abbreviations shown in the menus.

Figure 2.40

Keyboard shortcuts indicated

Selecting and Manipulating Content

Using the Mouse

Although using the mouse may seem like a fairly basic function of any software, Revit has some built-in enhancements that let you take full advantage of the graphical interface. Revit was built around the use of a Windows mouse like that shown in Figure 2.41. Additional enhancements include some keyboard and mouse routines to allow you to maximize workflow.

Figure 2.41

Windows mouse with a scroll wheel

Left Mouse Button

To select an object, use the left mouse button. This button also allows you to specify a starting point when drawing an element, navigate through the GUI, and select different tools.

Right Mouse Button

Right-clicking an object opens the context menu with various additional tools specific to the selected object. There are some changes in the context menus in Revit 10. Right-clicking a selected element now gives you some new tools.

In the free space of the View window, right-clicking opens a menu specific to the navigation of the particular view (Figure 2.42). Note the View Properties option. This is something you'll use regularly, and we'll go into more detail about its specific functions later.

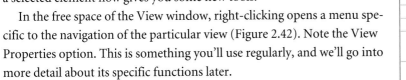

Figure 2.42

A context menu with view-specific information and options

Scroll Wheel

The scroll wheel can be rolled, held while moving the mouse, or used with modifier keys to alter your view:

Zoom Scrolling the mouse wheel while in a view invokes the Zoom command so you can zoom in and zoom out, depending on the scrolling direction. Ctrl + pressing the wheel also invokes Zoom but with a slightly smaller zoom factor.

Pan Moving the mouse while pressing and holding the mouse wheel invokes the Pan command.

Spin When in a 3D axonometric view, holding the Shift key with the mouse wheel depressed allows you to spin the entire model. When an element is selected, the model spins around that element.

Dynamic view navigation Although a three-button scroll mouse is recommended for Revit, you can achieve all of these behaviors with a two-button mouse as well.

To do this, you need to select the Dynamically Modify View icon on the toolbar (Figure 2.43) and use the commands in the Dynamic View dialog box:

Scroll + depressing the left mouse button scrolls (pans) the view in any direction.

Zoom + depressing the left mouse button zooms in and out on the current view.

Spin + depressing the left mouse button rotates the camera eye over the entire model or selected objects. (This feature is applicable to 3D views only.)

Figure 2.43

Click the Dynamically Modify View icon to edit mouse behavior.

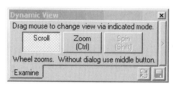

Before you go forward, try this behavior on any of the sample files you've used up to now. Open a 3D view; and using the mouse and keyboard combinations, familiarize yourself with the scroll, zoom, and spin commands. You'll use them frequently throughout the model and documentation process.

Selecting Content

To select an individual element, left-click on it. To select multiple elements, several options are available. The easiest way to select multiple elements is with a selection window. Depending on the direction that you drag the mouse, you can select different elements. If you are an AutoCAD user, this will be very familiar.

With mouse down, dragging a selection window from left to right (Figure 2.44) results in the selection of only those elements that are entirely within in the selection window.

Dragging the selection window from right to left (Figure 2.45) will result in the selection of elements that intersect or are entirely within the selection window. Note that the check box in the option bar "Press + Drag" will drag element when mouse is down during drag. If you find that you accidentally drag an element when creating a window selection, uncheck this option to prevent dragging elements.

To be more specific about what you want to select, you can select all elements of a particular type by using the right-click menu when an element is selected. Choose Select All Instances from the menu, and all elements in the model of that type will become selected. You can then make changes, delete all the elements, or swap the element with a new type.

Right-clicking Select All Instances lets you select all instances of a particular element type in the project. This will select all instances in all views.

You can also limit selection to categories by using the Filter tool, located in the Options bar. Once you've selected some elements, press the filter button, and you will get a dialog that shows which categories are selected. To de-select categories, uncheck them.

You can select all elements of the same category in a view by right-clicking an element and choosing Select All Instances from the menu.

Right-clicking Select All Instances lets you select all instances of a particular element type in the project. This will select all instances in all views.

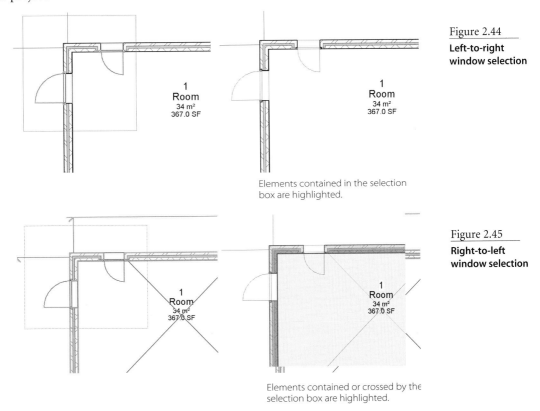

Elements contained in the selection box are highlighted.

Figure 2.44

Left-to-right window selection

Elements contained or crossed by the selection box are highlighted.

Figure 2.45

Right-to-left window selection

Manipulating Objects

Grip Editing

Many elements display blue grips when selected that allow you to modify their size or location. Selecting and dragging the grip provides a preview (like the one in Figure 2.46) of the final outcome prior to completing the drag operation.

For walls and lines, blue-filled grips are displayed at the ends of selected element in plan view, and along the ends, bottoms, and tops of selected walls in elevation and 3D views, where they're labeled as shape handles. You can click and drag these controls to resize an element, as shown in Figure 2.47.

The blue grips also have additional functionality. In the walls, by right-clicking and going to the context menu, walls have a control over the wall joins (the way the walls connect) so you can use the grips to disallow joins between two walls. By default, the walls join automatically, but this behavior may be undesirable in different conditions (see Figure 2.48).

Figure 2.46

Dragging a grip enables a preview of the movement's outcome.

Figure 2.47

Wall grips and shape handles

Figure 2.48

Using grips to edit wall joins

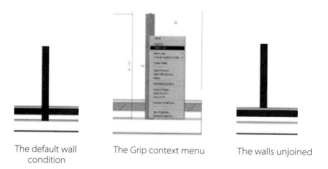

The default wall condition

The Grip context menu

The walls unjoined

You can right-click the wall-end controls and use the context menu to allow or disallow wall joins.

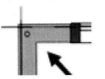

Figure 2.49

Wall grip when multiple walls are selected

When a chain of walls or lines is selected (Figure 2.49), drag controls are displayed at the coincident endpoints; you can drag these to change the layout of the chain. Touching walls are selected at the same time, and the blue-filled grip turns into an empty blue grip. Dragging this grip drags both walls at the same time, as shown in Figure 2.50.

Figure 2.50

Manipulating multiple walls using the grips

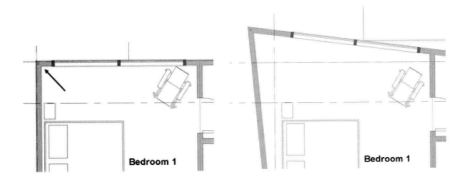

Bedroom 1   Bedroom 1

Move

Each object, when highlighted, can be moved without invoking the Move command in the toolbars. When you move your mouse close to the element, a set of crosshairs appears(✛). By clicking and holding the left mouse button, you can dynamically move the element selected.

Smart Constraints

Revit has many embedded help tools to make your life easier when creating or editing objects. One of these is the dashed green line shown in Figure 2.51. This line displays each time a movement is constrained to a plane, as with walls and lines in plan views.

The line helps you maintain the same plane of the wall when extending it, without the necessity of holding down the Shift key or using any other auxiliary tool.

A similar green dashed line helps you place a new element, similar to an adjacent one, by taking a reference from the nearby element. Figure 2.52 shows how placing new level lines in section or elevation references the start or end of another an existing level line.

Figure 2.51

Manipulating the wall constrained to a plane

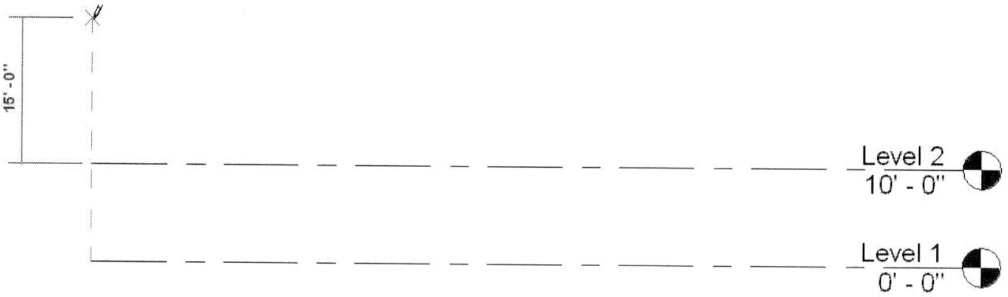

Figure 2.52

Figure 2.52

Referencing similar elements

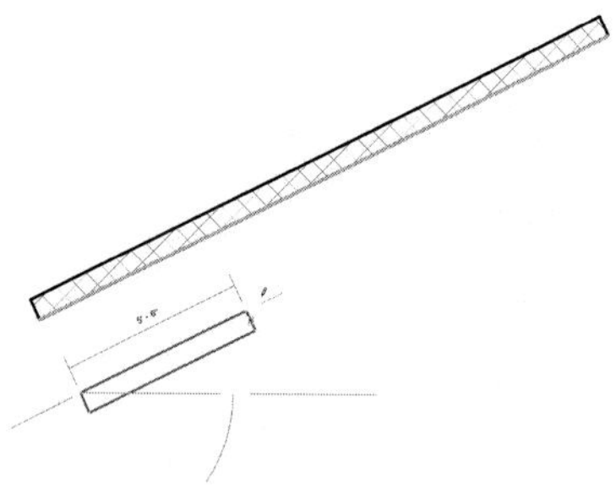

Figure 2.53

A new element is constrained when created near a similar one.

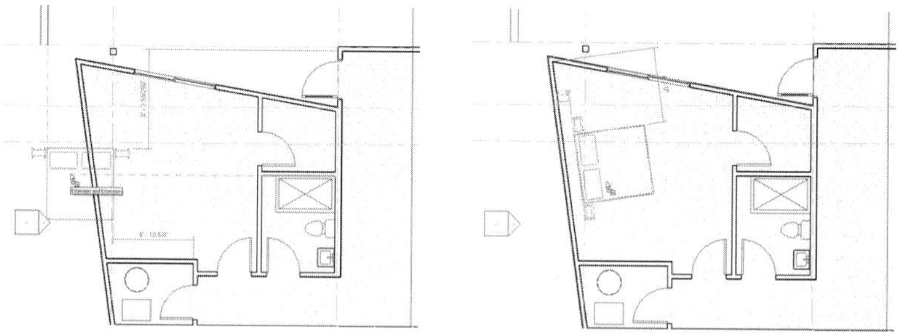

Figure 2.54

Using the spacebar to modify elements

When you're drawing or editing elements, Revit lets you orient them with respect to other elements without changing coordinate systems. This is a neat advantage of Revit.

If you want to draw a wall parallel to another that is already drawn, Revit will recognize the angle of that wall and will offer it as a constraint. This lets you draw the second element, keeping it parallel to the first wall during its creation (see Figure 2.53).

Using the spacebar will also help you orient elements during creation or while editing them. During placement, pressing the spacebar lets you rotate elements at 90-degree intervals. However, if you mouse over a non-orthogonal reference (such as the wall in Figure 2.54), the spacebar will start rotating the element, adding the angle for reference. For example, a bed placed next to a non-orthogonal wall can be quickly oriented to the angle of the wall. Just imagine how cool this is after all the trouble you may have had in the past defining UCS locations!

Flip Control

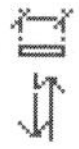

You click a flip control to change the orientation of an element. Flip controls are shown by two opposing blue arrows.

For example, when you flip a wall, you reverse the order of its component layers. Figure 2.55 demonstrates how to use a flip control.

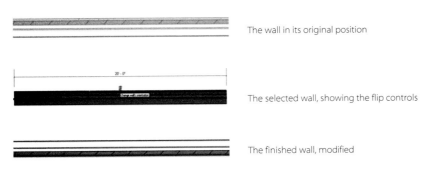

The wall in its original position

The selected wall, showing the flip controls

The finished wall, modified

Figure 2.55

Editing a wall using a flip control

Swinging doors have two flip controls: "Flip facing" (which controls whether the door swings in or out) and "Flip hand" (which controls whether the door swings right or left, as shown in Figure 2.56).

The flip control applies not only during creation of an element but also when an element is edited later. Note that flip controls are displayed only when applicable: They don't appear for items that don't need to be flipped (a table, for example).

Manipulating Objects Using Dimensions

In Revit, dimensions are much more than static forms of documentation. They can be used to interactively adjust the model at any time. Temporary dimensions are displayed each time an object is selected, inserted, or edited. Revit allows you to type a value in the temporary dimension string that will determine the position or size of an object. Permanent dimensions work the same way: you can edit the location of elements directly by changing dimensional values.

A wall 32′ (10m) long displays a 32′ (10m) temporary dimension. However, if you enter a 20′ (6m) dimension, the wall will become 20′ (6m) long (see Figure 2.57).

New Revit users are sometimes confused about which elements change or move when you use temporary dimensions. When you use temporary dimensions to change distances between elements, the selected element moves. If you select the wall on the right in Figure 2.58 and type a value in the temporary dimension area, the wall at the right will move, not the left one.

Figure 2.56

Door flip controls

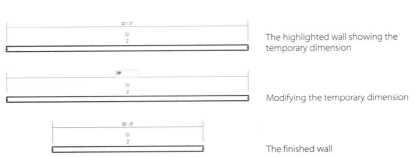

The highlighted wall showing the temporary dimension

Modifying the temporary dimension

The finished wall

Figure 2.57

Modifying a wall using temporary dimensions

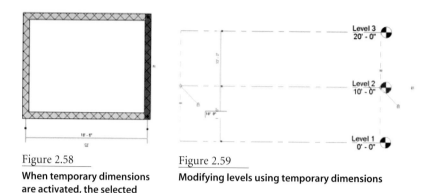

Figure 2.58

When temporary dimensions are activated, the selected element moves.

Figure 2.59

Modifying levels using temporary dimensions

It works the same way for levels. If you need to modify the height between levels, select the level you wish to move, and modify the temporary dimension. Regardless of whether you're changing the upper dimension or the lower dimension, in each case Level 2 is modified, as shown in Figure 2.59.

Padlocks

Revit is one of the rare architectural authoring applications that allows you to embed your design intent in the form of locks and constraints that persist until you consciously remove them.

- You can tell a door to be a certain distance from a wall so it fits a closet and lock that relationship so when you move the wall or the door, that relationship is maintained.

- You can space windows equidistantly along an exterior wall so that even if you change the length of the façade, the windows will keep their positions relative to the wall's length.

- You can keep an exterior wall attached to the roof so that if you change the height of the roof, the walls will also move, reflecting that change.

In the example in Figure 2.60, the door is constrained to a 1′4″ (40cm) distance from the wall to accommodate space for a cupboard. To constrain a distance, you set it by placing a dimension, selecting the dimension, and locking it with the Padlock command. After having locked the door to the wall (Figure 2.61)at a distance of 1′4″ (40cm), if you move the wall in the drawing, the door will always move with it, retaining the locked distance.

Pin

The Pin tool is another way to set a constraint for an element. In this case, the element isn't constrained with respect to another element in the model, but geospatially. You can pin your grid system so it doesn't move from its location, or pin elements from an existing building so they aren't mistakenly modified while you're working on new additions. You'll find the Pin command (📌)in the editing toolbar.

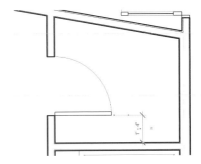

Figure 2.60

Temporary dimensions at a closet door

Figure 2.61

Locking the door location

Pin also appears in element types like the predefined curtain walls shown in Figure 2.62. By default, the pins exist here because there are embedded rules in a type-based curtain wall that you don't want to inadvertently change. If, however, you consciously decide to change the type or a distance (like the space between the mullions), you can unlock the pin at any time by clicking it. This undoes the constraint and allows you to freely change the element from now on. Locked and unlocked pins in a curtain wall are shown in Figure 2.63.

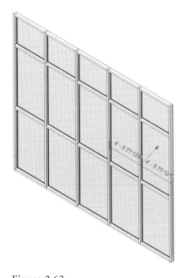

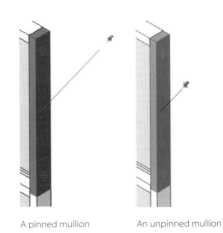

A pinned mullion   An unpinned mullion

Figure 2.62

Pins in a curtain wall

Figure 2.63

Using the Pin tool

Move with Nearby Elements

Another type of constraint is designed for logical relationships between elements. When furnishing a space, you probably want to align the bed or dresser with a wall. If you change your design, you want the furniture to follow the wall to the new location. For this purpose, Revit has a command called Move with Nearby Elements. When you select a furniture element, like the bed in Figure 2.64, this option appears in the Options bar. It lets you check a box to move the associated elements. By selecting this option, you create an invisible relationship between the bed and the wall so that each time you move the wall, the bed moves with it.

Instance Parameters

Figure 2.64

Moving an element with nearby elements

When elements appear with editable drag controls, these are considered *instance parameters*. This means you can modify the geometry on an instance-by-instance case rather than change the definition of a type and have all occurrences of the type in the model update at once. Many elements in Revit are driven by type parameters, but this doesn't restrict making and using content that is more flexible and driven only at the individual instance level.

This type of instance-level behavior may be desirable for windows and doors. Once a window or door is placed in a wall, there seems to be no way to change its size aside from going to the properties of that object and changing type parameters. When you select a window, blue grip controls do not appear as they do when you select walls. You might wonder: why can I not drag windows and doors to be any width and height I want? Essentially, the dimensions of windows and doors are defined as type parameters by default, and will not let you manipulate these dimensions on a per-instance basis. This is done intentionally, because you typically want to use a standard range of door sizes, and keep this information stable and predictable. Nonetheless, it is possible to create windows and doors that vary in size and shape on a per-instance basis. Remember that Revit makes some assumptions about desired behavior, but in most cases will allow you to move beyond the typical and not be hindered.

Should you want the ability to change the dimensions of windows and doors with direct editing (using the blue grips), you must change the parameters for width and height from *type parameters* to *instance parameters*. This can be done in the Family Editor with a few clicks. Note that this method of working takes away the advantage of having all windows and doors changed at once via a single parameter change. You also need to be careful not to create any odd custom sizes unintentionally. Figure 2.65 shows an example of a window as a type and an instance.

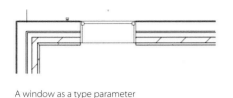
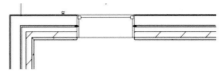

Figure 2.65

Type and instance parameters

A window as a type parameter

A window as an instance parameter has arrows to dynamically modify its size

Using Keyboard Shortcuts

Out of the box, Revit automates a variety of common commands using preset keyboard shortcuts:

Tab The Tab key is similar to the Cycle command you may know from AutoCAD. It allows you to cycle through various elements near the cursor when more than one is present. In Revit, this can happen frequently, so get used to using this key. The Tab key is useful when you're dimensioning because it allows you to cycle through various references of the elements dimensioned (dimension to wall center instead of wall face; opening of a door instead of outer frame; and so on). The Tab key is also used to select chains of connected lines and walls.

Shift-Tab This shortcut reverses the default order in which the Tab command cycles.

Ctrl The Ctrl key is used to add multiple objects to a selection at the same time.

Shift Unlike Microsoft conventions, which use the Ctrl key to deselect, Revit uses the Shift key to deselect an element.

Some elements in Revit are constrained to move horizontally or vertically only. Revit gives you visual clues indicating which way a selected element can move. You can remove this constraint by holding the Shift key while repositioning the element. At the same time, some elements can move in any direction by default, but holding the Shift key while moving them constrains their direction. For example, you can move a window freely in any direction in an elevation or a 3D view, but holding down the Shift key constrains the movement of the window so that it moves only horizontally. Likewise, you can normally move walls, lines, or gridlines freely in any direction, but the Shift key lets you constrain their movement to directions perpendicular to the wall or line.

Delete The Delete key is used to delete selected elements from the model. You can also use the Backspace key to delete elements.

Undo/Redo Commands can be undone and restored using Ctrl-Z (undo) and Ctrl-Y (redo). (These shortcuts are standard in many Windows-based applications.)

Multiple undo operations (Figure 2.66) can also be performed from the toolbar using the list of recent commands. Dragging the mouse down this list undoes all selected commands in one step.

Figure 2.66

Multiple undo

Spacebar The spacebar is mostly used to cycle through rotation of an element during or after placement. For instance, when you set a door in a wall, you can use the spacebar to cycle through choices including having the door open into or out of the room, and having it open from the left or right. The spacebar is also used to identify the direction in which walls will be placed and to edit their position after placement.

F1 This is a quick way to call the Help function. (Revit's embedded help menus are pretty good!)

Setting Up Your Project Environment

Now that you have an initial idea about the UI and the tools available, let's look how to predefine some settings in Revit. Many predefinitions and global settings are stored under the Settings menu. We'll cover some of the more important settings in this section.

Project Units

Revit has its default units fairly well defined; however, local standards or various projects may ask for different ways of documenting length, area, and other measurements. In the

Figure 2.67

The Project Units dialog

Settings → Project Units dialog (Figure 2.67), you can preset the measurement units, rounding convention (number of decimals), and suffixes for length, area, volume, and angle. You can also define the way you measure slopes—in rise or angle degrees—as well as the symbol used for the decimal division (point or comma).

As a rule, you should define all your units prior to starting a project; but if necessary, you can change any of them on the fly later in the development of the project.

By default, Revit inputs and displays in feet (imperial) or millimeters (metric). To change the input value to something you may be more familiar with, under **Settings → Project Units**, choose Length, and change the setting to fractional inches. Click OK. Next, choose the Dimension tool, and go to Properties. Choose **Edit → New**. Then, choose **Units → Format**. Deselect the "Use project settings" box, and change the units to read "Feet and fractional inches."

Snaps

Snaps are a great help for precise placement and modification of elements. In Revit, you can define snaps by choosing Settings ➝ Snaps. From the resulting dialog, you can turn the snaps on or off globally and also set a variety of snap types and the angular and length increments at which the system will snap. For the most part, these settings are adequate. Although they aren't represented in this dialog (Figure 2.68), different graphics and tooltips for each snap type appear in the view when you're drawing.

Lineweights

Revit has a global setting to display the line thicknesses on the screen and the printed page. Revit provides independent control over cut and projected lineweights on a per-category basis, giving you a great deal of flexibility. For example, cut lines for walls are often represented with thicker lines than walls in elevation. You can choose from sixteen preset lineweights that range from very thin to very thick. Revit does an excellent job of pre-setting these lineweights to produce a good graphical display of your model on the printed page. We don't recommend manipulating the dialog shown in Figure 2.69; however, if you're unhappy with the print quality of the lineweights, you can access the values in this dialog and make changes by going to **Settings ➝ Line Weights**.

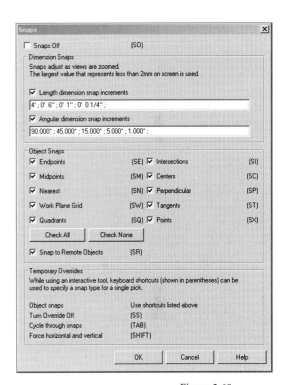

Figure 2.68

The Snaps dialog

Figure 2.69

The Line Weights dialog

	1 : 10	1 : 20	1 : 50	1 : 100	1 : 200	1 : 500
1	0.1800 mm	0.1800 mm	0.1800 mm	0.1000 mm	0.1000 mm	0.1000 mm
2	0.2500 mm	0.2500 mm	0.2500 mm	0.1800 mm	0.1000 mm	0.1000 mm
3	0.3500 mm	0.3500 mm	0.3500 mm	0.2500 mm	0.1800 mm	0.1000 mm
4	0.7000 mm	0.5000 mm	0.5000 mm	0.3500 mm	0.2500 mm	0.1800 mm
5	1.0000 mm	0.7000 mm	0.7000 mm	0.5000 mm	0.3500 mm	0.2500 mm
6	1.4000 mm	1.0000 mm	1.0000 mm	0.7000 mm	0.5000 mm	0.3500 mm
7	2.0000 mm	1.4000 mm	1.4000 mm	1.0000 mm	0.7000 mm	0.5000 mm
8	2.8000 mm	2.0000 mm	2.0000 mm	1.4000 mm	1.0000 mm	0.7000 mm
9	4.0000 mm	2.8000 mm	2.8000 mm	2.0000 mm	1.4000 mm	1.0000 mm
10	5.0000 mm	4.0000 mm	4.0000 mm	2.8000 mm	2.0000 mm	1.4000 mm
11	6.0000 mm	5.0000 mm	5.0000 mm	4.0000 mm	2.8000 mm	2.0000 mm
12	7.0000 mm	6.0000 mm	6.0000 mm	5.0000 mm	4.0000 mm	2.8000 mm
13	8.0000 mm	7.0000 mm	7.0000 mm	6.0000 mm	5.0000 mm	4.0000 mm
14	9.0000 mm	8.0000 mm	8.0000 mm	7.0000 mm	6.0000 mm	5.0000 mm
15	9.0000 mm	9.0000 mm	9.0000 mm	8.0000 mm	7.0000 mm	6.0000 mm
16	9.0000 mm	9.0000 mm	9.0000 mm	9.0000 mm	8.0000 mm	7.0000 mm

Figure 2.70

The Object Styles dialog

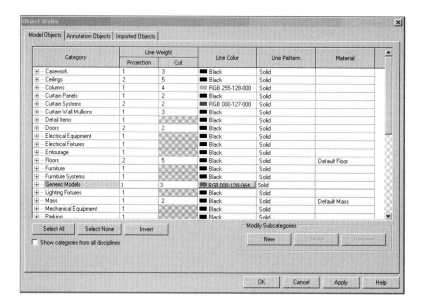

Object Styles

Line colors and styles are defined in the Object Styles dialog, which you can access from **Settings → Object Styles**. As you'll notice in the Object Styles dialog (Figure 2.70), each Revit element has an assigned lineweight number that corresponds to what is defined in the Line Weights dialog that we addressed previously. The lineweights chosen for Projection (elevation) and Cut can vary depending on your requirements. You can also define line color and line pattern for each category from this dialog. We'll dig deeper into this in the next few chapters.

Options

The Settings → Options dialog box (Figure 2.71) has a variety of other options for using Revit. Listed below are the tabs for this function:

General Here you can set your save-reminder intervals and your user name. By default, your user name will be the same as your Windows login name.

Graphics This is where you can change some of the settings for your graphics card and the screen colors in Revit. As you may have noticed, Revit by default has a white screen with black lines (the inverse of AutoCAD).

File Locations This tab stores the location of your default paths for templates, user files, and most importantly paths to your family libraries. **File → Load from Library →**

Load Family brings you to the location where you see all available folders in which families are logically stored. You can add libraries to that menu here. If you create new file locations, they will show up as quick-links on the left hand pane of the standard file open dialog.

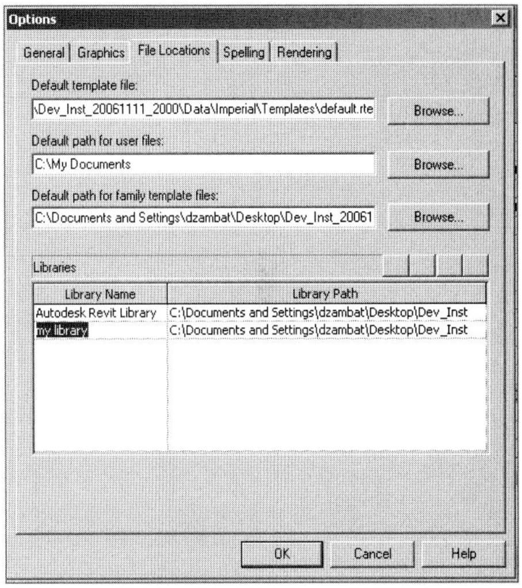

Revit File Formats

Revit introduces some new file formats, as discussed in the following sections.

.rvt: Revit File

Each Revit project is saved with the file extension `.rvt`. When you save a project in using the `.rvt` extension, all project information is saved in that one file. This file includes all library components used

Figure 2.71

Miscellaneous Revit options

in the project and imported DWG, DGN, or image files. Don't be too surprised to see the size of your project file grow significantly as you begin adding more detail to the model. It isn't unusual for file sizes to exceed 50 and even 100 MB. If you want to share your project with another person or office, you won't need to send them any files other than your project `*.rvt` file.

.rfa: Revit Family

The RFA file format is used for Revit elements that can be loaded into a project. These are also referred to as *families* in the project browser. A library of loadable content has been provided with the standard Revit installation. These libraries are starting points, and represent only a small sampling of what is possible to create in Revit. For this reason, everything you need to create your own content is provided with Revit in the form of a content-creation environment known as the Family Editor. You don't need any other software or knowledge of scripting or programming languages to build your own content. Revit families are created in the Family Editor and then loaded into a project. You can edit and make modifications to a family within the project environment at any time, minimizing workflow interruptions.

Unless you consciously changed the default installation,, Revit installs all library objects in this directory: `C:\Documents and Settings\All Users\Application Data\Autodesk\Revit Architecture 2008`. This is the location of the default content that ships with Revit, and where the Load from Library dialog will take you. (See Figure 2.72)

You can also load families from a web library to which Revit provides a direct link (Figure 2.73). Here you can find some additional international libraries.

Revit families can be two-dimensional or three-dimensional. Annotations and title blocks are obviously 2D, but you're welcome to create (or reuse from your CAD libraries) 2D symbols for real objects as well (toilets, furniture, and so on).

Double-clicking an RFA file from Windows opens the family file in Revit's Family Editor.

Figure 2.72

Revit library-object library

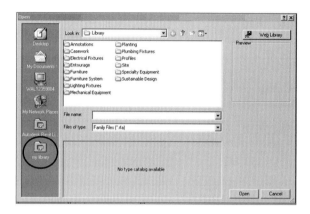

Figure 2.73

Revit web library

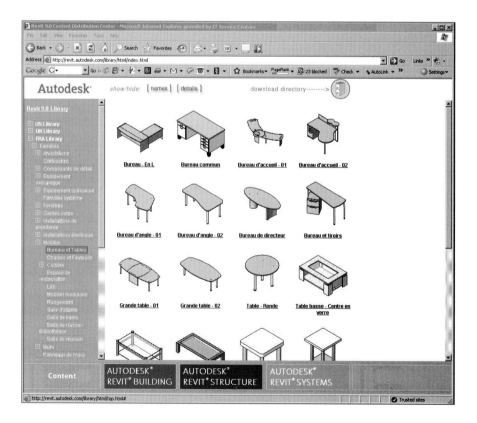

Figure 2.73

continued

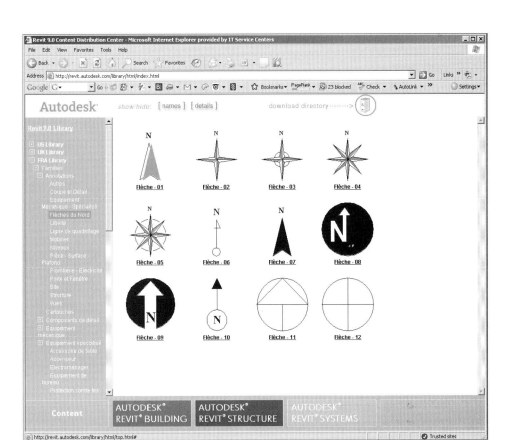

.rvg: Revit Group

To group elements together and repeat them throughout a project (imagine a table with chairs, or typical bathroom or hotel room fixtures), Revit has a tool called Groups (🔲 Group). It's somewhat similar to the Block concept in AutoCAD, but with a higher level of intelligent behavior. The file extension for Revit groups is .rvg. You create a group in Revit by selecting several objects and then clicking the Group button on the menu bar

Groups can be saved from one Revit model and loaded into another. Double-clicking an RVG file in Windows opens the family file in Revit's Family Editor.

> The RVG file format became obsolete beginning in Revit 2008. When a group is saved in Revit 2008 and later, it's saved as an RVT file. However, groups created in previous versions of Revit that are still in the RVG file format can be used and loaded in a project.

.rft: Family Template

This file format indicates a family template, which is used to create custom families. These are hard-coded in Revit. To see the full selection of available templates, choose **File → New → Family**. These templates have embedded behavior and intelligent parameters relevant to the type of object you're creating. For example, a template for creating a window has a different set of requirements than a template for creating a room. You can't create your own family template as you can a project template.

.rte: Revit Template

Templates are preconfigured empty drawings in which standard settings and content can be predefined so that each time you start a new project using that template, you have a predictable starting point that incorporates your office standards.

A template file allows many users working in the same company to start with a baseline set of graphic standards and a preloaded set of commonly used model and annotation elements. This is crucial for achieving a similar look and feel for all documents produced by your office. Architectural firms can have one office template or many, depending on the type of job they're engaged in. For example, a residential template may have different content preloaded than a commercial template, but the annotation and linestyle standards may be identical. Templates allow this kind of flexibility when defining a starting point for any given project.

You can preset the following in a template:

- Default title blocks used for your sheets
- Loaded families
- Linestyles
- Lineweights
- Line patterns
- Fill patterns
- Materials
- Units
- Snaps
- Dimension styles
- Temporary dimensions
- Object styles

The location and selection of the default template used in Revit is defined in **Settings →
Options → File**, as discussed earlier in this chapter.

If you've created a few templates and you want to start a new project using a template
other than the default one, you can go to **File → New → Project** and select from the drop-
down list or browse to another template. Revit includes a selection of preloaded templates,
but you can also create and save your own templates so the selection is extended. Note
that choosing **File → New** opens the default template and won't allow you the option of
choosing or browsing to a template file.

To create and save your own template, open any of the existing template files, and save
it under a new name; then, modify the settings, units, fonts, and library objects that you
want to see each time you open a new project using the template. Starting a new project in
Revit can be easy. Choose **File → New → Project**, and Revit will open a dialog box with the
following options:

Browse From here, you can change the default template predefined in Settings Options
and select another template.

Project This option is selected by default. It means you're starting a new project using one
of the templates selected.

Project Template Choose this option if you want to create your own template. Select the
template that is most similar to what you want to create, and make changes to it.

CHAPTER 3

Views

This chapter discusses how to look at a Revit model using the views set up in the default template, as well as how to create new views. We'll explore how to create plans, levels, sections, elevations, and 3D views. This chapter also discusses how to create simple schedules and how to customize a schedule to show a wide range of information available in a building information model.

- ■ **Data visualization in Revit**
- ■ **Creating views**
- ■ **Working with views**
- ■ **Schedules**

Data Visualization in Revit

Now that you have an understanding of the basic Revit interface, let's discuss the primary data visualization components of Revit: You'll notice immediately that Revit has been designed with architectural drawing conventions in mind. The displays that Revit generates should be familiar: floor plans, sections, elevations, details, perspectives, and even schedules. Each of these is a way to display the building model in what Revit calls a *view*. Although the names of these views follow a long tradition, the act of creating them with Revit is quite different from traditional drafting and CAD practices.

There is an important difference between Revit and CAD applications to keep in mind as we delve into documenting and viewing a building information model. In Revit, views are dynamic, living images taken from the same database that you created as you built your model. In CAD, views are represented by line drawings that are independent of one another and need to be manually created from scratch. Each drawing is a manually generated artifact. In Revit, when you create a view, you draw nothing. It's as if you're taking a picture of the 3D model from various vantage points.

As you learned in Chapter 1, in Revit a wall drawn in any view is represented in other views automatically. There is no need to draw the wall as lines in every view. This feature is incredibly powerful because it allows you to rapidly generate your building geometry and have all the information necessary to begin laying out a drawing set much earlier in the design process. From a very early stage, you have enough information to place plans, sections, elevations, and details onto sheets for documentation. From that point forward, sheets will auto-update as the design progresses and moves through iterations. When the design solidifies, you'll add the necessary level of construction detail and annotations to your views.

Figure 3.1

The View tab

Creating Views

Many view types are available in Revit. These appear in the Project Browser under Views. Each view type is defined by a collection of parameters that provide control over values such as view depth, scale, object visibility, and level of detail. Right-clicking any view in the Project Browser lets you access the properties of a view and change its parameters. As you'll see, view properties allow you be extremely versatile in what information you present in any given view.

Most of the different views in Revit can be created using the View tab (shown in Figure 3.1). There are some additional ways to create views, which we'll be exploring throughout this chapter. Any number of views can be preset using project templates. When you use Revit's default templates, a number of views are already established when you start a new project.

Navigating Views

As new views are created, they dynamically populate the Project Browser. When you create new views or delete views, they're added to or removed from this list automatically. Double-clicking any view in the Project Browser opens that view and makes it active. Once a view is active, you can close it using the Close icon in the upper-right corner of the view. Doing so doesn't delete the view; it closes it in the view window. To delete a view, use the right-click menu when the mouse is over a view in the Project Browser.

In addition to using the Project Browser to navigate between views, you can also use view reference graphics including section marks, elevation tags, and levels as hyperlinks. When a view is created, the view tag is shown in blue (see Figure 3.2). Each of these blue elements can be double-clicked to take you directly to the view it references. You must double-click the arrow (in the case of elevations) or the flag (for sections and callouts).

Figure 3.2
Section flag

Make sure you double-click within the blue section tag to open the corresponding view (See Figure 3.3). Double-clicking the section line will not open the associated section.

Figure 3.3
Where to click

The hyperlinking of section and elevation tags works only when they aren't selected. If they're selected (highlighted red within Revit), no matter how many times you double-click, it won't lead you to another view.

Levels

Let's start with the first view you'll typically use: plan view. In Revit, the default plan is referred to as a Level 1. A level typically represents one story in a building; but as you'll see later, a level can also be used to reference other elements (split levels, roof edges, and so on). Levels are typically created for each story in the model.

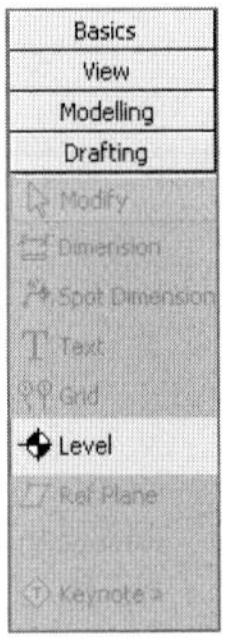

Creating Levels

You can select the Level command from either the Drafting or Basics tab in the Design toolbar when you're in an elevation or section view (Figure 3.4).

Figure 3.4
The Level command in the Drafting toolbar

When selected, this command allows you to draw a level and thus add it to a model. It's important to note that the Level command is grayed out unless you're actively in an elevation or section view.

To create a level, select the Level tool and draw on the screen. When you draw a level, Revit automatically generates a floor plan and a ceiling plan for that story. To add another story, repeat the process.

You can also create a level by copying an existing one. To do this go to a section or elevation view, select a level in the view and, using the Copy command, copy the existing level creating a new one.

Copied levels react differently than those drawn with the Level command. One difference is that they appear black instead of hyperlinked blue. Another difference is that a copied level doesn't automatically create a new view; it only gives you another datum in the project that shows in elevation or in section. This is intentional, and it's useful when you need another benchmark in elevation to show heights but don't necessarily want another level in plan. A good example is the top of a wall in a foundation drawing.

Working with Views

This section discusses a few tasks and challenges you may encounter in your first Revit projects when adding or manipulating views.

Adding a Plan View

What do you do when you create a level that isn't associated with a plan, and you later decide that you want it to become a plan view? It's not too late. **Go to View → New → Floor Plan**. You'll see a dialog box that allows you to select a level and create a new floor plan based on that level (Figure 3.5). Make sure to check "Do not duplicate existing views" at the bottom of the dialog box. (This process is the same for ceiling plans.)

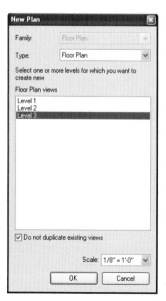

Figure 3.5
New Plan dialog box

Duplicating Views

What happens when you want to create a new view based on an existing floor plan? Say that you need a presentation plan of Level 1 as well as a typical floor plan for your documents. You can achieve that in Revit by duplicating views. To duplicate a view, right-click the view's name in the Project Browser, and choose Duplicate View from the menu that appears (see Figure 3.6).

Duplicate makes a duplicate view in which only the model data of that view is copied. This can be useful when you don't wish to copy any tags, dimensions or annotations from one view to the next.

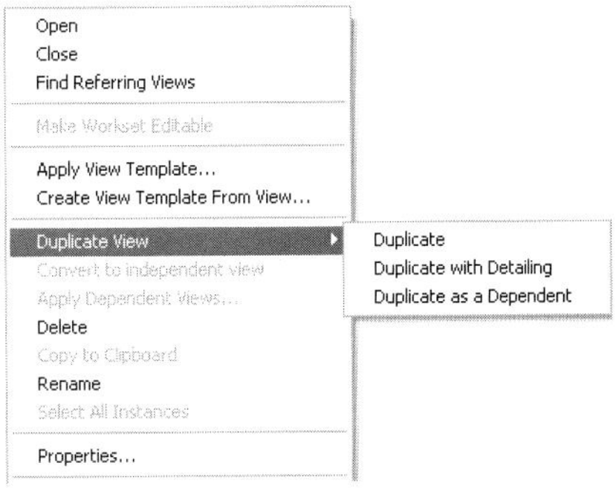

- Duplicate makes a duplicated view in which only the model data of that view is copied.

- Duplicate with Detailing makes a copy of the model data and any 2D information (such as text, dimensions, or keynotes) in the view. When this method is used, annotations and detailing that are added or edited in the original view after the duplication aren't propagated in the duplicated view. Only model-data modifications show in the new view.

- Duplicate as a Dependent not only creates a duplicate of all the model and drafting data, but also creates a dependency between the detailing information of the duplicated view and the original view. When this type of duplication is used, model as well as drafting changes in the original view propagate in the duplicated view.

Figure 3.6
Duplicate View menu

You can not have dependent view be in a different scale then the original. Use cases: Working with big floor plate projects that you need to split in separate segments for printing or placing the VERY same view on many sheets.

Types of Views in Revit

Revit uses many types of views. Following is a list of commonly used views:

Floor plans   There are a number of different floor-plan view styles in Revit. We've discussed the most common type, which is associated with the levels.

Ceiling plans   Ceiling-plan views behave in a similar fashion to floor plans, with the exception that they give a view upward to the ceiling of a level.

Site plans   Site plans by default are at 1:20 (1:250) scale and are views from above your model. The site plan typically contains the physical and topographic features of the model and doesn't show certain annotations that normally would not appear at scales greater than ¹⁄₁₆″ (1:200).

Callouts   A *callout* is a plan, section, detail, or elevation view showing a cutout of a view that is dependent on the parent view from which it's generated. If the parent view is deleted, the callout view or views dependent on that parent view are also deleted. For example, if you have a plan view of a kitchen, and you want to create another view that represents only part of the kitchen at a larger scale to see more detail, you use this command. The new view shows up in your Project Browser under Floor Plans and by default is called Callout of [*view name*].

Elevations

Placing elevation tags lets you create elevations of a portion of the model. These are orthogonal projected views as opposed to 3D views, which are axonometric or perspective. There is no distortion of vanishing points in an elevation view.

In previous versions of Revit, it wasn't possible to duplicate an elevation without adding a new tag to the documents. While it is still possible to add elevation views in this manner, you can now also add elevations by right-clicking the view in the Project Browser and choosing **Duplicate View → Duplicate**. This will make a new non-dependent elevation view. What's great about Revit is that when you insert an elevation tag, it dynamically positions itself perpendicular to the wall or any other object you want to elevate.

> Try drawing a few walls that are non-orthogonal and placing an elevation tag, moving the mouse around the walls. See how the elevation tag orients itself according to the wall that it references. If you have a series of walls at different angles to each other, it selects the one closest to being perpendicular to it.

Figure 3.7

A highlighted elevation tag. Note that the active elevations' associated boxes are checked.

Each elevation symbol is capable of creating four elevations, each facing a different direction. This is designed purposely for interior elevations. By highlighting the middle of the elevation tag after inserting it, you get the option to activate the other elevations. Check or uncheck one of the boxes to turn the elevation on or off (see Figure 3.7).

> Revit understands the differences between interior and exterior elevations. When creating interior elevations, Revit draws the elevation of the room and cuts it where the bounding walls, floors, and ceilings are located.

Highlighting the activated elevation arrow gives you additional options and displays the width and depth of the elevation. In Figure 3.8, the bar represents the width of the elevation, and the dashed line shows the depth. Both of these properties can be modified either in plan or in the actual elevation.

You can double-click any of the elevation arrows to navigate directly to the corresponding view. Once the elevation is placed on a sheet, the sheet number appears inside the elevation box (see Figure 3.9), and the view number appears in the elevation arrow. Deleting the elevation tag deletes all the corresponding elevations from the model.

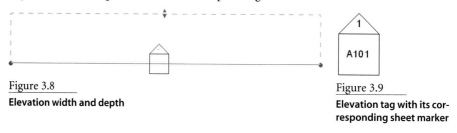

Figure 3.8

Elevation width and depth

Figure 3.9

Elevation tag with its corresponding sheet marker

Sections

Sections show a vertical slice of the model. The properties of section tags are similar to those of elevation tags. The view width and depth are defined by the dashed lines, as in the elevation, and opposing arrows dynamically change the direction of the section cut (see Figure 3.10).

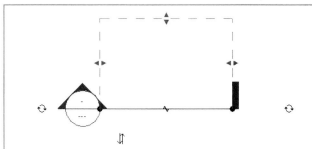

Figure 3.10

A typical section symbol

You often need broken section cuts through a project—for example, when you want to cut through a staircase that isn't in the cut line of the section. To do this, you need to create staggered section lines.

To properly display a particular section, you may want to stagger the section cuts. To stagger a section cut follow these steps:

1. Draw a section line where you need to establish a view.

2. Highlight the section, and choose Split Segment (Split Segment) from the Options bar.

   This opens the Split tool and allows you to split the section flag at any point along the cut plane.

Note that now each segment of the section cut is editable for location and depth. Grab a portion of a section line that you've segmented, and move it up or down to arrive to a desired position. A section can be cut multiple times in a model.

> For best performance, make sure to limit the depth of your section and elevation cuts to what you really want to see. For example, if you are cutting a wall section, there is no reason to set the section depth past the back wall of the room in which you are cutting the section. Revit will calculate all of the information whether you see it or not, so make your section depth as shallow as possible.

Area Plans

Area plans can be used for gross area, rentable, or BOMA (Building Owners and Manager's Associations) area calculations, to name a few. To create one of these plans, click the Room and Area tab, and choose Area Plan. Area plans are most effective when you have areas that span multiple rooms.

Drafting Views

Drafting views are 2D views specifically designed to show information that is not created with the model. They're usually used to show information like standard details or information that is typical of a certain area but doesn't necessarily have a connection with the model. Drafting views can also be used to display detailed 2D information about something in the model.

A plenitude of 2D details and elements by various manufacturers is available on the Web. You can also reuse details from your previous CAD projects. Drafting views let you import CAD files of standard details and create 2D details by drawing with drafting tools such as lines and fill patterns.

It's important to understand that drafting views, even if created separately from the model or imported, can be referenced in the model and linked to a callout so your drawing sheets always maintain a parametric relationship to their associated details. You should also understand that Revit can create dynamic details that are generated out of the model with 2D drafting elements overlaid on top. Unlike drafting details, these details are connected with the model elements, so any model changes are reflected in the details.

Drafting views can be inserted onto sheets and can also be referenced to sections or elevations as a similar (SIM) condition. To reference a drafting view to a model, follow these steps:

1. Create your new drafting view, and name it using the Drafting View button (⚸ Drafting View..) from the View tab.

2. Import a DWG file, or in the empty view using detail lines, filled regions, and other Drafting tools, create the 2D detail.

3. Go to the View tab and choose Callout (🔲 Callout   ).

4. Prior to drawing the callout bubble in the model where the detail explains the condition, from the Options bar select "Reference other view" and choose the drafting view you just created (see Figure 3.11).

   The resulting reference brings you to more detailed information about the portion of the model that you describe in the drafting view.

As discussed in Chapter 1, you don't need to model every detail of the building. Each project needs to define an acceptable level of detail to model, based on the project parameters.

View Range

Most of the time, Revit's default settings cover the usual cases. However, there are situations in which you may want (or need) to modify the View Range settings. Here is an elementary description of how this tool works.

Working in a modeling environment, a plan view is nothing but a horizontal slice of your building. Architects slice the building at what is called a *cut plane* of 4′-0″ (1.20m). That's easy. But once you cut the building, how deep do you want to see? How do you want to represent the objects below the cut plane: Hidden? Cut through? Dashed? What about the objects above you: Do you want to see four cut table legs in plan view when you cut the plan low to capture a certain aspect of your room? This is where the View Range options come in handy.

These options are applicable only to floor and ceiling views. Modifying these properties influences the visibility and appearance of the elements in the project. To access the View Range dialog box, right-click in the View window and choose **View Properties → View Range**, as shown in Figure 3.12.

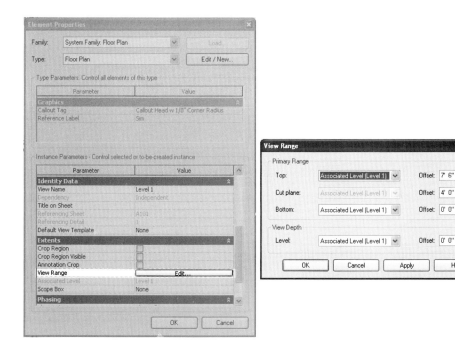

Figure 3.12

Accessing the View Range dialog box

Primary Range

The following list describes the Primary Range features in the View Range dialog box (see Figure 3.13). These features can be a little complex to understand initially, but as you modify them and see the results in your model, they will become easier to understand:

Top plane The top plane defines the uppermost plane above the cut plane up to which elements will be considered. If an element is above the cut plane but still in the primary range (partially or fully), the element is visible in the plan view as if it were seen from below the element.

Cut plane The cut plane defines the height at which the 3D elements of the model are physically cut, as shown in Figure 3.14.

Bottom plane By default, the bottom plane is coincident with the view depth plane, but it doesn't have to be. If an element is below the cut plane and is wholly in the primary range, it's still shown. Note that only a few Revit elements are considered here: windows, furniture systems, and generic models.

View Depth View depth defines the extent to which you want to view what is below the cut plane.

Figure 3.13

View Range dialog box

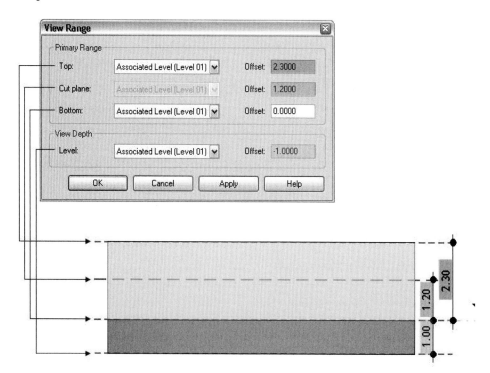

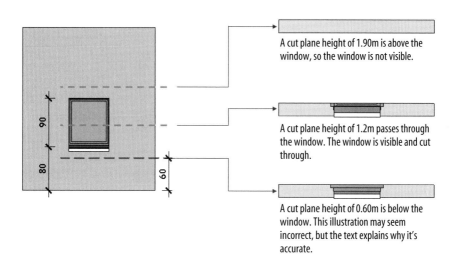

Figure 3.14

Cut plane functionality

A cut plane height of 1.90m is above the window, so the window is not visible.

A cut plane height of 1.2m passes through the window. The window is visible and cut through.

A cut plane height of 0.60m is below the window. This illustration may seem incorrect, but the text explains why it's accurate.

Figures 3.15 through 3.18 demonstrate the use of the View Range. Different settings for the bottom plane and cut plane result in different ways to see a split view.

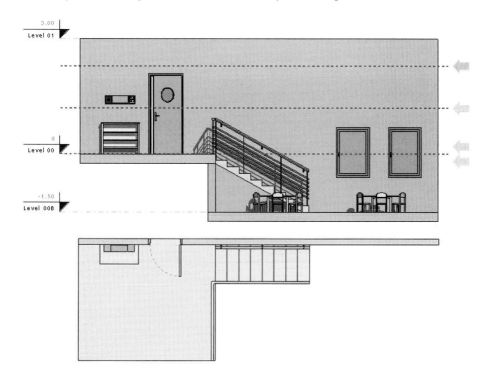

Figure 3.15

Cut plane and bottom plane shown at the upper floor level

Figure 3.16

Cut plane and bottom plane shown at the lower floor level

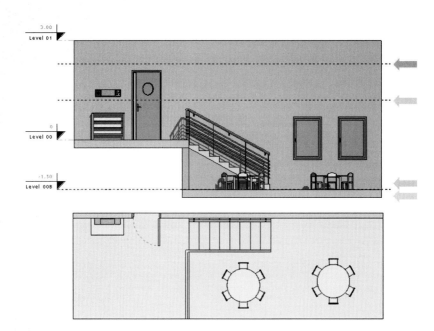

Figure 3.17

Cut plane and bottom plane shown at 1 meter above the lower floor level

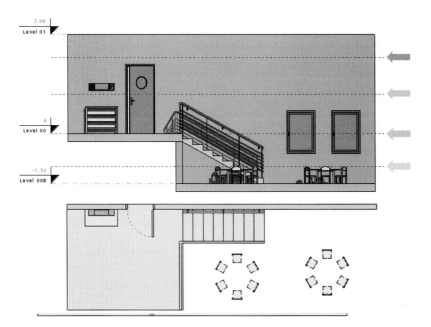

Figure 3.18

Cut plane and bottom plane shown below the lower floor level

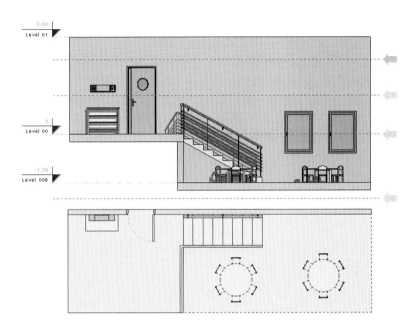

Figure 3.19

Cut plane application

Revit doesn't cut all 3D elements. When you cut furniture, regardless of the cut plane, the furniture is always cut at the same height. To understand which Revit elements are cut, choose **Settings → Object Styles**, and note that some elements are grayed out in the Cut column (see Figure 3.19). These objects aren't affected by a change of cut height.

Legends

Legends are a special type of view in Revit. They're graphic representations of elements in the model that explain the symbology used in the project. Examples include demolition notes on a title block, a key to symbols in a site plan, and typical wall and window types used in a project. Unlike all other views, which you can place only once on a sheet, legends are used for views you want to replicate on multiple sheets. Legends are 2D linework; in spite of the fact that they look like the elements they represent, allow match properties, and possess other smart behavior, they don't increment quantities of the elements they represent and thus aren't computed in the schedules. For example, adding a door or a door symbol to a legend won't be reflected in the schedule or overall project door totals. This is one of Revit's most sophisticated features (see Figure 3.20).

Figure 3.20

Legend and plan notes

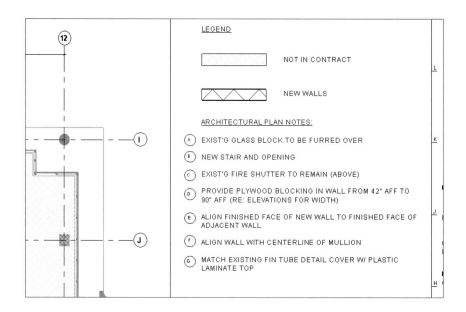

Figure 3.20

Legend and plan notes

Legends are the only view type in Revit that can be placed on multiple sheets.

To create a Legend view, go to the View tab on the Design bar and select the Legend tool. You can then give the Legend view a name and associated scale and you will be presented with an empty view window. To add information to this view, simply go to the Drafting bar and use the Legend Components or Symbols tools.

Axonometric Views

Axonometric views of the entire project model can be generated by clicking the 3D icon (🏠 3D) on the toolbar.

Once a view is created, you can use the mouse or the Dynamic View bar to rotate the view to reflect a position you'd like to capture (see Figure 3.21). To save the axonometric view after manipulating the orientation or other view parameters, click the Dynamic View icon in the same bar, and then click Save at the bottom of the Dynamic View dialog box. You'll be prompted to give the 3D view a name.

Perspective and Camera Views

Another type of 3D view is the perspective view (see Figure 3.22). Once created, these views appear in the 3D Views folder in the Project Browser. Such views can be taken from anywhere in the model.

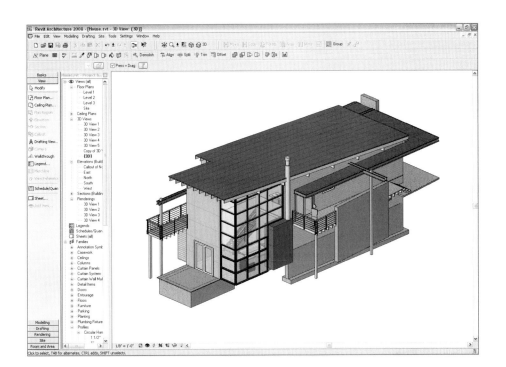

Figure 3.21

Axonometric view

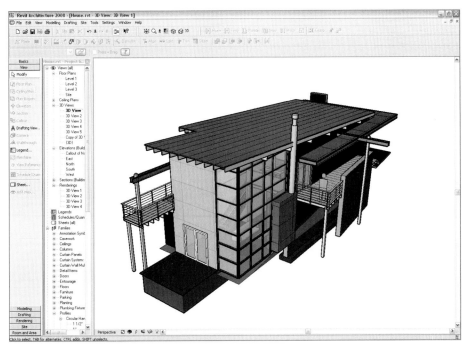

Figure 3.22

Perspective view

Camera Views

To place a camera view, open the floor-plan view or level where you want the camera to be placed. By default, the camera view is 5´-6˝ above the floor and looks straight ahead. To create a camera view, follow these steps:

1. Make sure you're in a floor-plan view. Go to the View tab, and choose Camera (📷 Camera).

2. Select the location where you'd stand in the model and then the direction in which you want to look. You can manipulate the view range once the camera is located. Figure 3.23 shows the camera after it has been placed in a view.

3. When your camera is placed, it automatically opens the 3D view of the model that you just created. At this point, you can expand the view range vertically and horizontally to make more or less of the model appear in the view.

4. Once you are in a perspective view, unless the view window of the perspective is active, the camera you have placed will not be visible in other views. To see the camera placement, open the perspective view and highlight the crop box surrounding the view (the border of the view) or right-click the view name in the Project Browser and choose 'Show Camera.'

Figure 3.23

A camera view placed within the model

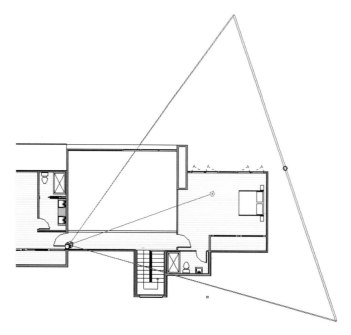

5. Go back to the plan where you created the camera view. The camera is highlighted in red. The extent of the new view range is shown graphically in this view. To modify it textually, highlight the view or go to Properties. Doing so pulls up the properties for the view and allows you to modify the camera's head height, target height, and view depth.

Walkthroughs

A *walkthrough* is an animation of a camera that follows a path. It's an effective method to create a sense of walking through a building that you can communicate to a client.

You can create a walkthrough by placing a series of cameras in a chosen order on a chosen path in plan view and then viewing the created walkthrough as an animation. You can also save a walkthrough file in AVI format to share with your client.

> To toggle through multiple open views, use the Ctrl-Tab command.

Schedules

Schedules are lists of entities and objects within the model. They enumerate things that can range from building objects such as walls, doors, and windows, to sheets, textnotes, and keynotes. The ability to dynamically create and update schedules is a core aspect of BIM and Revit.

Creating schedules of objects, areas, or material quantities in a project is one of the most painful tasks for architects. Needless to say, performing a manual calculation takes a long time and can result in errors. Using CAD systems, this process may be partially automated, but the calculation can only count the number of blocks that are predefined in a file. In Revit, all elements have information about their physical properties, and you can add information to individual elements. For example, doors can have properties like size as well as material, color, fire rating, exterior/interior, and so forth.

Revit lets you schedule any element on any of the properties it holds. Almost anything placed in a Revit view can be scheduled. Additionally, because the schedule is linked to the objects in the model, you can use the schedule to locate objects within the model and change types and properties. As we often state, it does not matter in which view you add or change something. The changes will be reflected in all the views. Schedules are easy to create and use and they are intuitive.

To create a schedule, go to the View tab, and choose Schedule/Quantities (▦ Schedule/Quantities...).

NOT ALL SCHEDULES NEED TO APPEAR ON SHEETS

You can use schedules to document doors and windows, but you can also use the schedule to look for inconsistencies within your model. For instance, you can keep a schedule of textnotes only within a model and not use them on sheets. This schedule can then be used to look for odd items inserted into the model. You can schedule the textnote name and the number of times it appears in the model. Perhaps the schedule indicates that a particular note is used only one or two times in the model. You can then decide if the note was inserted incorrectly into the project and determine whether it's inconsistent with the other notes in the model. The same thing can be done for wall types or anything else you can schedule.

The resulting dialog box has a list of possible schedules:

Multi-category   This schedule is for objects that don't normally appear together. For example, you may want to create a list of windows and doors in the same schedule. You may also want a schedule showing all the casework and furniture in a project. A multi-category schedule allows you to combine a number of different items in separate categories into one schedule.

Area (gross building)   This schedule lists the gross building areas created with the area plans.

Areas (rentable)   Rentable area plans can be created with a rentable plans schedule. Later in this chapter, we'll walk through an exercise demonstrating how to create a simple schedule.

Other schedules

The following shows some of the other schedules you can create within Revit.

Figure 3.24

Other Schedule Types

Casework	Plumbing fixtures
Ceilings	Property line segment
Curtain panels	Property lines
Curtain systems	Railings
Curtain wall mullions	Ramps
Doors	Roofs
Electrical equipment	Rooms
Electrical fixtures	Site
Fascias	Slab edges
Floors	Specialty equipment
Furniture	Stairs
Furniture systems	Structural columns
Gutters	Structural foundations
Lighting fixtures	Structural framing
Mass	Structural trusses
Mechanical equipment	Topography
Parking	Walls
Planting	Windows

Although this list is long, it doesn't include all the schedules available in Revit. Navigate to **View ▸ New**, and you'll see yet another list of schedules, shown in Figure 3.24 and described here:

Material Takeoff This type of schedule can list all the materials and subcomponents of any Revit family and allow an enhanced level of detail for each assembly. You can use a material takeoff to schedule any material that is placed in a component. For example, you might want to know the cubic yardage of concrete within the model. Regardless of whether the concrete is in a wall or floor or column, you can tell the schedule to report the total amount of that material in the project.

View List This schedule shows a list of all the views in the Project Browser and their properties.

Drawing List This schedule shows a list of all the sheets in the project, sorted alphabetically.

> The drawing list can also be used as a sheet index to the documents. Because Revit sorts sheets alphabetically, it's typically not desirable to prepare the sheet index in the traditional fashion, with civil sheets first, then architectural, and so on. One way to customize sheet sorting is to add a field to the schedule and number the sheets so civil is 1, architectural 2, and so on. You can then sort by that number column.

Note Block This schedule lists the notes that are applied to elements and assemblies in your project. You can also use a note block to list the annotation symbols (centerlines, north arrows) used in a project.

Keynote Legend This schedule lists all the keynotes that have been applied to materials and objects in the model. You can either use this list as a complete index of all the notes in the drawing set or filter it by sheet. This legend can then be placed on multiple sheets.

These views are separated from the main list of schedules because they aren't commonly used in building documentation. These schedules are primarily for data coordination that happens outside of the project documentation.

Making a Simple Schedule

Now that we've discussed the variety of schedule types, let's make a simple schedule. When you begin a new schedule, you're presented with a number of format and selection choices. These will help you set the font style and text alignment as well as organize and filter the data shown in the schedule. Remember that Revit at its core is a database, so many of the same functionalities that are available in database queries are also available in

Schedule/Quantities...
Material Takeoff...
View List...
Drawing List...
Note Block...
Keynote Legend...
Revision Schedule...

Revit. If you're unfamiliar with database concepts, don't worry; we'll explain the options in the New Schedule dialog box.

The schedule choices for a new schedule in Revit are shown in Figure 3.25.

You're first given the option of choosing a schedule category from the menu. You're also prompted for a name for the schedule (you can change this later) and given the option of a phase filter. This filter allows you to schedule new construction or existing construction in conditions where you may be working on a renovation and want to schedule only the new or existing materials.

The following example walks through the options in the New Schedule dialog box while creating a new door schedule:

1. Open the `Station.rvt` file found on the CD.

2. Navigate to **View → Schedule/Quantities**.

3. Choose Doors from the Category menu, and name the schedule **Door Schedule**.

4. Click OK. You'll see a series of tabs that allow you to choose the graphics of the schedule and exactly what data is shown. We'll discuss these tabs and how they control the information and visibility in the schedule in Chapter 8. For the time being, we'll only discuss the use of the Fields tab.

5. You can add fields either by double-clicking the name of the field or by highlighting the field and clicking the Add button. Doing so moves the field from the left to the right column. Alternately, you can remove a field by highlighting it in the right column and clicking Remove.

6. Choose the fields Family and Type, Type Mark, and Level, described in Table 3.1.

7. Click OK. Revit will show you the complete schedule in table form. (See Figure 3.26.)

Table 3.1

**Some Door
Schedule Fields**

FIELD	DESCRIPTION
Family and Type	The name of the door family and its type name
Type Mark	The number or letter that appears in the door tag
Level	The level the of the model on which the door appears

Door Schedule		
Family and Type	Mark	Level
04106-pocket_door_658: G.1	1727	LEVEL 4
04106-pocket_door_658: G.1	1736	LEVEL 5
04106-pocket_door_658: G.1	1745	LEVEL 6
04106-pocket_door_658: G.1	1722	LEVEL 3
04106-pocket_door_658: G.1	1730	LEVEL 2
04106-pocket_door_658: G.2 Pocket Door	805	LEVEL 5
04106-pocket_door_658: G.2 Pocket Door	838	LEVEL 6
04106-pocket_door_658: G.2 Pocket Door	839	LEVEL 6
04106-pocket_door_658: G.2 Pocket Door	759	LEVEL 2
04106-pocket_door_658: G.2 Pocket Door	782	LEVEL 2
04106-pocket_door_658: G.2 Pocket Door	783	LEVEL 2
04106-pocket_door_658: G.2 Pocket Door	784	LEVEL 2
04106-pocket_door_658: G.2 Pocket Door	804	LEVEL 2
04106-pocket_door_658: G.2 Pocket Door	820	LEVEL 2
04106-pocket_door_658: G.2 Pocket Door	822	LEVEL 2
04106-pocket_door_658: G.2 Pocket Door	939	LEVEL 5
04106-pocket_door_658: G.2 Pocket Door	957	LEVEL 5
04106-pocket_door_658: G.2 Pocket Door	958	LEVEL 6
04106-pocket_door_658: G.2 Pocket Door	968	LEVEL 6
04106-pocket_door_658: G.2 Pocket Door	977	LEVEL 6
04106-pocket_door_658: G.2 Pocket Door	978	LEVEL 6
04106-pocket_door_658: G.2 Pocket Door	1060	LEVEL 2
04106-pocket_door_658: G.2 Pocket Door	914	LEVEL 4
04106-pocket_door_658: G.2 Pocket Door	917	LEVEL 4
04106-pocket_door_658: G.2 Pocket Door	1076	LEVEL 5
04106-pocket_door_658: G.2 Pocket Door	1115	LEVEL 6
04106-pocket_door_658: G.2 Pocket Door	1118	LEVEL 6

Figure 3.26

Schedule in table form

You've just created a schedule that shows all the doors in the project and the levels they appear on. You can see how easy it is to create simple schedules in Revit. These schedules can, at any time, be modified, re-sorted, filtered, or copied with out re-creating an extensive amount of work and the quantities will always be up-to-date.

CHAPTER 4

Modeling Basics

This chapter of the book focuses on the creation of the basic modeling elements. Walls, floors, and roofs are covered as well as windows, curtain walls, doors, stairs, and railings. In the following chapter, we'll take you through an exercise. In this exercise, we'll build a small house and cover the following basics:

- **Levels and grids**

- **Basic walls**

- **Floors and roofs**

- **Doors and windows**

- **Components**

- **Stairs and railings**

- **Getting started with a project**

Levels and Grids

Levels are horizontal planes that represent major floor-to-floor divisions in a building. Just about every model element in Revit has a relationship to a level, making levels an extremely powerful agent of change. When a level height is changed, all elements associated with that level also change. Elements such as walls have top and bottom relationships to levels, so that when floor-to-floor heights change in the model, walls won't start to stick through floors or appear too short. These smart relationships with the levels reduce the need to manage the vertical position of elements in the model on an individual basis (see Figure 4.1.).

To find out what level an element is associated with, select the element and check its properties. The word *Level* will appear for most content. Walls can be constrained to two levels: one for the base of the wall and one for the top. These parameters are named Base Constraint and Top Constraint, as shown in Figure 4.2. Figure 4.3 shows an object's properties (in this case, a desk) and its constraint to Level 1.

Creating Levels

Levels generate new plan and ceiling views when created interactively. They're displayed and created in the model in perpendicular views (sections and elevations) as lines with a symbol and name attached to them. To draw a level, use the Level tool ( ) in the Basics or Drafting tab in the Design bar. You enter a two-pick placement mode. Your first pick defines the beginning of the level graphic, and the second click sets the end. At the end of the level are a symbol, a name, and an elevation value. These are interactive edit fields that allow you to change the height and name in context.

Figure 4.1

Levels drive floor-to-floor heights.

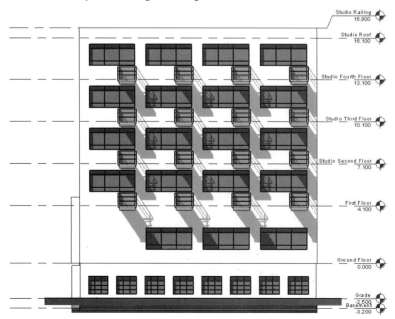

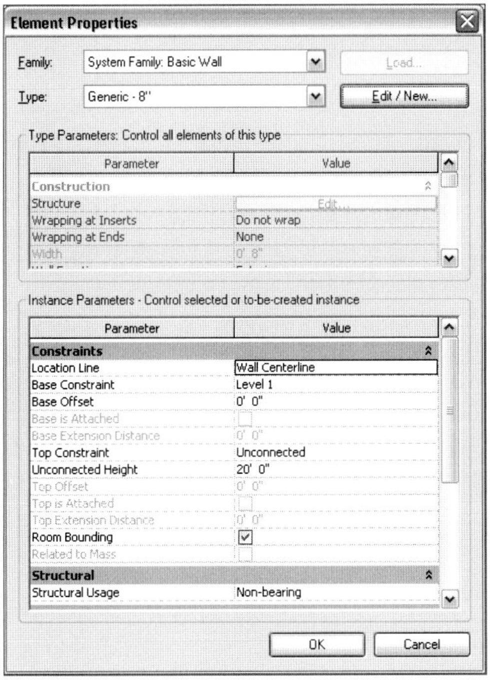

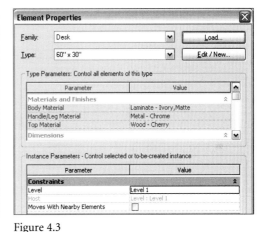

Figure 4.2

Base and Top Constraints of a wall

Figure 4.3

Level parameter for a desk

When a level is selected some text turns blue, and some additional controls appear. Blue text indicates that text is editable. Clicking the text allows you to edit values directly.

The blue dots are drag handles and are used throughout Revit. With your mouse over the control dot, drag the mouse: The level will dynamically adjust its length with the mouse movements. With levels and grids, dragging a control often drags other aligned levels and grids. This is indicated by the blue lock and green reference line. When you see the lock and reference line, it means that when one control is dragged, other controls will also be dragged. To free a level from this implicit constraint, click the lock icon to unconstrain the alignment.

The check box icon turns the symbol and associated text on or off. You can turn the symbol on or off at either end of the level line using the check box, as shown in Figure 4.4.

When a Level is selected, you will also notice the "add elbow" control—a small break sign icon between the top and bottom text. Clicking on this icon will break the level and add a new drag control so that text can fit in tight situations. The same control is available for Grids, which we cover next.

Figure 4.4

Symbol visibility

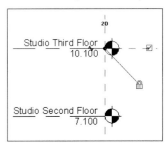

Grids

Grids are vertical planes used as standard references in the construction industry for creating location grids on the site. These construction datums are used to accurately define locations for elements such as columns and beams. In Revit, when columns and beams are placed on grids, they're automatically constrained to grids and grid intersections. As with a level, when a grid is moved, associated elements move with the grid. The creation, graphic representation, and control editing of grids is similar to that of levels (see Figure 4.5).

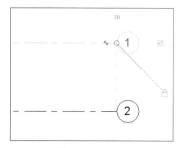

Figure 4.5

A selected grid symbol

When a grid line is selected, you will see a small icon indicating if moving the grid end is a 2D (view-specific) or 3D (model) change. If the icon shows as 3D, then moving the end of the grid line will propagate to all other views where that grid end is visible. Clicking on the icon will turn the 3D control into a 2D control. Then, if you move the end of the gridline, you will only be affecting the appearance of the grid in your active view.

A grid is composed of a line, a symbol and a unique grid number/letter. Revit does *not* let you give two separate grids the same name, just as it won't let you call two separate levels by the same name. It reduces the possibility of uncoordinated data.

Basic Walls

Walls are one of the basic building blocks of architecture and are easily constructed with Revit. Walls are built up from layers of materials that give the wall thickness—they aren't a mere collection of parallel lines. Each material has a user-definable representation for cut and projected geometry, which makes it possible for walls to be represented properly depending on the type of view the wall appears in. For example, when you draw walls in plan view (see Figure 4.6), you see the wall as if it were being cut, with materials represented as abstract hatch patterns. When you look at the same wall from an elevation or in 3D view, you see materials represented with a more realistic expression.

The materials in walls can be designed to provide automatic layer routing, greatly reducing the need to manually deal with wall intersections. Stud layers connect with other stud layers and bypass finish layers, creating clean join representations.

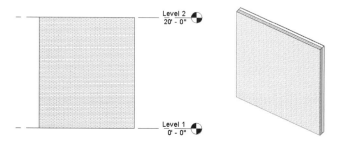

Figure 4.6

Wall representations

Wall layers are properties of each wall type (see Figure 4.7) and can be accessed via the Element Properties dialog. When the properties dialog is open, click the Edit/New button to access type properties. From this dialog, you can the access the Edit Wall Assembly dialog by editing the Structure parameter (see Figure 4.8).

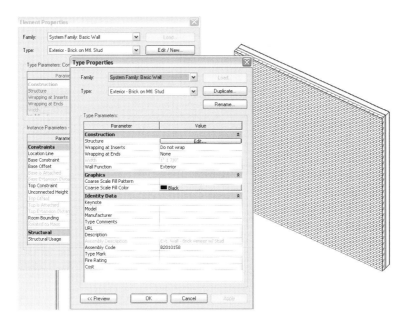

Figure 4.7

Wall properties

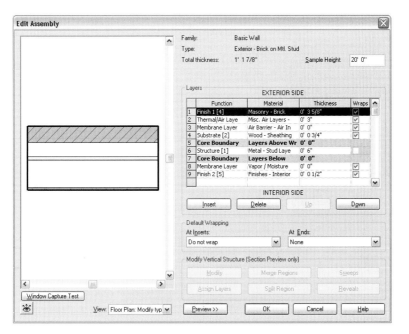

Figure 4.8

Wall layers and materials

Figure 4.9

**A stud wall joining
to a brick wall
in plan**

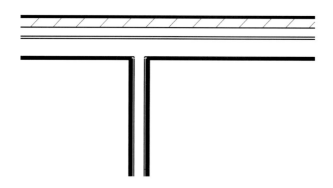

These properties allow you to define a hierarchy of materials so that when the walls in Revit dynamically join (see Figure 4.9), Revit knows how to properly show the joint condition.

Curtain Walls

Curtain walls are a special type of wall (usually known as a *hung* façade) that allows you to divide the wall into a grid that regulates panel and mullion placement. An example curtain wall is shown in Figure 4.10. Panels and mullions can be customized to meet most any design requirement, from metal panels to structural glazing. As with basic walls, curtain-wall height is controlled by setting Base and Top Constraints to levels or offsets from specific levels.

Figure 4.10

**A customized
curtain wall**

Creating Walls

The Wall tool is located in the Basics and Modeling tabs of the Design bar. With this tool, you can create both basic walls and curtain walls in plan and 3D views. Making a wall involves using one of three methods: draw, pick line, and pick face. The most common method is to draw walls using a multipick interaction—defining a start and end point for each wall as if you were drawing it. You can also pick existing lines and generate walls with a single pick. Using the pick-face method, it's possible to place walls on more complex geometric faces with a single pick. The specific methodologies will be covered in more detail in exercises throughout the book.

Floors and Roofs

Floors, Roofs, and Ceilings are similar to walls in that they're built of layers of materials and are constrained to levels. The interface for creating and editing layers of construction is nearly identical, as you'll see in the exercise. Floors and roofs also use the same layer routing as walls, making connections between walls, floors, and roofs appear correctly (shown in Figure 4.11).

Creating Floors and Roofs

These tools can be accessed from either the Basics or Modeling tabs in the Design bar. All of these elements are sketch-based elements, in that they are made by first defining a 2D boundary in what is called the sketch editor. When you activate these tools, the Design bar is replaced with a set of tools specific to sketching 2D shapes. In this mode, lines are drawn that represent the extent of the element as if it were projected onto a two-dimensional plane. When you finish drawing a closed loop of lines, and finish the sketch, Revit generates 3D geometry for you.

Figure 4.11
Walls join with floors and roofs

In the case of floors, the geometry is co-planar with the sketch and has a predictable outcome. With more complex forms, such as hipped roof configurations, the resulting geometry is less obvious from within the sketch mode. Nonetheless, the underlying 2D sketch is always just a click away and can be easily manipulated to achieve your design objectives. Figure 4.12 shows some common roof forms that can be made using sketch mode.

Roofs can also be made by picking faces or by extrusion. These methods are suited for arc roof forms and more complex shapes that cannot be reduced to a 2D projected sketch plane.

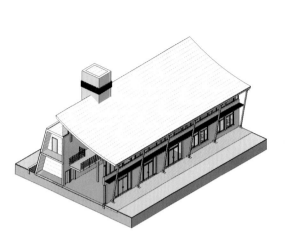

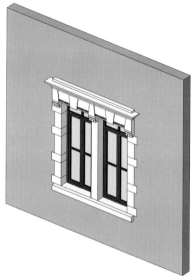

Figure 4.12

Roofs by Footprint on the left, and roof by extrusion on the right

Figure 4.13

Example showing a window hosted by a wall

Doors and Windows

Revit makes adding doors and windows to your model a snap. The key thing to under-stand about inserts (windows and doors) is that they're hosted by walls. Without a host wall, doors and windows can't exist in your model. Figure 4.13 shows a window hosted by a wall.

Inserts always stay in-line with a wall; when the wall is moved or rotated, the inserts also move and rotate. Likewise, if a wall is copied, all inserts in the wall are copied. Like everything else in Revit, windows and doors are associated with a level in order to stream-line the design process and remove obstacles to iteration by reducing the need to manually fix the model.

These elements have specialized representations that are specific to the view in which they're placed. For example, in plan view, a door can be shown as open with an abstract door-swing graphic, whereas in elevation it appears closed and the door swing is shown as diagonal lines indicating the hinge side (see Figure 4.14). Given the fact that graphical symbology varies across the world, Revit is designed to allow you to represent these how-ever you see fit; whether you want a door swing to be an arc or a straight line, or to be shown at all, is at your discretion. Customizing content to suit your needs is always just a few clicks away.

Creating Doors and Windows

To place a window or door, use the tool in the Basics or Modeling tab in the Design bar. Move your mouse into the view. A preview graphic of the element appears on your cursor when it hovers over valid hosts. Pressing the spacebar will rotate the element prior to placement. When you're ready to place the window, click to place it; it will automatically cut out material from the host wall. Inserts can be placed in any view except perspective views. If you need to change the swing direction, press the spacebar when door is selected, and it will cycle through all possible configurations.

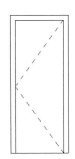

Figure 4.14

Door representations

Components

Windows and doors are just a subset of the possible components that can be created using Revit. Revit will allow you to design, create, and place just about any kind of component you can dream up. The predefined categories of component types include everything from casework to structural framing. Components are a bit more flexible than windows and doors, in that they do not need a wall in order to exist in the model. However, it is possible to design elements that have dependencies on walls. Lighting fixtures are a good example that shows this flexibility in Revit. For something like a wall-mounted light fixture (Figure 4.15), you'd expect it to move with the wall and get deleted with the wall just like a window or door would. Revit allows for this. At the same time, a free-standing floor lamp has no dependency on a wall. Again, Revit lets you determine these types of interaction behaviors for components.

To place components, use the Component tool in the Modeling tab of the Design bar. You can also drag and drop components from the Families node in the project browser.

Figure 4.15

Wall-mounted light fixture

Stairs and Railings

Most buildings have stairs, and where there is a stair, you're likely to encounter a railing. Revit provides specially designed tools for the creation of stairs and railings that give you control over their basic constructive parts. With stairs, we set up design rules for elements such as stringers, treads, and risers, then Revit goes to work building the 3D geometry for us. The same is true for railings. Using design rules, we establish a pattern of rails and balusters, and then draw a simple 2D path. Revit fills in the path with 3D geometry based on the rules we established. Figure 4.16 shows a Revit stair.

The Stair and Railing tools are located in the Modeling tab of the Design bar. When activating these tools, you enter a special sketch mode where you sketch 2D lines. When you're finished, Revit builds the 3D geometry for you. Changing the appearance and design rules for stairs and railings is done through the element type properties interface.

A final note about Revit stairs: They can be set to be Multistory. If your building is a six-story building out of which five are the same floor-to-floor height, you can draw the stair and the railing on one floor only. Then, by setting the Multistory parameter in the stair properties (see Figure 4.17), you can make the stair repeat itself on all the other floors. If the stair was drawn with a railing, the railing is also drawn. If you later decide to make any changes to the stair, you'll need to change it only once, and the change will propagate throughout all floors. Figure 4.18 shows a staircase spanning multiple floors while being one element.

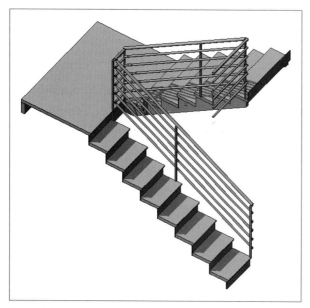

Figure 4.16

A stair

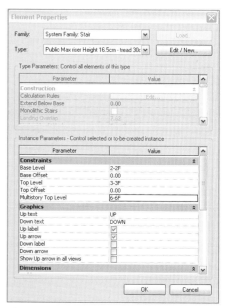

Figure 4.17

The Multistory setting

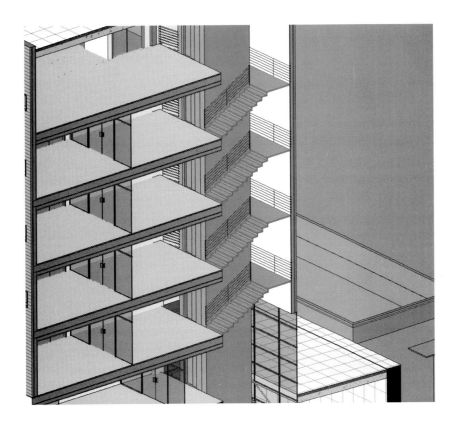

Figure 4.18

A multistory stair

Getting Started with a Project

In the following exercise, you'll use some pre-drawn lines to help you begin laying out exterior and interior walls. This does not mean that you'll always need or have such lines to begin using Revit. We do it here to facilitate moving through the exercise efficiently, and do not burden you with typing in every last dimension value. In real life, there are many different ways to start a project—from an existing 2D import (covered in Chapter 7), from a conceptual massing form, from an imported image, or from scratch. As you will see, Revit has many useful features when laying out walls, especially the smart listening dimensions that let you see dimensions of elements before and during creation.

In the exercise, we will start with a set of lines, and construct 3D walls using these lines as guides. In fact, the lines are named Guides, and are located in the Line Styles dialog, if you feel the need to edit their appearance. To follow along with the process of building exterior and interior walls throughout the rest of this chapter, open the exercise base file named Source_House_Walls_Start.rvt. The model opens with the Level 1 plan view active. Several levels are pre-defined for first and second floors as well as for some roof planes.

Wall Options Bar

Click the Wall tool in the Basics tab to begin the process of drawing a wall. Before you start drawing anything, focus your attention on the horizontal Options bar (Figure 4.19) just above the view. The options you see here are always specific to the selected tool—in this case, the Wall tool. Get accustomed to looking at the Option bar for tool-specific options, because many features show up in this thin strip of interface. We covered some of the basics of the available options in Chapter 2, but the following paragraphs talk more about the wall-specific options.

The first part of the Options bar is the Type Selector, which lets you choose the type of wall element to create. Go ahead and choose the Basic Wall: Exterior Wall. The nice thing about the type-selection list is that even if you place a generic wall initially, you can change the type of wall later by selecting it and changing the type with the same mechanism. I mention this because often, when new users start using BIM, they wonder what level of detail they should start modeling to, at this early stage. It's OK to not know that right from the start. Revit is designed to easily change any wall type to another later in the process without losing any intelligence or relationships with other elements. It's natural to use more generic, abstract wall types when beginning a design process and refine the model later. At the same time, Revit also allows you to be specific from the get-go. If you know your interior walls are wood studs with gypsum wall board, you can start placing those immediately.

The next set of options are methods for making the wall (▱◩◉). You'll use the default option, which uses a drawing metaphor and allows you to draw walls as you would lines. The next two options let you select existing lines or geometric faces to auto-generate a wall without drawing. These are generally used if you're working from an imported set of lines, an imported solid geometry, or a massing form made of geometric faces.

Next comes the height of your wall (Height Level 2 ▾). You define which level the top of the wall is constrained to, or if you want the wall to have a specific fixed height that isn't tied to a level. In Revit, when the top of a wall is not tied to a level, this is referred to as its "unconnected" height. A knee wall is an example of a wall that isn't necessarily tied to a level at the top but needs an explicit height from the Base Level.

Next on the Options bar is the Loc Line parameter. This is short for Location Line, which is really the wall's justification. The Loc Line allows you to set a fixed axis for the wall based on the built-up construction of the wall. The most common use of this is to draw with either the interior or exterior core boundary (as in Figure 4.20) or structural layer when laying out walls. For example, you can draw walls relative to the stud face, rather than the finish face, of gypsum board. Whatever is set here determines where your cursor is relative to the wall construction during creation. You'll notice this when walls are selected, as well: The drag control is located at the location line.

Figure 4.19

Wall Options bar

Basic Wall : Exterior Wall ▾ | ▱◩◉ | Height: Level 2 ▾ | Loc Line: Wall Centerlin ▾ | ☑ Chain ⟋ ▢ ⌐ ▾ Offset: 0' 0" ☐ Radius:

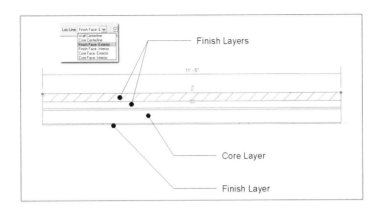

Figure 4.20

This wall has Loc Line set to Finish Face: Exterior.

Next is the Chain check box. When this is selected, it means you can keep making connected walls after every click of the mouse. When it's deselected, extra clicks are needed to snap to the end of the previous wall in order to start the next wall. Chain is selected by default, based on the assumption that when you're making walls (and, as you'll see later, this is the case for sketch lines as well), you generally make a series of connected walls. If this isn't the case, deselect the box, and Revit will remember this setting the next time you use the Wall tool.

Figure 4.21

Wall-shape options

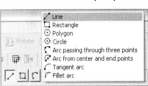

Finally, we get to some options for different types of wall shapes you can draw, shown in Figure 4.21. This includes an obvious suite of line-generation options: lines, rectangles, polygons, circles, and various types of arcs.

Figure 4.22

Here's the house you'll be designing.

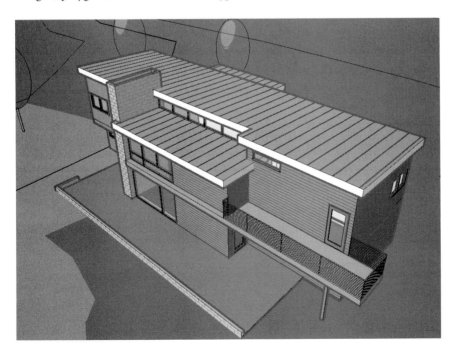

Exterior Walls: Drawing Exterior Walls

Let's start the exercise. In a few chapters, you'll make the small house shown in Figure 4.22! Follow these steps:

1. Select the Wall tool from the Basics tab. From the Type Selector, set the wall type to Basic Wall: Exterior Wall.

2. Using the Options bar, set the Loc Line to Core Face: Exterior. This will allow you to draw the wall using the structural core edge as a baseline, rather than a finish layer or wall centerline.

3. Starting in the upper-left corner of the sketch, begin tracing the outer edge of lines with your wall. Move in a clockwise direction, drawing walls from left to right. (See Figure 4.23) As you do this, take note of snapping as you move the cursor from point to point. Snap your walls to intersection points of the guide lines. Zoom and pan while drawing walls --try this by scrolling the middle mouse button zoom, and holding the middle mouse button down to pan while drawing your walls. To avoid snapping to the wrong points, zoom in and trace the sketch. Revit provides snapping that lets you be precise in your wall creation by looking for endpoints, midpoints, and perpendicular edges (among others).

Figure 4.23

Starting a sketch

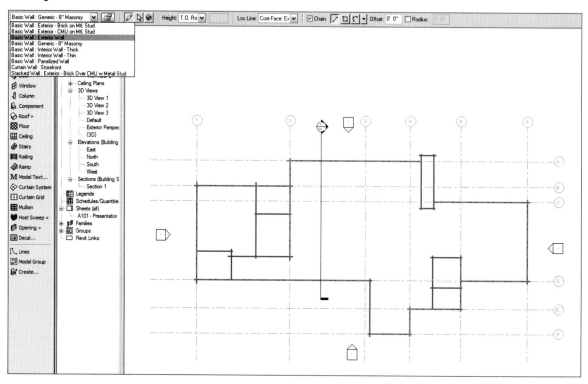

Notice the dimension strings that appear as you draw the walls. These are temporary dimensions that indicate the dimensions of the objects you're drawing and, more important, can be used to specify explicit length and angular values. (To try them, click one point as the start of a wall, and start typing a value on the keyboard. Revit won't need any units or x, y coordinates.) Use snap intersections to place walls. Temporary dimensions can be used to get a more precise placement, as shown in Figure 4.24.

Note that the blue guidelines are obscured by the wall as you draw the walls. This is because the walls you're drawing have a physical height in the model and are being represented as if cut at 4′ above Level 1. What you see isn't just line, but the cut face of the wall geometry, which obscures the lines below. This type of display is called *hidden line*. It means that geometry is displayed relative to your point of view. Elements closer to you will obscure elements farther away.

Figure 4.24

Snaps and temporary dimensions

4. Continue drawing walls until you complete a circuit of lines around the perimeter. If you want to stop drawing walls, press the Esc key twice, or click the Modify tool in the Design bar.

> Drawing walls from left to right on the screen places the exterior face of the wall facing the top of your screen by default. If this isn't the desired orientation, press the spacebar while drawing the wall, and it will flip.

5. Once you complete the walls around the perimeter, toggle the view display to Shaded with Edges using the keyboard shortcut SD (press S then D), and the display mode will change to Shaded with Edges. This option also appears at the bottom of each view in the View Control bar, as shown in Figure 4.25.

6. Use the Tab-selection method by hovering mouse over one of the walls without clicking it, and then press the Tab key once. You'll see the chain of connected walls highlight. Click once to select the walls. Use this method to quickly select connected walls, rather than picking walls individually (See Figure 4.27). Now that all these walls are selected, you can change the wall type with one click. To see this, Tab-select all exterior walls, and then use the Type Selector and change them from Basic: Exterior Wall to Basic: Exterior - Brick on Mtl. Stud.

Figure 4.25

View-display modes can be changed using the View Control bar.

7. All the walls became thicker. These aren't the walls you want, so press Ctrl-Z to undo the type change.

Figure 4.26

**Connected walls can
be selected by using
the Tab key prior to
selecting**

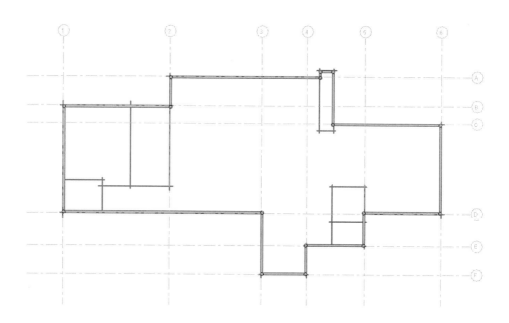

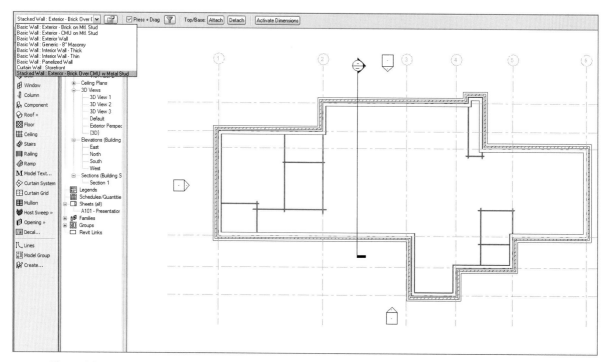

Figure 4.27

Swapping wall types

Drawing the Fireplace Walls

Let's use a similar method to make the fireplace walls:

1. Zoom into the area between gridlines 4 and 5, where we will put the fireplace. Hold down the Ctrl key and select the three walls, as shown in Figure 4.28. Note that the cursor changes to show a + symbol, indicating that each selection will add to the current selection.

> To remove elements from a selection, press Shift and then pick elements that are already selected. To add new elements to selection use the Ctrl key when making selections.

2. Use the Type Selector to change the walls to Generic - 8″ Masonry. The walls maintain their exterior face justification and expand inward. Notice that the cut graphic changes as well—to a diagonal crosshatch. See Figure 4.29.
3. Select the far left shortest segment of the fire place wall and extend it by dragging the blue end grip control.
4. Continue by selecting each wall individually, and dragging the end controls until they snap to the guide line intersections. (Figure 4.30)
5. Select one of the masonry walls and from the right-click menu, select Create Similar. This command puts you directly into drawing mode. Draw the remaining section of the fireplace. If you start drawing from the left corner, the wall is drawn inside-out. To resolve this, press the spacebar to flip the wall on its location line while drawing. Figure 4.32 shows the wall before it's flipped and after it has been corrected.

> Even if you draw the wall inside out to begin with, you can always flip it later by selecting it and pressing the spacebar. The spacebar is a generic method for flipping objects about one or more axes. This is one of the beauties of Revit: There are no rules for when you do what; everything is changeable and replaceable later.

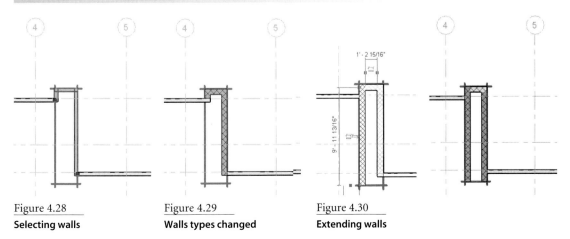

Figure 4.28
Selecting walls

Figure 4.29
Walls types changed

Figure 4.30
Extending walls

Figure 4.31

Choosing Create Similar using the context menu and the toolbar

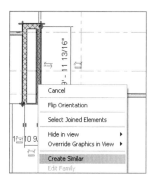

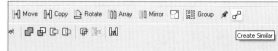

Figure 4.32

Flipping a wall

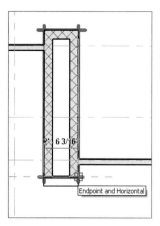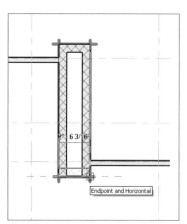

6. Let's change the height of the fireplace walls to go up to a predefined level in the model. Using the chain-selection method mentioned earlier, hover the mouse over one of the masonry walls and press Tab once. The four walls highlight. (If this doesn't happen, select the walls individually pressing the Ctrl key, or window-select them—whichever method works best for you.) Click to select them.

7. Right-click the fireplace walls, then choose Element Properties.

8. Change the Top Constraint parameter to T.O. Chimney, as shown in Figure 4.33.

9. Press the Modify button, or hit Esc key twice to exit the wall creation mode.

Changing Wall Types

Let's now change some walls to more specific types using the Type Selector. You'll see how easy it is to deal with design change using Revit. Follow these steps:

1. Select the walls as indicated in Figure 4.34, and change them from Basic: Exterior to Basic Wall: Panelized Wall using the Type Selector .

2. Let's see what the 3D view looks like. Click the 3D button (⌂3D) at the top of the toolbar to open the default 3D view (see Figure 4.35).

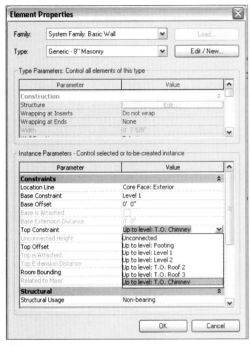

Figure 4.33

Properties dialog box

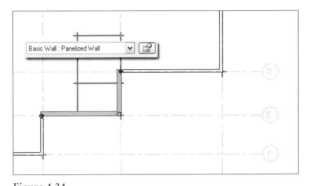

Figure 4.34

Changing walls to Panelized Walls

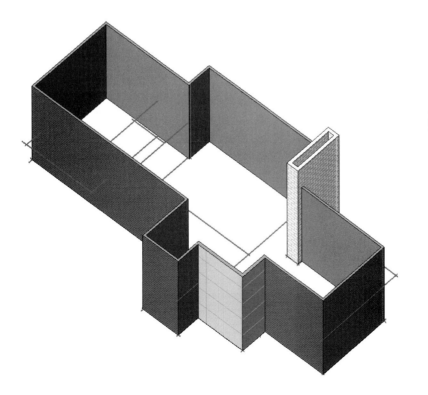

Figure 4.35

The default 3D view

Exterior Walls: Level 2

Let's add some exterior walls to the second floor, to give the model a bit more interest:

1. From the 3D view, select the wall running into the fireplace, as shown earlier in Figure 4.31. Go to the element properties dialog, and change the Top Constraint to Level 2. You do this because the bedroom on Level 2 needs to cantilever over Level 1, and you don't want that wall going through the bedroom. Figure 4.36 shows the wall before and after the constraints have been changed.

Figure 4.36

Modifying the Top Constraint

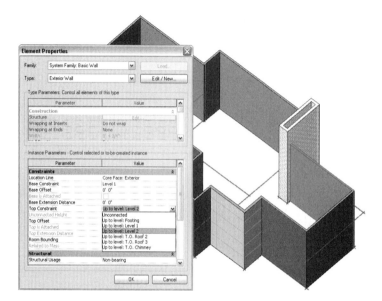

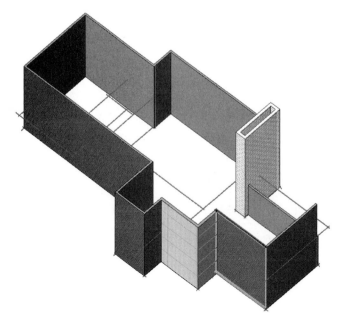

2. You can add some walls to the model directly from the 3D view—a nice benefit of working with a building model. Activate the Wall tool and choose Basic: Exterior wall. Set Level to Level 2, and set Height to T.O. Roof 3 (see Figure 4.37). Make sure the Loc Line is still set to Core Face: Exterior.

3. Start drawing the wall from the intersection of the guideline and the fireplace, and turn the corner to meet the other wall as shown in Figure 4.38.

Figure 4.37

Set the wall parameters before drawing the wall.

Figure 4.38

Adding walls to Level 2

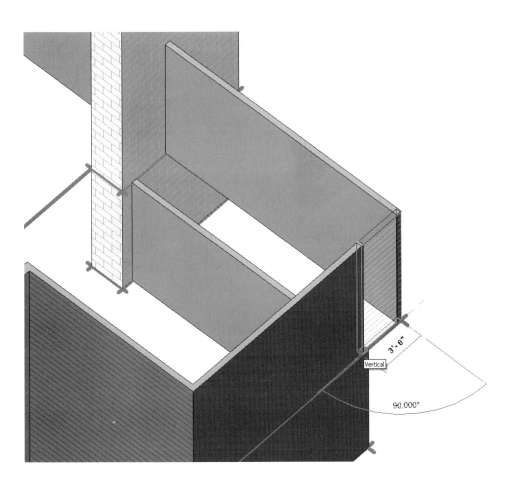

4. Perform a similar operation to create a bump-out for the master bedroom; this will become a closet later (see Figure 4.39). Before you start drawing, make the wall type Basic: Panelized Wall, and draw it from right-to-left so that the panel material faces the exterior.

5. To give the house a bit more variation, let's bring down the height of walls for the front entry and the walls in the back, shown in Figure 4.40. Multi-select the walls as indicated, using the Ctrl key, and then go to the Element Properties and change the Top Constraint to T.O. Roof 2.

Figure 4.39

Adding closet walls

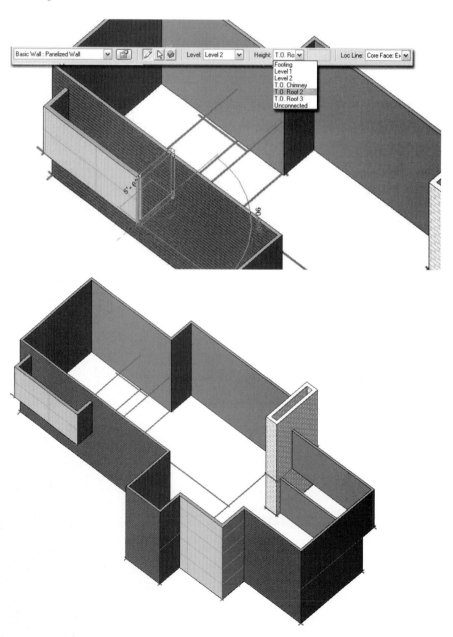

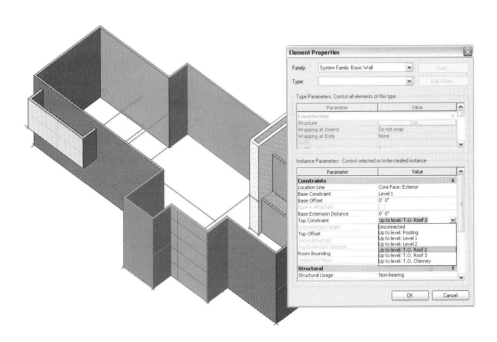

Figure 4.40

**Modifying
wall height**

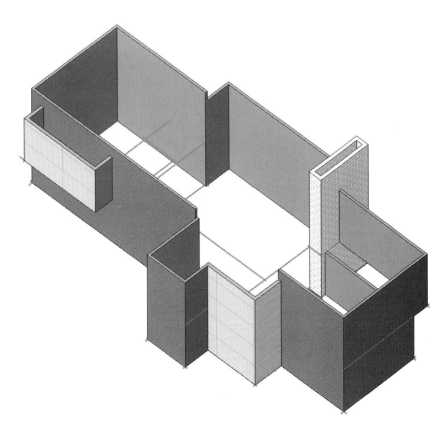

Interior Walls: Level 1

Looking good so far.

1. Open the Level 1 Plan.

2. Select the Wall tool and choose Basic: Interior - Thin.

3. In the Options bar, set Top to Level 2 and the Loc Line to Centerline. Begin laying out the interior walls using the guidelines provided in the view, as shown in Figure 4.41.

Figure 4.41

Creating interior walls

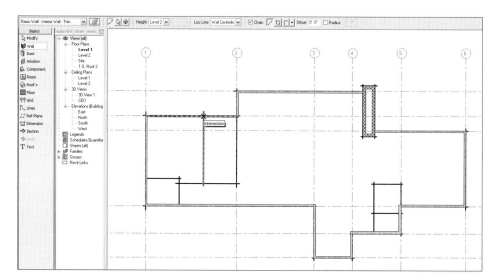

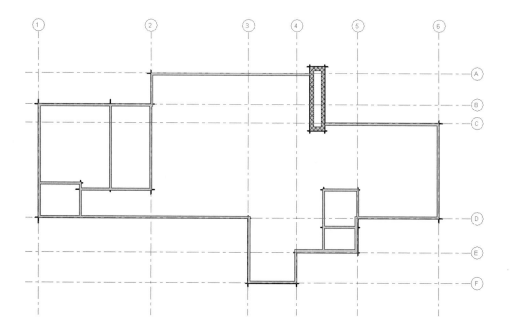

Wall Join/Face Resolution

Not all of the interior walls are lining up neatly with exterior walls. Let's fix that. You'll first change to a thicker wall and then unjoin the wall. You'll use the Align tool to make things line up, then rejoin the walls. Follow these steps:

1. Zoom into the grid 2 join condition where the interior wall hits the exterior, as shown in Figure 4.42. You need to clean this up.

2. Change the wall type to Basic: Interior Thick. You do so because this wall will span two levels and also act as a plumbing cavity.

3. Grab the wall-end control and drag it away from the join, as shown in Figure 4.43.

> If you don't detach the join, then you won't be able to realign the walls to the finish face. When dealing with complex joins such as this, the best practice is to pull the walls away from the join, make proper alignments, and then rejoin the walls.

4. Select the Align tool (⫶ Align ⫶) in the toolbar. You'll use it to align the finish faces of the two walls. This tool allows you to make alignments between elements and constrain that alignment if you desire. Walls that are connected automatically attempt to stay aligned. (Users often comment that the Align tool is one of the most useful tools in Revit. The thing to remember is that the first pick is where you want to align to, and the second click chooses which element you want to move [align].)

5. Select the geometry (the horizontal wall) that you want to align. This is the target that you want other geometry to align with. Then, choose the geometric edge that you want to align, as shown in Figure 4.44—in this case, the thick interior wall face.

6. Drag the wall end back into the join. The walls clean up, and you get a nice-looking image like the one in Figure 4.45.

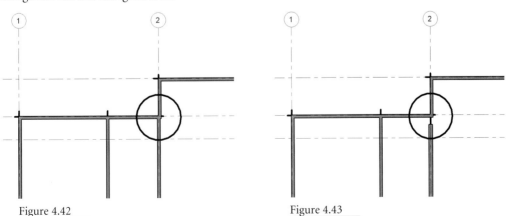

Figure 4.42
An example of a bad wall join

Figure 4.43
Modifying the wall join

7. Now that the wall looks good, change its height so that its Top Constraint is T.O. Roof 3. Check out your results in the 3D view; see Figure 4.46.

8. Using the technique you just went through, clean up the condition shown in Figure 4.47.

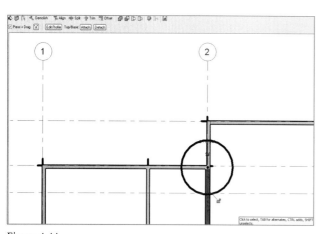

Figure 4.44

Aligning the wall

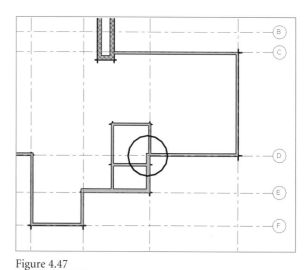

Figure 4.45

Finished walls

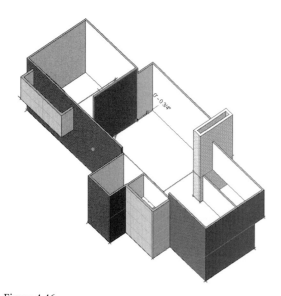

Figure 4.46

Interior walls extending to T.O. Roof 3

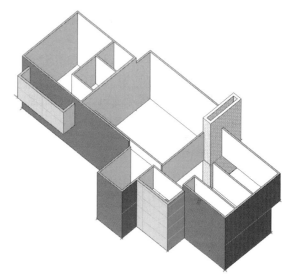

Figure 4.47

Clean up this join condition also.

Interior Walls: Level 2

Let's continue to add interior walls, this time to Level 2:

1. Open the Level 2 Floor plan and place interior thin walls using the guidelines as placement aids.

2. Using the Basic: Interior—Thin wall type and the Pick tool, pick the lines in the view. Before picking, use the options bar to set the Loc Line to Wall Centerline, and the Height set to T.O. Roof 3.

3. Make sure to clean up the walls highlighted in Figure 4.48 to get aligned walls and clean joins. Use the same technique used in Level 1 by pulling the join apart and then using the Align tool as shown in the figure.

4. The model has a large double-height volume for the main living space. A knee wall will be used to bridge the two bedrooms on either side of the volume. To change the height of the wall, select it and change its Top Constraint from T.O. Roof 3 to Unconnected (see Figure 4.49).

5. Set the Unconnected parameter value to 3′-0″(90cm).

Excellent job! Now you have the beginnings of a small house (see Figure 4.50). The next exercise will pick up from this point and continue to add more detail to the model.

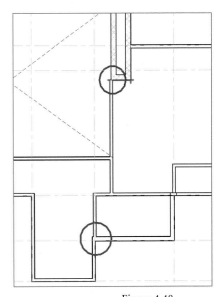

Figure 4.48

Align the finished faces of these walls.

Figure 4.49

Change the wall height.

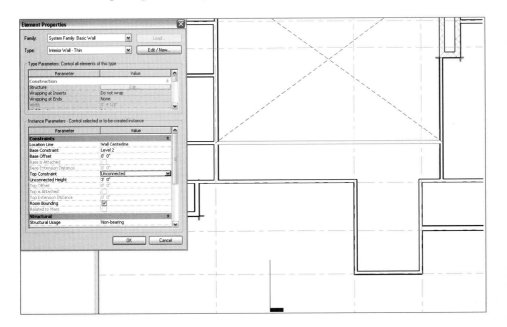

Figure 4.50

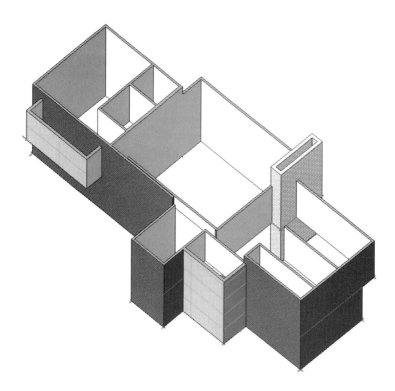

Adding a Floor to Level 1

Now that you've built the exterior and interior walls, let's continue to build out the model by adding floors and roofs. You can continue where you stopped on your file, or open the file Source_House_Floor-Roofs.rvt.

Figure 4.51

Sketch tab for floors

1. Open floor plan Level 1. From the Basics tab in the Design bar, select the Floor creation tool. The view and interface change into sketch mode.

   In sketch mode, the model becomes halftone and non-editable. A specialized set of tools replaces the normal Design bar. Depending on the type of element that is being edited, different options appear in the Sketch tab. The Sketch tab for floors looks like Figure 4.51.

   The default state puts you into the Pick Walls command. This allows you to create the sketch of the floor by picking walls in the model to create a parametrically associated floor boundary. A *sketch* is a series of connected lines that form closed shapes. Sketches can form multiple closed shapes, but lines can't intersect or be left unconnected at an end. Revit uses the term *loop* to define a closed sketch.

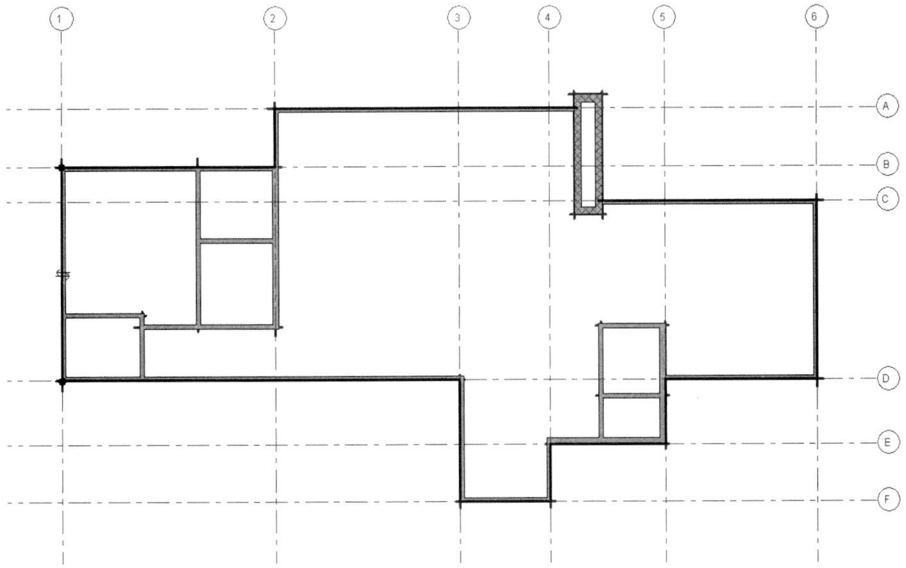

Figure 4.52

**Walls used to gener-
ate sketch lines**

A sketch must follow some basic rules in order to generate geometry: It needs to be form a closed loop of lines that do not overlap or have unconnected ends. Lines cannot be left floating around, and disconnected, or the sketch cannot be finished. If you sketch is invalid, Revit will warn you, and even highlight the problem areas.

2. Using the Pick Walls option, hover your mouse over an exterior wall; don't click it. Press the Tab key; a chain of connected walls highlights. Click the mouse. Sketch lines are generated from the walls, as shown in Figure 4.52.

3. Not all the walls along the perimeter were selected. This is because the fireplace walls aren't connected at their *ends* with other walls in the selection. To finish the sketch to be a closed loop, you need to select the fireplace walls and clean up the sketch. If you attempted to finish the sketch without adding lines around the fireplace, you'd get the warning seen in Figure 4.53, indicating that the sketch isn't valid.

4. While still in sketch mode, Pick the three exterior fireplace walls using the Pick tool, being sure to pick on the exterior face of the walls, as shown in Figure 4.54.

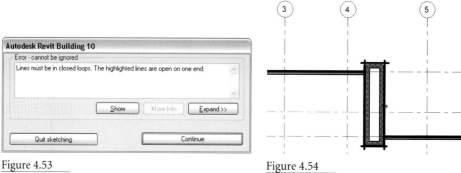

Figure 4.53

The warning if lines don't form closed loops

Figure 4.54

Pick the remaining exterior walls.

The lines in our sketch intersect and will need to be cleaned up in order to complete the sketch. The Trim tool is great for these conditions, let's continue:

5. Select the Trim tool in the toolbar (⊬ Trim).

6. Select pairs of lines to trim. The first pick is any line you want to trim. The second pick is the line you want to trim to; and shows a preview of the result, as shown in Figure 4.55.

7. Do the same for the other overlapping lines to complete the sketch (see Figure 4.56).

8. Now that the sketch looks good, click the Finish Sketch button in the sketch Design tab.

9. Open the 3D view, and you'll see the floor. Select it by hovering mouse over an edge of the floor and clicking when it highlights. (You can press Tab to select it if it doesn't highlight immediately.) The floor can be re-edited using the Edit button on the Options bar. Figure 4.57 shows the floor in 3D.

Figure 4.55

Trim lines

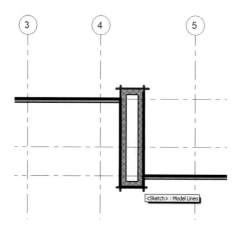

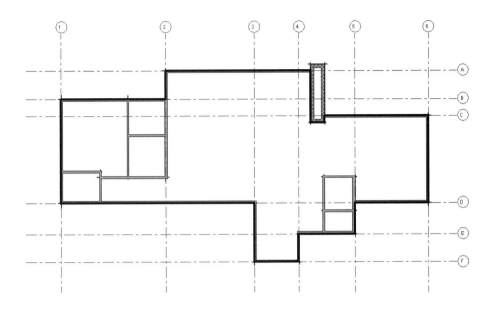

Figure 4.56
A closed-loop sketch

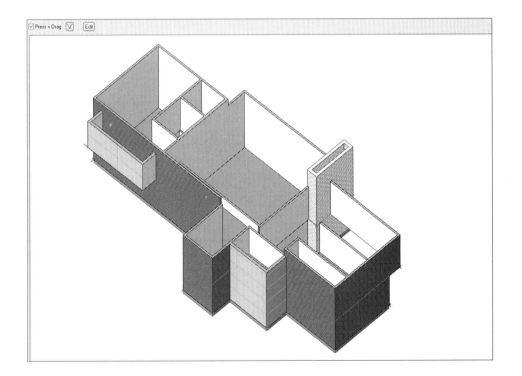

Figure 4.57
The 2D sketch generates a 3D floor

Copying Floors from Level 1 to Level 2

Revit has some great copy and paste features that allow you to paste elements from one view into another with relative ease and also keep elements lined up in 3D space. In this section, you'll copy-paste the floor from Level 1 into Level 2 and then edit the sketch to match the design:

1. Select the floor in the 3D view, and copy it to the clipboard using Ctrl-C.

2. To paste the floor, choose **Edit → Paste Aligned → Select Levels** by **Name → Level 2**, and click OK (see Figure 4.58). The floor is pasted into Level 2.

4. Select the floor, and click the Edit button in the Options bar. At this point, you're back in sketch mode.

5. Switch the view to Level 2 plan so that it's easier to visualize the relationship of the lines to the walls (see Figure 4.59).

6. Using the Pick Walls tool, select the two interior walls.

7. You'll get a warning about keeping elements joined when picking the cantilevered wall (see Figure 4.60). Click the Unjoin Elements button to continue.

8. Using the Trim tool, clean up the lines to form a continuous loop of lines. The un-trimmed lines are shown in Figure 4.61. After trimming the lines, delete the leftovers.

9. You need to continue editing the sketch to include the bump out in the lower-left corner of the model. To do this, first pick the walls using the Pick Walls tool. If the pick puts the line on the inside of a wall, click Flip Arrows to toggle the line to the outside face.

Figure 4.58

Pasting Level 2 in a 3D view

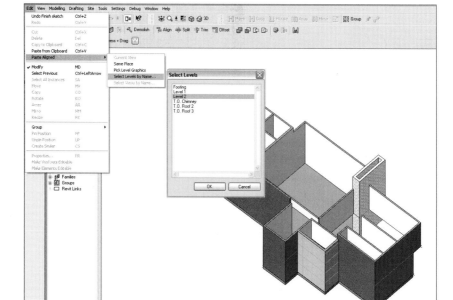

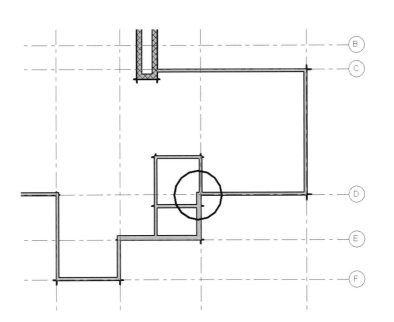

Figure 4.59
Level 2 plan view

Figure 4.60
Error message example

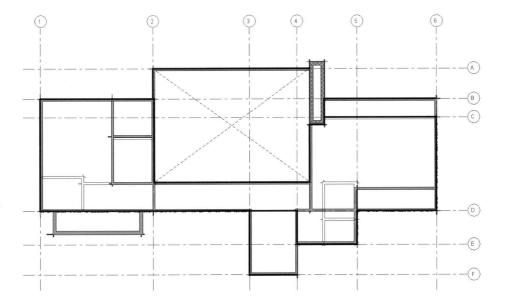

Figure 4.61
Before the lines are trimmed

Next, you'll clean up the lines so the sketch forms a closed loop. Here are the steps:

1. Use the Split tool to split the horizontal line into two segments, as shown in Figure 4.62.

2. Complete the sketch by trimming the lines to one another.

3. Click Finish Sketch in the Sketch tab. A dialog box appears, asking if you want the walls to attach to the bottom of the floor (see Figure 4.63).

4. Click Yes. The interior walls will connect to the bottom of the floor. This ensures that section views of the model look correct. When walls are attached to floors, they dynamically adjust their height to match the bottom of the floor, even when floor thickness is changed or given an offset from a level.

5. The next dialog asks if you want to join the floor with wall geometry (see Figure 4.64). Click Yes.

Figure 4.62

Split the lines, and then trim.

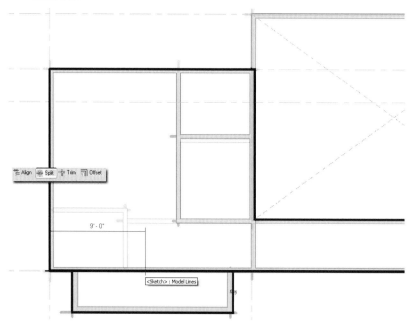

Figure 4.63

Dialog box asking if you want to attach the walls to levels

Figure 4.64

Joining floor and wall geometry

This option automatically joins walls that overlap with the floor—in this case, the exterior walls. The resulting graphics manifest in section views, producing a cleaned-up relationship between the layers in the walls and floors.

Adding the Main Roof

Now that you've created the basic floors, let's add some roofs. Roofs are created in the same manner as floors: as sketches that relate to a level in the project. As you'll see, roofs allow you to specify slopes for each line in the sketch, which lets you rapidly create hipped, gable, shed, and flat roof configurations. Follow these steps:

1. Open the Level 2 floor plan.

2. From the Basics tab in the Design bar, select the Roof tool. A flyout menu appears. Select the option Roof by Footprint. Just as with floors, you're placed in a sketch-editing mode where you can use existing geometry to construct the sketch boundary lines or draw the desired shape with lines.

3. Use the Pick Walls option. Look at the Options bar, and set the roof overhang to 1′-0″ (30cm). This offsets the sketch line from the wall to produce a parametrically associated overhang distance.

4. Hover the mouse over an exterior wall and press Tab. When the perimeter walls are highlighted, click to select them. The beginning of the sketch is created, as shown in Figure 4.65.

5. Delete unneeded lines, and use Trim to form a closed loop (see Figure 4.66).

6. Add lines for the cut-out around the fireplace. Use the Split tool and the option to Delete Inner Segment. Make two split marks at each intersection, and the middle section will be removed.

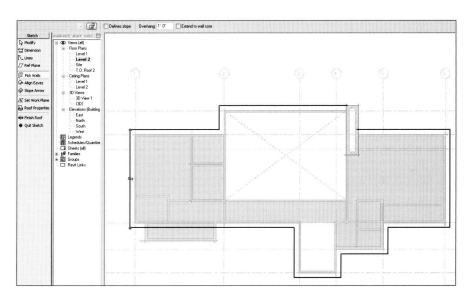

Figure 4.65

Using the Tab key to select sketch lines

7. Before finishing the sketch, let's set its Base Constraint. In the sketch Design bar, click the Roof Properties button. Set Base Level to T.O. Roof 3 (see Figure 4.67).

8. You've just created a flat roof. However, you want the roof to have a slight slope, creating a gently sloping shed. Select the bottom horizontal sketch line. In the Options bar is a toggle for setting lines to define slope: Toggle it. The sketch line gets an icon indicating that it's slope-defining. Finish sketch. If you get an error that you have overlapping lines, check where that Revit indicates the problem and clean up the lines. (this happens on the right side of the building).

Once you've define a slope in a roof, this can be changed from outside of sketch mode. Simply select the roof, open the Element Properties dialog, and then change the Slope value.

Figure 4.66
Delete the high-lighted sketch lines.

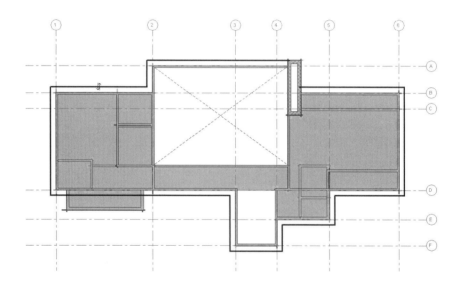

Figure 4.67
Roof properties

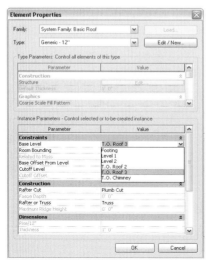

9. To toggle a slope-defining line, use the Options bar when a line is selected, and uncheck the Defines Slope option.

10. The slope is auto-set to be a 9/12 pitch, which is too steep for this design. Select the number, and change the 9″ to 1″ (see Figure 4.68).

11. Click Finish Sketch, and look at the model in 3D.

12. Select the roof, and change its type from Generic – 12″ to Metal Roof. A pattern of lines appears that represents standing seam roof panels (see Figure 4.69).

    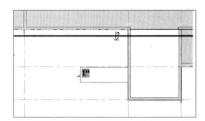

    Figure 4.68

    Changing the roof pitch

    If you spin the model to the side, you'll notice a gap between the walls and the roof. This is easily rectified using the Attach to Roof tool. In Figure 4.70, you can see where the walls aren't attached to the roof.

13. Spin the model a bit, and then use the Tab-selection method to select the exterior walls.

14. Click the Attach button in the Options bar, and then select the main roof. The walls extend up to meet the underside of the roof. When you get the warning message shown in Figure 4.71, click Detach Target(s). This detaches walls that aren't entirely below the roof (the walls in the foreground). The resulting geometry should look like Figure 4.72.

The great thing about the Attach tool is that if the roof pitch is changed, the walls will parametrically adapt to the new slope! To experiment with this, select the roof and go to the Element Properties. Change the roof slope, and watch as the walls dynamically update.

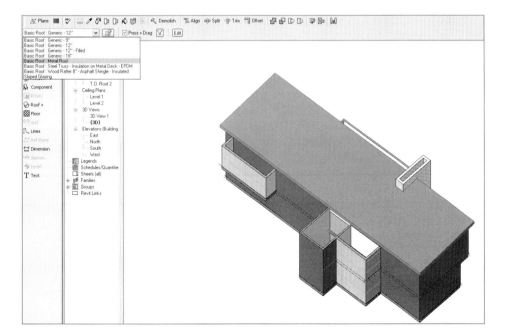

Figure 4.69

Modifying the roof type

Figure 4.70

Walls before being attached to the roof.

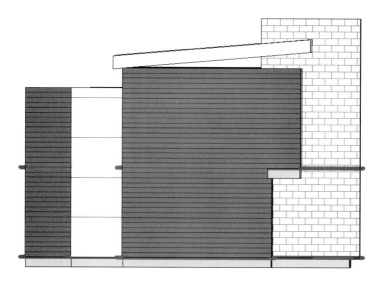

Figure 4.71

Warning message

Figure 4.72

Walls are now attached to the roof.

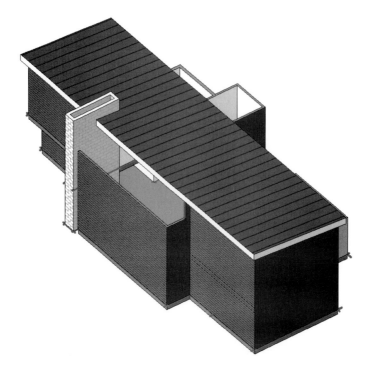

Adding Other Roofs

You'll now add the remaining roofs and make walls attach to them:

1. Open the plan view T.O. Roof 2 using the Project Browser.

2. Start with the roof in the lower-left in Figure 4.73. Use Roof by Footprint, pick the three exterior walls, and then draw the last line to make a closed rectangle. (Switch to Draw mode by picking on the pencil icon in the options bar). Also using the Options bar, set the overhang to 0′-0″, and make sure all the lines are non -slope defining.

3. When you're got a closed loop of lines. Press Finish Sketch.

4. Create additional roofs over the entry and the main living space (see Figure 4.74) using the same techniques. Make one roof for each condition.

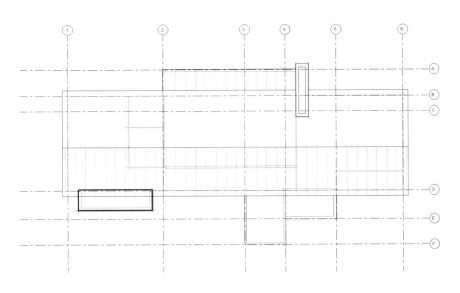

Figure 4.73

Adding a roof with no slope

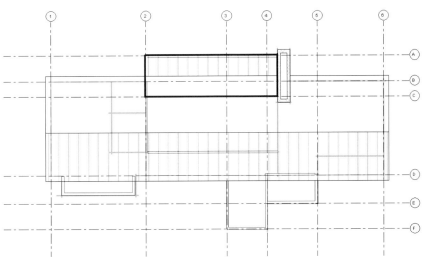

Figure 4.74

Adding more roofs

Figure 4.74

Adding more roofs
(continued)

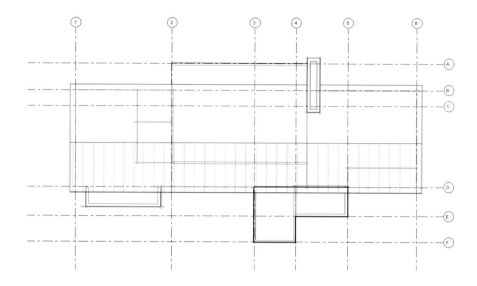

Use Pick Walls when walls are present. Then, switch to drawing lines to finish the sketch. Use the Trim tool to clean lines and get rid of any overlapping or unconnected lines.

Modifying an Existing Roof

Go to the 3D view. If the roofs aren't the Metal roof type, you need to change them. Using selection and the Type Selector is a common method, but there is also a nice tool that lets you pick a target type and then push that type into other elements with a few clicks.

This tool (✎) is called Match Properties, and it's located in the toolbar. To use the Match Properties tool, you first select the type of element you want to convert other elements into. You then select elements of the same category, and they will change type with each subsequent mouse click. Try it out:

1. Select the Match Properties tool in the toolbar.

2. Select the main roof. Note that the cursor appears filled—as if you sucked that type into your dropper. With each selection, you can change types belonging to the same category (in this case, the category Roof; see Figure 4.75).

3. Select the three roofs. You'll give them a negative offset from the level to make room for some clerestory windows.

4. Go to the roofs' Element Properties, as shown in Figure 4.76.

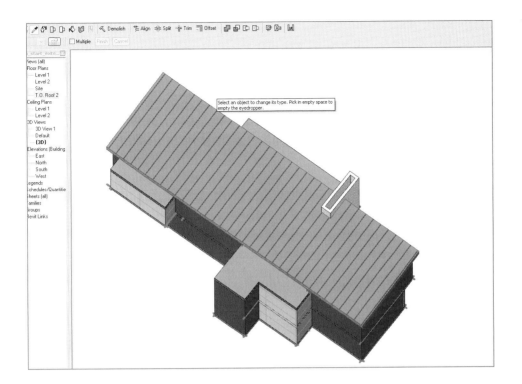

Figure 4.75

Select the roof with the Match Properties tool.

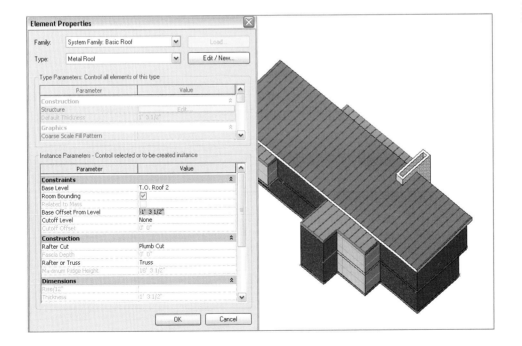

Figure 4.76

The remaining roofs modified

5. Change the Base Offset to 1′ 3½″ (40 cm) (the thickness of the roof).

6. Select the walls below the roofs you just created, and attach them to the roof as shown in Figure 4.77.

7. When you get the error message shown in Figure 4.78, click the Detach Target(s) button. This changes the attachment of the wall so that it connects with the lower roof.

Figure 4.77

Attach the walls to the roof.

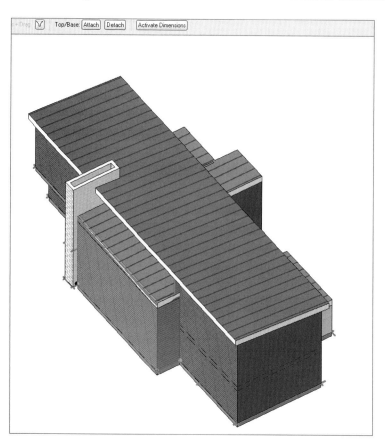

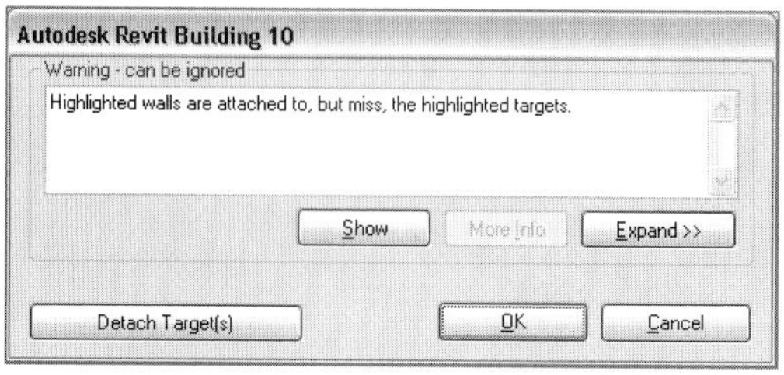

Figure 4.78

Detach Target(s) error message

Attaching Interior Walls to the Roof

In order to attach interior walls to the underside of a roof, you need to be able to select them first. With the roof in the way, this is a problem. To resolve this issue, you can temporarily hide the roof, select the walls, and then unhide the roof and attach the walls. There is one caveat to this workflow: Selection gets lost when you reset the view. However, using the Select Previous command, the selection can be reclaimed. Follow these steps:

1. Select the main roof and then access the right-click menu, Override Graphics in ViewBy Element. Check the option to make the roof Transparent, then open the Surface Patterns node and uncheck the Visible option. The roof will turn 100% transparent, and the surface patterns will be turned off. Figure 4.79.

2. Select the interior walls on Level 2 using the Ctrl key when picking.

3. With walls still selected, press the Attach button in the Options bar, then select the roof.

4. Select the roof, and open the Element Overrides dialog again. Press the Reset button to clear all the overrides (Figure 4.80) and press OK to finish.

To see the effect of the wall meeting the roof, rehide the roof.

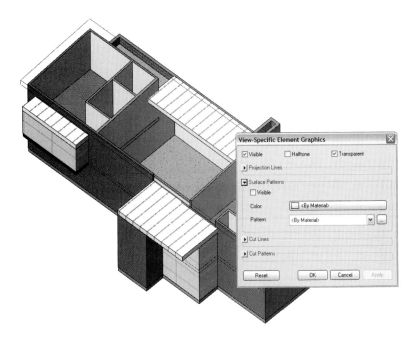

Figure 4.79
Model with the roof hidden

Figure 4.80
Resetting the Hide command

> ### A TIP ABOUT SKETCH DESIGN
>
> With a sketch-based design, an element is created from a closed loop of lines. More than one loop is allowed. If you draw a loop of lines within the boundary of another loop, then the shape defined by the interior loop will be negative. This makes it easy to create openings for stairs, chimneys, and so on—just draw a second loop of lines in the shape of the opening, and voila!

Making Curtain Walls

To add some clerestory windows to the design, you can use the Curtain Wall tool. Curtain walls are a special wall type that lets you place mullions and panels on a grid surface. Each gridline divides the wall into sections, which become panels. Mullions separate individual panels and are placed on curtain grids. For this exercise, you'll use a curtain wall where the mullions and panels are predefined in the wall type. This makes layout extremely quick and easy to manage. You can continue with the file you created so far, or open the file Source_House_CurtainWall_Start.rvt. Follow these steps:

Figure 4.81

The Hide Element option for the roof

1. In the default 3D view, hide the main roof using the Temporary Hide/Isolate located in the View Control bar. Select the roof then choose the option to Hide Element (see Figure 4.81).

2. Once the roof is hidden, use the Wall tool in the Basics tab to set the wall type to Curtain Wall: Storefront. In the Options bar, set Level to T.O. Roof 2, and Height to T.O. Roof 3.

3. Draw the curtain wall, as shown in Figure 4.82. Use snapping to get the correct placement.

4. Add a similar curtain wall to the opposite side of the model (see Figure 4.83).

5. Choose Reset Temporary Hide/Isolate from the View Control bar so the roof reappears.

6. Select the curtain wall at the back of the house, and attach it to the roof above using the Attach command in the Options bar.

7. You'll get a message about elements becoming invalid. Click the Delete Element(s) button (see Figure 4.84). This isn't a problem; Revit is just letting you know that it needs to delete the elements in order to re-create them. The mullions will be regenerated once the curtain wall is attached to the roof.

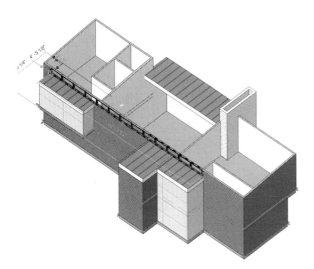

Figure 4.82

Draw the curtain wall as shown.

Figure 4.83

Clerestory curtain walls

Adding Curtain Walls to the North Façade

Now that you have the clerestory windows in place, let's use the same tool to add a glass wall to the façade:

1. Open the Level 1 plan view and choose the Storefront curtain wall type again.

2. Set the Height to T.O. Roof 2.

3. Draw the wall from the edge of the fireplace to the center of the wall (see Figure 4.85). A triangle snap icon appears when the wall's end hits the center.

4. Add a curtain wall on the other side of the fireplace as well, as shown in Figure 4.86. Set this wall's Height to Level 2.

5. Open the north elevation. In this view, you can see the effect of the curtain walls you just made, as shown in Figure 4.87.

6. Select each curtain wall, and attach it to the roof above using the Attach tool you used for the interior and exterior walls (the button on the Options bar). To select the curtain wall, hover the mouse over an outer boundary of the curtain wall until a dashed frame appears. Note that selecting a mullion or panel doesn't select the curtain wall.

7. You'll get the message shown in Figure 4.88 about mullions being removed. Again, this isn't an error; it's Revit alerting you to its process. Click the Delete Element(s) button to continue.

Figure 4.84

Delete Elements dialog box

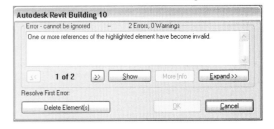

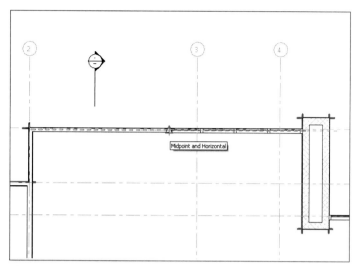

Figure 4.85

Draw a curtain wall from the chimney to the wall midpoint.

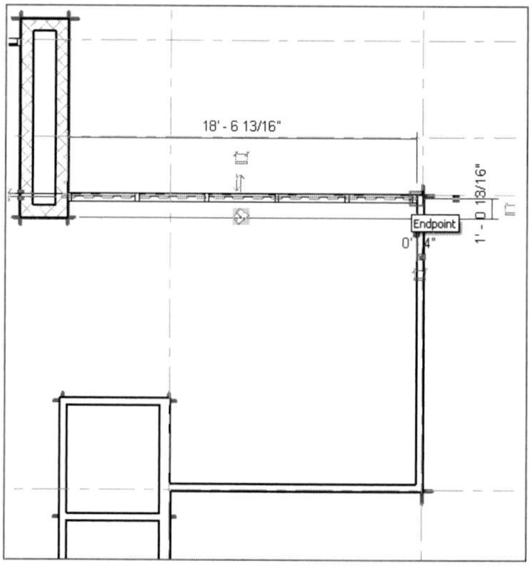

Figure 4.86

Adding the second curtain wall

Figure 4.87

The north elevation

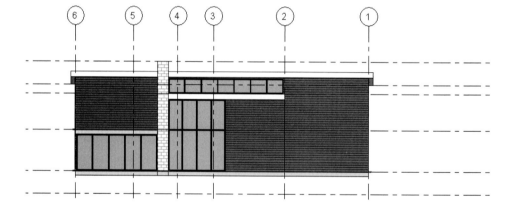

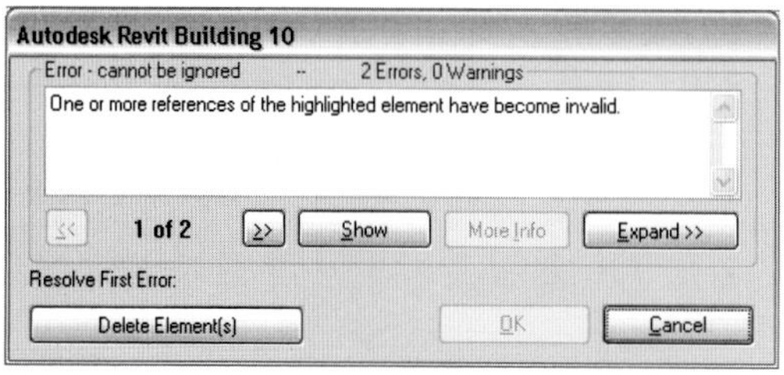

Figure 4.88

Mullions being removed

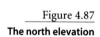

Changing the Grid Pattern

The curtain walls you've been placing preset the spacing of grids, which in turn determines the spacing of mullions and panels. You can deviate from the pattern interactively to make patterns that are more irregular:

1. To align the curtain wall with the clerestory windows, activate the Align tool. Select a curtain grid in the clerestory first, and then select the edge of the curtain wall. When selecting a grid, make sure you select a GRID not a mullion (pres tab when mouse is over a mullion until the dashed line representing the grid shows up and then click) The two curtain walls are now aligned.

2. Remove some grid segments and mullions to give the wall more interest. To do so, hover the mouse over the vertical mullion nearest gridline 4. Press the Tab key to cycle the selection until a curtain gridline highlights (be careful: *not* the mullion, but the curtain grid). Select this grid.

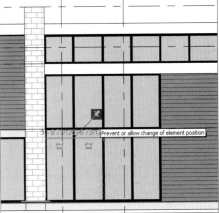

Figure 4.89

Curtain wall modifications

3. Note that the gridline has a pin icon associated with it. This indicates that the grid is locked into place and can't be moved interactively. The grid can be unpinned and then moved interactively, if you desire. Click the pin to unlock it, and drag the grid. For now, let's leave the grid pinned, and only deal with removing segments of grids. You can see the pins in Figure 4.89.

4. With the curtain grid selected, click the Add/Remove Segments button on the Options bar (Add or Remove Segments). You can now add and remove segments of grid that span between other grids. Remove the bottom grid segment by selecting it. You'll notice that the mullions are also removed. Do the same for the adjacent grids until the picture looks like Figure 4.90 (two bottom grid segments and two top segments removed).

Figure 4.90

The completed curtain wall

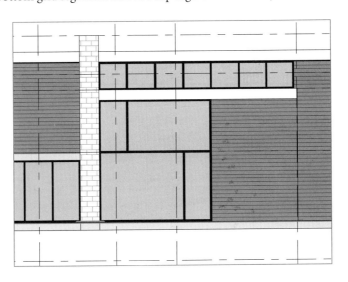

Figure 4.91

**The completed
curtain wall in the
3D model**

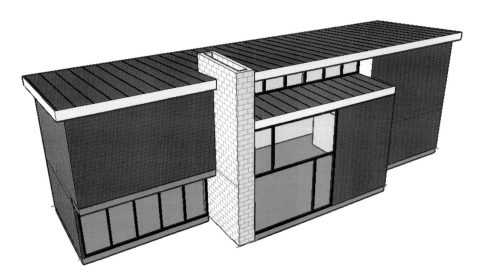

5. In order to replace grids and mullions on the curtain wall, select a curtain gridline, and use the Add/Remove tool again. Selecting on a dashed grid segment puts back the segment as well as the mullion.

6. Open the Exterior Perspective 3D view, and look at your model in 3D (see Figure 4.91). Remember, you can use Shift+middle mouse button to orbit the model in 3D.

Adding Doors and Windows

Now that you've constructed the basic envelope of a small house, let's move back to the inside and place some windows and doors. Follow these steps:

1. Go to the Level 1 floor plan.

2. From the Basics or Modeling tab, select the Door tool.

3. Set the door type to Single-Flush 34″ × 84″ (85 × 210cm).

4. Move your mouse over walls in the model—note that the door previews before it's placed. If the mouse isn't over a wall, no preview appears, and the door can't be placed.

5. Place the door as shown in Figure 4.92.

Note the helpful dimensions that appear during placement.

Figure 4.92

Adding a door

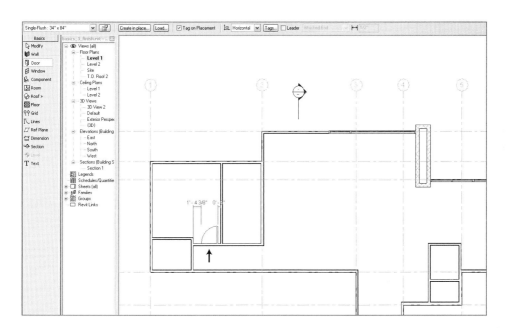

Temporary dimensions show up during and after placement to aid you in locating the door. Once the door has been placed, the dimensions become active controls that you can use to precisely position the door relative to nearby references such as walls, grids, or other doors:

1. To edit a dimension value, click the numeric value, and it becomes an editable text field.

2. Clicking the blue squares of the temporary dimension cycles the dimension between centerlines and opening conditions.

   For example, after placing the door, select the blue control for the temporary dimension that snaps to the door centerline, and move it toward the door leaf. Note that the dimension jumps to a new location. Now, click the dimension value and set the distance to be 6″ (15cm) (see Figure 4.93).

You'll notice that the door was given a tag when it was placed. This is an option available in the Options bar during placement. For this exercise, you don't need to see tags yet. Go ahead and delete the tag (hover the mouse over the tag; if you can't select it, use the Tab key to cycle to it), and start the Door tool again. This time, uncheck the option Tag on Placement on the Options bar. This will prevent the doors from being tagged automatically from here on out.

Figure 4.93

Locating the door

Let's continue to place doors. When you're placing doors, get used to using the space-bar to flip the door orientation and get the door facing correctly. If you don't place a door correctly, no problem—select the door and press the spacebar until the door looks right. For now, place the same door so the image looks roughly like Figure 4.94.

Once the doors are placed, you can create constraints between the doors and nearby walls. This is useful if you want to maintain a specific relationship between a door and a wall so that if the wall moves, the doors move with it.

To do this, you'll convert a temporary dimension into a permanent dimension and then lock the dimension to create a constraint. You'll then delete the dimension but leave the constraint in place. Here are the steps:

1. Choose **Settings → Temporary Dimensions**.

2. In the Walls options, select Faces of Core; in the Doors and Windows options, select Openings, as shown in Figure 4.95.

3. Go back to the view and select a door, and notice that the behavior of the temporary dimensions is different—the dimensions follow your new rules when initialized. This will let you set distances between door openings and the stud faces in your walls with a few clicks.

4. Use the temporary dimensions to get door opening 6″ (15cm) from the stud face of the wall, as shown in Figure 4.96.

5. Click the icon that looks like a blue dimension string (⛶). This converts the temporary dimension into a regular dimension.

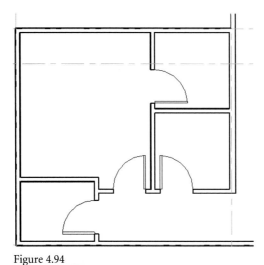

Figure 4.94
Placing more doors

Figure 4.95
Change the temporary dimensions for walls to Faces of Core; and for Doors and Windows, change them to Openings.

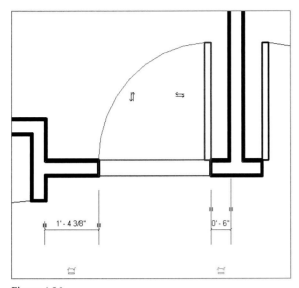

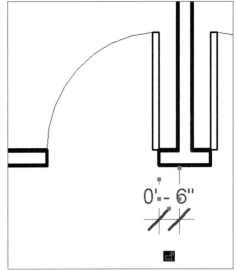

Figure 4.96

Temporary dimensions at the door

Figure 4.97

Use the lock icon to create a constraint.

6. Select the dimension and click the lock icon. This creates a fixed constraint between the door and the wall (Figure 4.97).

7. You don't want to have that dimension when you print later—you just used it to set a rule. You'd like to delete the dimension but keep the rule you defined. When you select and delete the dimension, you'll get a warning message (see Figure 4.98); you can either unconstrain the condition or click OK and keep the constraint but still delete the dimension. Click OK.

8. Do the same thing for the door on the other side of the wall.

9. Select the wall, and the locks show up again, indicating the presence of a constraint. Clicking the lock (unlocking it) deletes the constraint. Figure 4.99 shows the constraints.

10. If you move the wall by dragging it or using the temporary dimension, the doors will also move. Go ahead and change the temporary dimension from 4′-8⅜″ to 5′-0″ (130cm to 150cm) to see this work.

Figure 4.98

This allows you to keep or remove your constraints.

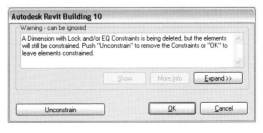

11. Place more doors in the project: glass doors for the exterior doors and smaller doors for the bathroom and the closet near front entry. Figure 4.100 shows additional door locations.

12. Changing door types is just like changing wall types. Select the door and use the Type Selector to swap the door with a different type.

    For the moment, don't worry if you don't find the exact type of door you wish to use. We'll explain later how you can find more doors or adjust existing ones to serve your needs.

Figure 4.99

Locks indicate a constraint.

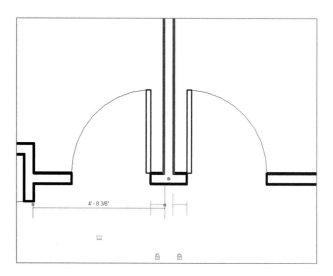

Figure 4.100

Additional door locations

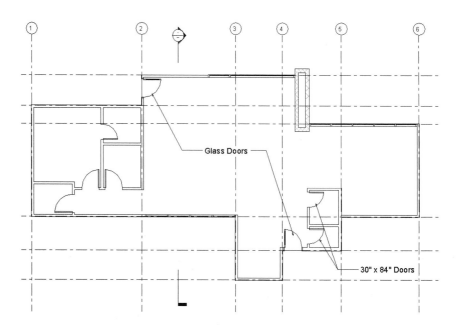

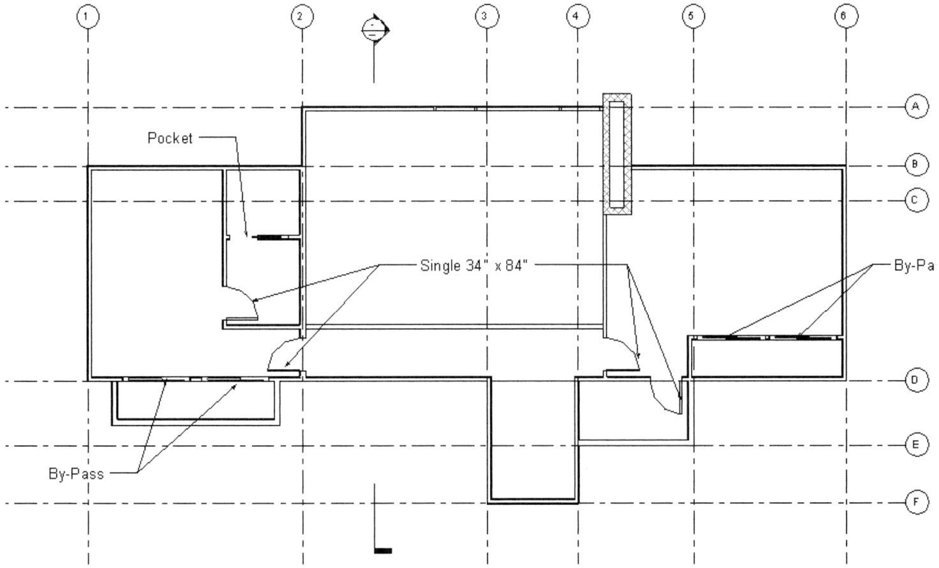

Figure 4.101

Second-floor doors

Adding Doors to Level 2

Let's continue to place doors in the model:

1. Open the Level 2 plan view.

2. Place the following types of doors in Level 2, as shown in Figure 4.101:

   - By-Pass sliders

   - Single-Flush 34″ × 84″ (85 cm × 210 cm)

   - A Pocket door

   Use temporary dimensions to place door openings 6″ (15cm) from stud faces, as you did on Level 1.

Placing Windows

Placing windows is just like placing doors. Use the Window tool in either the Basics or Modeling tab. You'll start by placing some sliders and then some fixed openings. The sliders have a fixed size set in the type properties, and the fixed windows have instance-based sizes. We'll explore the behavior of both type and instance families. Let's start placing windows:

1. In the Level 2 plan view, select the Window tool from the Basics tab. Choose the type Slider with Trim: 7′ 0″ × 4′ 0″ (215cm × 120cm). Uncheck the Tag on Placement option. Place windows in the walls as indicated in Figure 4.102.

2. Place windows of type Fixed – Size Varies in the locations shown in Figure 4.103.

Figure 4.102

Figure 4.102

Placing slider windows

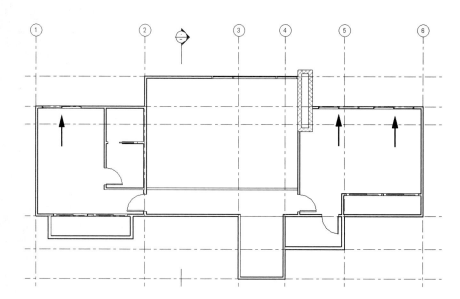

Figure 4.103

Placing the remaining windows

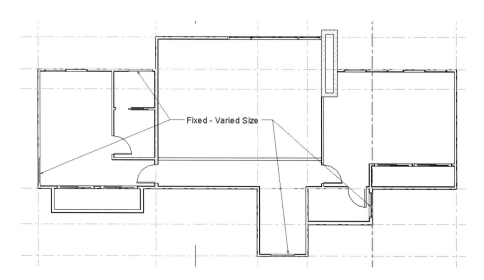

Resizing Windows Dynamically

The Fixed – Size Varies window is designed such that its width and height are set to be instance parameters, as opposed to the window you previously used whose width and height were set to be type parameters. Setting the dimensions of an object to be instance parameters gives you the advantage of working with more flexible, directly editable elements; you can modify them with the blue grips that display when they're selected.

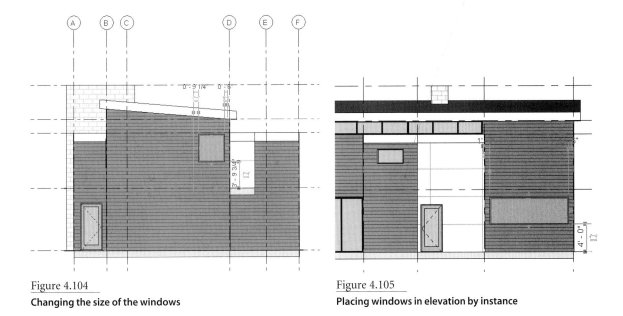

Figure 4.104

Changing the size of the windows

Figure 4.105

Placing windows in elevation by instance

To see how to dynamically size a window using the blue grips, select the window and make it wider.

> Be aware that instance parameters, when changed, don't propagate that change throughout all similar elements in the project. The change is applicable only to that one instance of the element.

To adjust the height of the window, open the West Elevation view and select the window. Similar controls appear. Dragging the controls resizes the window dynamically.

Feel free to change the size of the other windows you just placed by opening each elevation and making adjustments, as shown in Figure 4.104.

Let's place one more window. Open the South Elevation, select the Window tool, and choose the Fixed – Size Varies type. Place the window in the façade and adjust its size as shown in Figure 4.105.

Getting Additional Content Online

The windows you've placed are fairly generic. The beauty of Revit is that these windows can be swapped out with different window types on the fly. Content from the default libraries, from the Web, or your own custom-made elements can be loaded into the project and swapped. Try searching the web library for additional window and door types, and load them into the project:

1. Select the Window tool.

2. On the Options bar, click the Load button.

3. Click the Web Library button in the upper-right corner of the dialog (see Figure 4.106).

   Doing so launches a web browser to the Autodesk online library. (this will open behind Revit --so it may not be obvious you're opened a website). From the web site, you can navigate to doors and windows families, and save them to your machine. Note that Revit elements can be dragged and dropped from Windows Explorer but not from the Web. To load the element in your project, choose **File → Load from Library → Load Family**, and browse to the place where you saved the downloaded family.

> You can also open a family directly using the Open option when downloading families. Doing so opens the family in the Family Editor—the tool used to design and build families. To get the family into your project, you can then use the Load Into Projects button on the Design tab.

> If you create library elements on your own or download them from the Web, make sure you create a separate folder to store these in. You can then specify this location as an additional path when loading content that shows up in the left hand pane of the file open dialog. To add a new library, use Settings → Options dialog. Open the File Locations tab and add a new Library location.

Figure 4.106

Autodesk online families

Placing Components

For the next step, you're going to add furniture, plumbing fixtures, and other interior equipment in the building. You can use the file that you have created until now or open the file that we have prepared for you named Source_House_ Components_Start.rvt.

Placing Furniture

To place free standing furniture is simple. Using the Component Placement tool in the Basics or Modeling tab populates the Type Selector with available components. The list doesn't include windows and doors, but it does have a mixture of other categories of elements. For example, furniture, plumbing fixtures, and plantings appear on the list. An example is shown in Figure 4.107.

If you can locate the type of family you want to place, this method works fine:

1. Open the Level 1 plan view.

2. Choose the Dining Table and Chairs family from the drop-down list.

3. Move the mouse into the view. A temporary graphic representing the table and chairs appears on the mouse (Figure 4.108).

4. Press the spacebar prior to placement to rotate the table by 90 degrees.

Next, continue placing more furniture components in the model: couches and tables. Follow these steps:

1. Place the Sofa Loveseat, Sofa Couch, and Coffee Table using the component tool. Create furniture arrangement in the living space.

Figure 4.107

Content in the Type Selector

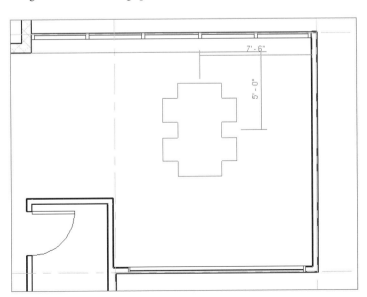

Figure 4.108

Inserting a dining-room table

Figure 4.109
Furniture placement

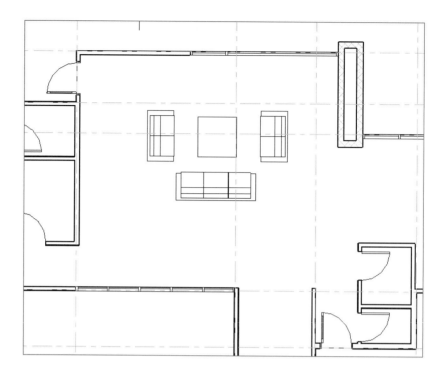

2. To mirror the loveseat across the coffee table, select the loveseat, and then select the Mirror (Mirror) tool in the toolbar at the top of the interface.

3. Select the center reference of the table as the mirror axis. The loveseat mirrors across this axis, creating a new instance (see Figure 4.109).

To place additional furniture elements, such as beds and nightstands, use the same technique. Use the Component tool, and choose appropriate families from the Type Selector. Open the Level 2 plan view, and place some beds to get familiar with this behavior.

Placing Plumbing Fixtures

Placing plumbing fixtures follows the same paradigm as placing other components. However, for this exercise, you'll use the Project Browser rather than the Component tool to place your components:

Figure 4.110

Fixtures under the Families node

1. Open the Families node in the Project Browser.

2. Open the Plumbing Fixtures node: This represents the category of element you wish to place.

3. Open the Shower Stall-2D node: This is the family name. The family types show up under this node (see Figure 4.110).

4. To place a component from the browser, drag the family type from the browser into the view. The visual feedback is exactly as if you chose the type from the Type Selector—the element appears on your cursor, ready for placement.

5. Drag the family into the view, and press the spacebar to rotate it.

6. Place it so that it snap-aligns to a wall. To see this, hover the component over a wall: The wall edge highlights.

7. Using the same method, place the sink (Sink-Hand) and toilet (Domestic-Low profile). The completed bathroom looks like Figure 4.111.

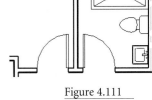

Figure 4.111

The finished bathroom layout

> Remember to use the spacebar before placement, and hover the mouse near walls to orient the object correctly.

Using the same technique, you can finish the other bathrooms in the model. Be sure to take advantage of the Place Similar tool by first selecting the component you want to duplicate (such as the sink and/or toilet) and then clicking Place Similar. This puts the component onto your cursor, and you can bypass the need to search for content in the Type Selector or family browser.

Some additional families are loaded into the project, which you can experiment with. Using the furniture components in the project, attempt to create a kitchen configuration.

Stairs and Railings

Stairs in Revit are created using a sketch mode where you can define stair boundaries, risers, and runs by drawing a 2D line sketch. Those sketches are then used to automatically generate a smart parametric 3D stair element of any complexity level. A number of stair-type variations are shown in Figure 4.112. Figure 4.113 shows a stair in sketch mode and 3D view. Different colors are automatically assigned to risers, boundary, and runs.

Stairs are considered complex architectural elements because their construction is dependent on local building rules defined in building codes. Revit allows you to accommodate by setting different rules for stair creation.

Just as with walls and floors, stairs are constructed using relationships to levels: All stairs have a Base Level and a Top Level that are used to calculate tread depth and height based on min/max rules. These parameters, shown in Figure 4.114, change from stair to stair and are the most important parameters used for constructing stairs.

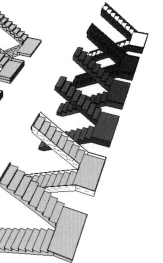

Figure 4.112

Stairs

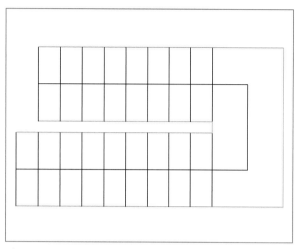 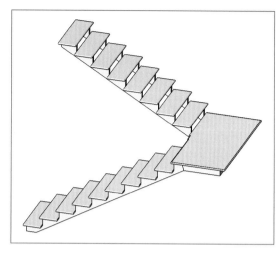

Figure 4.113

Stairs in sketch mode and in 3D view

Geometric variation of the individual elements of a stair (threads, riser, stringer, and so on) is managed with Type properties that provide dimensional and material parameters. Figure 4.115 shows those type values.

The most important parameters are rules that establish minimum tread depth and maximum riser height. These values are used to automatically guarantee minimum and maximum distances to keep your stairs within the constraints of what your building codes dictate. Revit won't break these rules. Your stairs start and end where you want them, and the correct number of risers and treads are auto-generated for you when making the stair. You'll see this in the exercise.

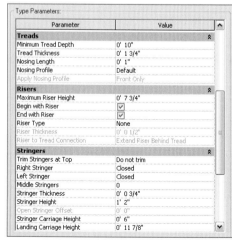

Figure 4.114

Stair levels

Figure 4.115

Stair properties

Adding a Stair

You need to add a stair from Level 1 to Level 2 in your model. From the Chapter 4 folder on the companion CD, open `Source_House_Stairs_Start.rvt`. You'll start by sketching the stair in Level 1 and making sure it's going up to Level 2. You'll then look at the stair using a 3D sectional view and change the type.

Start the Stair tool from the Modeling tab (Stairs). You'll enter the stair sketch editor. Note that the Design bar is replaced with new tools specific to stair creation (shown in Figure 4.116).

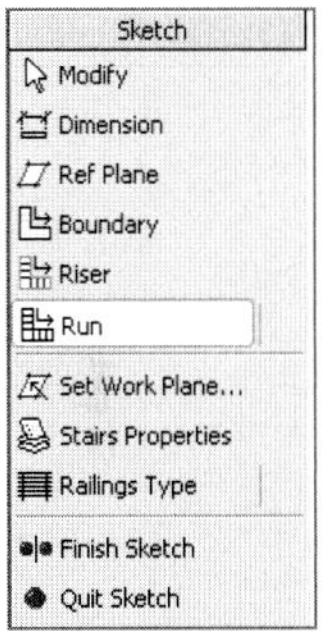

Figure 4.116
Stair design tools

Revit puts you into the Run tool by default. This tool auto-creates boundary and riser lines as you draw a run line.

Now, let's discuss something briefly. When Revit prompts you to draw a stair run, it always uses the middle of the run as a justification point. Often, however, you won't have a reference to the location of the stair centerline. So, you need to either draw help lines at the distance from the wall that represents half the stair width or draw the stair in an approximate location and then move it into place.

To make this exercise useful for teaching you about other Revit editing tools along with the Stair tool, you won't use a help line; instead, you'll draw the stair in a position close to the correct one and then adjust it to the right location using other tools. Follow these steps:

1. Start drawing the riser line by snap-aligning to the horizontal gridline to begin the run. (The green dashed line indicates that snap.) As mentioned, the line is drawn through the center of the stair, with boundaries shown offset. A half-tone text graphic also appears as you drag the run line. The text shows how many risers have been created and how many remain to get the stair from Level 1 to Level 2.
2. Drag the line until the text shows `8 RISERS CREATED, 8 REMAINING`, and click the mouse once. This is where you'll break the stair for a landing. It should look similar to Figure 4.117.
3. Begin a new run line to the left of the first stair; snap the beginning of the run to the end of the last riser.
4. Draw the run until you see `16 RISERS CREATED, 0 REMAINING`. This should be a point that is aligned with where you started the stair. You've created a stair return; your drawing should appear similar to Figure 4.118.
5. By default, railings are added to stairs when created. You can pre-set a railing type, or choose to not auto-generate railings. In the design bar, choose the Railing Types button, and then choose None.

Figure 4.117
Starting the stair

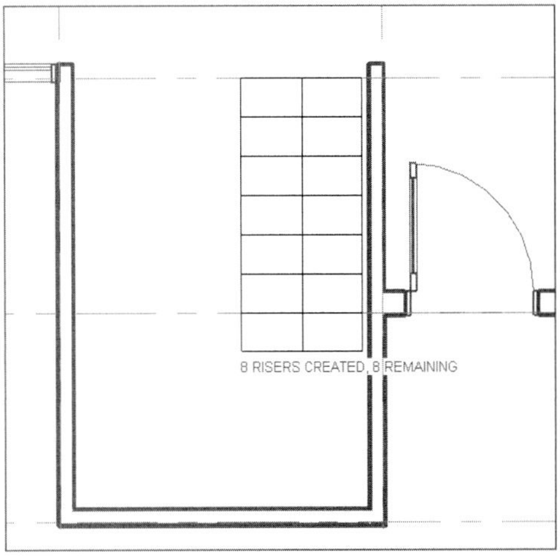

Figure 4.118

Start the return run; at right, the completed command.

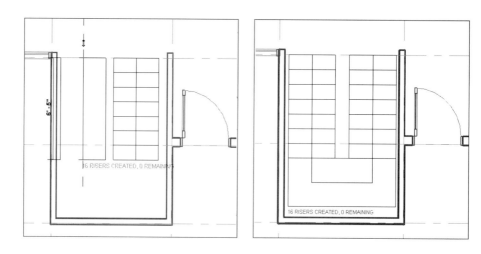

In order for the railings to work properly, you need to adjust the sketch a bit. Let's add a riser to the bottom of the stair and remove one from the beginning of the next run:

1. Drag the blue run line at the bottom segment of the stair until another riser appears. Revit will tell you that an additional riser is present (-1 REMAINING).

2. Delete the riser at the top of the first run of stairs, as shown in Figure 4.119.

   There is a gap between the outer boundary of the stair and the bounding walls. You need to adjust the boundary lines to fit the model.

   The initial width of the run is set in the stair properties. This stair is set to 3′-0″ (90 cm), but you could change that to any value prior to drawing the run lines.

3. To make the stair fit between the walls, align the outer boundary lines to the bounding walls. Still in sketch mode, align the landing by selecting the Align tool, then the interior side of the wall at the bottom of Figure 4.120, and finally the landing boundary.

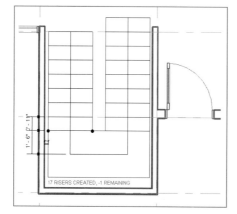

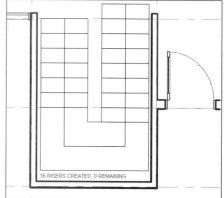

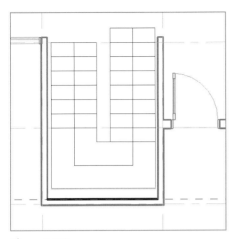

Figure 4.120

Align the stair boundary to the wall.

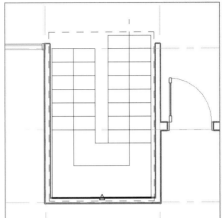

Figure 4.121

Center the stair.

Next, you'll move the stair so it's centered in the stairwell. Using a crossing selection, select all lines in the sketch. Because you're in sketch mode, no other model elements are selected, so you don't have to be too careful about what you select—Revit will grab only what's in the sketch. Now, follow these steps:

1. With the sketch lines of the stair selected, click the Move tool.

2. With the first pick, select the center of the stair boundary by the landing side, and then select the middle point of the wall. This should place the stair in the center between the two walls. You'll know you've moused over the center of the stair line and the wall when you see the triangular snap shown in Figure 4.121.

3. Use the Align tool to align the left and right boundaries to the wall. Select the Align tool, the inside edge of the wall on the right, and then the right edge line of the stairs. Doing so aligns the right run to the wall. Repeat for the left run. Figure 4.122 shows the stairs, properly located.

4. You can also preset a railing type to be added to the stair and drawn automatically when you finish the stair sketch. Click the Railing Type button (▦ Railings Type), and then choose Handrail – Pipe from the Railing Type dialog.

5. Finish the sketch to see the resulting 3D geometry. To do that, click the Finish Sketch button from the Design bar (◉|◉ Finish Sketch).

Figure 4.122

The located staircase

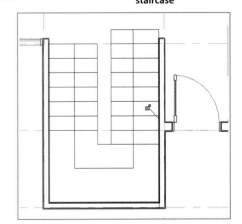

Users often forget to finish a sketch; then, they wonder why everything is grayed out and not all the tools are available. Always check on the left side to see whether the Finish Sketch button is available. If it is, click it to finish the operation.

Sectional View of the Stair

A great way to see the stair in an isolated 3D view is to create a section through the stair and then orient a 3D view to the section view. Here are the steps:

1. Use the Section tool in the View Design tab to draw a section, as shown in Figure 4.123.

2. Right-click the section, and choose Element Properties. Rename the view by changing the View Name property from Section 2 to Stair Section.

3. Open the default 3D view by clicking the 3D icon.

4. Choose **View → Orient → To Other View**.

5. Select the section that you just created: Section: Stair Section.

   The 3D view reorients and becomes cropped to the same crop extents as the section view. The view you see looks like a section through the stair, but it's a 3D cropped portion of the entire stair. Figure 4.124 shows the finished view.

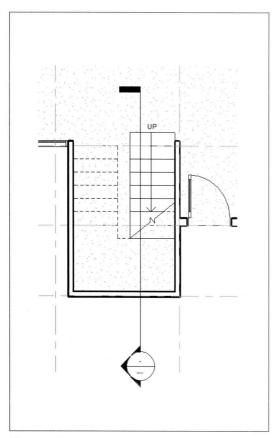

Figure 4.123

Cutting a section through the stair

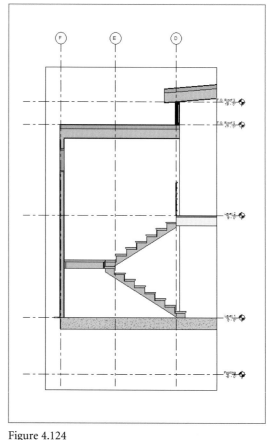

Figure 4.124

The completed section view

6. To see the stair in 3D, press Shift+middle mouse button, and slowly spin the model (see Figure 4.125).

7. Right-click the view name {3D} in the Project Browser and rename the view 3D Stair. Alternatively, click the eye icon on the View Control bar, and use the Save command in the resulting dialog box. Either way, save the view. Should you forget to do so, each time you create a new 3D view it will be oriented to this section view.

   Saving with a new name saves the view as a unique view. The next time you click the 3D icon, a new default 3D view that shows extents of the model will be generated for you.

Railings

Railings are also sketch-based elements that are generated from a 2D path (sketched line) and a set of design rules. Figure 4.126 shows some of the elements of a railing, the primary ones being the path, rails, and balusters. The path is made from 2D lines.

Rails are 2D profiles that sweep along the length of the path. There can be many horizontal rails in a railing.

Balusters are 3D geometry that is arrayed along the length of the path. Don't think of a baluster as something that has to be vertical and rectangular. In Revit, a baluster can be any geometry you wish to have a vertical repetition.

Balusters consist of a main pattern (a unit that is repeatable) and posts. Posts can be start, corner, or end posts. They can also have varying geometry.

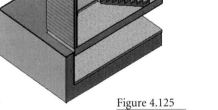

Figure 4.125

Resulting 3D image

Figure 4.126

Railing elements

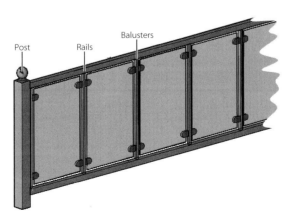

Adding a Railing to a Model

To draw a railing, use the Railing tool in the Modeling tab (▤ Railing). You'll be put into a sketch mode in which the path is drawn. The path can be composed of multiple lines, but within one sketch all lines must be connected. If you draw a path with lines that aren't connected, Revit will give you a warning.

You can have a single line as a railing (imagine a railing in a middle of a stair). But the moment you draw a second segment in the same sketch, Revit will expect you to connect them in a chain.

Once you've drawn the path, the rail geometry is constructed and conforms to the path. An endless number of railings can be defined using the combination of custom profiles and balusters. For this exercise, you'll add a predefined rail to the project and then change the type to make a different configuration. Follow these steps:

1. Open the Level 2 plan and start the Railing tool.

2. Using the Lines tool, draw a railing along the edges of the exterior deck, as shown in Figure 4.127.

3. Finish the sketch.

4. Open the 3D view and spin the model to see the railing.

5. Select the railing and change its type to CABLE RAIL – CABLES using the Type Selector. The railing changes to a cable-style rail and looks like the railing in Figure 4.128.

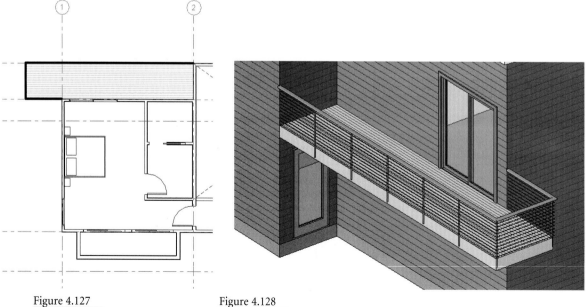

Figure 4.127

The railing path

Figure 4.128

Cable railing

Modifying Existing Railings

Looking at the model, you can see the result of your sketch. Note also the presence of railings; Revit automatically places railings on stairs that can then be changed or deleted as desired. You'll also notice some modeling issues that need to be resolved. For example, the stringers are embedded in the wall, and you don't need that railing along the outside edge where you have the wall.

To fix the railing problem, select the railing in the wall and delete it (make sure you're selecting the railing, not the wall or the stair, help yourself using the almighty Tab key). Don't delete the internal railing.

To fix the stringer problem, let's change the construction a bit. Rather than have the stringers on the outside edge of the treads, you can move them under the treads—a more typical method for wood construction:

1. Select the stair, and go to Type Properties.

2. Scroll down to the Stringers parameters.

3. Change Right Stringer and Left Stringer from Closed to Open (see Figure 4.129).

4. Click Apply to see the effect in the model. The stringer geometry changes.

Feel free to experiment with other parameters available in the stair-type properties. It's possible to create treads with nosing profiles, have slanted risers, and change the materials of each subelement in a stair or change the construction of the stair to monolithic.

Note that you're editing type properties when changing how treads, risers, and stringers are defined—meaning that other instances of that stair (if you've drawn a couple of staircases in the building) will update as a result of type changes. To avoid undesirable changes, duplicate the stair first, name the new type, and then begin your experiments.

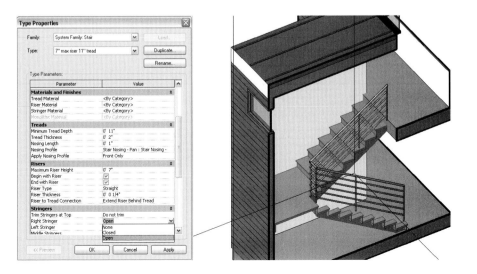

Figure 4.129
Modified stair stringers

Setting Hosts

Railings can be freestanding or hosted by floors and stairs. Often, a railing that was originally hosted by a stair needs to be deleted and later redrawn. You can become confused

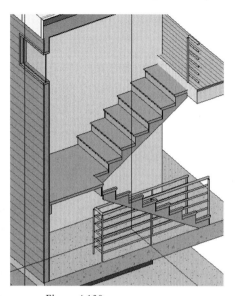

trying to place the railing on the stair, because it always ends up on the floor below the stairs. To re-place a rail so that it's hosted by a stair, start the Railing tool and sketch a railing path that is on top of the stair. Use the Set Host tool (⊕ Set Host) to attach the railing to the stair. Do this before finishing the railing sketch. When you finish the sketch, the rail will wind its way up the staircase. This is also possible after drawing the railing: Select the railing, click the Edit tool in the Options bar, and select the Set Host tool, and Revit will set the railing on the stair. Figure 4.130 shows what happens when you don't set the stair to host the railing.

Model Started…Now Have Some Fun!

We just went through a series of exercises meant to get you familiar with the basic modeling tools available in Revit. Obviously, we did not get into the nuts and bolts of every tool, but with time you will begin to dig deeper and experiment with more of the features.

Figure 4.130

The stair without the railing hosted

Also, we will revisit some of these tool in the chapter on Extending Modeling. Now that you have a basic model started, feel free to experiment with it: change the roof, lay out a kitchen, load some additional doors and windows. Most of all, have fun, be creative, and be patient with yourself and the software.

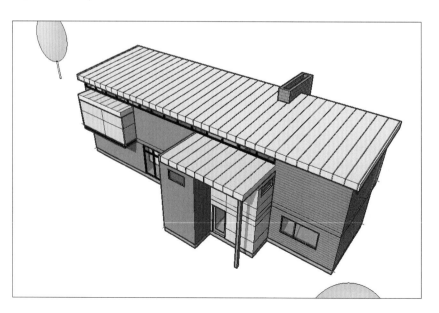

CHAPTER 5

Modifying Elements

Once you've started modeling with Revit, you'll immediately need to make changes to the elements in your model. Swapping types of elements is one way to change them, but once you have the desired types in place, you'll often need to reposition, copy, hide, and even change the graphic representation of these elements. This is where the editing tools and graphic override features come into play. The basics of these tools will be explained in this chapter.

This chapter reviews the essential modification tools available in Revit:

- **Standard tools**
- **Edit tools**
- **Graphic and visual overrides**

Standard Tools

This section describes some of the standard tools in Revit:

- Move tool
- Copy tool
- Rotate tool
- Array tool
- Mirror tool
- Resize tool

Windows Copy/Paste

Copy-paste is a familiar tool that is used in almost all software applications, and Revit has the basic features that you'd expect with a copy-paste interaction (Ctrl-C and Ctrl-V). It also has some surprising time-saving options when you're pasting elements that are driven by the nature of a building model.

To copy any element to the clipboard, select it and press Ctrl-C. Elements are now ready to be pasted. To paste, press Ctrl-V. In the majority of cases, Revit will place your selection into a bounding box that represents the size of your selection and let you paste it to a new position. In some special cases, Revit may prompt you to select a work plane on which to paste the copied element.

Paste Aligned

Once elements have been copied to the clipboard, they can be pasted into other views with a variety of options. This allows you to quickly duplicate elements from one view to another (from one floor to another floor, for example) while maintaining a consistent location in the XY coordinate plane. After selecting elements and copying them to the clipboard using Ctrl-C, choose **Edit → Paste Aligned** from the main menu, as shown in Figure 5.1.

Five options are available. Depending on the view from which you copy and what elements you copy, the availability of these options will change. For example, if you select a model element in a plan view, you'll have all the options shown in the figure:

Current View This pastes the elements on the Windows clipboard in the currently active view, in the same relative spatial location. For example, if you copy a series of walls in a view, Revit remembers the walls and their location. Using this feature, you can copy elements from one view and then switch to another view of the same type and paste the elements into that view.

Figure 5.1

The Paste Aligned submenu

Same Place This option places an element from the clipboard into the exact same place from which it was copied or cut. One use for this tool is copying elements into a Design Option. (Design Options are covered later, in Chapter 12.)

Pick Level Graphics This is a mode you can use to copy-paste elements between different floors. Once you select the elements, you're placed into a pick mode where you can select a level in section or elevation. You must be in elevation or section view to have this option available. The level you select determines the Z location of the paste and preserves the XY location. You might use this type of paste to copy balconies on a façade from one floor to another.

Select Levels by Name This method is similar to the previous one, but the selection of levels doesn't happen graphically. Instead, you choose levels from a list in a dialog box, and you can paste to multiple levels at once. This is useful when you have a multistory tower; in such a case, manually selecting levels in a view can be tedious. Similar to other options, the XY position is maintained, and the pasted elements are translated in the vertical dimension.

Select Views by Name This option allows you to copy elements to other views by selecting views in a dialog box. In the list available for selection, you don't see levels listed, but rather a list of parallel views. For example, if elements are copied from a plan view, all other plan views will be listed. Likewise, if you copy from an elevation view, only elevation views appear as possible views to paste into.

Move

Projects are changeable. You move and reshuffle elements from one place to another, especially in the initial phases of a project. Thanks to parametric constraints, many objects tend to move in relation to other objects in an automatic manner, but you also need the ability to move things manually. There are a couple of ways to accomplish this in Revit: using an explicit two-click operation or the nudge command.

The Move tool (⊞ Move) is located in the toolbar and becomes active when elements are selected. Once the tool is activated, you select a start point and end point to determine a move distance and vector. The start and end point can be anywhere in your active view; these picks establish the distance and direction of the move. For example, to move a desk to the left by 3″ (90cm), you select the desk, click the Move tool, pick a start point, and then drag the mouse to the left 3″ (90cm) using the temporary dimension as a reference. You then click to finish the command. If you know the distance you want to move, you can also type in the value—just be sure you give the move a vector by dragging the mouse in the direction you want to move, and then start typing a value. Revit automatically understands that you're telling the element to "move" by the distance you type and will finish the command when you press Enter on the keyboard, as shown in Figure 5.2.

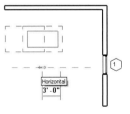

Figure 5.2

Using the Move tool

☐ Constrain ☐ Disjoin ☐ Copy

When the Move command is active, it gives you several options in the Options bar:

Constrain When this option is selected, it constrains movement to horizontal and vertical directions.

Disjoin Hosted elements such as windows and doors can't change host and move to another host without explicitly being disjoined from their host. This is what this tool does. If you need to move a door from one wall to another, select the door, select the Move tool, check the Disjoin option in the Options bar, and move the door to another host.

Copy This option makes a copy of the selected element and then moves that copy to desired location. The original element stays in place.

Nudge

You use a nudge move when you need to move an element with less dimensional precision. Any time an element is selected, you can use the arrow keys on the keyboard to move the element horizontally and vertically in small increments. Each press of an arrow key nudges the element a specific distance based on your current zoom factor. The closer you zoom, the finer the nudge distance will be.

Copy

This is an interactive tool that is nearly identical to the Move tool but makes a copy of the selected element at the location of the second pick (⋈ Copy). Note that this isn't the same Copy tool as Ctrl-C (the one found in the Edit menu that copies elements to a clipboard). This tool doesn't copy anything to the clipboard; it copies an instance of an element or selection of elements in the same view. To activate this tool, first choose the object(s) you want to duplicate, and then select the tool.

Rotate

To rotate an element, select it and click the Rotate tool (▱ Rotate). You'll notice that the Rotate tool in Revit isn't entirely like other Rotate tools you may be use to. A round rotate icon indicates the center of the rotation and appears at the center of the element's bounding box (shown in Figure 5.3).

More often than not, the center of the element isn't the point around which you want to rotate. In these cases, you need to reposition the center of rotation. To do this, select the icon and drag it to the point you wish before rotating the element—this temporarily relocates the origin. Once the origin is established, begin rotating the element using the temporary dimensions as a reference or typing in the angle of rotation explicitly.

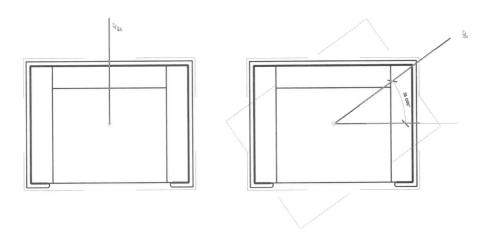

Figure 5.3

**The Rotate
command**

Array

An *array* is a way to make multiple instances of an element with consistent spacing between each element. Revit arrays are smart and can be parametrically grouped and associated such that the array spacing and number of elements in the array can be modified after you make the initial array. The Array tool (📋 Array) is one of the standard tools available for model and drafting elements.

The steps to create an array depend on the settings in the Options bar (see Figure 5.4).

You have two ways to array: linear and radial. Linear array is set as the default. A linear array arrays a series of elements in a line; that line can either use a set distance between each element or equally space a number of elements over a given distance. The radial array works in a similar fashion, but it revolves around a center point.

The Group And Associate option allows you to treat the array as a group that can be modified later to adjust the number and/or spacing of the array. If this is unchecked, then the array is a one-off operation, and you have no means of adjusting the array after you create it.

In the Number field, you set the number of elements to be arrayed. This option is active when Move To: 2nd is checked. For example, if you type **7** as the number and check Move To: 2nd, the element will be arrayed seven times. The distance between each element is determined by the distance between two subsequent clicks in the view.

Figure 5.5 shows two arrays drawn from A to B, number 5, illustrating the difference between choosing Move To: 2nd and Move To: Last.

Figure 5.4

**The array
Options bar**

Figure 5.5

Top: Array by number; bottom: an array between two points

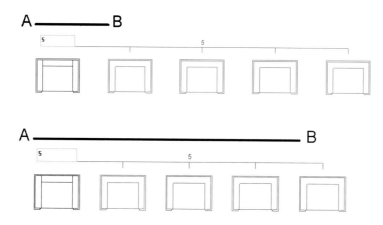

In both examples, Group and Associate were activated. When an element in the array is selected, a control appears, indicating the number of elements in the array. This allows you to change the number of elements in the array by directly editing the number. If you select any element, it behaves as a separate element rather than part of a group that is editable at any point, which is the case when Group and Associate are selected.

Mirror

The Mirror tool (▪ Mirror) allows you to mirror elements across an axis to create a mirror image of an element, like the chairs in Figure 5.6. The tool lets you either pick an existing reference in the model (the arrow icon) or draw the axis interactively (pencil icon).

Figure 5.6

The Mirror command

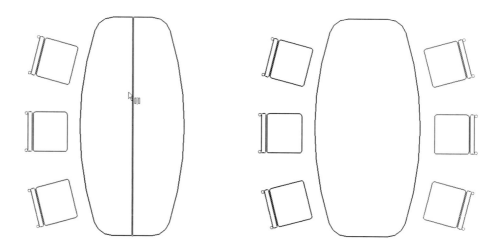

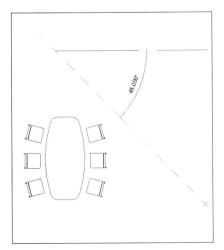 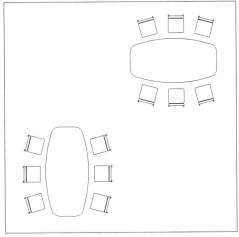

Figure 5.7

Mirror using a chosen axis

Use the pick method ( ) when you have an existing element with a meaningful center axis. If nothing in the model exists as a mirror axis, use the draw mode ( ) and draw your own axis, as shown in Figure 5.7.

Resize

When placing and dragging elements, Revit auto-creates temporary alignment lines to similar types of elements in the model. Use these alignment lines to place elements in relation to other elements. When you drag elements around, take note of these helpful alignment lines—and use them to line things up. This works for all categories of elements, including annotations. Figure 5.9 shows auto-alignment when placing a tag.

These alignments are great for lining up annotations such as room tags. Select a tag and drag it—note how it will align to other tags in the view, making it a snap to create organized drawings. Figure 5.10 shows auto-alignment while interactively dragging.

This tool is well suited for working with imported images that need to be scaled to match real-world dimensions. Say you've scanned a drawing of an existing building that you wish to convert into a model. Chances are, the image isn't at any reasonable scale when imported and needs to be scaled relative to some model element.

The Resize tool is active once you select an image. After you select the Resize tool, click a point to enter an origin (say, the left corner of the image); the second point you click is the width of the image that you want to fit within a certain size; finally, the third click is the new length you want (see Figure 5.8).

Figure 5.8

The Resize tool

Edit Tools

Another set of editing tools is available in Revit. You'll find them in a separate toolbar ( ).

Align Tool

The Align tool is one of the favorites among Revit users. It makes lots of common manipulations easy and precise. The Align tool matches the edge of one element precisely to another.

Auto-Alignment

Revit has embedded placement and can modify the alignment between elements of the same category. That is to say, when you drag elements around, they locate nearby similar elements, and alignment graphics are drawn to aid you when laying out the model or adding annotations. Figure 5.9 shows auto-alignment during tag placement.

If you wish to put room tags in order on your drawing, and you start moving one to align with another, Revit shows an align line and snaps to the other tag. Figure 5.10 shows auto-alignment during editing.

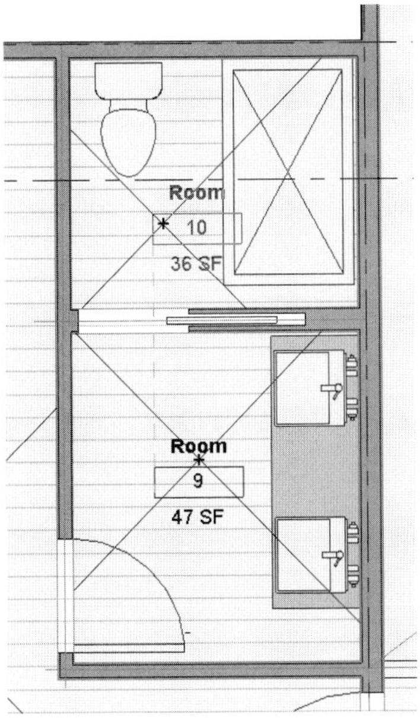

Figure 5.9

Alignment during placement

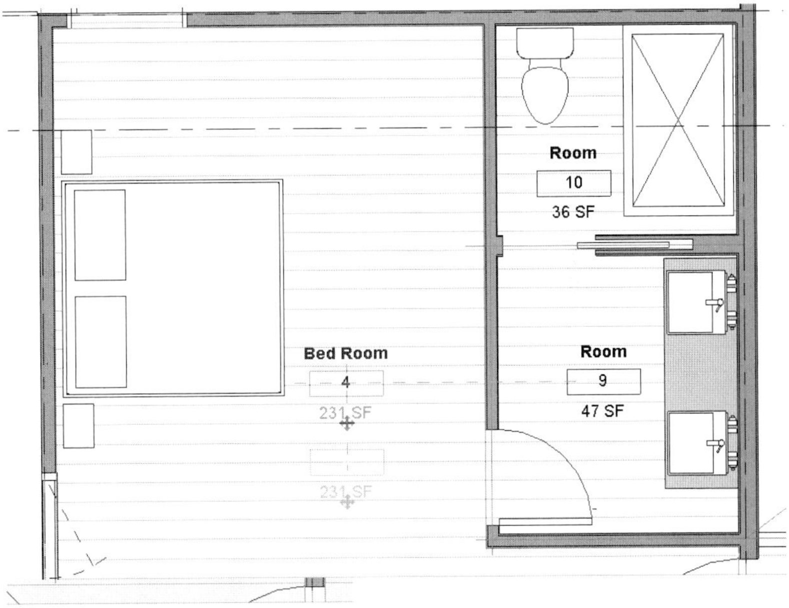

Figure 5.10

Alignment during editing

Manual Alignment

You can explicitly align references from one element to another. For example, you can align windows in a façade in an elevation view to line up their centerlines. To use the Align tool, select a target line and then select what you want to align to that first pick. The second element picked moves into alignment. Whenever an alignment is made, a blue lock icon will appear. Clicking that icon locks the alignment, creating a constraint between the two elements. Once constrained, if either element is moved both elements will move together.

Locking elements together is a powerful part of Revit. However, locking too many elements together can over-constrain your model. Be careful when you choose to use this tool.

Figure 5.11 shows the use of the Align tool to align windows on a façade. The top window's mid-axis is selected as the alignment reference. After that, the mid-axes of the lower windows are clicked, and the lower windows automatically align to the top window.

The Align tool also works for aligning geometry with surface patterns like brick or stone. Figure 5.12 shows how you can align the edge of a window to an expansion gap.

The Align tool is useful in the Family Editor environment, where you can align an element to a reference plane that will control the behavior of that element and lock it.

Figure 5.11
Manual alignment

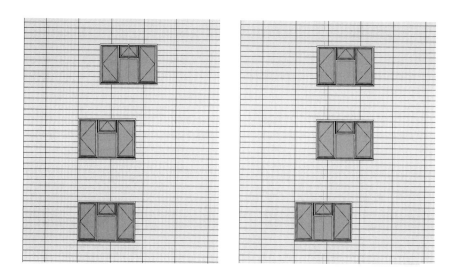

Figure 5.12
**Aligning windows
and patterns**

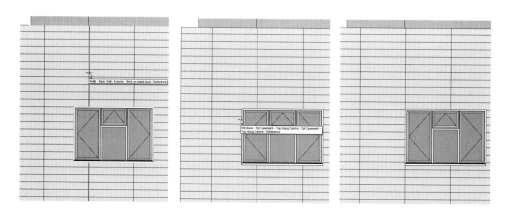

Split

The Split tool is used only on lines and walls and is used to split these elements into separate entities. When activated, hover the mouse over a wall or line. A Knife icon will appear; clicking will split the wall or line into two separate segments. If you need to make two splits, with the intention of removing the segment between the two splits, use the Options bar checkbox: Delete Inner Segment. See Figure 5.13.

Trim/Extend

You can trim and extend lines and walls to one another using the Trim tool. The behavior is a bit different from the previous tools we've discussed, in that you don't select elements first and then perform an operation on them; instead, you select the tool first and then operate on elements.

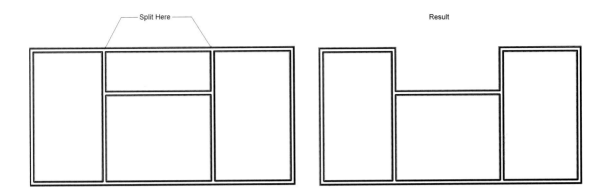

The Trim tool has several options, which are expressed in the Options bar as you select the tool and then the elements.

The first option is the default, Trim/Extend to Corner ( ). It trims elements to one another, creating a connected end-join condition when you finish. For example, to clean up the T intersection shown in Figure 5.14, use the Trim tool.

Figure 5.15 shows two walls before and after using the Trim/Extend Single Element tool ( ).

Figure 5.16 shows multiple walls before and after using the Trim/Extend Multiple Elements tool ( ).

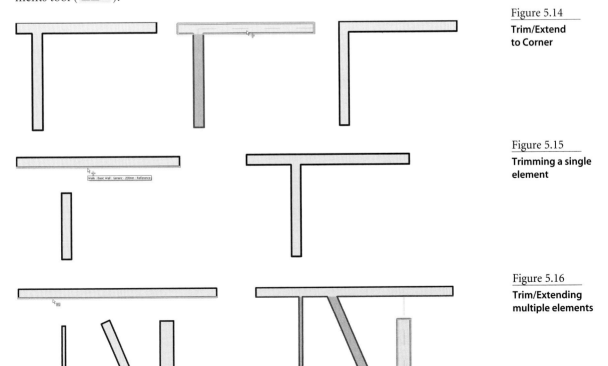

Figure 5.13

Splitting the wall where the two perpendicular walls intersect will produce the following image with just two clicks when the Delete Inner Segment option is checked.

Figure 5.14

Trim/Extend to Corner

Figure 5.15

Trimming a single element

Figure 5.16

Trim/Extending multiple elements

Figure 5.17

**The Offset tool (left)
on the Edit toolbar
and (right) on the
Options bar.**

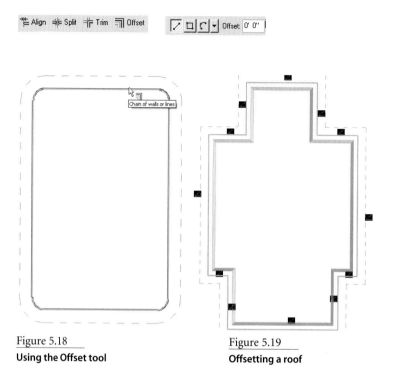

Figure 5.18

Using the Offset tool

Figure 5.19

Offsetting a roof

Offset

Offset is similar to the Move and Copy tools: It makes a copy of a selected element parallel to the edge you select as a reference for offset. You can find the Offset tool either on the Edit toolbar or on the Options bar (Figure 5.17) when you're sketching lines or walls.

This tool is great in the Family Editor when you're making shapes that are a consistent thickness in profile, such as an extruded steel shape. Offset is also handy when you're making roof forms or soffits with known offsets from a wall. You can either offset a line and maintain the original (copy) or offset the line and remove the original. Figure 5.18 shows the offset of a loop of lines using the Copy option.

Figure 5.19 shows how you can use the Offset command to make the roof boundary wider in every direction.

Graphic and Visual Overrides

Revit provides a rich set of controls that allow you to change the graphic appearance of elements on a view-by-view basis. Every element belongs to a category, which provides a baseline graphic appearance for any given element. However, the category graphics may need to deviate, depending on what you're trying to convey in a drawing. For example, the furniture category uses a solid black line by default. This is set in **Settings → Object Styles**. Changing the default values in the Object Styles dialog affects furniture in all views, as shown in Figure 5.20.

Let's say you need to create a plan view where all furniture is shown as halftone, dashed, or as hatched. No problem. With Revit, this is handled with view-specific graphic overrides that can be applied to entire categories or individual elements.

Each view is a unique view of the model that can be graphically tailored to meet your needs. Graphically overriding an element or a category doesn't mean you're changing the element—you're changing its appearance. To override graphics in a view, you can use the Visibility/Graphic Overrides dialog or the view-specific element overrides dialog:

- To access the Visibility/Graphic Overrides dialog, you can either go directly to the dialog from the menu: **View → Visibility/Graphics Overrides** or right-click in the view and choose View Properties from the context menu. You'll see the Visibility/Graphics Overrides parameter in this dialog as well.

- You can also access the dialog when an element is selected using the right-click menu. Select an element, and choose Override Graphics in **View → By Category** (see Figure 5.21).

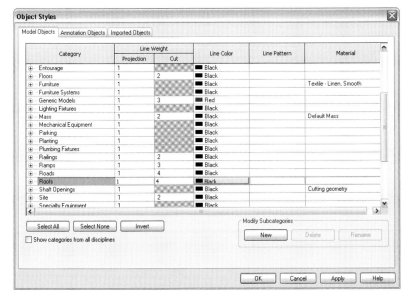

Figure 5.20
Object Styles

Figure 5.21
Accessing the Visibility/Graphic Overrides dialog when an element is selected

Figure 5.22

Overriding an element

When you access the dialog from the context menu, the dialog preselects the category for you based on the elements you selected. For example, to override the furniture category, select a piece of furniture and use the right-click menu to access the override options.

Figure 5.22 shows a long chaise chair in elevation: default mode and overridden with line pattern dashed.

Once you're in the Visibility/Graphic Overrides dialog, you see a list of all the categories and the various ways of manipulating the graphics. To get a handle on this, we'll walk through the override options from left to right, as they appear in the dialog.

Categories

Top-level tabs divide elements based on type: Model, Annotation, and Imported. The Filters tab is also available as a way to manipulate graphics based on parameter criteria. If a view includes imported or linked files, there will be tabs for those as well, which will allow you to change the visibility and appearance of imported layers. This dialog allows for total control over the graphics of anything in your view.

Visibility

The first column combines a list of categories and subcategories with a visibility toggle. To turn off the visibility of a category in the view, uncheck the box next to the category, as shown in Figure 5.23.

Each category has a list of subcategories; to turn off any particular subcategory, uncheck it.

> You may want to turn off the Primary and Secondary contours from your toposurface to have line-less presentation of the toposurface. You may also wish to turn off Door Swing or Door Panel in certain views.

Figure 5.24 shows an example of controlling visibility by unchecking subcategories from the Visibility/Graphic Overrides dialog box. The first image shows the view with the doors turned on, the second image shows what you uncheck, and the final image shows the result.

The lines and surfaces of elements in projection can be overridden. With these controls, you can change the line style of any element and also apply hatches to surfaces.

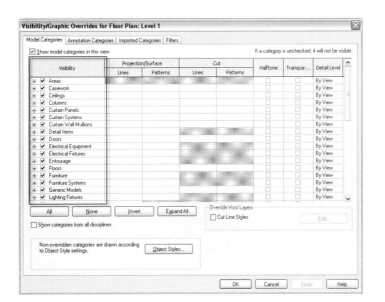

Figure 5.23
Controlling visibility

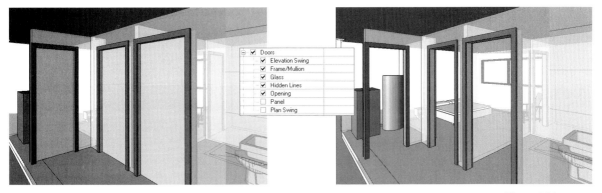

Figure 5.24
Visibility examples

Line and Pattern Overrides

For most model categories, you can apply overrides to projected and cut lines as well as surface and cut patterns (shown in Figure 5.25). Using these overrides allows you to alter line color, thickness, and pattern. You can also apply a hatch pattern override to any surface, whether projected or cut.

To add an override, click the desired override for the category you want to change. The row will then display a series of buttons, as shown in Figure 5.26.

Clicking Override takes you to dialogs where graphics can be overridden. Figure 5.27 shows the Line Graphics override dialog box and the Fill Pattern Graphics override dialog box. Note that the options in the dialog boxes vary based on what you're trying to manipulate.

The controls are fairly self-explanatory. Feel free to experiment with the behavior.

Figure 5.25

Line and pattern overrides

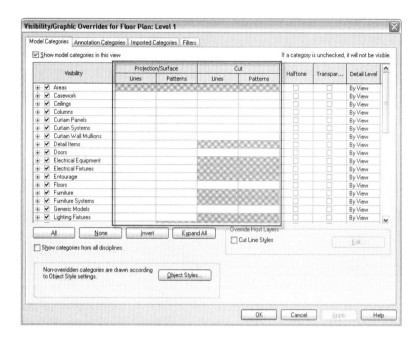

Figure 5.26

Element choices

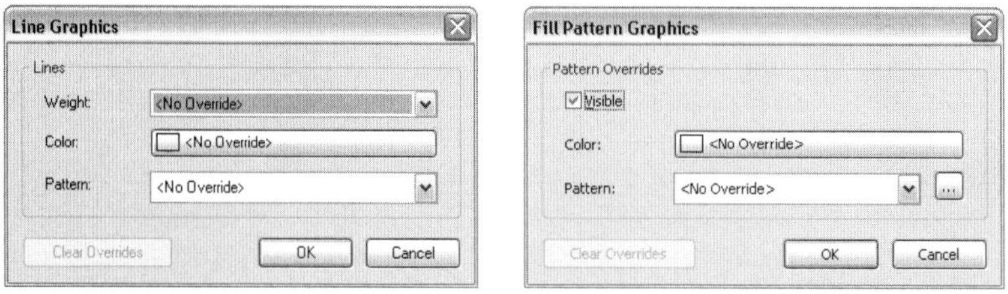

Figure 5.27

Line Graphics and Fill Pattern overrides dialog boxes

Here's something important to note about the Fill Pattern Graphics dialog box: If you want to hide the pattern of a category, use the Visible check box in the Pattern Overrides options. Don't change the pattern color to white, because doing so can cause problems if you end up exporting the view. The lines are still there—they just don't appear, due to the screen background color.

Halftone and Transparent

These columns (shown in Figure 5.28) are check-box controls that change lines and surfaces. The Halftone option takes the line color and tones it down by 50 percent. The Transparent check box makes all surfaces of the category 100 percent transparent, so that you can see through these elements in the view.

Detail Level

The last column controls the Detail Level appearance for categories. This allows you to show fine levels of detail for some categories, even if the view is set to coarse. Until you get into sophisticated content creation, this level of overrides can be safely ignored.

Override Host Layers

The Visibility/Graphic Overrides dialog box contains an additional override feature that is specific to host layers. You can see it at lower right: the Override Host Layers section. Using this edit control, it's possible to override individual layers within wall/floor/roof elements. For example, this will let you make the structural stud layer of walls appear in a heavier line weight than the finish layer.

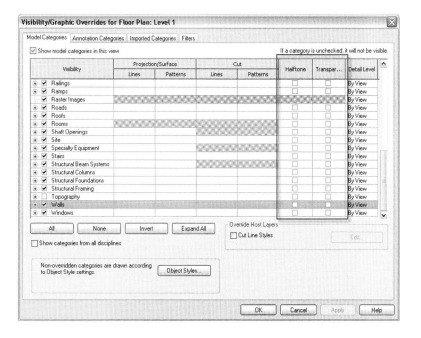

Figure 5.28

Halftone and Transparent overrides

Element Overrides

New to Revit Architecture 2008 is the ability to change the graphics and visibility in individual elements. When element(s) are selected, you can hide them in the view and also override their graphics. This allows you to change the visibility of individual elements, not just entire categories. To do so, select any element, and then use the right-click menu option **Hide in View → Elements**, as shown in Figure 5.29.

The selected elements are hidden in the view. Figure 5.30 shows an example of hiding only few elements of a category in a view. In this case, the trees are obstructing the camera view, so a few of them have been overridden for visibility.

Figure 5.29

Element overrides

Figure 5.30

Hiding elements in a view

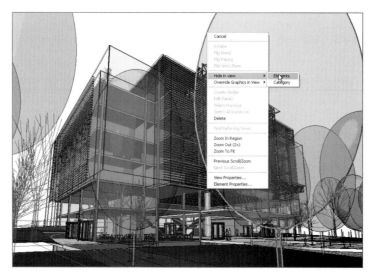

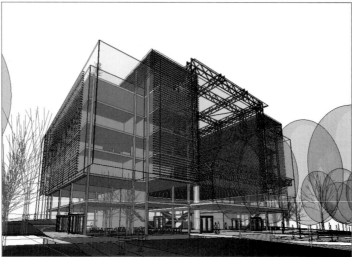

Image courtesy of Architect Kubik & Nemeth

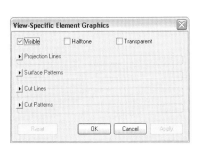

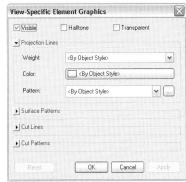

Figure 5.31

View-Specific Element Graphics

Figure 5.32

Projection Lines override group expanded

To override the graphics of a selected element, choose Override Graphics in **View → By Elements** from the right-click menu. Doing so brings up a dialog with the same graphic overrides available in the Visibility/Graphic Overrides dialog box, in a collapsed state (see Figure 5.31).

Along the top of this dialog are check boxes for making an element visible, halftone, and transparent. Below that are groups of controls for overriding lines and patterns. Clicking the small arrow button opens and closes groups of controls for each kind of override. Figure 5.32 shows the dialog box with Projection Lines expanded.

Figure 5.33 shows various element overrides: The bed is set to Transparent, the doors to Halftone, and the shower to Invisible.

Figure 5.34 shows an example using a Transparent override per element in a 3D view; the roof and the front wall are transparent.

Figure 5.33

Uses for graphic overrides

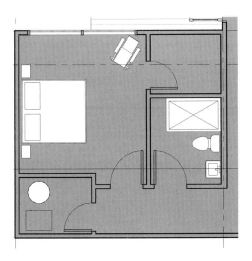

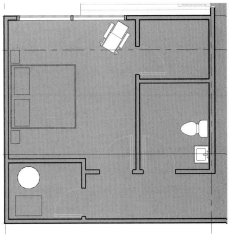

Graphic overrides per view allow you to quickly turn a working drawing in a presentation drawing. You can override in solid fill color all elements that are cut and get another level of presentational drawing. Figure 5.35 shows how you can modify the color of the wall in plan view.

Figure 5.34

Graphic overrides using transparency

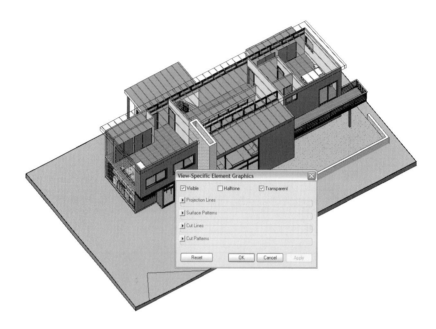

Figure 5.35

Graphic overrides for walls

Unhiding Elements/Categories

After an element or category has been hidden, you can use the Reveal Hidden Elements toggle to see hidden elements and then unhide them. To do this, click the light bulb icon in the View Control bar(1/8" = 1'-0"   □ ⊗ ∅ 🗮 🗲 ⊗ 💡). This is a new feature of Revit Architecture 2008.

The view halftones all visible elements and draws hidden elements with a magenta color. A magenta border is also drawn around the entire view to make it more obvious that you're in a special mode. Hovering the mouse over hidden elements displays a tooltip that explains how the element is being hidden: Hidden Category or Hidden Element. Figure 5.36 shows some examples of hidden elements and categories.

To unhide the element, use the buttons in the Options bar (Unhide Element Unhide Category) or the right-click option Unhide in **View → Element**. To return the view to its normal display, click the light bulb icon again.

As you can see, Revit provides a full range of tools that give you control over how your model looks and feels. Using the interactive editing tools, you can manipulate elements spatially and then make decisions about how elements should be displayed, depending on what you're trying to convey with your drawings.

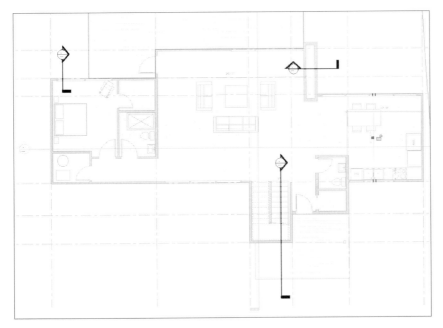
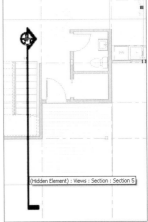

(Hidden Element) : Views : Section : Section 5

Figure 5.36

Hidden elements and categories

CHAPTER 6

Extended Modeling

In the previous chapters we covered basic modeling techniques to construct a simple building. We skipped over many additional features so that you can get a handle on essential workflow, the user interface, and making modifications to the model. In this chapter we'll cover more-advanced features that are available any time you're modeling in Revit. As you'll see, with a little refinement and creativity, you can make almost anything using standard creation tools. With that said, let's take a deeper look at

- Walls: advanced modeling features
- Curtain walls: advanced design techniques
- Roofs and Slabs: advanced shape editing

Walls: Advanced Modeling Features

Walls are made from layers of materials that represent the construction materials used to build real walls. In Revit, these layers can be assigned functions, allowing them to join and react to other similar layers in the model when walls, floors, and roofs meet. The wall *core* is one of these special layers, and understanding it will help you when designing your walls.

Figure 6.1

Wall assembly materials

Revit has a unique ability to identify a wall core that is much more than a layer of material. The core influences the behavior of the wall and how the wall interacts with other elements in the model. Every wall type in Revit has a core material with a boundary on either side of it. These core boundaries are references in the model that can be dimensioned and snapped to. When other host elements (walls, floors, ceilings, roofs) are drawn, you can use wall-core boundaries to generate sketches and maintain a relationship with that boundary. For example, a floor sketch can be constrained to the structural stud layer of walls by using the wall-core boundary to create the sketch. If walls change size or are swapped, the floor sketch maintains its relationship to the core boundary and will auto-adjust.

To access and edit wall-core boundaries and material layers, select a wall, go to Element Properties, press Edit/New to get to Type Properties, and then select to edit the Structure parameter. This will open a new Edit Assembly dialog. From here you can define materials, move layers in and out of the core boundary, and assign functions to each layer (see Figure 6.1).

To get a feel for how core layers are used in relation to a floor, start a new session of Revit and follow these steps:

1. Open a new project, and draw a simple floor plan using walls. Select a multilayered wall type in order to understand the value of the exercise—the Brick on CMU wall type works well. Draw some walls in the shape shown in Figure 6.2.

2. Use the View bar to switch to fine or medium view so you can see all wall layers. (In coarse views, wall layers are never displayed.)

3. From the Modeling Design Bar, select the Floor tool, keep the default Pick Walls option, and in the Options Bar (Figure 6.3) check the "Extend into wall (to core)" option.

Figure 6.2

Create brick walls in this configuration.

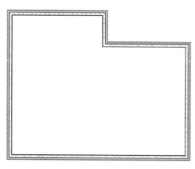

4. Position your mouse over an edge of the wall, (do not click the mouse yet), press Tab to highlight all the walls, and then click to select. Zoom in. A sketch line indicating the shape of the floor will be created. This sketch line indicates the position of the floor relative to the wall—it's drawn at the exterior edge of the wall core. Make sure you've selected all walls as a reference to create the floor, and click Finish Sketch.

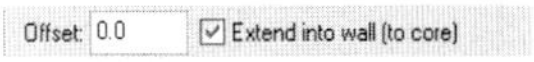

5. Create a section through the wall, and open the section view. Again, make sure your view is set to medium or fine. You'll see the edge of the floor and how it aligns with the wall construction (Figure 6.4).

6. Go back to the floor plan, and select all elements in the view. Click the Filter button in the Options bar, and uncheck all but the Floor category. Click OK. In the Options bar, click the Edit command to edit the floor. You'll be put back in sketch mode.

7. Tab-select the floor lines to pick all lines in the sketch. In the Options bar, set an offset of 6″ (150mm).

8. Finish the sketch.

9. Switch back to the section view (Figure 6.5). The floor now extends 6″ (150mm) beyond the edge of the core.

10. You can continue by changing the wall type to another type and see that the floor always follows its position relative to the core of the new wall. If you change your design and move your walls to make the floor plan bigger or smaller, the floor will always adjust with the change.

Offset: 0.0   ☑ Extend into wall (to core)

Figure 6.3

Floor sketch option allows you to constrain lines to wall-core boundaries

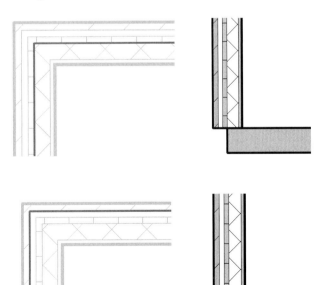

Figure 6.4

On the left, the floor sketch in plan view; on the right, how the floor looks in section in relation to the wall.

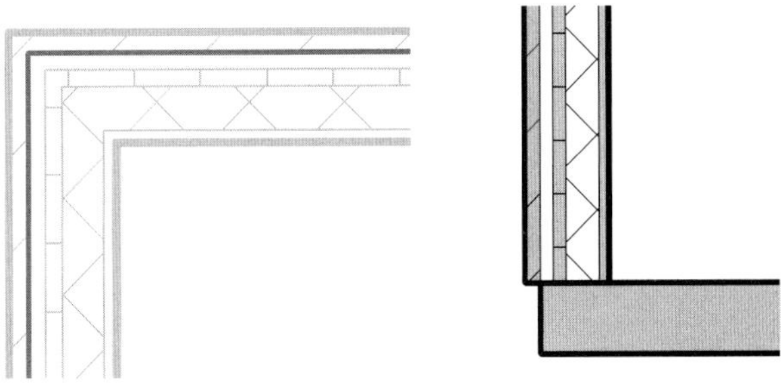

Figure 6.5

Floor with offset from the wall-core boundary

Layer Join Cleanup

As mentioned in Chapter 4, the wall-layer priority determines the interaction and cleanup of joins between walls of different types. There are six functions (levels of priority of wall layers), with Structure having the highest priority (as shown in Figure 6.6).

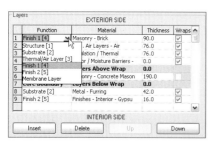

Figure 6.6

Wall functions

When you create a new wall type and begin adding layers to the wall, you need to assign a material, thickness, and priority to the layers. When you're assigning a priority, think about the function of the layer in the wall—is it Finish? Substrate? Structure? This decision will help clean up your walls down the road.

If you encounter situations where the automated wall cleanup doesn't correspond to your expectations, Revit will let you cycle through a range of possible layer configurations using the Edit Wall Joins tool, located in the Options bar.

Editing Wall Joins

The Edit Wall Joins tool lets you edit wall-join configurations (🔲 🔲). The default wall join is set to Butt join. Activate the Edit Wall Joins tool, and place your mouse over a wall join. (This can be a corner where two walls meet.) The Options bar shows some alternative configuration options: Miter and Square. A Miter join is shown in Figure 6.7.

Disjoining Walls

Disallow Join is another tool designed to provide more flexibility in wall-join behavior. If you select a partition wall that cleans up with your exterior wall, but that isn't the desired behavior for that partition wall, you can right-click the blue control dot at the end of the wall and select Disallow Join from the context menu. Doing so breaks the auto-join cleanup. Figure 6.8 shows the walls intersecting in a Disallow Join condition.

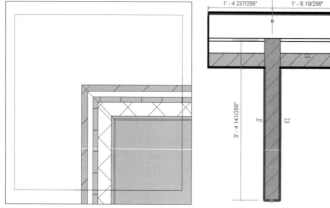

Figure 6.7

A Miter join

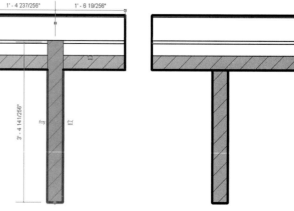

Figure 6.8

Disallow Join

Stacked Walls

Walls in a building, especially exterior walls, are often composed of different wall types that vertically stack on top of one another over the height of the façade. At the very least, most walls sit on top of a foundation wall. To guarantee that if the foundation wall moves, the walls above it also move, you can use a special wall type in Revit: Stacked Wall.

Stacked walls allow you to create a single wall entity composed of vertically stacked different wall types. The wall types need to be existing types already available in the project.

To understand how stacked walls work and how to modify one, follow these steps:

Figure 6.9

Stacked walls

1. Open a new session of Revit, and make sure three levels are defined (if you don't have three levels defined, go to an elevation view, add a third level, and then go back to your floor plan view).

2. Pick the Wall tool and select the Stacked Wall: Exterior - Brick Over CMU w Metal Stud (located at the bottom of the list in the type selector). Go to Element Properties, select the Edit/New button, then duplicate the wall type to create a new stacked wall (Figure 6.9).

3. Edit the Structure parameter, and press the Preview button to see the wall in section (Figure 6.10). When you're editing the Stacked Wall type, you'll notice that the UI is slightly different than when you're working with a basic wall. Rather than editing individual wall layers, this dialog allows you to stack predefined wall types.

Figure 6.10

**Modifying a
stacked wall**

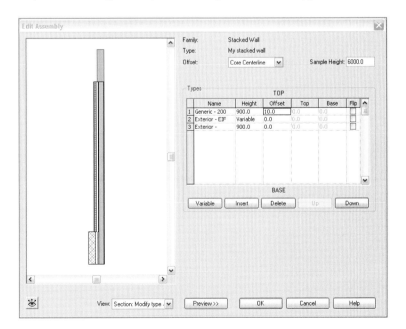

4. Click the Insert button to add a new wall. A new row appears in the list and allows you to define a new wall. Select the Generic wall type from the Name list, and set the Height value; you also may need to define an Offset value to make the three walls flush with the interior face. With a new row selected, press the Variable button. This will allow the wall to vary in height to adjust with levels.

5. Go back to your plan view and draw the new wall, setting its top constraint to Level 3.

6. Cut a section through the model and change the heights of Level 1 and Level 3 to see the effect this has on the wall. (Make sure the level of detail is set to medium/fine to see the wall layers.) You'll see that changing Level 2 does not change the bottom walls, as they are fixed in height. However, changing the height of Level 3 will change the height of the variable wall (see Figure 6.12).

Note that in Revit it is never too late to add or change something. There is no need to rearrange things to accommodate late changes to the project because that is exactly where Revit excels—it revises instantly when you apply a change to one place.

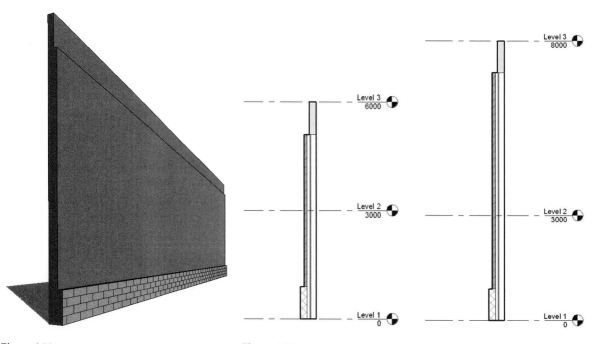

Figure 6.11

A finished stacked wall

Figure 6.12

Variable instance in a stacked wall

Vertical Compound Wall

Walls are often complex and articulated in their composition. Cornices, reveals, corrugated metal finish, and other projections are used all the time. Revit can accommodate any of these types of design articulation. Some examples of compound walls are shown in Figure 6.13.

From the type properties of any basic wall, you can enable a preview of the wall. This preview allows you to view the wall in either plan or section. When the section preview is active, additional tools also become active and allow you to place geometric sweep/reveal components on the wall (see Figure 6.14).

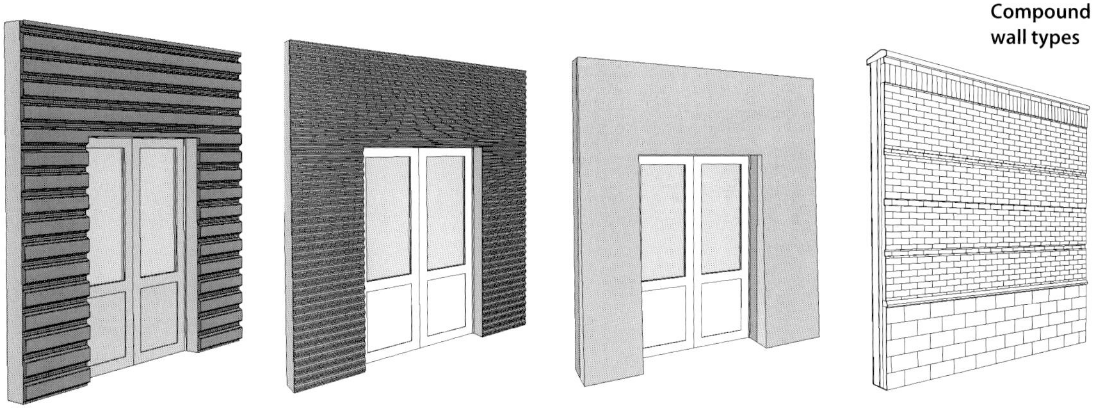

Figure 6.13

Compound wall types

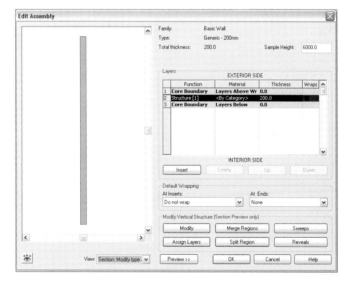

Figure 6.14

Wall-section preview

Sweeps and Reveals

Clicking the Sweeps or Reveals button in the Edit Assembly dialog opens a new dialog box where you can define profile families to use as sweeps or reveals. These profiles, which are no more than 2D shapes made out of simple lines, are then swept along the length of the wall at a specified height. Many profiles representing cornices, skirting, and chair rails ship with Revit; but if you need to create a custom profile, you can use the Profile Family template. Choose **File → New Family → Profile** to access the Revit Family Editor. From here, you draw one closed loop of lines at the desired real-world scale and load the profile back into your project. Note that you cannot have more then one closed loop of lines when creating profiles. Follow these steps:

1. Click the Wall tool and select Generic Wall.

2. Go to its properties, select Edit/New, and click Duplicate. Give the wall a new name.

3. Using the Insert button, add new layers as shown in Figure 6.15. Use the Up and Down buttons to move layers in the assembly.

4. In the preview view, switch to section view. The six Modify Vertical Structure options become active at the bottom of the dialog box, as shown in Figure 6.16.

5. Click the Sweeps tool to open the dialog box shown in Figure 6.17. At present, no sweeps are defined in your wall, so let's add some.

6. Click the Load Profile button, browse to the Profiles folder, and load these two profiles as shown in Figure 6.18:

   • Cornice profile: Traditional (1)

   • Skirting profile: (Base 2, Ogee or similar)

Figure 6.15

Layers in the wall

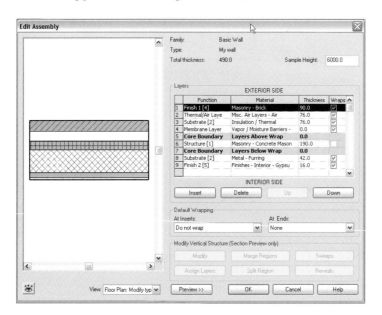

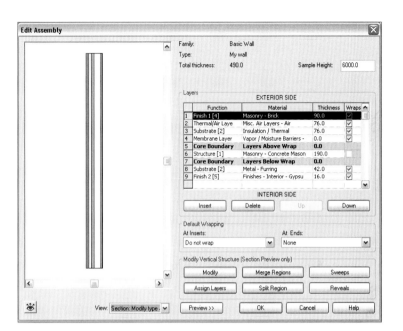

Figure 6.16
Wall in section view

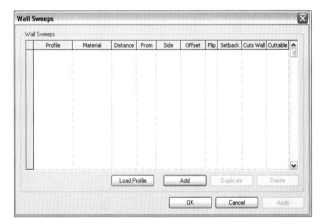

Figure 6.17
Wall sweeps

Cornice profile: Traditional (1)   Skirting profile: Ogee

Figure 6.18
**Load these
wall profiles.**

7. Click the Add button. This adds a row in the dialog box that lets you select one of the loaded profiles and set its position relative to the wall geometry. Figure 6.19 shows the profiles loaded in the wall.

8. Add both profiles. Set the Traditional profile's From value to Top and the Ogee profile's From value to Base. Doing so attaches the profiles to the top and bottom of your wall. Figure 6.20 shows the profiles attached to the top and bottom of the wall.

9. Click OK. Draw a segment of this wall in the drawing area. Check out the wall in section and 3D views to see the resulting wall.

> Another useful feature available when you're working with a wall in section preview is the ability to unlock wall layers. To do this, click the Modify button and zoom in to the bottom of the wall. Hover the mouse over the bottom edges of the layers in the preview, and they will highlight. With the help of the Tab key, select one of the bottom edges and a lock icon will appear. By default, all top and bottom edges of layers are locked into place; however, if you unlock this edge it becomes free to move up and down. You can then manipulate individual layers dynamically or with parameters. When you unlock layers, the instance parameters for Base and Top Extension Distance become enabled. Figure 6.21 shows the lock and the ability to unlock the material and extend it further than the wall base.

Figure 6.19

Adding the profiles to the wall

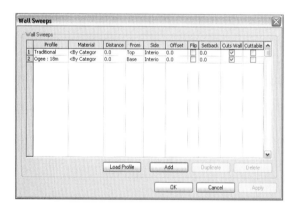

Figure 6.20

The profiles on the wall

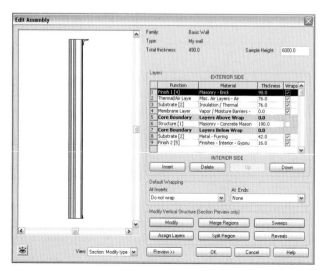

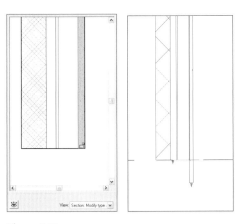

Figure 6.21

Extending wall materials

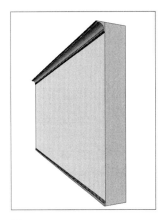

Figure 6.22

Finishing the wall

Using the same principles outlined for adding traditional looking elements, you can get creative and add any type or profile you want. Figure 6.23 shows a wall with a corrugated siding added as an integrated wall sweep.

Reveals

Reveals can be added to a wall using the same workflow as with sweeps, the only difference being that but the profile is subtractive rather than additive.

When you're working on traditional architectural projects, the wall sweeps usually wrap around door openings in thick walls. Revit can accommodate that using the Change Sweep Return command.

Wall sweep returns

When you're working on traditional architectural projects, the wall sweeps usually wrap around door openings in thick walls. Revit can accommodate that using the Change Sweep Return command.

To understand this feature, follow this simple exercise:

1. Open a new Session of Revit and place a generic wall.

2. Rather than placing a sweep in the wall type, we can use another method for placing sweeps: the Host Sweep tool in the Modeling tab (shown in Figure 6.24). Choose Wall Sweep, and then select a wall sweep from the Type Selector. These sweeps can be placed either vertically or horizontally using options in the Options bar.

3. Add a horizontal sweep to the middle the wall. Use the temporary dimensions to place the sweep at the desired height.

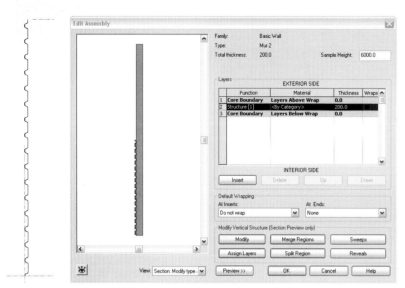

The profile　　The wall in Edit Assembly　　　　　　　　　　The finished wall

Figure 6.23

A corrugated metal wall

Figure 6.24

Host Sweep

4. Using the Opening tool, also located in the Modeling tab, draw an opening that intersects the sweep, as shown in Figure 6.25.

5. Select the sweep—it will display a blue grip at the end (edge of the opening). Click the Change Sweep Return command on the Options bar; the mouse turns into a knife symbol, and when you click somewhere on the profile, it creates a new segment that wraps around the edge of the opening. Press Esc or use the Modify tool to exit the command. You will need to zoom in close to the end of the sweep to really see the effect. If you zoom very closely, the lines might become very thick and ugly—in that case, click the Thin Line Mode button that we explained earlier in the book (▤)

6. Select the sweep again, and drag the control to adjust the length of the sweep. Figure 6.26 shows some examples of modifying an instance Host Sweep.

Figure 6.25

Wall with a sweep and opening, prior to applying the Change return functionality

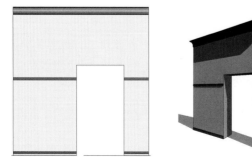

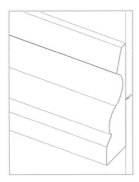

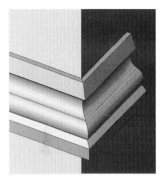

Figure 6.26
Modifying a sweep return

Wall sweeps created using the Host Sweep Tool from the Modeling Design bar can be scheduled. Integral wall sweeps created from within the Wall properties cannot be scheduled in Revit at present. That is the main difference between these two types of sweeps.

Creating Special Walls Using the Create Tool (In-Place Walls)

When you're working on traditional architecture or restoration of historic buildings, you'll often need to create walls that are irregular in shape. The Create tool, found under the Modeling Design tab, lets you address such wall styles; Figure 6.27 shows an example.

This tool allows you to draw solid geometry using one of four modeling methods. Each created form is assigned a specific category that is later used to control visibility and behavior in the model. For example, assigning a swept from the category Wall allows the wall to host inserts such as windows and doors.

Figure 6.27
Create in Place showing a series of connected blends; images courtesy of A.U.S. Italy

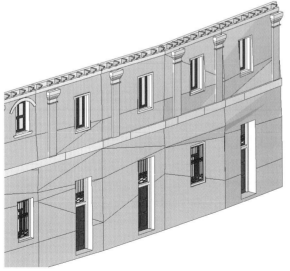
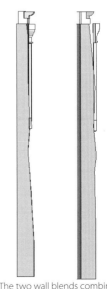

The finished wall

The two wall blends combined
to make the wall

The wall in Figure 6.28 is created using a series of blends assigned to the Category Wall. It still behaves as a wall: You can make doors and windows, and they cut through the geometry of the wall as with standard walls. Various wall types can be created using this method.

The beauty of Revit modeling tools is that you can always go back to the sketch and change your idea (the sketch), and all related drawings will update. You do not need to redraw the profile. Same applies for the path—if you used the sweep technique, you can at any point edit the path while keeping the profile.

A wall created using the sweep modeling technique

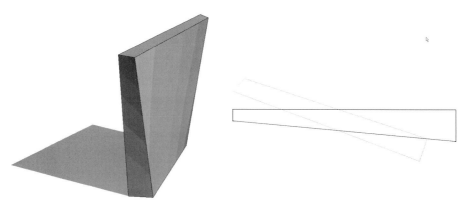

A twisted wall created using the blend technique—drawing the base and the top shape, and setting a distance between them

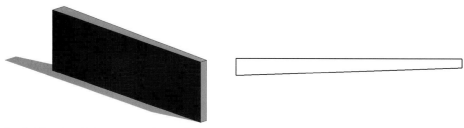

A wall with various thicknesses created using the extrusion method

Curtain Walls: Advanced Design Techniques

The Curtain Wall tool is designed with flexibility in mind. You can use it to generate anything from simple storefronts to highly articulated structural glass façades. In this section, we'll look at the basic principles and how to extend these principles to create a range of designs.

As we mentioned in Chapter 4, the composition of a curtain wall is divided into four primary elements, shown in Figure 6.29:

- The wall and its geometric extents
- Curtain grids
- Mullions
- Curtain panels

The wall A curtain wall is drawn like a basic wall and is available in the Type Selector when the wall tool is active. It has top and bottom constraints, can be attached to roofs, can have its elevation profile sketch edited, and schedules as a wall type.

Curtain grids The curtain grid is the layout grid: the design of your façade that defines the physical divisions of the curtain wall and sets the rules of behavior. The layout grid can be designed freely as a combination of horizontal and vertical segments or can be a type with embedded rules that specify regular divisions. Figure 6.30 shows two dramatically different types of curtain wall systems.

Figure 6.29
**Taxonomy of
a curtain wall**

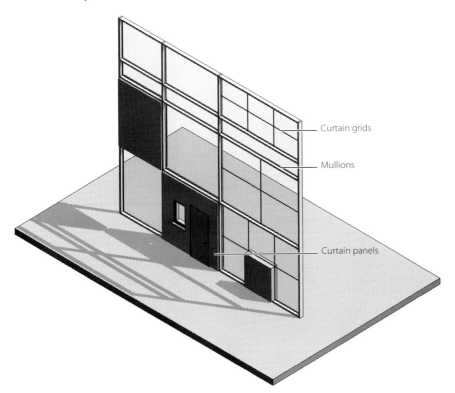

Curtain grids

Mullions

Curtain panels

Figure 6.30
**Curtain wall
examples**

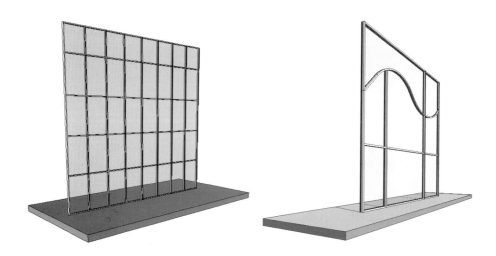

Mullions The mullions represent the metal or PVC profiles on a glass façade, and in Revit they follow the geometry of the grid. They can have any shape that is based on a mullion profile family.

Curtain panels The curtain panels fill in the space between gridlines and are always one of the following:

Empty panels are just that: empty. No panel is placed in the mullions.

Glazed panels can be made out of different types of glass that can have any color or transparency.

Solid panels and panels with wall types can take on any geometry you wish and thus create most interesting structures, like the one shown in Figure 6.31.

Figure 6.31
**A curtain wall
system with formed
panels; image cour-
tesy of Edward
Phillip Read**

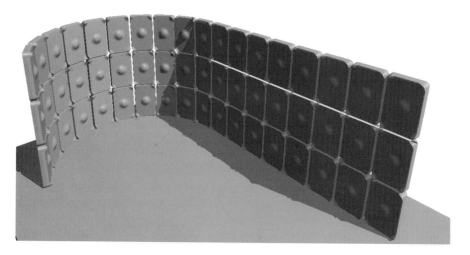

Designing a Curtain Wall

In this simple exercise, we'll walk through the creation of a simple curtain wall. To draw a curtain wall, you can either draw a standard wall and then change its type to Curtain Wall or select a Curtain Wall type from the Wall Type Selector first. Follow these steps:

1. Select the Wall tool.

2. From the Type Selector, select Curtain Wall.

3. In the Level 1 plan view, draw a curtain wall. Use the wall type Curtain Wall 1.

4. Toggle the view to see the result in 3D.

5. To divide the wall into panels, use the Curtain Grid tool on the Modeling tab. Mouse over the edges of the wall to get a preview of where the grid will be placed. Revit has some intelligent snapping built into grid placement that looks for midpoints and points that will divide the panel into thirds.

6. You can place one mullion at a time by selecting separate segments; or, if you want to apply the same mullion on all segments, hold the Ctrl key and click a gridline to select all segments and apply the mullions. The series of images in Figure 6.32 shows the approximate results you should get.

7. Let's say you want to add more mullions, but this time you don't want them to extend the entire height of the curtain wall. Select the Curtain Grid Line tool, and place new grids as shown in Figure 6.33.

8. Before applying a mullion to the new gridline, delete the segments of the gridline where you don't wish the mullion to occur. Exit the grid-placement tool, and select the newly created gridline. Click the Add/Remove Segments button in the Options bar, and click the segment you want removed. Remove the top and bottom segments; you should have an image similar to Figure 6.34. Place mullions on the gridline to finish.

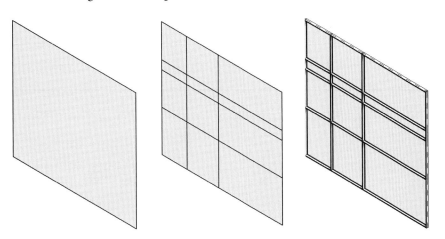

Figure 6.32

Making the curtain wall and adding mullions

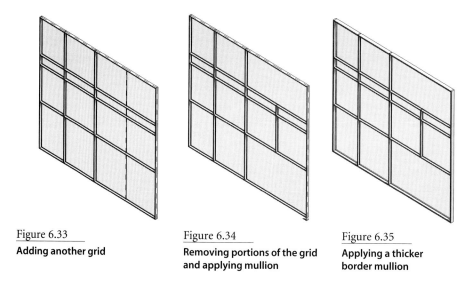

Figure 6.33

Adding another grid

Figure 6.34

Removing portions of the grid and applying mullion

Figure 6.35

Applying a thicker border mullion

9. To change mullion types—in this case, the border mullions—use the right-click menu to isolate mullions for selection. Hover the mouse over a mullion, right-click, and select **Mullions → Border Mullions** to select all border mullions.

10. Swap them for another type using the Type Selector. If you don't find a mullion type with the dimensions you need, no worries: It's easy to create a new one on the fly:

   a. Open the mullion properties.

   b. Select **Edit → New**, and then click Duplicate.

   c. Name the mullion type. In the Type Properties, change the thickness to the new value to 8″ (200mm) and the two parameters for Width (this represents half the width of the mullion) to 1.25″ (35mm). Figure 6.35 shows the finished exterior mullions.

   The result shows thicker mullions on the border of your curtain wall.

Curtain mullions are usually rectangular, and you can make new types of different sizes on the fly, as shown in the previous exercise. However, not all mullions are simple rectangles. With Revit, you can use complex profile shapes as extruded mullions. Mullion profile families can be made with the Family Editor.

The default library provides some mullions that use custom profiles. To use these, load them into your project, duplicate an existing mullion type, and set the type parameter Profile to one of the newly loaded profiles. A list of available profiles loaded into the project appears in the field shown in Figure 6.36.

Figure 6.36

Modifying the mullion profile

In reality, curtain-wall mullions can have complex internal details from a manufacturing perspective. Many curtain-wall manufacturers provide DWG details showing the actual manufactured look of the mullions. You'll probably want to show more of those details when you do detailed drawings.

Curtain Panels

Curtain panels fill the space between the curtain grids and mullions. These elements are created in the Family Editor using the Curtain Panels family template. They can be found under **File → New Family → Curtain Wall Panel.rft**. The Revit default template has a couple of curtain panels preloaded: System Panel Glazed and System Panel Solid.

You can duplicate different types of these families and change the material, thickness, and offset to customize the appearance.

Selecting the Elements within the Curtain Wall

Revit provides specially tailored selection options in the right-click menu to aid with workflow and interaction when working with curtain walls. When you hover over or pick an element in a curtain wall, take note of the Status bar in the lower-left corner of the screen: It tells you exactly the type of element you're about to select or have already selected. Depending on what the mouse is hovering over, various selection options are available. The elements you can select include the following:

- The entire curtain-wall entity (this selection is indicated by a green dashed line surrounding the curtain wall)
- A gridline
- A mullion
- A curtain panel

To select the element you want, use the Tab key until the element of choice is highlighted.

By default, Revit applies glazed curtain panels as panels for the curtain wall.

Using the method explained earlier, select one of the curtain panels and use the Type Selector to change it to System Panel Solid. It will look like Figure 6.37.

Doors and Windows

Curtain walls can host specially designed doors and windows. Keep in mind that standard doors and windows cannot be hosted by a curtain wall. These specially designed elements are recognizable by their name that indicates that they are curtain wall doors/windows, they schedule as doors and windows, but their behavior is dependent on the

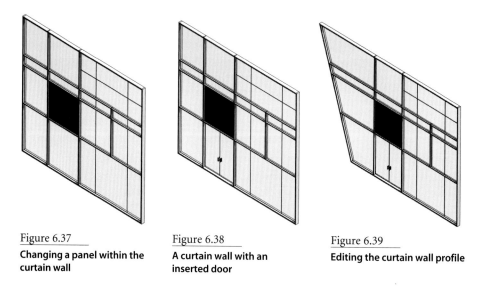

Figure 6.37

Changing a panel within the curtain wall

Figure 6.38

A curtain wall with an inserted door

Figure 6.39

Editing the curtain wall profile

curtain wall. Curtain-wall doors and windows adapt their width and height to fill in grid cells. Essentially, they behave exactly like panels—they've just been made to appear and schedule as doors or windows.

To insert a door within a curtain wall, choose **File → Load Library → Load Family.** Navigate to the Doors folder, and select a Curtain Wall Door (Single or Double). A door is added to the curtain wall, as shown in Figure 6.38.

Be sure you make the distance between gridlines/mullions reflect a standard door size. You can do this before or after the placement of the door. The curtain wall is highly parametric, so changes are allowed at any time during the design process.

Parametric Behavior

You can edit the profile shape of a curtain wall, just like a basic wall. Select the curtain wall and click the Edit Elevation Profile button in the Options bar to start editing the sketch outline of the wall.

1. Draw four walls on Level 1 in shape of a rectangle.

2. Add a Roof by Footprint on Level 2, picking all four walls with the Tab key (be sure to select the outside face of walls, and go ahead and give the roof an overhang using the Options bar).

3. Switch to 3D view.

4. The resulting curtain wall should be as shown in Figure 6.39.

For the sake of the next exercise, undo this last profile edit.

Curtain walls also share some of the other behaviors of standard walls, such as Attach and Detach Top/Base.

Attaching the Curtain Wall to a Roof

Curtain walls have a highly parametric relationship with other modeling elements. Like a basic wall, when a curtain wall is attached to a roof, it maintains its connection to the roof as the roof shape adjusts. To see how this works, start a new drawing and do the following steps:

1. Draw four walls on Level 1.

2. Add a Roof by Footprint on Level 2, picking all four walls with the Tab key.

3. Switch to 3D view.

4. Toggle two ends of the sketch to be non–slope defining, using the Options bar. This will generate a gable roof when the sketch is finished.

5. Change one wall to the Curtain Wall: Store Front type.

6. Select all the walls, and attach them to the roof using the Options bar's Attach/Detach button.

7. Select the roof and drag the blue arrow on the top to make the roof pitch higher. The curtain wall automatically readjusts its size and shape to accommodate the change, as shown in Figure 6.40.

Curtain walls can also use standard wall types in lieu of panels. Using the same method described previously, select a curtain panel and exchange it with a wall using the Type Selector.

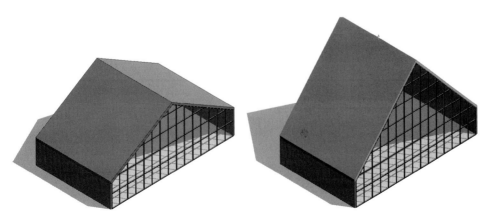

Figure 6.40

Curtain wall conforming to roof changes

Complex Curtain-Wall Panel Gallery

Look at the complex-shaped curtain panels in Figure 6.41. You may think, "Oh, I can *never* do that!" Well, Revit can help you do it—and do it easily. To be fair, you'll need to have some mileage in using Revit before you can create such a curtain wall. But isn't it inspiring to look at all the possibilities that you'll be able to master one day?

The creation principle behind any of these types of curtain walls is the same as we just reviewed. All that differs is the geometry of the curtain panel.

The curtain walls in Figure 6.42 were created with curtain panels that—instead of a standard rectangular solid shape—are made of a solid extrusion that is perforated with four corner openings. An additional solid geometry represents one quarter of the spider clamp.

Figure 6.41

A complex curtain wall designed in Revit

Figure 6.42

A spider-clamp curtain wall

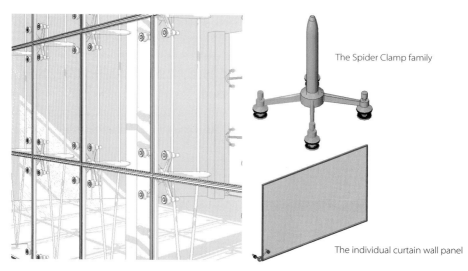

The Spider Clamp family

The individual curtain wall panel

Roofs and Slabs: Advanced Shape Editing

No flat roof is ever really flat! Creating roofs with tapered insulation over flat roof (Figure 6.43) is no longer a challenge with the new roof/slab modifier tool introduced in the 2008 version of Revit. This powerful tool is a modifier that is applicable to roofs or floors with straight edges and offers the ability to model concrete slabs with multiple slopes, often referred to as warped slabs.

Figure 6.43

Flat roof with sloped insulation

UI

The modification Tools appears in the Options bar when a roof or floor is selected (Figure 6.44).

Here is what each tool is for (left to right):

Figure 6.44

The new Shape Edit modifying tools

- **The Direct Editing tool** edits of element geometry using selection and modification of points (vertices) and edges.

- **The Draw Points tool** adds points on the top face of a roof or floor. Points can be added on edges or surfaces.

- **The Draw Split Line tool** allows sketching directly on the top face of the element, which adds split lines to the floor and roof so that hips and valleys can be created.

- **The Pick Supports tool** allows picking linear beams and walls to create new split edges at the correct elevation automatically.

As you can see, there is also a Reset Shape button. This button will remove all modifiers applied to the floor/roof that is selected.

Let's do a short exercise that shows how to make a sloped roof as shown in Figure 6.45.

1. Open the drawing Modifying Roof Shape start.rvt.

2. Select the roof that has been already prepared for you.

3. Activate the Draw Split Line tool—(note that the color of the rest of the model greys out).

4. Sketch ridge lines to divide the roof into areas that will be independently drained.

5. Using the same tool, draw diagonal lines within those areas to create the valleys.

Figure 6.45

A roof plan showing a roof divided in segments with drainage points

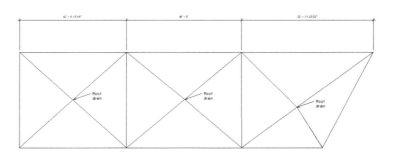

What you have done is split the roof surfaces in many subslabs, but they are still all at the same height/inclination. You should have roof that looks like Figure 6.46.

6. Switch to a 3D view.

7. To add a slope (height of the drainage points), Tab-select the crossing point of the diagonals. New controls that allow you to edit the text appear and you can either move the arrows up and down or type in a value for the point height. Type in -0′ 5″ (-13cm) as shown on Figure 6.47.

8. Repeat the same for all 3 drainage points.

9. If needed (as it often happens to accommodate what's happening in the room below the roof) to move the point to another position, which is easily done by a simple select and drag-and-drop of the point. See Figure 6.48.

10. Make a section through the roof—if possible somewhere through the drainage point. Open the section; change the detail level to Fine to see all layers. What you will see is that the entire roof structure is sloped towards the drainage point. See figure 6.49.

Figure 6.46

Using the Draw Split tool, ridges and valleys are created.

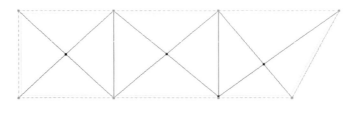

Figure 6.47

Edit points to change the height.

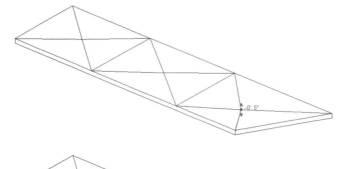

Figure 6.48

Drainage point moved to a new position

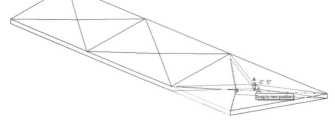

Figure 6.49

Section through roof showing the slope

What if you wanted just the insulation to be tapered but not the structure? For that, there is additional capability added to the layers of the roofs that now can have variable thickness.

11. Select the roof and go to its Type Properties to edit its Structure.

12. Activate the preview. You will notice that in the roof-structure preview you do not see any slopes. That is correct and will not change: This preview is just a theoretical preview of the structure and will not show the exact sloping. You'll see a Variable column under Layers. This allows layers of the roof to vary in thickness when slopes are present. Check the insulation material to be Variable (Figure 6.50).

13. Go back to the section view and take a look at the difference that this change provoked: As you will see, only the insulation is tapered now while the structure remains flat. See Figure 6.51

You can find a final state of this exercise on the CD as Modifying Roof Shape End.rvt.

If you want to see what the Reset Shape functionality does, select the roof and press the Reset Shape button in the Options bar.

Currently this modifier cannot be applied to any floor or roof that has a nonstraight segment. However, you can work around that by using a vertical opening (see Figure 6.52).

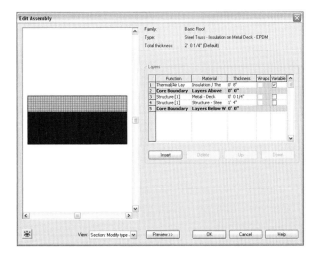

Figure 6.50

Roof assembly dialog box

Figure 6.51

Section of the roof with variable thickness

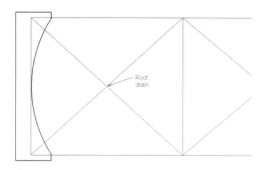

Figure 6.52

Apply a vertical opening in plan view to cut the roof in curved shape.

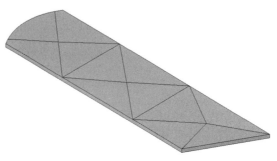

Figure 6.53

Axonometric view of the final roof shape with curve and tapered insulation

You need to start with a simplified straight segment floor/roof shape that contains no arcs. You add the arc as a subtraction in the form of an opening. By using the opening tool in the Modeling tab and choosing the Vertical option, you can then sketch the arcs you need. See Figures 6.52 and 6.53.

> You could achieve similar results without using the Draw split line tool by simply adding points in the middle of the flat roof. Try it out to see how that simplifies the process.

Warped Surfaces

Warped surfaces can also be created using this tool. Draw a flat roof (no slopes) and then select the roof. Using the Modify tool in the Option bar, you can start moving edge points up and down (Figure 6.54).

Rotate the 3D view to understand what you have just created. See the final result in Figure 6.55.

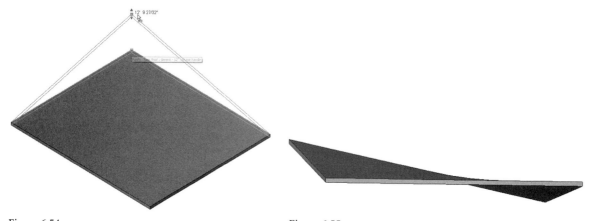

Figure 6.54

Edit the edge point to warp a flat roof.

Figure 6.55

Axonometric view of a warped roof

CHAPTER 7

Working with Other Applications

Now that we have developed a language for working within Revit, let's look at how you can use it to work and communicate with others. The building industry is a complex organism with many moving parts and participants. Partners, consultants, contractors, sub contractors, and owners are all involved in the process and need the ability to exchange vital design information. Because of the robustness of information within the Revit model, it's possible to do things with data that weren't possible with basic 2D drafting. Even so, the need for data exchange with other applications is still a requirement. Revit provides tools to import and export a wide range of information.

In this chapter, you'll learn how to export your Revit model in forms that others can read and how to import information that is relevant to your project from other sources. We'll first review all the possible export and import file formats and then dig into more detailed use cases. Topics covered in the chapter include:

- **Exporting your data**

- **Importing and linking**

- **Working with imported files**

- **Different ways to start a project**

- **Utilizing CAD libraries**

Exporting

You can find the export options under **File → Export**. Revit offers several different export formats depending on the format and type of data you want to export.

Here's a list of the types of files that Revit can export using information from the Revit model:

- CAD formats
- Animations, including walkthroughs and animated solar studies
- ODBC database tables
- Images
- Schedules
- gbXML
- Room / area reports

CAD Formats

CAD Formats lets you export a view or sheet of the model into a 2D or 3D CAD format. The following CAD file formats can be exported directly from Revit: `.dwg`, `.dxf`, `.dgn`, and `.sat`.

DWG

DWG refers to the original patented Autodesk object, RealDWG. DWG is the established standard for exchange of digital data in the construction industry for the last 20+ years. Revit can export an entire project, collections of sheets and views, or any individual sheet or view to the DWG format. DWG has become the industry standard for 2D digital file types in the last 20+ years.

Revit exports views to DWG in a 2D DWG drafting format. Only the 3D views are exported as 3D DWGs. These can be viewed in a 3D environment in AutoCAD or any other application that reads DWG. When exporting to DWG, some of the metadata (property information) of elements is also exported and can be read within AutoCAD.

Exporting DWG files is discussed in more detail later in this chapter.

DXF

Data Exchange Format (DXF) is a format for storing vector data. DXF is regarded as a legacy standard and is almost out of use in the industry. However, Revit still supports exporting to DXF. If you haven't used DXF files in the past, be careful exporting 3D data to DXF. A file can get very large very quickly!

DGN

DGN is the name used for CAD file formats supported by Bentley Systems' Microstation and Intergraph's Interactive Graphics Design System (IGDS) CAD programs. Note that Revit supports export to DGN file formats only up to Microstation version V7.

SAT

SAT stands for Standard ACIS Text. ACIS can store modeling information in external files called *save files*. These files have an open format so that external applications, even those not based on ACIS, can have access to the ACIS geometric model. Revit exports to version 7 of SAT.

Exporting Animations: Walkthroughs and Solar Studies

You can create walkthrough animations in Revit and save them as `.avi` files. To export a walkthrough, choose **File → Export → Walkthrough**.

Revit lets you make Animated Solar Studies, and those can also be exported as `.avi` files. To export an Animated Solar Study, choose **File → Export → Animated Solar Study**. Creation of solar studies is covered in Chapter 8.

ODBC Database Tables

You can export almost all the information embedded in your Revit model to an open database connectivity (ODBC) table. Doing so creates a link between your Revit file and another external database such as Excel, Access, Filemaker, or SQL. ODBC gives you the opportunity to download data from any of the tables in Revit directly to a database using the Microsoft ODBC connector. An example of this functionality is the cost-estimating software add-on packages that get material quantity take-offs directly from the model.

ODBC is an advanced topic that won't be covered in depth in this book. However, if you do need to export to a database, here's how to use the Microsoft ODBC connector:

1. Open the file Station.rvt supplied on the sample CD.
2. Select **File → Export → ODBC Database**.
3. Select New to create a new data source name (DSN).
4. Select a driver. This driver will normally be associated with the software program you export to: for example, MS Access, dBase, or Paradox.
5. Click Next.
6. Type a DSN name, and, if necessary, navigate to the directory where you wish to save it. Click Next. A confirmation dialog appears. If any information is incorrect, click Back, and correct it.
7. Click Finish.

Next, create the database file:

1. Click Create in the ODBC Microsoft Setup dialog.
2. Navigate to the directory where you're saving the database, type the database name, and click OK.
3. Click OK in the confirmation dialog.
4. Click OK in the ODBC Microsoft Access Setup dialog.
5. Click OK at the Revit Building confirmation dialog.

Schedules

Revit will let you export schedule tables, view lists, material take-offs, key legends, and note blocks as a delimited text (.txt format) file that can then be read by Excel or any other spreadsheet/database application. Note that none of the formatting created within a Revit schedule, such as column spacing or font style, will be maintained. To export to .txt, open the schedule you want to export, then choose **File → Export → Schedules**. To make an .xls out of it, open Excel and open the .txt file.

gbXML

Green Building XML (gbXML) is an XML data type that was created to support the growing trend of sustainability and green building design. gbXML is an export function within Revit and other BIM applications that allows you to export specific data about a model for the purpose of performing energy analysis and evaluating building performance. There are a number of different applications on the market that can read gbXML formatted files. You can find more information on them at http://www.gbxml.org.

Room/Area Reports

Room/Area Report is a tool that creates a graphical and mathematical HTML report as a proof of the digital calculation of rooms in your project. Some authorities in Europe require these area reports as a part of permit documentation. Each room surface is divided into basic geometrical shapes (triangles, rectangles, arc segments), and each shape is described with a name that, in the table, has the geometrical formula used to calculate area.

You have the option to report the window area as a percentage of the room area. To comply with certain standards in different countries, you can choose to exclude columns from the total room area calculations by making your columns non room bounding. This is done through the element properties of individual columns.

To create such reports, select **File → Export → Room Area Report**, select the view or project, and define your graphic settings. You'll receive an HTML page of the report. A sample report is shown in Figure 7.1. These reports are not parametrically connected with the Revit model. If you make changes in the model, you will need to re-export the report.

Figure 7.1

Room area report example

#	Calculation	Area
	Triangles	
1	½ * 10' - 8 1/16" * 13' - 8 31/32"	73 SF
2	½ * 12' - 11 3/4" * 12' - 7 29/32"	82 SF
3	½ * 12' - 11 3/4" * 7' - 1 11/32"	46 SF
4	½ * 5' - 1 15/16" * 19' - 1 1/32"	49 SF
5	½ * 8' - 10" * 4' - 0"	18 SF
6	½ * 8' - 10" * 15' - 10"	70 SF
7	½ * 10' - 8 1/16" * 13' - 8 31/32"	73 SF
8	½ * 10' - 8 1/16" * 10' - 3 1/32"	55 SF
9	½ * 8' - 10" * 4' - 0"	18 SF
	Gross area is 484 SF.	

Total Windows	0 SF

Industry Foundation Class (IFC)

Industry Foundation Classes (IFCs) allow for exchange of intelligent data between architectural and downstream applications, based on STEP. IFC is a nonproprietary file format that has been recently resurrected as a possible BIM interoperability standard. The goal is to allow the transfer of information between models that have been created using different insert BIM authoring packages. More information on IFCs and their current and future uses can be found at `http://www.iai-na.org/technical/ faqs.php`.

Revit Architecture 2008 supports first-stage IFC 2x3 Certification Import / Export. Revit also has full (second-stage) IFC Singapore Code Checking (BCA) certification, which is export only. IFC can be imported into any other BIM or CAD application that accepts IFC class files.

> If you decide to use the IFC for import or export of data, there are a few items to keep in mind. Although multiple industries have made great advances with the IFC 2x2 data-exchange standards, no IFC file will be as robust as the parent file from which it was created. There will always be some data loss as you migrate your data to a more uniform data type.

Exporting DWG Drawings

DWG is the industry standard and is used by the majority of applications as a data-exchange method. We'll review some of the specific options and use cases for DWG exports.

In the majority of cases, you'll need to export 2D DWG drawings for owners and consultants or other engineers who will work with the file directly or use it as an underlay. You may also need to export the Revit model to a 3D DWG to make a compelling rendering or animation in a more sophisticated visualization package like Autodesk 3ds Max. Let's review all the options you should be aware of when exporting to DWG.

Select CAD Formats from the export options, and you'll see a dialog box like that shown in Figure 7.2.

Under the "Save As Type" menu, you have the option to select to export to the following CAD file types: `.dwg`, `.dxf`, `.dgn`, and `.sat`. For a DWG export, you can choose to export to an AutoCAD 2000, 2004, or 2007 file format (Figure 7.3). After you select an export file type, you have a few additional options:

File Naming   This section allows you to have Revit name the file for you in a short or long format. Alternatively, you can name it yourself with the Manual option:

Automatic   If you choose the Automatic option, the Short format grays out the "File name" text box and applies the view name or sheet name (depending on what you're exporting) to each of the exported views. The Automatic option with the Long button selected activates the "File name" text box and allows you to put in a prefix for all the files you export. You can enter a project name, a date, or something else as a prefix. With the Automatic option, you can choose to add a short system-defined prefix or a long user-defined prefix to the export file.

Manual If you choose the Manual option, you must name the exported file.

Export each view or sheet as a single file When you select this option, Revit combines each view on the sheet into a single file. This option is automatically selected for DXF files; it isn't available for DGN or SAT files.

With this box unchecked, Revit exports each view on a sheet into a separate file. If you're exporting a single view, using this feature won't make much difference; but if you're exporting a series of sheets with a number of views on each sheet, this feature will have a very different effect. In this case, with the box *unchecked*, Revit exports each sheet as separate file, then those separate files are combined via XREF within a parent file. For example, if you start with a sheet with four views on it, five DWGs will be exported. With this option checked, the views and parent sheet will be a single file with all of the views in the drawing as blocks.

Export Range The Export Range box allows you to select either your current view or a range of selected views and sheets. If you chose the latter, Revit will give you a dialog box showing all of the views and sheets currently in the model. After you select the views and / or sheets you want to export, you have the option to name and save that selection so you can quickly export those same sheets again, later on in the design process.

Figure 7.2

Export dialog box

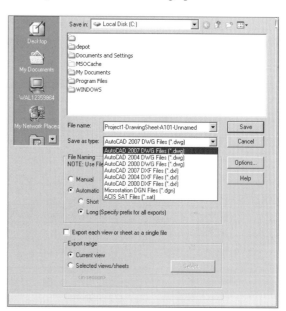

Figure 7.3

Export options

Export Options

The Export Options dialog box, shown in Figure 7.4, gives you some advanced options for exporting to CAD formats:

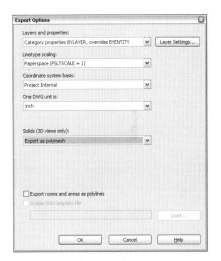

Layers and properties   The "Layers and Properties" setting determines what happens to a Revit element if it has attributes that differ from those defined for its object style category. In AutoCAD 2008 and in Revit Architecture 2008, view-specific element graphics are referred to as "overrides". This option allows you to control how categories are exported and their layer controls. The override options depend on the overrides you've set in the individual views you're exporting. If no view overrides are defined in your exported views, this menu won't change your export.

Layer Settings   (Layer Settings...)Revit automatically maps categories and subcategories to preconfigured layer names for export to DWG. Selecting Layer Settings lets you view or define the layers to which each object or component will be exported.

Figure 7.4

Export Options dialog box

By default, the U.S. version of Revit shows an export list linked to the standard AIA layering schema. If you scroll down this list (see Figure 7.5), you'll notice that you can define the layer name and color for each of the categories and some subcategories of the elements in your model. It's important to point out that this list is dynamic. As you add elements and entities to the Revit model, this list will grow to include them as well as linked and imported CAD and Revit files. This list is also available directly from the File menu under Import/Export Settings.

You can access a few preset Export Layer standards by clicking the Standard button. The predefined standards options are shown in Figure 7.6. Once you've gone through this list and specified the layers to which you want your Revit file to export, you can save the list to a separate .txt file to be used in other projects. Alternatively, you can load other .txt files into your project that have been exported from other projects.

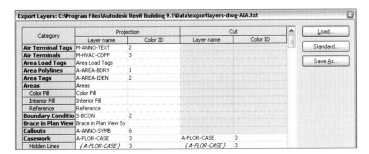

Figure 7.5

Export Layers

Figure 7.6

Export Layer Standards

> In a default template file, go through the export list and modify it to suit your standard layer settings. Then, perform a Save As to a .txt file, and keep that as an export template for other projects.

Linetype scaling This control sets your paperspace linetype setting in AutoCAD (psltscale) to either 1 or 0 or scales the linetypes by definition. This setting ensures visual fidelity between the linetype scales used in Revit and those in the exported DWG file.

Coordinate system basis This option lets you choose between project-internal or shared coordinate system. It ultimately sets a 0,0,0 point for your CAD file based on the selected coordinate system (either by the internal project 0,0,0 point or by the shared coordinates between multiple project files).

> The Shared option isn't available for Microstation files; only the Project Internal option is available for SAT files.

One DWG unit is CAD packages typically deal with measurements in units, unlike Revit, which builds the model in real dimensions. This menu allows you to correlate export units with Revit data. You can specify the export units: inches, feet, millimeters, centimeters, or meters.

Solids (3D views only) To export 3D solids, you need to have a 3D view active. Revit provides two types of solid exports: as Polymesh or as ACIS solids.

Export rooms and areas as polylines If you're exporting area or room plans, checking this option means that in AutoCAD, the room/area bounding lines will be polylines rather than normal lines (the default option).

Enable DGN template file This option is available only when you're exporting to a .dgn format. This means you can include a .dgn template file in the exported .dgn. Thus you can export to a Microstation template file to control the levels at which objects and components export.

Exporting Images

It's possible to export any of the views within Revit to an image file. To export a Revit view to an image file, open the desired view and choose **File → Export → Image**.

In the Export Image dialog box (Figure 7.7), many of the options are similar to the other export and printing functions. Export Range, for example, gives you the option to export either the current view or a series of views, similar to the Print dialog box.

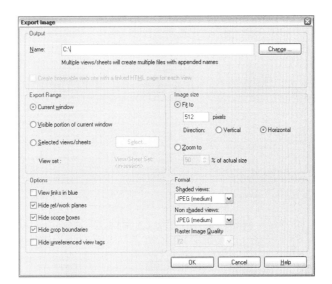

Figure 7.7

**Export Image
dialog box**

The Name box allows you to browse to a path in any of your folder directories to place the image. By default, the image name is the same as the view name. Similar to the options available when printing, you can choose to exclude elements such as crop boundaries, scope boxes, and work planes. This will give you nice results without having to worry about turning on/off categories every time you want to print or export an image.

Revit can export any view or sheet in several image file formats: `.bmp`, `.tif`, `.tga`, `.png`, or `.jpg`. Revit can also export any rendered scene to an `.ivr` or a `.pan` file. These are 360-degree panorama images that let you navigate and "feel" a space from all angles.

Creating a Browsable Website from the Revit Model

When more than one view is selected for export to image, an option becomes active in the Output section of the Export Image dialog box that lets you create a browsable website with a linked HTML page for each view, as shown in Figure 7.8.

Revit exports every view as an image and collects them in a HTML file, all packaged neatly into a folder. This allows you (or someone else) to scroll through the project views quickly and easily.

This technique is practical when you create PowerPoint slides for a project presentation and need all views exported in image formats.

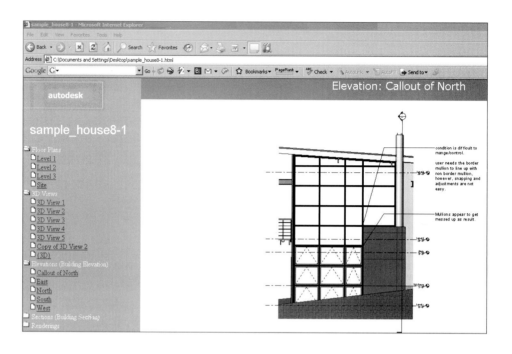

Image Size

This section in the Export Image dialog box allows you to set the size of the exported image. You can either fit it to specific pixel dimensions or zoom the image to a proportion of its actual size. Keep in mind that is a proportion of the view size, not the model size. So, if your view dimensions are 10″ × 10″ (25×25cm), and you're zooming to 50 percent, your exported image will be at 72 pixels per inch (ppi) and 5″ × 5″ (10×10cm), not at 1:2 scale.

Format

This section in the Export Image dialog box allows you to choose your export file type from the list shown in Figure 7.7 above. It also gives you the option to raise the ppi exported from 72 ppi to a higher density. The more ppi, the longer the export time will be, and the larger the final image file. As some general rules of thumb, 72 ppi is print quality in a newspaper picture. Most book images are printed between 150 and 300 ppi. It's widely assumed that the human eye can't differentiate beyond 300 ppi. Figure 7.9 shows an example of an exported image.

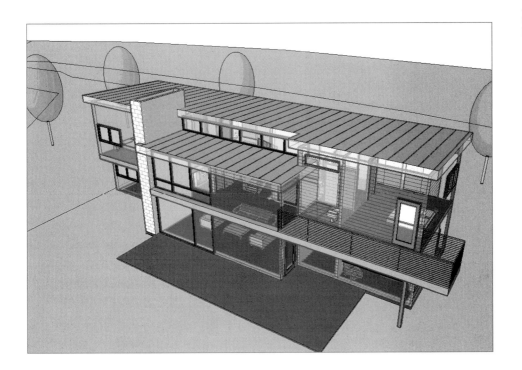

Figure 7.9
Exported Image

Importing and Linking

Now that you know what you can export from the Revit model, let's discuss the types of files you can import into Revit.

Choose **File → Import/Link** (Figure 7.10). The resulting submenu contains all the file types you can import into Revit, many of which we've already discussed in this chapter in the export context:

- CAD Formats: .dwg, .dxf, .dgn, .sat, and .skp files

- Image: .jpg, .bmp, and .pgn files

- Revit: .rvt files

- Link DWF Markup Set: Single- or multi-paged .dwf files

- IFC: .ifc files

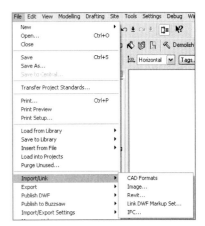

We'll explore the uses of each of these options. Before drilling into details, we want to make clear the distinction between importing and linking.

Figure 7.10
Import / Link

Linking

Linking creates a live connection to a file on disk. This allows you to work on the linked file, and then have the Revit model update to reflect the changes in the link. This behavior is similar to an XREF in AutoCAD.

Linking CAD Formats

The ability to link one file into another can be helpful in a collaborative environment. Perhaps someone on your team—a person working on details within your office or an external consultant—is working in an AutoCAD environment while you build up the project in Revit. Linking lets you have her latest work updated in your Revit model. If you import without linking, you get a static file that will not update. When you link, however, it's possible to always get the latest state of the DWG by updating the link within Revit.

From **File → Manage Links** (Figure 7.11) you can reload, unload, import, or remove a CAD link or see what is already loaded.

Linking Revit Models

Linking files can be used for either a large campus project where buildings are distributed among separate project teams or one project that is being worked on by multiple teams in the same office.

Figure 7.11

Managing links

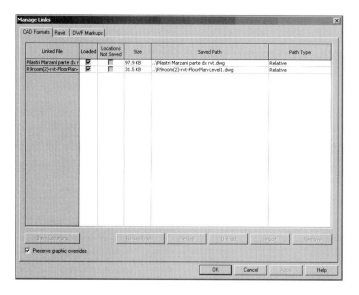

When you're working on a campus-style project that contains more than one building, you should consider making separate models for each building and later connecting them in one file via the linking method. Doing so gives you some flexibility to model individual buildings while still having the versatility to see the campus or building groupings as a combined site plan. You can also cut sections or make elevations in which you can see all the buildings or schedule elements across all linked files.

> When you're doing campus-style projects, linking optimizes system performance. Working on several smaller files for individual buildings is less memory-intensive than working on one large file with many buildings.

Another use of linking is for collaboration in a full BIM project team where the structural engineer is using Revit Structure and the mechanical, engineering, and plumbing (MEP) engineer is using Revit MEP. Using the linking methodology, you can view their models within yours. You can even select and read the properties of the structural or MEP elements from your model, although you can't modify them.

Additionally, these three products—Revit® Architecture, Revit® Structure, and Revit® MEP incorporate tools that let you copy and monitor changes among linked models. This, however, is an advanced topic not covered in this book.

When you link two or more Revit models together, you're linking more than just the model geometry. Linking Revit models allows you to do the following:

- View the content of a Revit file that comes from another discipline (The Structural engineer who made the structure with Revit Structure or a piping system made with Revit Systems).

- Combine scheduled elements of your building in a single schedule, regardless of whether they come from the parent file or from the linked file(s).

- Control the visibility of what is displayed from the linked file or imported DWG files in the linked file.

There were some significant additions to the linking capability added to version 2008. Here are just some of them:

- Ability to schedule the elements by link instance name so that if an element appears in multiple instances of identical building, Revit can identify which instance comes from which link.

- Dimension to or from elements and objects in the linked or parent file and establish user-defined relationships and constrains between the two (example: distance between a property line that is in the main file and the edge of the building that is linked).

- Copy paste elements from the linked to the parent file.

- Control and change the visibility properties not only of the linked file but of the nested links as well, without modifying the primary file.

- Nested links (a linked file in a Revit file that is linked into another Revit file) can be displayed in the host file and can have two different states; Attach or Overlay.

- Bind a Revit link within the parent model. This is similar functionality to the Bind option in AutoCAD: when using the Bind option, the Revit link turns into a Group and becomes fully integrated in the host model.

- Copy Revit links across documents.

- Display areas and area boundaries in linked files and schedule them.

- See linked as well as nested links in the Project Browser from where you can Unload, Reload, Open and unload, copy to another level by drag and drop, and access the linking manager.

EDITING A LINKED FILE

If you've linked a Revit file into your model, you cannot open that link file and start working on it in the same session of Revit. However, if you launch another session of Revit, you can open and edit the linked files. Each session of Revit will show up as a separate application running on your machine.

How to Link Files in Revit

To link a RVT file, choose **File → Import/Link → Revit**. The resulting dialog box looks like Figure 7.12. This dialog is a standard file open/navigation format, with a few options specific to Revit: Open Worksets and Positioning. We'll look at each option and explain what they mean.

Figure 7.12
Add Link dialog box

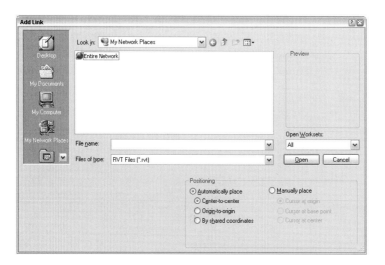

There aren't a lot of options in this dialog box. That's good, because you don't need many. This dialog box reacts like an average Microsoft dialog box with some predefined navigation options on the left and the Look In drop-down menu that allows you to browse to the location of the file to be linked. The items that differ here are the Open Worksets and the Positioning. We'll discuss them one at a time.

Positioning

The Positioning section asks you where to place the linked model. You can choose Automatically Place or Manually Place. Automatically Place gives you these options:

Center-to-center aligns the 3D center points of both models.

Origin-to-origin places the world origin of the linked file at the model's origin point. If the linked model was created far from the origin point, linking with this option may put the linked file far away from the main model.

By shared coordinates places the linked file geometry according to the shared coordinate system created between the two files. If no shared coordinate file has been created, Revit will alert you. The Shared Coordinates settings can be found in the Tools drop-down menu and it gives you the following options:

> **Acquire Coordinates** allows you to take the coordinates of the linked file into the host model. There is no change to the host model's internal coordinates; however, the host model acquires the true north of the linked model and its origin point.
>
> **Publish Coordinates** allows you to publish the origin and true north settings to your linked model. Revit understands that there may be other things in your linked file and you may not want this to be a global change to the linked file. An additional dialog box appears that gives you the option to name separate locations for each set of coordinates.
>
> **Specify Coordinates at a Point** allows you to manually key in x, y, and z coordinates relative to the origin point or define where you want your 0,0,0 point to be.
>
> **Report Shared Coordinates** shows the E/W (East/West) (x), N/S (North/South) (y), and Elevation (z) coordinates of any point in the model (Figure 7.13).

Figure 7.13

Reported coordinates

WHAT ARE SHARED COORDINATES?

Every Revit project has an internal origin that can be related to other projects. When a project location is moved, or rotated, this information is used to create relative positioning between files.

Manually Place gives you these options:

Cursor at origin puts the origin point of the linked model at your cursor location.

Cursor at base point puts the base point of the document at your cursor location. This is primarily used for files that have a base point, such as CAD files.

Cursor at center puts the 3D center of the building at your cursor location.

Open Worksets

Worksets are used to divide a model into user-defined groups so that a team of collaborators can simultaneously work on the same Revit project. Worksets can be used to cluster chunks of a building together, and the Open Worksets option lets you choose which Worsets to link in. This technique is practical when working on big projects where performance may be an issue. By only linking in a sub-set of a linked file, the graphical and memory resources are not taxed as much.

Importing or Linking CAD Formats

Site plans, consultant files, and details or drawings done with CAD technologies on prior projects all are examples of information you may want to link or import into Revit from a CAD format. This isn't limited to 2D data; you can link in 3D files and data, as well.

The data you import or link into your model can be view-specific (imported in *one* view only as opposed to all views), so start by opening the view into which you want to bring data. Choose **File → Import/Link → CAD Formats**. The CAD Formats dialog box includes additional options.

As we discussed previously in this chapter, you can link or import five types of CAD files in 2D or 3D in Revit:

- `.dwg`—Files made from AutoCAD, or other applications that can export to this standard format.

- `.dxf`—Drawing Exchange Format files. Most software packages write to a .dxf format.

- `.dgn`—Microstation native files

- `.sat`—Standard ACIS text files. Many modeling and fabrication applications can write to this file type.

- `.skp`—SketchUp native files

Here are the most common use cases for importing CAD files:

- To import a context of the surrounding with streets and buildings

- To import a civil-engineering file with your topography

- To use CAD detail previously created for another project or directly dragged and dropped from the manufacturer's web catalog

- To use Revit to continue a previous stage of the project that you did in CAD, building a 3D model based on the 2D imported CAD file

- To work with colleagues who deal with certain aspects of the project in another environment (CAD drafters working on details, principles working on massing studies with Sketchup, Rhino, or some other modeling tool)

Import or Link

In Figure 7.14, the "Import or Link" section of the CAD Formats dialog box gives you the option to import your file or link it. As explained previously, there are some pros and cons to each option:

Linking If you link a file, any changes made in that *original file* will be apparent in the Revit file in which it was linked. If your office or team workflow has personnel who are dedicated to working solely on details, they can continue creating and changing the details in AutoCAD, and you can update the link to reflect the changes automatically. You can also manipulate the linked file through the Manage Links dialog box found under **File → Manage Links**.

Importing An import is not tied to an external file, which will allow you to explode the file and modify the CAD drawing directly in Revit. You cannot explode or modify lines of a linked import. Once an import has been exploded, the import ceases to exist, and everything becomes lines. These lines are just that: lines, with no inherent intelligence. As lines, you can change their line-type, changing their graphic appearance.

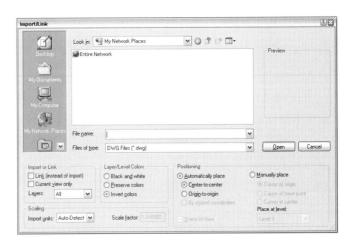

Figure 7.14

Import/Link dialog box

Regardless of whether you link or import a CAD file, you can always control the visibility of the lines in any view through the Visibility/Graphic Overrides dialog box. For linked files or CAD files that have been imported but not exploded, the lines appear in their own tab under Imported Categories. If the file has been exploded, the CAD lines are integrated into the model and appear under the Model Categories tab, under the Lines subcategory.

> One of the primary uses for importing CAD files is to use them as details in the Revit model. If possible, eliminate all the unneeded linework from your CAD file *before* you import it into Revit. We suggest cleaning up your CAD details in the native format first, then importing— rather than exploding your details in Revit and then cleaning up lines.

In Figure 7.14, the "Import or Link" section of the CAD Formats dialog box gives you the option to import your file or link it. As explained previously, there are some pros and cons to each option:

CURRENT VIEW ONLY

Selecting the "Current view only" check box brings the linked or imported file *only* into the view that is currently active. It's not always desirable to see your CAD files in all the views in your model. More often than not, you'll want to select this check box. Remember, if you import with this unchecked, the file will be visible in all of your views, and you'll need to manage its visibility via the visibility/graphics dialog, or with view templates.

> If you're importing a CAD file you want to use as a site, make sure you're importing it into all views; otherwise, you won't be able to convert it into a toposurface. It's now possible to convert any solid geometry created in other software packages into a toposurface.

LAYERS

The Layers drop-down menu gives you the option to import or link in all the layers, only the layers that were visible at the time the CAD file was last saved, or a selected group of layers. (Layers are a DWG-based naming convention. Revit allows the same functionality with levels from DGN drawings.)

Layer/Level Colors

The default view background in AutoCAD is usually black. So, the colors used in Auto-CAD are easily visible on a black background. When you import a DWG file in Revit that has a white background, many of the colors usually used in AutoCAD (yellow, light green, magenta, cyan) are difficult to read. Revit recognizes this issue, and in the Layer/Level Colors section of the Import/Link dialog box, it gives you the option to invert these colors into colors that are easier to read on a white background. It also gives you the option not to change the colors, if you prefer, or to convert them to black and white, which is Revit's default approach.

Scaling

The Scaling section of the Import/Link dialog box allows you to let Revit auto-detect the scale at which the imported or linked drawing was created and convert accordingly. Or, you can do the detection manually, and apply a scale factor.

Positioning

This section of the Import/Link dialog box is identical to the Positioning options described previously when we explained the linking of Revit models. However, you have two additional options:

Orient to view is available for non–view-specific imports and links and rotates the imported file in the same direction as the current view.

Place at level allows you to choose the level in the current view where you would like to place the linked or imported file.

Importing Images

In every project, you'll need to import an image—be it a photograph of the site and its surroundings; or background information, like scanned hand drawings of a historic building; or images that can represent advertising or marketing material (see Figure 7.15).

To import an image into Revit, use **File → Import → Image**. Navigate to the appropriate folder, and choose your image file. You can also drag and drop an image file directly from Windows Explorer into a Revit view. Imported images are specific to the particular view you've imported them into.

Once you've inserted the image, you have a few options to edit its size and proportion. Selecting the image highlights the corner grips and lets you resize the image dynamically. Doing so also highlights the Options bar and the Type Selector. The Options bar allows you to push the image forward or backward or bring it all the way to the front or back. The Background/Foreground selection tells the image that you want it above or below the model geometry. You can also change the shape of the image by deselecting the Lock Proportions check box.

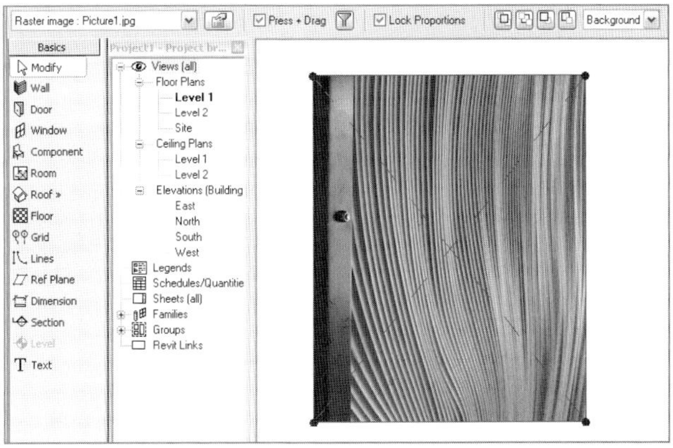

Figure 7.15

Inserted image

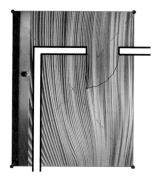

Figure 7.16

**Image properties,
and the image
placed in the
background**

The Type Selector allows you to toggle between different imported images just as you would any component family.

The Element Properties dialog shown in Figure 7.16 controls the same element parameters that appear in the Options bar (in Figure 7.15) when an image is selected, but provides a bit more precision. From here you can set the exact size of the image in project units. Figure 7.16 shows how the image looks when the Draw Order property is set to Background.

Decal

If you want to see images in perspective views, you can use the Decal tool, and render the view. A typical use case for this is to show signage on a façade. The Decal tool is located on the Modeling Design Bar, and you browse to an image to use. Note that the image won't show up in shaded view, but you will be able to manipulate its placement and size (Figure 7.17).

Figure 7.17

**Left, hidden-line
mode with decals;
right, the rendered
scene showing the
decals**

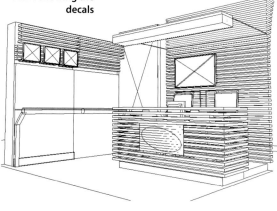

Working with Imported Files

Now that you've learned how to import and export drawings with Revit, what do you do with them? In this section, we'll explore the use of the various tools used to manage CAD files when they're in Revit.

As we've discussed a number of times, Revit doesn't build the model based on layers like other CAD packages do. Although layers offer an easy way to control the visibility of objects, they're also the reason other software packages can't guarantee quantities. Layers make it possible for an object to be duplicated on many layers and therefore appear more than once in the database. In Revit, every object can exist once and once only. As mentioned previously, Revit uses categories and subcategories for objects that exist in real life and uses annotation elements that describe them to control the visibility of what is presented where.

That may be good, but you work with—and need to exchange digital files with—people who give you information in a DWG layers structure. Therefore, you need to give them layer-structured drawings. Revit can understand imported drawings with layer structures and can also export drawings with a customized layer structure. When you import a file in DWG or other CAD formats in Revit, you can do the following:

- Turn layers on/off
- Change the default color of a layer
- Delete a layer
- Explode a DWG file so you can modify /delete elements

Managing Layers

Once your CAD file is imported into Revit, either as a link or as an insertion, you can begin to manage the layers and colors of the CAD objects as they appear in Revit. To do this, you need to go to the Visibility/Graphic Overrides settings. You can access this dialog box by typing **VG** (using the keyboard shortcuts), selecting the View pulldown menu/Visibility/Graphics, or using the context menu when right clicking in a View/View Properties/Visibility/Graphics Overrides/Edit. If you import a CAD file into your view, Revit adds an Imported Categories tab. Selecting that tab, shown in Figure 7.18, gives you a list of all the CAD files imported into this particular view. Remember, this list is view specific; Revit changes the list as you add or remove CAD files from the model and from this view.

Selecting the check box next to the name of your CAD file displays a list of every layer present in the file. Use the check box in front of the layer name to control its visibility. Here you can also override the line color and pattern of the layer or turn it to halftone.

Figure 7.18

Visibility/Graphic Overrides dialog box

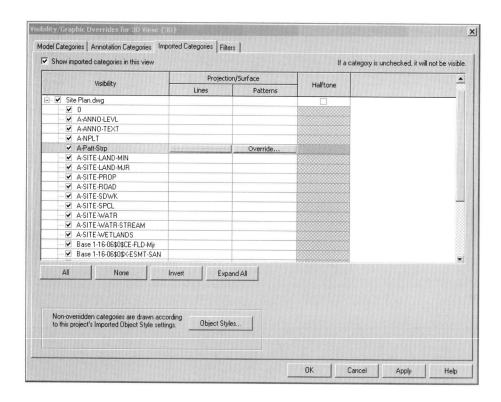

Modifying a CAD File

Often, you'll need to modify or delete some of the geometry in a CAD file that has been imported into Revit. Let's review how this works and all the options available.

Open the view your DWG is linked into, and click the DWG to select it. The Options bar (shown in Figure 7.19) will offer the following tools.

Delete Layers

This tool allows you to delete an entire layer from the imported file. With the DWG selected, click Delete Layer, and select from the list of displayed layers those you wish to delete. A sample dialog box with its associated layers is shown in Figure 7.20. As with most Revit dialog box lists, you have the option to select all or to select none as well as to invert the order of choices.

Figure 7.19

DWG Options bar

| Delete Layers... | Full Explode | Partial Explode | Visibility | Query... |

Full Explode

An imported DWG behaves as one entity when brought into Revit. If you want to modify any of the imported geometry in Revit, you need to perform an explode. The Full Explode option disassembles the entity as well as any blocks or attributes and simplifies it down to the lowest level of lines, arcs, texts, and hatch (filled regions).

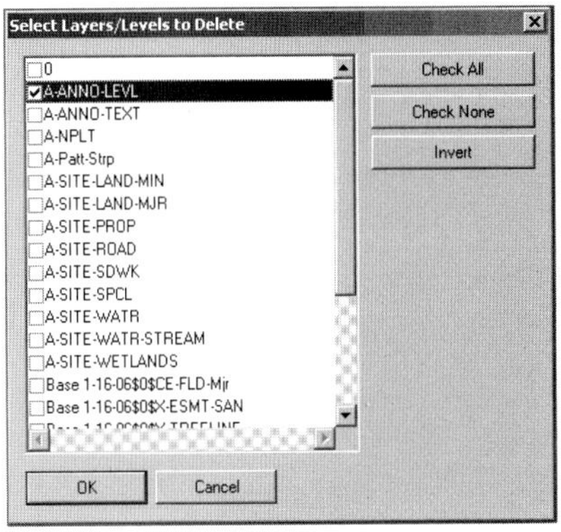

Partial Explode

This option disassembles the imported file to the first and highest level of entities: blocks, attributes, unassociated lines, arcs, and circles. Blocks remain as blocks and aren't converted to individual lines. In cases where you have blocks within blocks in your inserted CAD file, a first partial explode explodes the drawing, leaving the nested blocks combined. A second partial explode explodes the nested block, leaving the block within that block intact. A third partial explode turns everything into lines.

Figure 7.20

Select Layers/Levels to Delete

Given the fact that exploding DWGs can produce a multitude of elements that pollute the database and may affect the performance of the overall application, it's strongly recommended that you consider exploding only when you really need to modify the imported DWG. As an alternative, consider using Partial Explode, which may be sufficient to achieve the desired modifications.

Query

The purpose of the Query tool ( Query...) is to find the attributes of individual blocks/layers without having to explode the DWG. After you import a drawing into a project, you can query the inserted object for information about entities contained in the drawing. After you click Query and click an entity, Revit first highlights the lowest-level entities.

To select a block within the CAD file, use the Tab key to cycle through your selection options (see Figure 7.21).

Selecting an entity causes the following information about that block or line to be displayed:

- **Type**. Information about the type of the entity selected (line, text).
- **Block Name**. The name of the block that contains the entity, if applicable. (N/A means "isn't available"; the entity doesn't belong to any block.)
- **Layer**. The name of the layer containing the entity.
- **Style By**. Indicates whether the entity style comes from the layer or is defined by color.

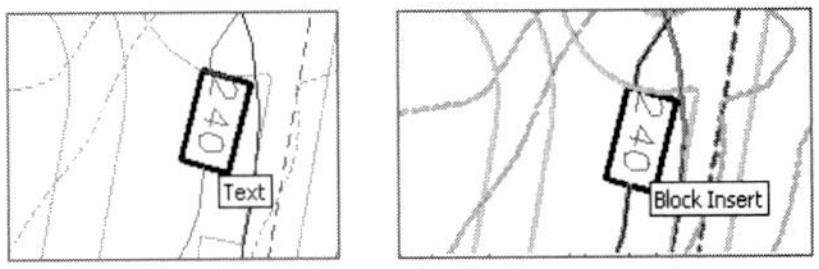

These results are reflected in an Import Instance Query dialog box (Figure 7.22).

Text query selection   Block query selection

Figure 7.21

Query selection

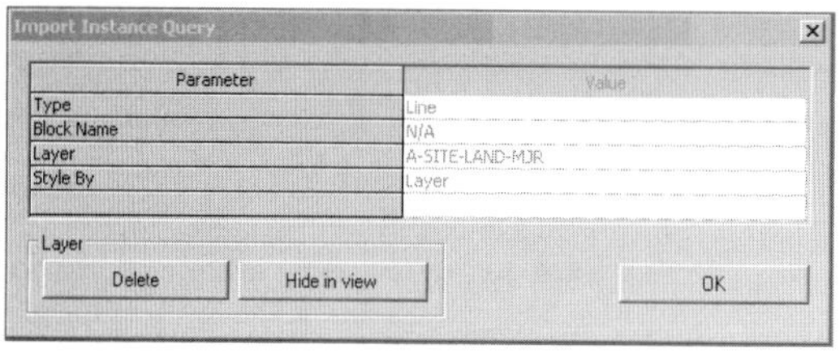

Figure 7.22
Reported query data

To find out the property information of the layer or instance, select the DWG, click the Query tool, and click the object/geometry that you want additional information about.

Once you have this information, you can do two things:

- Delete the layer on which that instance belongs.

> Once you delete a layer, you can't recover it from anywhere unless you use the Undo function or reimport the DWG.

- Hide the layer in that particular view.

> To turn the visibility of a layer back on after using the "Hide in View" command, choose
> **Visibility/Graphics → DWG/DXF/DGN Categories**.

Working with Civil Engineering DWG Files

Civil engineering plans are usually rich in data and information, not all of which is needed by architects. Architects constantly need to clean up civil engineering drawings, retaining only the data that is of importance to the architect for display in their drawings. Revit has a great way to import site information created by civil engineers in DWG file format and turning it smoothly into Revit topography.

Cleanup is one of the challenges when you import civil engineering data. DWGs have a plentitude of layers on which different data is placed (roads, utilities, vegetation, and topographic information). You need to know which layers contain the topographic information and select only those when creating the topography.

Another challenge is that the coordinate worlds of civil engineers and architects often differ. Creating a link between the two coordinate systems is important for a seamless workflow. Engineers typically have their maps facing north, whereas architects either orient them in whatever way is the most practical to work with or lay them out horizontally.

Transforming DWG Site Info into Topography

In this exercise, you'll transfer DWG data into Revit and make it into a Revit toposurface:

1. Start a new drawing (**File → New**).

2. Activate the site view by selecting Site in the Project Browser.

3. Import the DWG: Choose **File → Import → CAD Formats**. Choose the file provided on the companion CD named Site.dwg. Make sure you DO NOT select "Current View Only," and click OK. (See Figure 7.23.)

4. From the Site Design bar, select Toposurface (Toposurface).

5. Select **Use Imported → Import Instance** (Import Instance Points File).

6. Remember that you need to import topography information into the site view. If you forget to switch to site view and are still in a floor plan when you import the site DWG, you may get the message displayed in Figure 7.24. To correct this, do what the message says: Interrupt the import by pressing the Esc key, and then switch to site view to repeat the import.

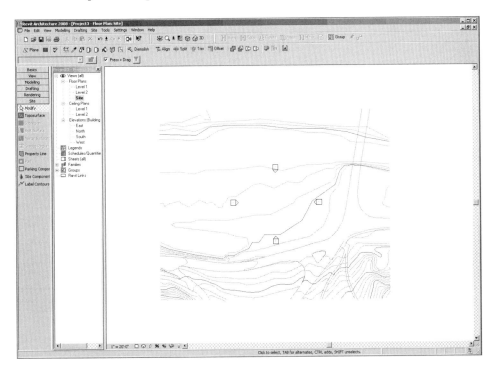

Figure 7.23

Importing the site DWG

Figure 7.24

Error message: file imported into the wrong view

In Revit versions 9.1 and later, you have to import the site in all views. If you select the option "Current view only", you won't be able to convert the DWG into a site plan.

7. Open the Site design tab, and select the Toposurface tool. Click somewhere over the DWG in your drawing area to highlight the site DWG (it will become red). A dialog (Figure 7.25) will open, and you'll see a list of all the layers included in the DWG. You need to know the layers on which the topography information is stored and select only those layers. In this case, click Check None (Check None), and select the layers called 3D contours. Press OK. A toposurface will be generated from the imported geometry. Press Finish Surface to complete the task.

Should you fail to do this and select all layers, Revit will probably fail to create a toposurface.

If you don't have a convention of layer naming with your civil engineer, and you're unsure which layer your contour lines lie on, you can find out by toggling various layers on and off using the Visibility/Graphics dialog box.

After you select the correct layers, Revit will highlight the points on the contours, and your drawing will appear as shown in Figure 7.26.

8. Select Finish Surface (●|● Finish Surface)from the Design bar. You'll see the image shown in Figure 7.27.

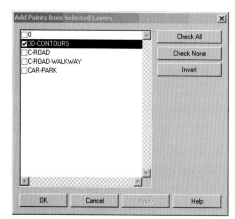

Figure 7.25
Select only the layers with contours when converting DWG to toposurface.

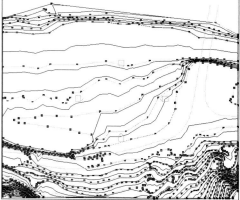

Figure 7.26
Highlighted topography points

Figure 7.27

**Finished
toposurface**

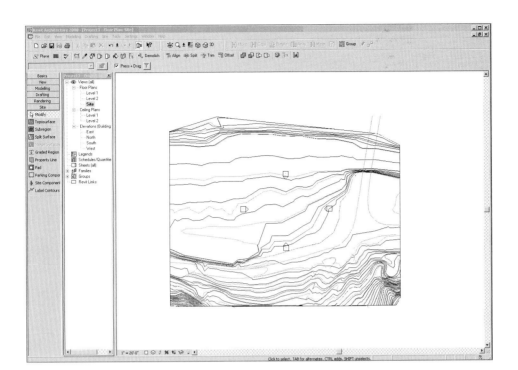

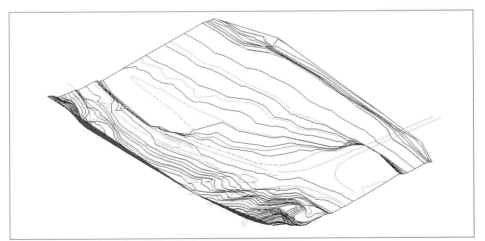

How anticlimactic: Figure 7.27 doesn't look much different from the DWG you started with. Now, switch to a 3D view, and activate the shaded view. Here you can see the topography you've created (see Figure 7.28).

The default material for the topography is Earth, as defined in the Object Styles shown in Figure 7.29.

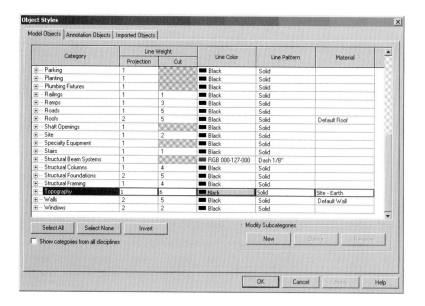

If you want to change the material of the topography, select the toposurface in the Object Styles dialog box, and go to its properties. Here you can choose another material (try Site - Grass). The topography will turn green.

All the site-related materials are listed under Site in the materials table Found at Settings →
Materials. In that list, Earth is labeled as Site - Earth, grass as Site - Grass, and so on.

You'll notice that there are many 2D lines you don't need. Those come either from the contour lines from the imported DWG or from the Revit toposurface primary and secondary contours. Revit allows you to control the visibility of those separately using the Visibility/Graphics Overrides dialog.

Open the dialog, scroll to the Topography Model category node, and uncheck all subcategories of topography, as shown in Figure 7.30.

Now, switch to the Imported Categories tab, and uncheck the entire imported site. To uncheck all the subcategories at once, you can deselect the parent heading, as shown in Figure 7.31. Click OK. This should look much better: You can see a nice smooth topography covered with grass.

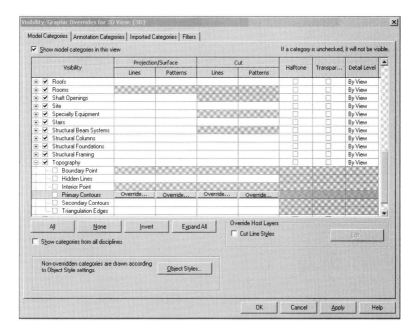

Figure 7.30

Visibility/Graphic Overrides for topography

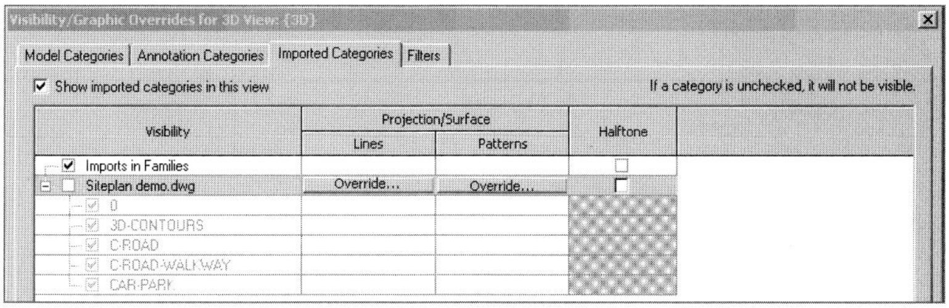

Figure 7.31

Visibility/Graphic Overrides for imported files

Other Ways to Create Topography

There are two other ways to create topography in Revit besides using an imported DWG:

- You can create a toposurface using an imported points file.
- You can create a toposurface from scratch.

Importing a Points File

You can automatically generate a toposurface based on a points file. A *points file* is a list of points described with their x, y, and z coordinates. It must contain x, y, and z coordinate numbers and be in a comma-delimited file format (.csv or .txt). If you receive a Points file from a civil engineer, you can view it in Notepad or Microsoft Excel. Here is a sample of a points file:

T-1	0	0	0.055
T-2	0	59.916	5.179
T-3	45.181	64.991	1.974
T-4	45.181	59.916	5.599
T-5	22.539	62.454	4.522
T-6	50.061	29.857	1.738
T-7	40.106	10.142	0.221
T-8	24.881	-0.008	0.06
T-9	44.986	42.739	2.917
T-10	24.296	45.862	2.665
T-11	8.875	62.844	4.462
T-12	1.848	26.538	1.815
T-13	24.686	16.974	0.459
T-14	32.494	12.289	0.962
T-15	8.095	15.607	0.686
T-16	33.274	29.661	1.146
T-17	51.037	28.1	0.981
T-18	46.743	56.598	5.875

Figure 7.32

Setting the unit format

To create a toposurface from a point file, follow these steps:

1. Click the Site Design bar.

2. Select Toposurface.

3. Select the Use Imported / Points file (Points.csv) included on the CD.

4. Open the points file in your Windows browser. (Note that only .csv or .txt file formats are recognized.)

5. In the Format tab, set the units in which the points file needs to be imported (see Figure 7.32).

6. Click the Finish Toposurface button. Figure 7.33 represents an editable toposurface in Revit and the completed toposurface.

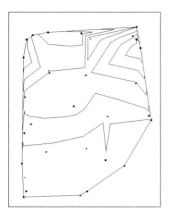
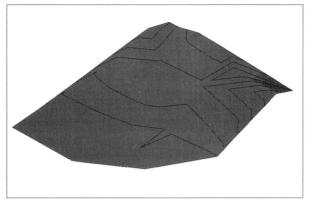

Figure 7.33

Left, an editable toposurface; right, the finished toposurface

Depending on the file you import, after the import you may not see anything on the screen. This means your site is outside of the crop region predefined for the site. To find your site, deactivate the crop region and choose Zoom To Fit All to find the site.

Creating Topography from Scratch: Drawing Points

When you don't have any civil engineering data to import and convert to topography, but you do have a paper drawing with points information, you can create your toposurface by drawing points and defining their heights. Revit will create a smooth toposurface out of them.

1. From the Site Design bar, click the Toposurface button (Toposurface).

2. Select the option Point.

3. Start drawing points that define your site contour. (Try it with four points to start with, as shown in Figure 7.34.)

Figure 7.34

Creating your own toposurface from points

4. Revit closes the points into a loop.

   If you don't change anything and just draw four points, all points have the same elevation of zero (z coordinate=0). You can give them a height coordinate during the drawing by typing elevations in the Options bar (Elevation: 0' 0").

   Alternatively, after you've defined the shape in plan view, you can start reselecting and defining elevation coordinates. For the moment, leave the four initial points at 0.

5. Without finishing the toposurface, draw an additional four points, select them all, and change their elevation to 20˝ in the Options bar (see Figure 7.35).

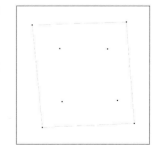

Figure 7.35

Adding contours to a toposurface

6. In the Design bar, select Finish Toposurface. Revit will grade the distance between the elevations with contour lines, as shown in Figure 7.36. You'll notice that some lines are stronger and some are lighter. Those that appear stronger are the primary contours. The lighter ones are the secondary contours.

7. Switch to 3D view, and activate the shaded view (Figure 7.37).

Like any other preset, the distance at which the secondary contours are placed is defined under Settings → Site Settings, shown in Figure 7.38. In this dialog box, you can define or change the material that appears in section when the toposurface is cut. It's also where you can control the height in elevation where the base of the toposurface begins to show in section view (see Figure 7.39).

The default settings place the primary contour lines at 10″ (3m) intervals. If you change that to 5′ (1.5cm), you'll see a site similar to that shown in Figure 7.40.

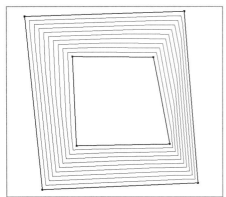

Figure 7.36
The graded toposurface

Figure 7.37
Completed toposurface

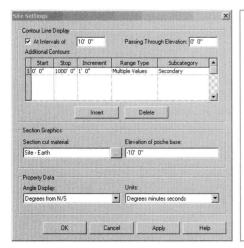

Figure 7.38
Site settings

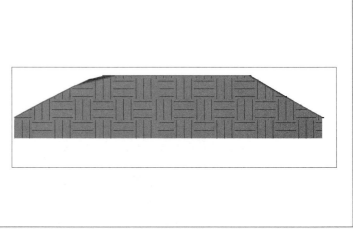

Figure 7.39
A toposurface in section

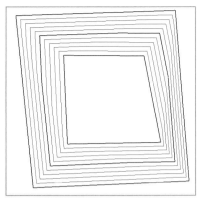

Figure 7.40

Toposurface with 10′ primary contours

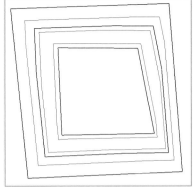

Figure 7.41

Toposurface with 2′ secondary contours

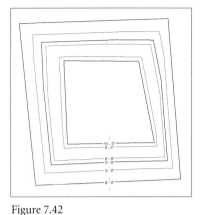

Figure 7.42

Toposurface with contour labels

Notice the placement of the secondary contour lines. Revit's default settings place them at 1′ intervals. Change that to 2′, and note the difference in the contours displayed in the model (Figure 7.41).

The contours can also be labeled to indicate their elevation. To label the contour elevations, select Label Contours ( ) from the Design bar, and click two points as if to create a section through the topography. Figure 7.42 shows what you'll see.

As with everything in Revit, you can edit the topography at any point later in the process. To do so, select the topography so that it becomes red, choose Edit from the Options bar, and modify the site as needed.

All three of the methods described show you how to create a toposurface in Revit. Of course, creating the toposurface is only the beginning. You still have to position your building at the correct location and elevation, create a pad for the building to sit on, and position the parking lot, the walkways, and other contextual features (Figure 7.43). Dealing with site tools, however, is a more advanced topic that won't be covered further in this book.

Figure 7.43

There's a long way to go from toposurface to finished site.

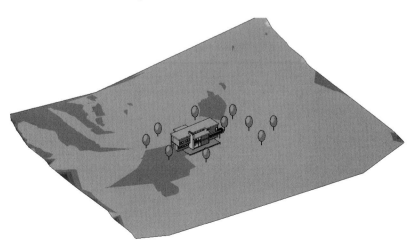

Converting 2D Drawings into a 3D Model

Here's a common situation: You have 2D plans, sections, and elevations, and you wish to transform them into a 3D building information model. When you first start to work on a project, you may have previously created DWGs available. Maybe your firm has just started using Revit, so the project was started in AutoCAD; or maybe you're working with an existing building created by another architect. Revit offers you the flexibility to incorporate legacy material in your model.

The development and adoption of intelligent software means that some day, redrawing will no longer need to be an option. Revit offers ways to maximize the reuse and referencing of existing data. Converting existing DWGs so they can be used in a Revit model isn't terribly complicated and avoids the need to retrace entire drawings.

You can create Revit objects three ways:

- Drawing ( )
- Picking references out of which the object can be created ( )
- Picking a face (this is an advanced topic not covered in this book)( )

These buttons appear in the Options bar when you select any of the host element tools, such as the Wall tool. Let's analyze the first two approaches.

The pencil tool ( ), when activated, indicates that you're in Draw mode. You can draw the shape of the object that will be created using standard drawing options. This is the default mode for all Revit tools that require you to draw something.

The second option, denoted with the arrow symbol, is Pick Lines ( ). Instead of manually drawing, this option gives you the ability to create elements by picking references. This means you can pick (and thus convert) any line of an imported drawing into an object. Note that the original line remains available.

Using a 2D DWG floor plan as starting point for generating a 3D BIM model is best explained using a concrete example, so let's do an exercise. Figure 7.44 shows a series of 2D AutoCAD files set on their corresponding levels in a Revit model and the 3D BIM model created from those plans and elevations.

Here's our strategy for this approach. Import the DWG of each floor into the corresponding level in Revit. In the Import/Link CAD Formats dialog box, under the "Import or Link" section select the "Current view only" option (see Figure 7.45). Note that if you forget to select this option, your ground floor DWG will appear in every level. This will be confusing, to say the least.

> A tip before you start: AutoCAD drawings can be busy, containing information that isn't relevant or creates visual clutter. When you want to quickly convert them to a 3D model, it helps to turn off the visibility of some of the DWG layers using Visibility Graphics/Imported Categories. Uncheck the layers you don't need, like dimensions, text, hatches, and so on. Doing so will speed up object selection and facilitate the conversion process.

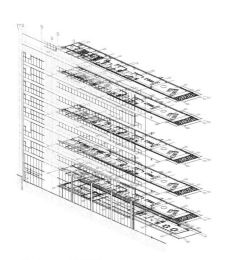

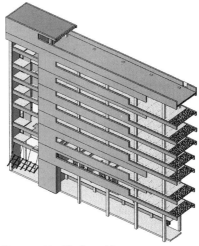

Figure 7.44

Converting 2D CAD files to a Revit model

The inserted CAD files   The completed Revit model

Starting a New Project

Start by defining the number of stories (levels) that your building will have and giving the levels floor-to-floor heights. To do this, open a new project, go to any elevation view (let's say south), and modify the project so it has three levels (if you're opening the default Revit template, you'll need to add one level). As we previously discussed, you do that by selecting the Level tool, drawing three levels, and placing them 10′ (3m) apart.

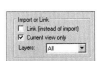

Figure 7.45

Using "Current view only"

You are now ready to import some DWGs into the corresponding levels. Follow these steps:

1. Activate Level 1, and import the DWG *Level 1* file found on the sample DVD in the Imports folder.

2. On Level 2, import the DWG *Level 2* file.

3. Open a south elevation, and import the DWG *Elevation South* file.

4. After the import, you may get a notification that none of the imported elements is visible in this view. As previously mentioned, this means the import is somewhere outside the boundaries of the crop region. To remedy this situation, turn off the crop region. Zoom all, and you'll find your DWG (![toolbar 1:100]).

5. Reposition the DWG as needed using the Move command.

6. In the south elevation view, you will need to reposition the levels so that they match the level lines in the DWG import. (Level 1 matches with Level 1-A from the DWG etc. If needed, rename the levels to match the naming of the levels in the DWG drawing).

Figure 7.46 shows approximately what the resulting drawing should look like.

Figure 7.46

**CAD files inserted
into Revit**

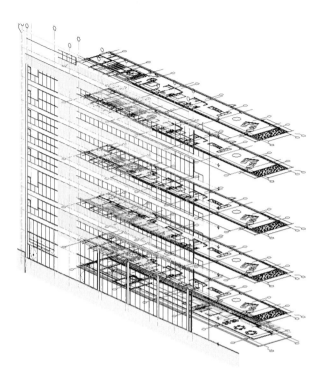

Converting DWG Gridlines into Smart Revit Gridlines

Most of the floor plan that you have imported as a reference drawing will have gridlines in it. To generate Revit gridlines from imported lines is simple: Select the Grid tool and set the creation method to Pick in the Options bar. Next pick any gridline in the import. Revit will create a gridline on top of the DWG gridline and number it. Revit usually starts with the number 1, but if the DWG grid uses lettered coordinates, you can change the Revit gridline on the first one you create. The remainder will number (or letter) in sequence, so they should append correctly. Otherwise, you can renumber them later.

Figure 7.47 shows an imported DWG image. In the second image, the gridlines have been converted to Revit grids using the pick method. Note that the grid bubbles in Revit change dynamically with the view scale. If the bubble sizes don't match, don't panic—just check your scale factor.

> You need to convert CAD gridlines to Revit gridlines in one level only. Gridlines in Revit span the entire building because they're *datums* that show up in every level. This is practical when the grid system is the same for each level.

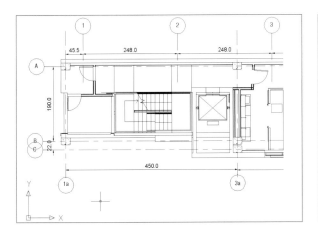

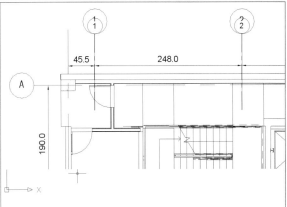

Figure 7.47
The image on the left shows view with DWG import. On the right, Revit Gridlines can be created using the import lines.

Working with Scope Boxes

If you have multiple floor plans where the gridlines aren't the same for all levels, you need to use the Scope Box tool. This tool limits the range in which datums (gridlines, levels, and reference lines) appear. Imagine that you have a building with a shopping center on the first three floors and a hotel tower above. Obviously, the grid systems for the lower and upper parts of the building will be different. You need to create two scope boxes, assign the grids from the first three levels to one scope box and the rest to the other, and control the area covered by each scope box so they show up correctly. Figure 7.48 shows how scope boxes work in a 3D view.

Scope boxes are also visible in 3D views (although not in camera views), and you can easily manipulate their extent directly using the grips. Assigning gridlines or other datums to a scope box is easy: Select the gridlines, choose **Element Properties → Scope Box**, and then select the scope box where the datums should belong. Figure 7.49 shows the Element Properties dialog box for the gridlines and the associated scope box.

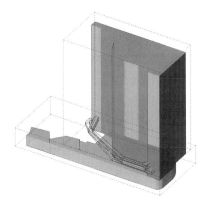

Figure 7.48
DWG layers list3

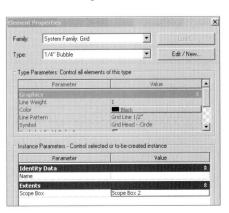

Figure 7.49
Highlighted topography points

Figure 7.47
The image on the left shows view with DWG import. On the right, Revit Gridlines can be created using the import lines.

Using DWG Lines to create Revit Walls

In a 2D CAD application, walls are represented with two parallel lines. You can use one of these two lines as your reference line for creating Revit walls. Create a wall type that is the same thickness as the one used in the DWG. Then use the Pick option when placing new walls, and pick on lines in the import. Be sure to set the Wall Location line to a meaningful value (Exterior Core, for example) to get correct alignment.

A rule of thumb when following this creation approach is to set your exterior and shaft walls' top constraint to the top of the building, and set your interior partitions to only go up to the next level. If you have repetitive floors with identical or similar floor plans, create the walls once, then leverage the copy-paste functionality to repeat the walls.

Figure 7.50 shows the beginning of a Revit model created using DWG floor plans as a base. DWG wall lines were used as a reference to create the walls with the pick method, and the wall Location Line was set to the insert Exterior face.

Using DWG lines to create Revit Floors

After you create the walls, the next step is to create floors. To create floors, select Floor from the Basic or Modeling Design Bar, and again, select the Pick option in the Options bar. Hover your mouse over the outer edge of the floor or walls and press the Tab key until the DWG floor lines are highlighted. Click to generate sketch lines. If the shape of t he floor isn't the shape you want, make corrections using edit tools. Remember, a sketch is a line drawing that has to form a closed loop so Revit can create an object out of it.

Figure 7.50

**Beginning the con-
version process**

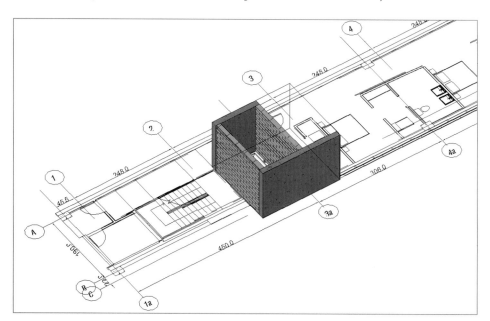

In Figure 7.51, the lines in the DWG that represented the outer wall faces have been selected, the magenta lines have been adjusted to a rectangular shape (using trim lines), and the floor has been created.

> If your workflow permits, draw interior walls before you create the floors so that when you create a floor, it will be attached to the walls and have a relationship with them.

Once you have your wall and floor structure, it's easy to starting adding windows, doors, and other elements.

Figure 7.51
Adding floors

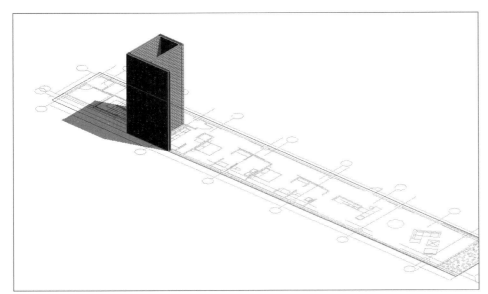

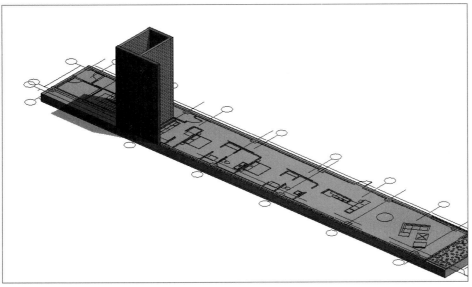

Working with Imported Library Components in DWG Format

Autodesk's i-drop technology allows you to drag and drop content (drawings) from the Web directly into a Revit drawing. This corresponds to the DWG import process and utilizes Revit's default import settings. From a workflow perspective, it's practical. As you work on your project, you can quickly go to the Web and search for a detail or piece of content in DWG format. Once you find what you need, you can drag and drop it into your Revit file.

Many manufacturers now have their content in i-droppable 2D or 3D DWG format. Figure 7.52 shows some sample i-drop content.

Figure 7.52

i-drop examples

Importing Library Components in SketchUp (.skp) Format

Another recently introduced source of downloadable library components that can be useful in Revit is Google's 3D Warehouse, which offers files in SketchUp (.skp) format. Revit can read SKP files, and you can import SKP files into an RFA (Revit family file) to create content. These families aren't always parametric—many families don't need to be parametric—because certain manufacturer content exists only in single dimensions and shapes. Figure 7.53 shows some samples of SketchUp content.

The best way to utilize this 3D content is to create a new family (**File → New → Family**) and select a family type, such as furniture or plumbing fixtures. You then can import a 3D SketchUp model into this family. If needed, you can quickly create simplified orthographic projections using linework instead of using a 3D object to generate those projections. This is useful if you need to show simplified versions of the 3D object in plan, elevation, or another orthogonal view. More details about family generation will be covered later in this book.

You can learn more about 3D Warehouse at http://sketchup.google.com/3dwarehouse.

Figure 7.53

Sample SketchUp content

 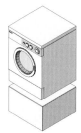

Starting a Drawing from a Scanned File

There are various ways for an architect to start a project. We have reviewed two of them: starting from scratch, and starting from an already available 2D digital document (CAD file). However, you may have old paper documents of the building that you need to work on.

This happens a lot on smaller projects, usually restorations or additions. An architect may get few floor plans and elevations to work from that they need to redraw before starting a new project. Let's review how you can use those as a basis to begin a new project.

You begin by scanning the floor plan and importing it in Revit as an image in the floor relevant to the drawing. Any of the image types we discussed previously will work fine for your scanned image. An example of a scanned floor plan is shown in Figure 7.54. Follow these steps:

1. Insert the scanned image into the appropriate level or view. So, if you have a first floor plan, insert it into your Level 1 view.

2. Scanned images are usually never perfectly orthogonal, so you need to rotate the image to square the lines of the walls. Use the rotation tool, and try to rotate the image as close to orthogonal as possible. To do that, select the image, click the Rotate button, and rotate the image. The rotated image is shown in Figure 7.55.

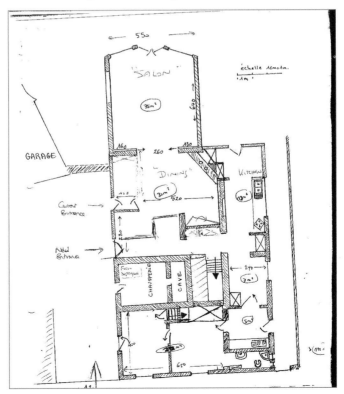

Figure 7.54

An example of a scanned plan

Figure 7.55

The rotated image

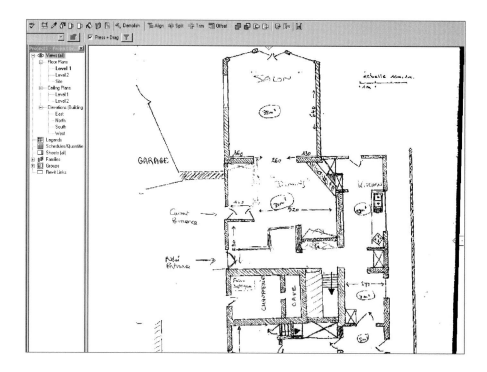

3. You need to verify the drawing scale or adjust the scan to fit the scale you're working in. To do so, zoom in on the image, and find at least one wall that has a dimensioned length. In this example, the original drawing was done in metric units.

4. Using the Resize tool, measure the length of the wall. The tool prompts you to choose two points, and a temporary dimension will show up indicating the length. Make your first two picks correspond to the length of the wall in the image, and then select a third point to re-size the image. Use the temporary dimensions to help visualize the change.

5. Click the wall and then across to the right to the end of the wall. The wall length in the scan is 160 cm and measures 3200 cm in the drawing. Bring your mouse back to the left, and watch the temporary dimension numbers get smaller (shown in Figure 7.57). When they reach 160 cm, click again, and your image will be resized.

You can now start tracing over the imported image and create the framework for your project. Obviously, scanned drawings can never result in total accuracy, so you'll probably want to field-verify your dimensions. However, this is a good way to get started. Figure 7.58 shows the project with all of the new walls located over the scanned image.

You just scaled the drawing. If you dimension the piece of wall, it should show 160 cm.

Once you've finished referencing the scanned image, you can delete it or hide it in the view.

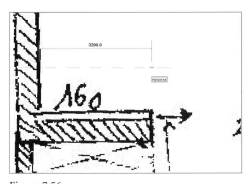

Figure 7.56

Resizing the scanned image

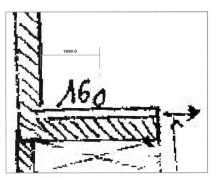

Figure 7.57

Finishing the image edits

Figure 7.58

The scanned image with Revit walls

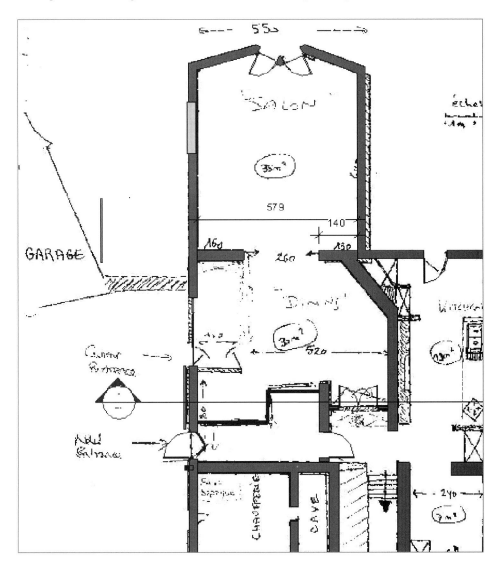

CHAPTER 8

Preparing Documents for Clients

There are many points in the design process where it's necessary to convey your ideas to others. As architects, we use a wide range of representational techniques, ranging from the loose napkin sketch to the photo-realistic rendering. We use 2D diagrams to convey plans and sections, and perspective views to convey a more human-scaled expression. This chapter will focus on a few techniques that you can use directly with Revit. We'll look specifically at creating color-coded area plans, presentation techniques for plans and sections, animated sun studies, and simple renderings that let you explore materials and lighting.

- Color fill plans
- Area plans
- Creating presentation graphics
- Shadows and solar studies
- Rendering a perspective

Color Fill Plans

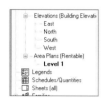

Figure 8.1

Area plans node in the Project Browser

In this section, we'll discuss two common types of graphical views: color fill plans and area plans. Both take advantage of a feature in Revit called Color Fill Schemes, which allows you to assign colors to parameter values and display them in the view.

Color fill plans are plan views that can be color-coded to represent room properties such as department, name, and usage. Area plans are used to convey building usage that extends beyond the shape and size of individual rooms, such as rentable area or office space. You access area plans from the View list of the Project Browser (Figure 8.1).

Revit's Color Fill Schemes feature is a fast, easy, and smart method for generating color-coded plans. It lets you apply color to room and area parameter values to help graphically illustrate spatial organization. For example, you may want to create a colored plan that represents units in an apartment complex, or show various departments with different colors (Figure 8.2) to distinguish space usage such as office, storage, and corridor.

One of the benefits of using color schemes in Revit is that the colors dynamically adjust as changes are made in the model. If a new department is added, a new color is automatically assigned, and the plan view updates immediately to reflect the change. Revit also makes it easy to change colors to match your aesthetic requirements if the auto-color isn't what you want. You can apply color fills from Plan using view properties. Right click in the view, and go to **View Properties**… There you will see a parameter for Color Scheme, with the option to edit it. A view can also be colored when placing a Color Scheme Legend from the Drafting tab in the design bar (🔲 Color Scheme Legend).

Figure 8.2

Color fill plan

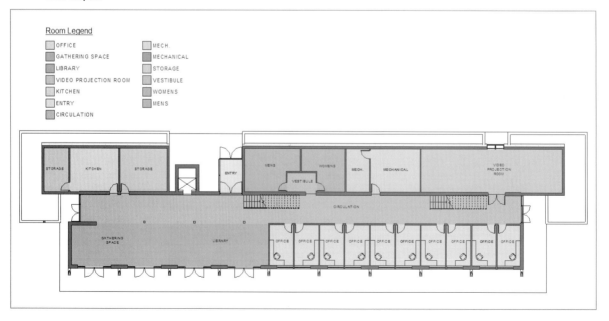

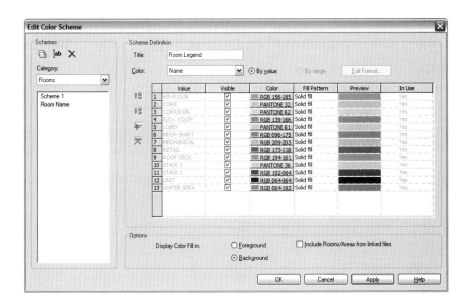

Figure 8.3

Edit Color Scheme dialog box

Defining a Color Scheme

A color scheme is defined once, and can then be applied to multiple views in a project. Using the Transfer Project Standards feature, you can transfer color schemes from project to project to maintain a consistent color palette.

To define and edit color schemes, choose **Settings → Color Fill Schemes**. The Edit Color Scheme dialog box, shown in Figure 8.3, has a number of options to help you format your color scheme. The right pane of this dialog box, Scheme Definition, allows you to specify what information you want to color code:

Title This text box lets you name your color legend. You would most probably use the same name that you gave the Scheme.

Color This drop-down list allows you to choose the criteria on which you'll color-code the plan from a list of all the room properties. By default this goes to Department, but you will most probably not have department defined in your rooms, so change it to Name to see the effect.

> **By Value** This option is checked by default and uses the value defined in the Color field to list and sort the rooms. For example, if you color by Name, it will list all names used in the project alphabetically and assign a color to each unique name.

> **By Range** This is a second option for sorting a Scheme definition and is ONLY active when the color criteria are set to Area or Perimeter. In that case, this option sorts all the areas by size range (from-to) ranging from smallest to largest. This is practical when you need to see how well your project matches a program with specific area goals.

Figure 8.4

Color by Range

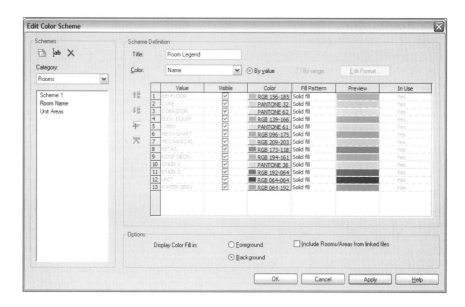

Figure 8.5

Color scheme definition

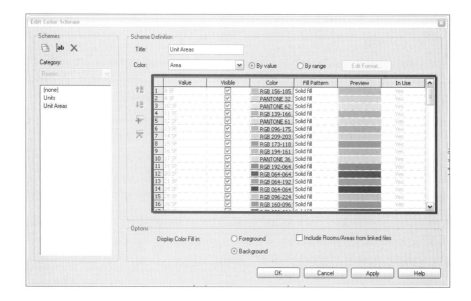

Let's review some of the fields available when the option By Value is selected, as that will be what you will most often need:

Value This is a non-editable field that displays a list of all the parameter values used that will appear in your color-fill legend. By default, this column will fill up with in-use values based on what is in the model. You can add values to this list by pressing the Add button. This allows you to pre-set some values and colors that can be used by rooms later in the design process. For example, If you have a common list of room names, you could fill this table out before starting to model anything, and then use the list when assigning names to rooms. When a row is selected, you can adjust the order of the values using the up and down arrow buttons. The order established in this dialog will be reflected in the color-fill legend.

Visible Although all the names are reported in this dialog box, you may not want the legend to show them all. This check box allows you to turn off individual values. This will likewise be reflected in the color-fill legend.

Color These colors are customizable and can be changed by clicking the color button. You have the option to define CMYK, RGB, or PANTONE values or to choose from the standard Microsoft color picker.

Fill Pattern lets you select the fill pattern from any of the drafting patterns available. By default, Revit chooses the Solid Fill pattern. To add or modify the fill patterns, choose **Settings → Fill Patterns**.

Preview This field gives you a visual preview of the color as it will appear on the screen in the view.

In Use This field tells you if the particular value is being used in the model. For example, if you add a value to the Value column but don't add it to a room in the model, Revit returns No in this column. This comes into play if you add rooms to a room schedule but don't add those rooms in the model. The color fill knows if rooms exist in the model or not. Note that only values that aren't in use can be deleted.

When the *By Range* option is selected, there is one more field that is available:

At Least In the At Least column, you can change the minimum area to 1000 square feet or whatever value you want to show. Revit automatically adjusts the colors in the view to reflect the changes for the color scheme.

In the lower portion of the right-hand pane of the Edit Color Scheme dialog box (Scheme Definition) are the fields shown in Figure 8.5 and described here:

Display Options At the bottom of the Scheme Definition pane are some additional options for color display. You can choose to include linked-room area information from other Revit models, and you also have the option to display the color fill in the foreground or the background. Displaying color in the background puts color beneath all model objects, whereas the Foreground option colors all model objects. The effect is illustrated in Figure 8.6.

Figure 8.6

Display Color Fill

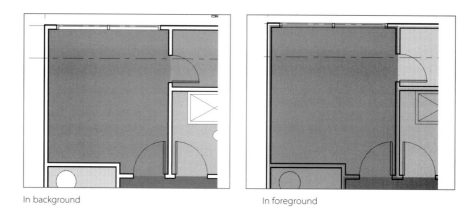

In background   In foreground

Adding a Color Scheme to a View

In this exercise, you'll create a color-coded plan and add it to a view:

1. Open the Station.rvt model found in the Chapter 8 folder of the CD that came with this book, and open the plan view called **Level 3 Pres**.

2. Define a new scheme in which you'll color the rooms/areas by Name. To do that, go to **Settings → Color Schemes.**

3. In the Schemes portion of the dialog box, click the **Duplicate** button located at the top of the dialog. Name the new scheme **Room Name.**

4. In the Scheme Definitions section, give the scheme a title by typing in **Room Legend**, then choose Name in the **Color** drop-down list.

5. The result will be a list of rooms sorted alphabetically by Name. If you wish to change the order to be non-alphabetical, use the Move Rows Up or Down buttons on the left of the list. These buttons become active when you click on any of the names. If you don't like the automatically assigned colors, change the colors by clicking on the color field.

6. Click OK.

7. You are back in the view—go to the Drafting Bar and select **Color Scheme Legend**.

8. Position the Color Scheme Legend somewhere close to the plan. You will be prompted to choose a color scheme: Choose the scheme you just created, named Room Name. The plan will automatically get colored based on the Names of the rooms in the plan view.

> The color fill tool assigns colors only if you have created Rooms in your project. If you work on a new project and have not yet defined Rooms, and place a color fill legend, it will report that no colors are defined. Select the Room Tool and start placing rooms in your spaces— you'll see the new rooms get colored in as you place each one and give it a unique name.

The Color Scheme Legend can display the colors used in the current view or all the colors used in the project. To toggle between the two, select the Legend, go to its Element Properties, and in the Type properties set the Values Displayed parameters By View or All. The usual case is that you will need to set it By View. The All option can be helpful when you make an overview legend for the entire project.

You can try a short exercise for color coding a plan using the Area/By range option:

1. Open **Level 3 pres** and duplicate the view, giving it a new name. Repeat these steps:

2. Go to **Settings/Color Schemes.**

3. In the Schemes portion of the dialog box, click the **Duplicate** button located at the top of the dialog box. Name the new scheme **Unit Areas,** and give change the title to **Unit Area Legend.**

4. In the Colors column select **Area** and check the **by range** option.

5. By default, the At Least column reads 20 SF. Highlight that value, and change it to **700 SF**.

6. While the At Least column is still highlighted, click the **Add** button to add a row to the column.

7. The new value defaults to 1400. Change it to **900,** and click OK. Add one more row using same method, and set the at least range to **1100** SF. Your settings should be similar to the ones shown in Figure 8.7.

8. In the Options at the bottom of the dialog box, set color to display in **Foreground** using the radio button.

Figure 8.7

Color scheme settings

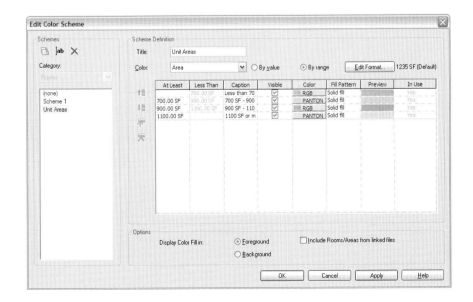

As the Color Fill Legend is a property of a view, you can at any point change the Color Fill from one type to another or set it to None. To access the Color Fill from the view, go to **View Properties → Color Scheme**.

Area Plans

Area plans are views of the model used to calculate the areas of rooms according to various calculation standards. Some of the standards for area calculations are as follows:

Gross area This is the overall area of a floor or footprint of the building.

Rentable area Different developers and leasing companies have different standards for rentable areas. One example may include all the spaces in a building except egress corridors, vertical transportation, and mechanical spaces. However, this includes the floor area taken up by columns and some walls.

Usable area This area defines only the usable space in a plan. It doesn't count areas taken up by columns, walls, mechanical rooms, shafts, and other nonusable space.

BOMA area BOMA is the Building Owners and Managers Association standard. Widely used in the U.S., it was created to help standardize office-building development. BOMA has its own set of standards used to calculate areas. More information on BOMA standards can be found at www.boma.org.

Revit allows you to choose among several predefined area schemes or to create your own scheme based on standard calculation variables. To add or modify the area settings, choose **Settings → Room and Area Settings**. Some of those settings, shown in Figure 8.9, include boundary locations such as wall finish and wall center, and the heights at which to calculate area.

> This dialog box gives you the option of calculating room volumes. This tool is useful in a number of applications but you should use it only when needed, because the additional calculations can create performance issues based on project complexity.

The Room Calculations tab allows you to change how the areas are calculated for each area scheme. You can set a height and boundary type that Revit uses to auto-generate room areas.

Figure 8.9

Room and Area Settings dialog box

The Area Schemes tab, shown in Figure 8.10, lets you add different schemes to calculate room areas, allowing you to calculate multiple area types in Revit.

To add an area plan to your model, open the **Room and Area** tab in the design bar, and click the **Area Plan…** button (Area Plan…). Doing so opens the **New Area Plan** dialog box (Figure 8.11), where you select area scheme, level, and drawing scale.

When you press OK, Revit automatically adds a new folder called **Area Plans** to the Project Browser and adds plans for each level you selected. In your view window, you'll see a duplicate plan view of the level you selected with purple lines defining the area boundaries. These lines are placed on the walls according to the type of area plan you selected (such as gross area or rentable area). You can move or delete the lines if they don't appear where you want them to be. To add additional area boundary lines, use the **Area Boundary** tool available in the "Room and Areas" tab (Area Boundary).

Area boundaries must be closed loops of lines (see Figure 8.12) in order for Revit to be able to calculate the area. Any breaks or gaps in the area lines, or lines that don't intersect, will result in Revit returning a Not Enclosed value for the area. (Should you get that error message, try trimming the corners.)

Figure 8.10

Area Schemes tab

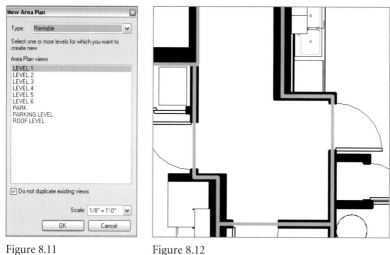

Figure 8.11

New Area Plan dialog box

Figure 8.12

Area boundary with closed loops

Creating Presentation Graphics

Creating compelling visual representations of architecture is an important device for conveying design intent and telling the story of your design. As you've seen, Revit lets you create standard forms of representation ranging from floor plans to perspectives. Using some simple techniques, it's possible to bring these typically flat drawings to life. In this section, we'll explore methods to help you make some great-looking drawings. We'll also touch on a more advanced tool set used to create semirealistic renderings.

Floor Plans: Making Walls Punch

Making clean, easy-to-read floor plans requires only a few steps. A typical plan view in Revit can become cluttered with lots of annotations and doesn't create striking figure/ground images. Figure 8.13 shows a typical floor plan in Revit.

To clean up this image, you can hide the annotations and override the cut for all the walls with a solid color. To do so, follow these steps:

1. Open the Visibility/Graphic Overrides dialog, go to the Annotations tab, and deselect the box to "Show annotation categories in this view" (see Figure 8.14). This hides all annotations with a single click.

2. Go back to the Model Categories tab, and scroll down to the Walls category.

3. Select the row, and override the Cut Patterns column by clicking the Override button. In the resulting Fill Pattern Graphics dialog box (shown in Figure 8.15), you're given options to select pattern and color overrides. Set Color to Black and Pattern to Solid Fill.

4. If you have Columns in your project, you may want to do the same for them as well. When you're finished, click OK to close both dialog boxes.

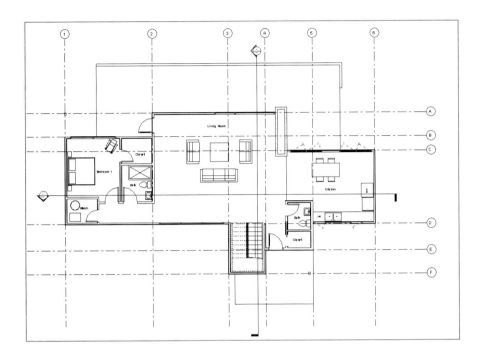

Figure 8.13

**Typical Revit
floor plan**

Figure 8.14

**Uncheck this box to
hide all annotations
in the view**

Figure 8.15

Fill Pattern overrides

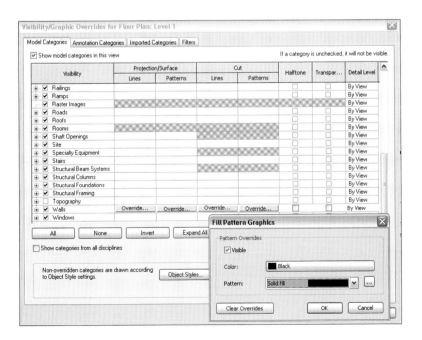

The effect on the plan view is immediately obvious, as shown in Figure 8.16. The same technique can be applied in section views. Be sure to override other categories relevant to section view, such as Floor, Roof, and Topography. Figure 8.17 shows a section with the same graphic overrides. Try these techniques in any of the sample files provided with the CD to get a feel for the interaction.

Figure 8.16

Plan view after applying graphic overrides

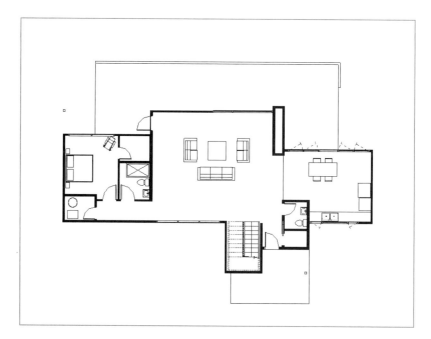

Figure 8.17

Section view with cut pattern overrides

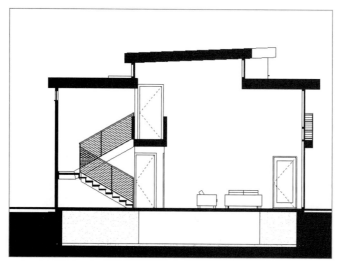

Making Elevation Graphics

Colored elevation views are a nice way to convey materiality, even if abstract. Change your elevation views to "Shaded with Edges" using the view controls at the bottom of the view to get a feel for this mode. A sample of this view style is shown in Figure 8.18.

Every material used in Revit refers back to an RGB value in shaded view; however, many users have noticed that color is rarely matched in the view, and will even look very different from view to view. To overcome this effect, and approximate the same colors set up in materials in the view, you can use "Sun and Shadows Settings" to control precisely where light is coming from, and thus improve the visual fidelity. A sample of this modified view style is shown in Figure 8.19 (the image in black and white is subtle, but will become readily obvious if you do this in Revit).

> To edit and adjust material colors and patterns, choose **Settings → Materials**. You can also access this dialog box from elements directly if the Material parameter is present. For example, if you aren't sure what material is on the exterior of a wall, go to the wall's Element Properties, then edit the **Type Properties → Structure** options. From here, you can select the Finish Layers Material, and you'll be taken directly to the Materials dialog box.

To get this effect, go to the Advanced Model Graphics dialog box from the View Control bar located at the bottom of your view (shown in Figure 8.20). Access to this dialog box is located with shadow controls.

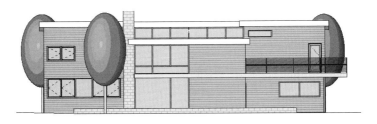

Figure 8.18

The default shaded view

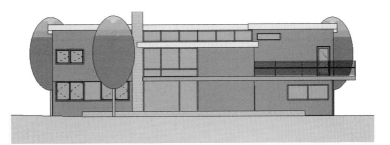

Figure 8.19

The same elevation with the sun repositioned

Figure 8.20

Shadow options in the View Control bar

Figure 8.21

Set the sun angles using the "Sun and Shadows Settings" dialog box.

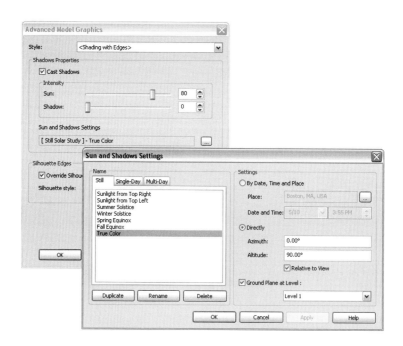

In the Advanced Model Graphics dialog, open the "Sun and Shadows Settings" dialog box by clicking the ellipsis button ( ). Then, do the following:

1. Create a new entry using the Duplicate button, and name it **True Color**.

2. Set the Sun to Directly, Azimuth to 0, and Altitude to 90.

3. Make sure the "Relative to View" check box is selected (see Figure 8.21).

4. Click OK to return to the Advanced Model Graphics dialog box.

5. Be sure shadows are enabled. Using the slider, change the Sun Intensity to 80, and turn Shadow down to 0. This way, no shadows will be cast, and the light source will always be directly above the model. The effect is that light won't cause unpredictable effects on material colors.

Using images in elevation views

Using images in elevation views is a great way to add some visual character to your drawings. Two useful techniques involve taking advantage of the draw order options for images when placed in a view. When you select an image, the Option bar gives you the ability to push the image to the foreground or background. By making a color-gradient image, then importing it into your elevation, you can then send the image to the background, and produce high-quality images right in Revit.

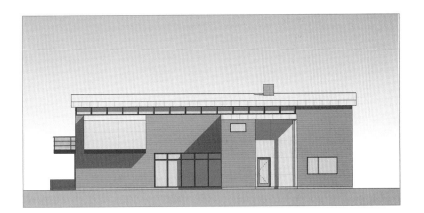

Figure 8.22

When image is selected, send it to the background using the options bar.

Figure 8.23

This PNG image is set to Foreground.

Another great technique is to use the transparency channel available in the PNG format. By making a color transparent, and pushing images to the foreground and background, you can add trees, people, and cars, and the image will not mask the model.

Shadows and Solar Studies

Using shadows can help articulate depth in your façade. You can toggle shadows on and off in any view using the view controls. A nice feature in Revit is the ability to orient shadows consistently from view to view.

Turn on shadows using the View Controls at the bottom of the view. From the same flyout menu, open the Advanced Model Graphics dialog box. Open the "Sun and Shadows Settings" dialog box and choose "Sunlight from Top Right." Close the dialog boxes to get a feel for the behavior. Change your view display to Hidden Line, and note that shadows are still cast. Go back to the Advanced Model Graphics dialog and experiment with the

"Sun and Shadow Intensity" settings. Increasing Shadow to 100 yields high-contrast images and dropping the value to 0 essentially turns off the shadow. A hidden-line view of the default sun settings is shown in Figure 8.24.

Creating a Solar Study

Understanding the effect your building will have on its environment is an important part of a design. Often, architects are required to show how a new building will cast shadows on its neighboring buildings and open space. For these purposes, Revit provides a tool that lets you generate an animated solar study that can show the effect of shadows over time, throughout the year. To access the feature, you'll first need to enable shadows in your view, and then set up some information about time and location of the project. The steps to create a solar study are described next. For the purpose of this exercise, any view can be used, but we suggest using a site plan, as it's a great view to use when visualizing shadows.

1. Go to the Advanced Model Graphics dialog, and click the ellipsis button (⬜) to open the "Sun and Shadows Settings" dialog box.

2. Choose the Multi-Day tab, shown in Figure 8.25.

Figure 8.24
Hidden-line view with shadows enabled

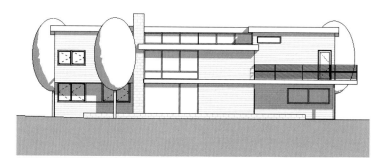

Figure 8.25
Multi-day solar studies

Figure 8.26

Previewing the solar study provides these animation controls.

Figure 8.27

Enabling the Section Box

3. The predefined options in this dialog box are good starting points. You choose a location on the Earth from a list of cities, a start date, an end date, and a time of day. Choose a time interval as well. Using the default settings for a Multi Day Solar Study, and change Place to a city near where you are right now.

4. Click OK, and go back to your view.

5. Once a multi-day study has been set up, new options appear on the View Control bar (see Figure 8.26). Click **Preview Solar Study** to activate animation controls in the Options bar.

Clicking the Play button starts the animation. In the view, you'll see a live animation of the shadows as the days of the month go by.

Once you're happy with the results, you can export the view as an animated movie. To do so, choose **File → Export → Animated Solar Study**. From here, you can choose a location to save the file, change the model graphic styles, and choose the size of the image in pixels. To make smaller files, try using the Microsoft Video 1 codec, and lower the quality settings. The resulting file can be played with a standard digital video player such as Windows Media Player. A sample solar study AVI is located on the CD accompanying this book.

3D Views

A great way to visualize the model is to use a perspective camera and enable section box. This allows you to create 3D sectional views that slice through the model, providing stunning graphics than can help better explain plan, section, and 3D in one view.

To take advantage of this form of representation, open a perspective view (or make a new one), and go to its **View Properties** using the right-click menu. Enable the **Section Box** parameter in the Extents parameter group, as shown in Figure 8.27.

A new 3D box appears in the view: This is the Section Box. Select the Section Box, and controls appear that you can use to clip the view from all six directions of the box. To experiment, drag the top arrows down until the box cuts through the model.

To hide the 3D cropping box, select it, and hide it by choosing **Hide in View → By Element** from the right-click menu. The same thing works with 3D axonometric views, but the camera views give different dynamics to the graphic presentation. A sample view of a 3D floor plan is shown in Figure 8.28.

Figure 8.28

**Perspective view
with the Section Box
enabled**

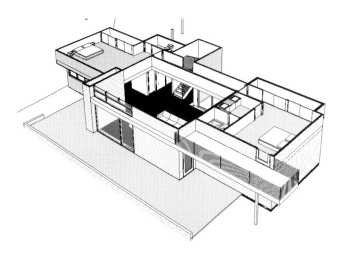

Figure 8.28

**Perspective view
with the Section Box
enabled**

You can apply the same graphic overrides to a 3D view as we outlined for plan and section views. This way, you can graphically override the color of everything that has been cut (walls, columns, roofs, etc.) and assign a solid fill color. Take advantage of these techniques to produce some really slick presentations!

Rendering a Perspective

Revit has an integrated rendering engine that lets you visualize the model with material texture maps and more realistic lighting effects. To fully delve into the depths of rendering is beyond the scope of this book, but we want to at least give you insight into its workflow and basic principles. With some quality material images, you can get decent images with relatively minimal time investment. However, if you don't have quality materials to work with, you'll get mixed results. Be realistic in your expectations: Clicking the Render button won't give you a high-quality image right out of the box. A great-looking, photo-realistic rendering always takes time and many iterations to get acceptable results.

If you're familiar with the Autodesk 3Ds Max or Autodesk VIZ, you can export a 3D view of a Revit model to DWG and link this file into either of these applications. The model retains its object model and materials so that you can create more advanced renderings and animations. Open the file Source_House_Complete.rvt located in the Chapter 4 folder on the CD.

The following exercise will take us through a simplified rendering workflow. Many of the materials in the model have already been pre-defined for you to make it a bit easier.

1. Open the file Source_House_Complete.rvt.

2. We've provided a material library for use with this file. In order for the rendering to process the files we've provided, you need to copy the folder named Materials to your

My Documents folder. Then, choose **Settings → Options** from the main menu. Open the Rendering tab. Click the New Path icon, and browse the folder My Documents\Materials. Your path structure should look like the highlighted line in Figure 8.29. When you're done, click OK. This guarantees that when you render, the texture maps provided will show up.

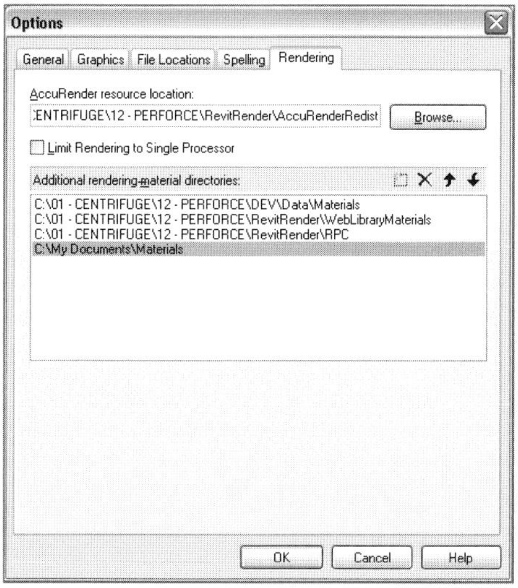

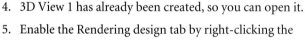

Figure 8.29

Option settings for rendering

3. To render a view, open or create a new perspective view of the exterior of the building. Any 3D view can be rendered, but you'll get the best results from perspective (camera) views.

4. 3D View 1 has already been created, so you can open it.

5. Enable the Rendering design tab by right-clicking the Design bar and selecting Rendering (shown in Figure 8.30). Doing so brings up the tools used for rendering. You use the first option, Raytrace, to initiate a rendering.

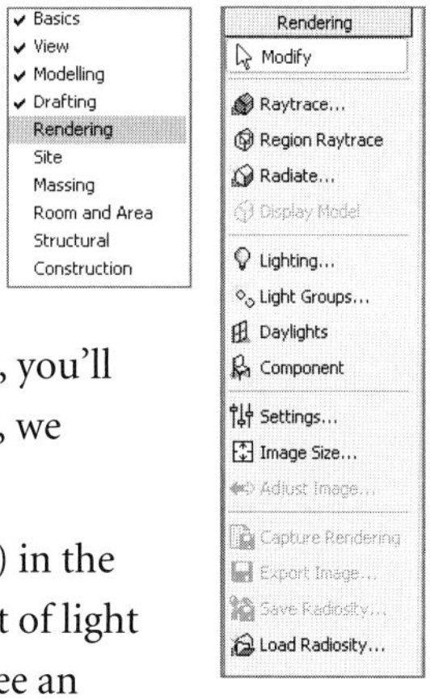

Figure 8.30

Activating the Rendering tab

6. Click **Raytrace**. If the view has not been previously rendered, you'll get a dialog box asking to create a new scene. In this exercise, we already have a default scene, so let's use it (see Figure 8.31).

7. To initiate the rendering, click the green **Go** button ( GO!) in the Options bar. Revit begins the process of calculating the effect of light on the model and displays texture maps in the view. You'll see an image start to appear in your view. The rendering can be cancelled at any time by pressing the Cancel button at the bottom of the screen near the progress meter. When the render is finished, the image should look like Figure 8.32.

This rendering, although exceedingly simple, illustrates some of the critical aspects of rendering: the camera, lighting, materials, and background/foreground. We'll step through each of these to give you an idea of where in the UI to find these features and how to make adjustments.

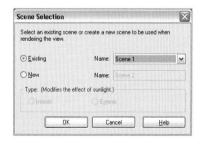

Figure 8.31

Selecting a scene

Figure 8.32

The finished view

The Camera

The Revit camera is easy to manipulate. When you're in a perspective view, click the (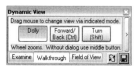) button in the toolbar brings up the Dynamic View dialog box shown in Figure 8.33.

Use the Walkthrough options to move the camera in space. The Dolly option moves camera in the vertical plane, and Forward/Backward moves the camera in the horizontal plane. The Turn option keeps the camera stationary and redirects where you're looking.

The "Field of View" options let you change the field of view as if you were using a zoom lens on a camera. The camera doesn't move; the zoom factor changes. Use the In/Out button to change zoom.

Lighting

It's possible to set highly specific date, time, and place information for your rendering. This allows you to generate accurate lighting studies. Click the Render Settings button (Settings...) to access the scene information.

The Scene Settings dialog box is used to set up values and parameters used when rendering the view. This includes the effect of the sun, lighting, and overall quality of the rendered image. The first group of controls lets you change the sun location. By default,

Figure 8.33

The Dynamic View dialog's Walkthrough and Field Of View tabs

Figure 8.34

Scene Settings dialog box, with the Sun button

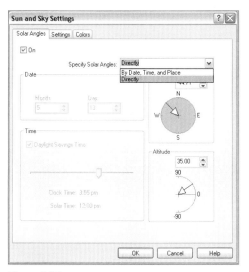

Figure 8.35

Sun and Sky Settings dialog box

Figure 8.36

Sun and Sky Settings dialog box: Place tab

the rendering will use the same shadow settings used in the view. To override that pre-set, uncheck the option Use "Sun and Shadows Settings" from view. Then when you click the Sun button, you will be given options to position the sun, as shown in Figure 8.34.

The next dialog that opens lets you set the sun angle either directly or by using the date, time, and place, as shown in Figure 8.35.

If you set Specify Solar Angles to Directly, you can adjust the altitude and azimuth to any angle you see fit. If you're attempting to show how the model would look at a specific time of year, choose "By Date, Time, and Place," and drag the slider controls to the desired values. A new Place tab appears; use it to choose the location of your building on the planet (see Figure 8.36).

Foreground/Background

Foreground and background are used to help give your model some context by using images or color gradients for the sky and choosing materials for your site. Placing trees and bushes and other site entourage such as cars and people helps fill in the foreground. Be careful when working with your camera so your model doesn't look like it's floating in an

abstract, empty plane. Tighten the shot using the field of view, or crop the view to reduce the amount of ground taking up space. To do this, select the crop boundary and drag the blue controls. You can also access the exact size of the crop boundary from the options bar by pressing the **Size** button when the crop boundary is selected. The button reports the actual size. Clicking on the button will bring up options to resize the boundary.

To set up a background for the rendered image, click the **Environment** button in the Scene Settings dialog box (Environment...) shown in Figure 8.37.

In this dialog box, you can choose from several different sky options. Selecting the Background Image check box in the Advanced section enables a new tab in the dialog box, from which you can browse to an image to use in the background. This can work out nicely if you've taken a digital photo of the site, and you know the position of your camera in the model is relatively close to the position where you took the photo. Note that Revit does not have a built-in method for exactly matching a photograph with a camera in the model.

Materials

Perhaps the most critical aspect of producing a convincing rendering is having good materials. Good materials convey characteristics of texture, color, reflectivity, and transparency that you expect to see in reality.

All elements in Revit have a material, but not all materials have rendering attributes assigned to them. To assign a rendering material, use the AccuRender field in the **Settings →
Materials** dialog box, a portion of which is shown in Figure 8.38. Follow these steps:

1. Click the launch icon to open the AccuRender Material Library editor.

2. This dialog box presents a list of libraries that contain predefined materials.

3. Browse to the "Samples" Library and select it. This is the library that was automatically added to the project when you added a rendering location point to the My Documents\Materials folder shown in Figure 8.39.

4. Select the Cedar Deck material, right-click the preview, and choose Edit.

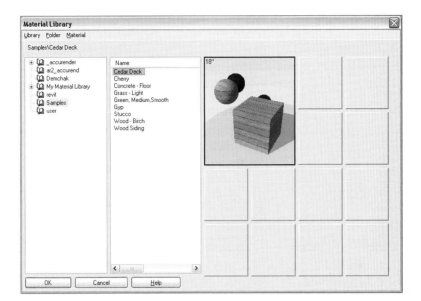

Figure 8.39

Material Library

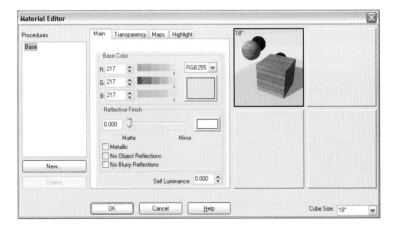

Figure 8.40

Material Editor

5. A new dialog box appears that defines the characteristics of this material. For example, you can set base RGB colors, adjust reflectivity, change transparency, and assign images to the material. All these options are shown in Figure 8.40.

6. This material uses an image file that is a digital photograph of wood decking and that has been tailored for rendering purposes. When the image repeats (tiles) on model geometry, it appears seamless; you shouldn't be able to see seams where the image starts and ends as it tiles.

7. Click the Maps tab.

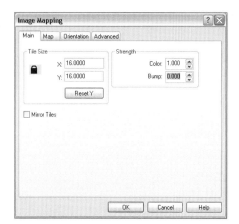

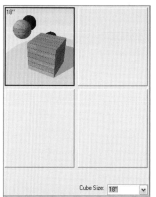

Figure 8.41

Image Mapping dialog

Figure 8.42

Material variations

8. Select the Path in the dialog box, and click Edit.

9. The next dialog box(shown in Figure 8.41) shows parameters for the image map. The tile size represents how big in decimal feet the image will be stretched to fit in the model. In this example, the wood image file will repeat itself on model geometry every 16′. The Map tab allows you to browse to the actual file location on disk. You can choose a different image if you want.

This is the basic process for setting up materials. To recap: Create a location of quality images on disk, and then create AccuRender materials from them. Experiment with the tile size to get the correct results. Use the preview cube in the AccuRender dialog boxes to help make decisions about the tile values. The cube represents a real-world geometric size and can be changed to different sizes to help visualize the tiling of an image when mapped to real-world sizes. For example, knowing that wood decking is spaced about every 3″ (8-10cm), you expect to see four or five boards on the 18″ (45cm) cube. Some examples of these variations are shown in Figure 8.42.

For materials such as glass, where an image isn't needed, choose from the default materials libraries that ship with Revit. Browse through the AccuRender Library, and you'll find a set of glass options as well as a host of other materials to choose from (see Figure 8.43).

Figure 8.43

Glass material options

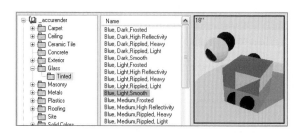

CHAPTER 9

Sheets

In previous chapters, we discussed how to create a model in Revit and how to make standard views to represent the model. We've explored how to create plans, sections, callouts, and elevations of a BIM model. This chapter starts by looking at the properties of views and what these all mean. We then move into sheets, and how to get your views onto sheets. In Revit, getting your views onto sheets is extremely easy: you simply drag and drop views from the Project Browser onto sheet views. Because every view has a scale, you see immediately the effect of this, and if you need to change scale, or crop the view, this can be done in the context of the sheet. These sheets can then be printed, exported, or published for use.

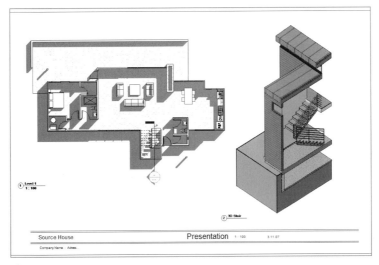

Figure 9.1

A presentation sheet with plan and 3D stair

Historically, the creation and delivery of document sets has been divided into three phases: schematic design, design development, and construction documents. The final CD set becomes the legal documents of record and is used by the contractor to physically build the building. With the advent of BIM, a discussion in the industry around this traditional division of documents is taking place, and new questions are being raised: Is this a viable and sustainable practice in the context of a BIM workflow? Can a BIM model redefine the types of documents that are created throughout the life of a project? Do we even need paper documents to build the building, or is a live, up-to date BIM model that actual deliverable? The divisions in BIM aren't as rigid as they have been in a legacy 2D workflow. An example of BIM deliverable packages might include:

- Conceptual model and documents, where the basic geometric forms of the building are created

- Design-development model and documents, where the building geometry and major building elements are completely modeled

- Construction model and documents, where the design-development model is embellished with annotations and dimensions and the construction document set is created

This is more than just an elimination of schematic design. It amounts to a restructuring of project deliverables and, more specifically, the deliverable timetable. The traditional percentages of time per phase also no longer apply. This is an important point to remember as you move forward in documentation, because you'll need to adjust your expectations and timeframe to a different delivery methodology. You'll find additional information in the Integrated Practice and Technology in Practice sections of the American Institute of Architects (AIA) website (www.aia.org/IP and www.aia.org/TAP, respectively.)

In Chapter 10, we'll discuss in more detail the creation of construction documents. This chapter will focus on:

> ▪ **View properties**

> ▪ **The sheet**

View Properties

Now that we've covered most of types of views you can create with Revit, we need to discuss how to place those views on sheets. But before you start placing views onto sheets, it's important to know about some critical properties of views that affect how they behave when placed on sheets. There are several ways to access view properties. You can get to the View Property dialog box the following ways:

- Right-click any view in the Project Browser, and choose Properties from the context menu.

- Right-click in the active view window, and choose View Properties from the context menu.

- Right-click any view once it's placed on a sheet, and choose Element Properties from the context menu.

- Select View on sheet and use Properties button to open properties.

- Select a view (left-click it with the mouse) in the Project Browser, and click the Properties button next to the Type Selector.

- Activate a view on the sheet using Activate View, and then use the keyboard shortcut (VP) to go to the view properties.

Element Properties Dialog Box

Like any other element in Revit, views have their own properties. Many of these properties can be displayed as parametric information about the view when views are placed on sheets. This is how Revit handles intelligent viewtitles. Other parameters control how the model is displayed graphically. Here is a list of common properties (Figure 9.2) and how they affect the view:

View Scale This sets the view scale of the drawing. You can similarly set the view scale in the View Control bar in the view window.

Scale Value This sets the drawing scale of the view that will be represented on the sheet.

Scale Value 1 This field is non-editable for the view properties. It shows what your scale value would be if it were translated to an AutoCAD paperspace view. This field dynamically changes as you change the View Scale value above it.

Display Model There are three settings for this field: Normal, As Underlay, and Do Not Display. In Normal, all the cut walls are shown in black. As Underlay grays out all the model contents in the view; it doesn't gray out 2D information like annotations, text, or dimensions. Do Not Display turns off all the model data and shows only the 2D information in the view.

Detail Level This offers three choices: Coarse, Medium, and Fine. Choose one depending on the level of detail you're trying to show in your model.

At larger scales ¼= 1′-0″ (1:20), set the detail level to Coarse. Typically, plans or sections printed at Medium or Fine at this scale have lines so close together that they can't be differentiated on the sheet. Also, a Medium or Fine setting on a complex model can drastically affect load time or print time of that view.

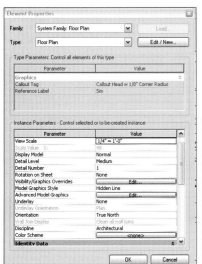

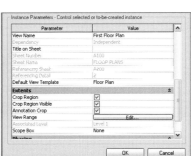

Figure 9.2

Element Properties for views

Detail Number This sets the detail number (such as A1) on the sheet. This number must be unique to each sheet.

Rotation on Sheet This setting gives you the option to rotate the view and view tag to read from the right side of the sheet rather than from the bottom. You might use this prefer-ence if you had a tall building and wall sections didn't fit in a traditional orientation. Note that you're rotating the view, not the model. Once a view is on a sheet, it can be rotated using the Options bar when the view is selected.

Visibility/Graphics Overrides This is an alternate way to access the Visibility/Graphics Overrides dialog box for this view. This dialog controls which elements appear in the view.

Model Graphics Style This controls how your model displays on the screen. By default, it's set to Hidden. Other choices are Wireframe, Shaded, and "Shaded with Edges." These options are discussed in Chapter 3.

Advanced Model Graphics This option brings up the Advanced Model Graphics dialog box, which controls shadows and shading. You can also access this dialog through the View Control bar at the bottom of the view window.

Underlay This option lets you choose another level of the building to be shown in a light-gray tone as an underlay to this view. This is especially useful if you're trying to align walls with a floor below or when you want to make a reference to a roof from the level above.

Underlay Orientation This option is available only if you've chosen to put an underlay into your current view. You can set whether you want to see the floor plan or the ceiling plan of your underlay.

> Underlays are thought of in the 2D drafting world as a layer of trace under your current draw-ing. This view is useful for seeing what is happening in another view while working in your active view. In a 3D modeling world, this underlay is a live look at the model—if you delete something shown as underlay, you're deleting the element, not an abstraction.

Orientation The model is typically shown orthogonal to the view you are working in, and this extends to how the view will appear when placed on a sheet. However, in many condi-tions a building doesn't align with the cardinal directions of your screen, and printed page. Orientation lets you align your view with either the project north (screen and sheet north) or to True North (how the building is located relative to the earth).

Discipline This sets the discipline (architecture, structure, mechanical, electrical, or coor-dination) of the view in the document set. This is useful for sorting views in the Project Browser.

Color Scheme This will add a Color Scheme to the view, and allow you to edit an existing Color Scheme. Use this to create color-coded plan views. This parameter is only available for plan views.

Dependency Views that are made as dependent views report which view they depend on. A dependent view displays the annotations of the parent view. If a view is not a dependent, it's listed as Independent.

Title on Sheet This field allows you to override the name of a view as it appears on the sheet. By default, or if this field is left blank, Revit will make the name on the sheet identical to the name of the view.

Annotation Crop This enables a second crop region that only hides/unhides annotations that are outside of it, or intersecting it.

Sheet information The following four fields in the view properties are noneditable in this dialog box:

- Sheet Number
- Referencing Sheet
- Sheet Name
- Referencing Detail

These values are reported from other views in Revit. Sheet Number and Sheet Name can be modified from the sheet they reference and tell you what sheet this view has been placed on. Referencing Sheet and Referencing Detail report which views this sheet references from. In the case of our example plan, we're referencing an elevation on sheet A200.

> If multiple references depend on one view, the first reference created is reported in the View Properties dialog box.

Default View Template This sets the default view template for this view. Creating and editing view templates is covered later in this chapter.

Crop Region This option activates the crop region for a view, which limits the extent of what is visible in the view.

Crop Region Visible This setting makes the crop region visible or invisible for the view.

Annotation Crop This shows the crop boundary of a parent view when views are linked.

View Range This opens the View Range dialog box discussed in Chapter 3.

Associated Level If the view is associated with a particular level (in the case of a floor plan or enlarged plan), it's reported here. This isn't an editable field.

Scope Box If you have scope boxes defined, you can apply them to this view.

Phase Filter This option lets you control which of the defined phase filters (basically, phase combinations) are implemented in this view. You can set the phase filters by choosing **Settings → Phases**.

Phase If you have phases set up in your project, you can change the phase visibility properties for the view here and set a specific phase, such as New Construction.

View Templates

View templates are powerful time savers when you're working on a project. The purpose of a view template is to capture view settings and then apply these settings to many views with the same graphical requirements. They are a great way to ensure graphical consistency between views. View templates can be found by choosing **Settings → View Templates**.

Figure 9.3

View Template dialog box

Different view templates tend to be used for plans, sections, elevations, and details. The View Templates dialog box (Figure 9.3) allows you to create a new view template or modify existing ones. You'll notice that view templates are a subset of view properties. By setting these values, you can create standard view characteristics and push them into other views. In the View Template dialog box, you can preset the following view properties:

- View Scale
- Display Mode
- Detail Level
- Visibility (through the Visibility/Graphics Overrides dialog box)
- Model Graphics Style
- Advanced Model Graphics (through the Advanced Model Graphics dialog box)
- View Range (through the View Range dialog box)
- Orientation
- Phase Filter
- Discipline

Figure 9.4

Create View Template context menu

Although it's possible to preset all your view settings through this dialog box, you may find it easier to set the settings interactively in a view. This way you can see the effects of settings immediately. When you like what you've set up, you can then create a new view template from your active view. Right-clicking any of the views in the Project Browser gives you the option `Create View Template From View` (see Figure 9.4). You can then apply this new view template to any other view.

To apply a view template to another view, select one or more views (not sheets) from the Project Browser, and right-click. Then, choose `Apply View Template` from the context menu. Choose the template you want to apply to the views and Revit will update them all to use the same view properties established in the template.

> Users are sometimes confused about how to delete obsolete view templates. You can do this by choosing **Settings → View Templates**, selecting the template from the Name list, and clicking Delete.

Creating and Applying a View Template

In this exercise, you'll create a new view template and apply it to a view:

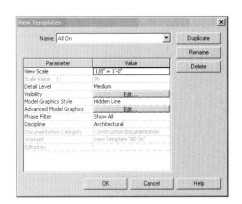

1. Open the Station.rvt model on the CD included with this book, and open the view called Level 3 Pres. Note that there is already a Level 3 view, but this view has been set up to be a presentation-styled view. You want to create a similar view for Level 4.

2. In the Project Browser, right-click the view Level 3 Pres, and choose Create View Template From View.

3. Name the view **Plan Presentation**. Click OK.

4. Right-click the Level 4 view, and choose "Duplicate with Detailing." Doing so creates a new view called "Copy of Level 4."

5. Right-click the view called "Copy of Level 4," and rename it Level 4 Pres. It resorts itself alphabetically in the Project Browser so it appears below the Level 4 view.

6. Right-click the new view, Level 4 Pres, and choose Apply View Template. Choose the new Plan Presentation view template from the list, and click OK.

Figure 9.5

View Templates dialog box

Revit allows you to apply templates to schedule views as well. The workflow is the same as with any other view, allowing automatic propagation of graphic definitions from one schedule to other schedules in the project.

The Sheet

Construction documents are how architects convey their ideas and designs on paper to the contractor or builder so that they can build the building. The information conveyed must be sufficient and organized well enough for the builder to understand the design intent of the documents. Conflicts, errors, omissions, and coordination issues can and will occur on any document prepared by human hands. These discrepancies are magnified on the job site as cost overruns, RFIs, or lost schedule time. The goal of a good set of documents is to minimize the number of errors and convey the design clearly. Revit excels in this process by automatically managing your views and references and thereby eliminating many common errors found in traditional document sets.

Perhaps the mostly widely used type of architectural sheet system is the ConDoc system supported by the AIA. This system has identifiers for sheet name and numbering formats. If you're new to creating architectural sheets, or you're looking for additional information about construction document standards, the AIA's "Best Practices" white paper for construction documents is a good starting point:

```
http://www.aia.org/SiteObjects/files/bp%2018_05_02.pdf
```

Most firms have a defined graphic standard for sheet layout. If you're responsible for creating office-standard content, such as sheets, you should take a bit of time to create Revit sheets that mirror your firm standards *before* you get started on a project. Not only will you then have them when you're ready to go forward into production, but you'll gain experience working with Revit families.

Before you load a sheet into your project, notice the sheet border. In the title block exercise in this section, the border is an invisible line that traces the extents of the sheet. If you move your mouse over the outside border of the sheet, the invisible lines highlight. Invisible lines are a line type that is similar to a nonplot line; they don't graphically interfere with the view on the screen.

Adding a Title Block to a Sheet

Title blocks in Revit are similar to any other family. You can create and edit them with the Family Editor. Like tags, title blocks use intelligent labels built into the family to pull data from the Revit model or the particular view and apply it to the title block. This can be in the form of the view scale, project name, project address, or any parameter you see fit to use in your title blocks. To get an idea of how these labels work, let's add one to an existing sheet. This exercise presents a basic description of how to add labels and other data to your sheets:

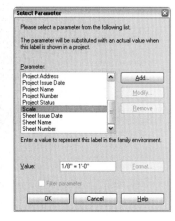

Figure 9.6

Select Parameter dialog box

1. Open the `Presentation - 11 x 17.rfa` file found on the CD included with this book. The file automatically opens in the Family Editor.

   This is a simple 11″ × 17″ title block. As with any sheet, you can add as much or as little detail as you want. In this sheet, you'll add a graphic scale.

2. Click the Label button (⊘ Label) on the Family tab, and choose Field Text from the Type Selector.

3. Click to drop the text in the desired location on the sheet.

4. The Select Parameter dialog box (Figure 9.6) opens and asks what kind of label you'd like to add. From this list, choose Scale.

This process adds a label to the sheet and shows its default value (in this example, ⅛″ = 1′-0″). As you bring views onto the sheet, this value parametrically changes to reflect the scale of the views on the sheets.

Your sheet border may fluctuate depending on your printer type. For instance, an 11″ × 17″ printer typically has a print range of 10.5″ × 16.5″, or ¼″ margins around the edges. On some printers, printing at paper size can lead to minor distortion of the scale of the printed views. Depending on your printer type, you may need to set your sheet size to fit within the printer margins rather than set it to the actual paper size. Once the sheet has been created, you can load it into your project by clicking the "Load into Projects" (⬆ Load into Projects) button on the Family tab; or, in your project, you can use the options under **File → Load from Library → Load Family**.

Adding a Revision Schedule

Revit allows you to add revision clouds and tags to sheets for tracking changes in the document set. These can be automatically tracked and displayed in a Revision Schedule on your titleblock. To place a revision schedule into a titleblock, follow these steps:

1. Open an existing titleblock family, or choose to make a new one.
2. From the Project Browser, open the Schedules node. You will see a Revision Schedule view. Drag and drop this view into your titleblock.
3. To modify the graphics and fields used in the revision schedule, right-click on the Revision Schedule in the Project Browser and open Properties. In the Fields parameter, you can use common fields such as Revision number, Description, Date, and Issued To. (Figure 9.7)
4. When the titleblock is loaded into your project, and you begin to add Revisions to your project, the table will automatically fill out. (Figure 9.8)

To add Revisions, go to **Settings → Revisions**. From this dialog box, you can add Revision information that will then show up in the revision schedule on your sheets. You can have revisions enumerate on a per-sheet basis, or on a project-wide basis. When you add Revision clouds to your sheets, set which revision it belongs to, and you'll be good to go.

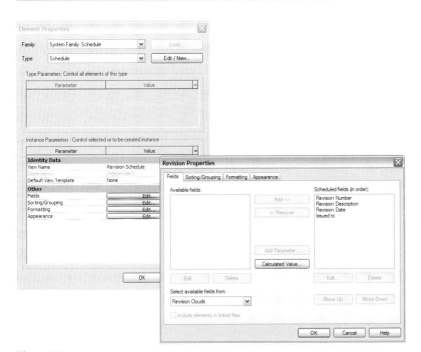

Figure 9.7

Fields available for use in a revision schedule

No.	Description	Date
1	Revision 1	3/11/07
2	Revision 2	4/12/07

Figure 9.8

The revision schedule will fill up as you add revisions to the project

The View Title

A key component of a view placed on a sheet is the view title. These elements are tags that live on the sheet (see Figure 9.9) and display information about the view. Common information includes view name, scale, and detail number.

> View titles are families like every other element in Revit, but they have a slightly different access point for editing the graphics. You can edit most families in Revit on the fly by selecting the family and choosing the Edit Family button from the Options bar. However, some families don't show this button when selected. These include view titles, level tags, callout heads, and section heads. To edit one of these types of families, locate it in the Project Browser under **Families → Annotations**. Right-click the family, and select the Edit option from the context menu. Doing so opens the family in the Family Editor. Editing options are similar to those available for sheets (explained earlier in this chapter) and other tags.

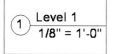

Figure 9.9

Sample view title

The view title appears automatically when you place a view on a sheet. When the view is placed, the labels are automatically populated with the correct information about the view. The detail number (in Figure 9.9, it's 1) automatically increases by 1 for each view placed on the sheet. (You can change this number to a letter, or a number/letter sequence like A1.) If the view placed on a sheet is referenced from an elevation, a section, or a callout, the detail number is automatically propagated into the view markers in the other views. If you change the detail number, it updates the tags in the other views. Basically, this means that your references are always correct on any sheet and in any view. It's impossible for views to be out of sync.

> Detail numbers must be unique on each sheet. Revit doesn't allow for duplicates.

View titles are tags that report information about a view. If you select a view title on the sheet and go to properties, you'll see information about the view it is tagging. The element is called the Viewport. From the type properties of the viewport, you can edit some graphic parameters for the view title such as color, whether to show the view title or not, and if the view title has an extension line.

Figure 9.10

Turning off the title

If you don't want a view title to display on a sheet (as in a presentation drawing), duplicate the view title from the Type Selector, and set the view title properties to show no title and no extension line (see Figure 9.10). You don't need to create a new view title family for this purpose.

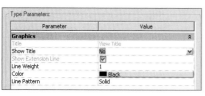

Take care when you modify the properties of a view title. Changing a view title type changes *all* the views on all the sheets of that type. That may not necessarily be the desired effect.

Placing Views on Sheets

To place a view onto a sheet requires a drag and drop from the project browser. You can drag views from the project browser onto a sheet name in the Project Browser, which will open the sheet view and let you place the view; or you can first open the sheet view, and then drag views onto the sheet from the Project Browser. If you don't have a sheet view set up, create a new sheet view by choosing **View Tab → Sheet**. Doing so opens a dialog box where you choose what type of sheet to make. Choose a sheet, and a new sheet view is created and opened. You can then start dragging and dropping any view name from the Project Browser on to the sheet (so long as the view has not already been placed on a sheet). You can place the view anywhere on the sheet, and it will be tagged with a view title.

With the exception of legend views, it's important to point out that you can't put a view onto more than one sheet. Each view is a unique, living picture of the model. Although this may not seem intuitive at first, it makes sense given that all views are guaranteed to report correct information about what sheet they're on.

If views placed on a sheet don't fit in the space you have available, there are a couple of ways to mitigate the situation. The size of the view relative to the sheet is based on two things:

- View scale
- View extents

The view scale determines the architectural scale and can be modified, as discussed earlier. In most cases, the scale is correct, but the overall size of the view may be too large. If this is the case, there are two ways to solve this problem.

First, you can move annotations and symbols closer to the model, and tighten up the graphics to reduce the amount of empty white space. This approach buys you some precious sheet real estate. See Figure 9.11 for an example.

Moving a view marker is different from moving the view itself. For example, you can move an elevation symbol by grabbing the view tag without moving the front clipping plane of the elevation. In Figure 9.12, the physical extent and location of the elevation remain the same, but the tag has been repositioned.

Figure 9.11

Tightening up a view

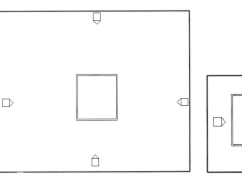

View before optimizing sheet usage   View after optimizing sheet usage

Figure 9.12

Clipping plane location in the elevation tag

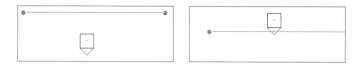

Section marks behave in similar fashion. The blue controls at the base of the head and tail graphics let you make the graphic footprint of the symbol smaller or larger without affecting the extent of the view it's referencing (shown as dashed lines in Figure 9.13).

The second option to make your views fit on the sheet is to modify the view's crop region. Turning the crop region on and off was discussed in detail in Chapter 2. Modifying the crop region changes the actual size of the view and can also hide areas you don't want to show on a particular sheet. In Figure 9.14, the crop region is described by the lines bordering the view. Although there is much more to see of the model at this floor, the crop region has been minimized to show only this unit. By drawing in the crop boundaries, you can make the view smaller to display only the information necessary for that view.

From the sheet view, Revit lets you edit views directly in order to make changes to view in the context of sheet layout. Select any view on a sheet, and right-click to bring up the context menu. Selecting Activate View grays out the sheet and other views placed on the sheet, and lets you directly edit the view as if you had opened the view normally. You can then manipulate annotations, model data, and the crop region. When you're done editing the view, right-click in the view to bring up the context menu, and choose Deactivate View. This drops you back into sheet view.

While you're creating documents, you may decide to move a view to a different sheet than the one it's on. To do so, grab it from the sheet list in the Project Browser, and drag and drop it to the new sheet name in the list.

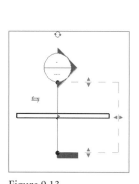

Figure 9.13

Clipping plane location in the section tag

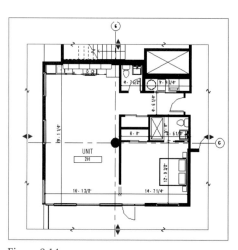

Figure 9.14

Crop region

Splitting views across multiple sheets

There are some view improvements in version 2008 that extend how you can place views on a sheet when the view is too large to fit on a single sheet. The improvements create a coordinated way to relate views to one another such that you can work in one primary view, and have your work appear in other, dependent views. They are available via the new way of duplicating a view called "Duplicate as Dependent."

To understand this, let us review in more detail the three methods of duplicating a view that we touched upon in Chapter 3.

DUPLICATE

Duplicate will make an exact copy of the model elements in a view and will ignore any annotations and view-specific detail work existing in the original view. The resulting duplicated view will have no annotations or details in it. It will show 3D annotations such as levels, grids, and reference planes.

Dependency Model changes that happen in either the original view or in the duplicated view will propagate to the other. Annotations added in any of the two will NOT propagate to the other view.

Use case You will select this method of duplication when you need to make a presentation drawing of a plan in which you do not wish to see any dimensions, tags, or text existing in the original view. This method is applicable when you need to produce nice images of a project for publication purposes or marketing material ordered by your client.

DUPLICATE WITH DETAILING

"Duplicate with Detailing" will make an exact copy of the model, annotations, and detail elements. The new view will look exactly like the original.

You use this method when you wish to continue developing a plan to a different level of detail than the original.

Dependency Model changes that happen in either the original view or in the duplicated view will propagate to the other. Annotations added in any of the two will *not* propagate to the other view.

Use case Examples for this would be when you need to make a detailed plan of a typical hotel room from a hotel floor, or a technical detail of a how a column penetrates a wall, and so on.

DUPLICATE AS DEPENDENT

"Duplicate As Dependent" will make an exact copy of model, annotations, and detail elements. This type of duplication also maintains a dependency between the view that is duplicated and the original view. If an annotation is deleted in either view, it is deleted from both views.

Dependencies: Whatever changes happen in *any* of the two views (the original or the duplicated view) will propagate.

Use case scenarios: Use this method when you work on very large projects when the plans you wish to print in a certain scale do not fit the maximum sheet/plot sizes. You would in this case split the plan in many portions but they will maintain the dependencies with the other parts so they are all coordinated in both model as well as annotation aspect. Another use scenario is when you need to place the same view on different sheets. Note that when we say same it really means same: you cannot change scale or any other view properties of a dependent view, and not have these propagate. The only allowed and possible differences between dependent views are per view visual and graphical overrides (hiding an element or category or graphically overriding an element or category).

As Duplicate As Dependent is new to the 2008 release and has some extended capabilities, let us review this concept in detail.

Scenario: You have a large project and you drag the floor plan onto a sheet. You realize that the plan is too big for that sheet and that splitting it into separate pieces will be necessary.

You *duplicate as dependent* the original floor plan. If you need more than two spilt views in order to fit the plans onto sheet, then duplicate as many views as you think you need. In the example shown, two dependent views will be needed but as you can imagine, in bigger projects this could range from to 6–8 dependent views.

Figure 9.15

Dependent View allows you to split views and place them on separate sheets

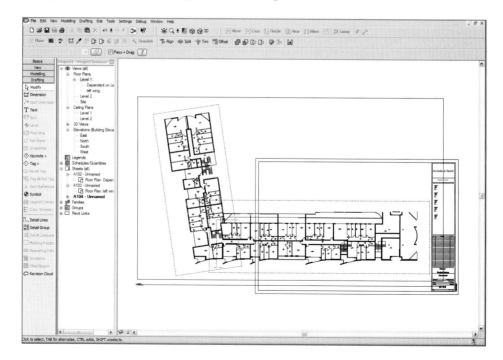

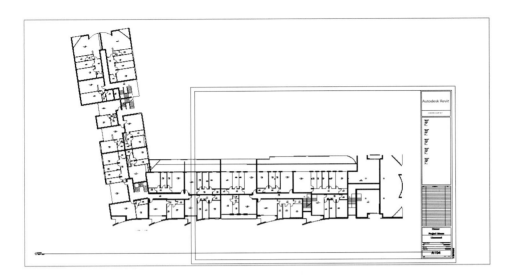

Figure 9.16

The plan does not fit on one sheet

After creating duplicate views as dependent views, each view is cropped so that it will fit the sheet. You will notice with dependent views that the annotation crop is enabled by default. This is to keep annotations from other parts of the parent view from showing up in your cropped view. After manipulating the crop region of both views, you will end up with two dependent views, each focusing on one section of the building:

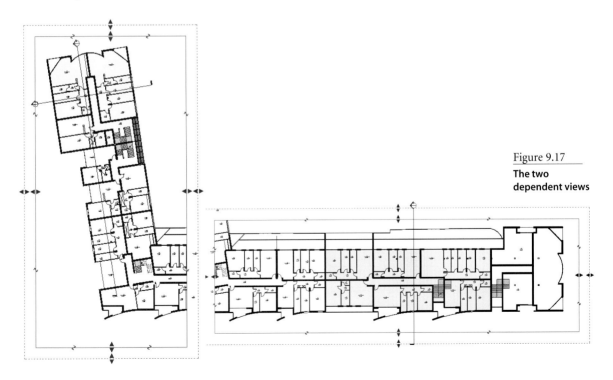

Figure 9.17

The two dependent views

Note the double crop region: the outer boundary is the annotation crop; the inner is the model crop. When you drag the blue grips of the model crop, the annotation will follow along at a preset offset distance. Manipulating just the annotation crop has no effect on the model crop, and you cannot drag the annotation crop inside of the model crop.

If you go back to the original view and press the Show Crop toggle in the view bar, you will see both the crop regions of the dependent views, and thus see how they relate to one another.

In our example, and this can be quite typical, one wing of the building may be at an oblique angle relative to the screen, and by extension, the sheet. Revit provides a way to orient each dependent view so that it can better fit a sheet.

Figure 9.18

Original view with crop region visibility turned on

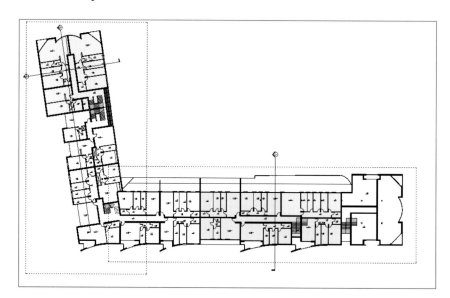

Figure 9.19

This wing of the building needs to be oriented to better fit the sheet

To accomplish this task, in Sheet View, Activate the dependent view, select the crop region of the dependent view, and rotate it. During the rotation you will notice a green help line that finds angles of reference and can help you rotate the view parallel to the main axis of the wing.

You can accomplish the same rotation by opening the Dependent View itself, and then rotating the crop region. Do not attempt to rotate dependent view crop regions from the original "parent" view.

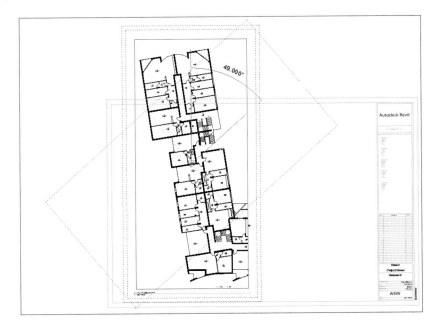

Figure 9.20

The crop region can be rotated such that the view is rotated parallel with the model.

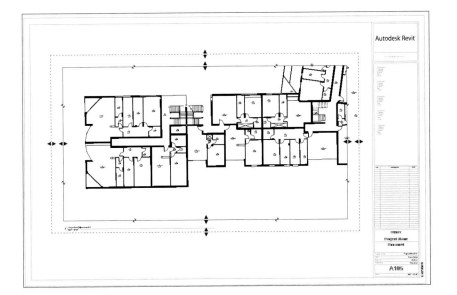

Figure 9.21

The plan now fits the sheet.

You will also notice that rotating a dependent view will also reorient the tags in the view so they remain readable on the sheet.

Whenever you are in any of the dependent views, you can see the other view by selecting the Crop/Do Not Crop view option in the View bar. This will turn off the cropping and the other views will show up displaying the crop boundaries that are inactive.

As you continue working with a project divided between multiple dependent views, you will notice that any addition or change to annotation as well as model elements will appear in all views associated with the original parent view.

One very neat detail: Imagine your project has 20+ floors and the size was such that you needed to divide it into 4 dependent views. After you have spent time dividing the first 4 on Level 1, you need to do the same thing for the remaining 20+ floors. Revit streamlines this process for you. In the right-click menu of the original view that you made the dependent views from, there is an option to Apply Dependent Views that will open a dialog box where you select all the views you wish to apply the same dependent view division to. With one click, this will create dependent views in the same manner of each selected view you selected.

Figure 9.22

Tags have been smartly rotated to be legible.

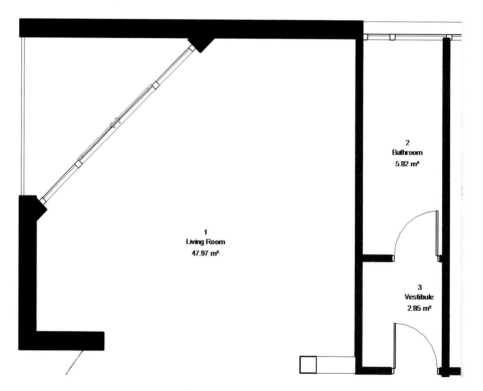

MATCHLINES AND VIEW TAGS

Matchlines are graphic indicators in plan views that depict a split in the drawing because the whole building could not fit on a sheet. In Revit, the Matchline is a 3D line that extends (as grid lines do) through the entire project.

The Matchline tool can be found in the Views design bar and is drawn as you would any other line in Revit. In the properties of a Matchline you can define the top and the bottom constraint. This is needed when the building does not have the same floor plan so that the division in dependent views might not be applicable to all views in the same way.

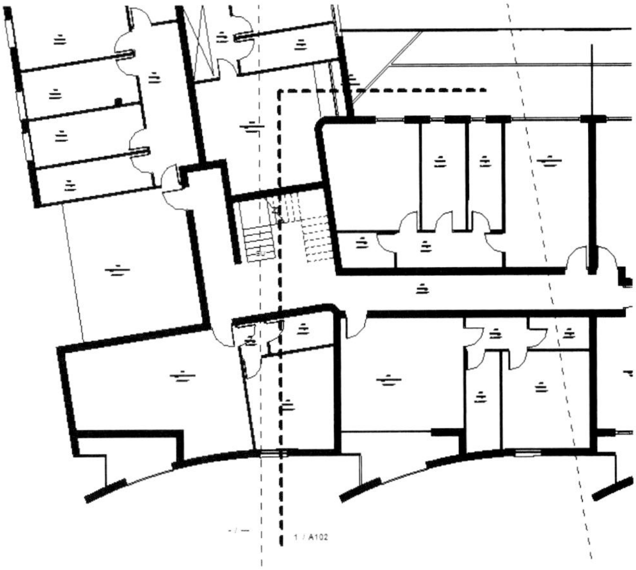

VIEW REFERENCES

View references are a special type of annotation applicable to views only. What they do is reference other dependent views and hyperlink to them.

You will find the View reference under the Views design bar. If you are in dependent view, and select a view reference, it will instantly recognize the other dependent view and create a reference and hyperlink to it. If you are in the original view when more dependent views are present, you can select the view reference tool, hover over a crop region of a view you want to reference, and place the view reference.

Note: the view reference will be empty if the dependent view is not placed on a sheet. The moment you place it on a sheet it will fill in the number of the reference.

Figure 9.23

The matchline indicates a break in the view.

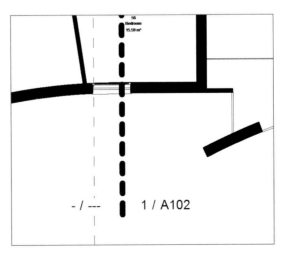

Figure 9.24

View reference tags for two dependent views: one placed on a sheet and another one not.

A few more tips about dependent views:

- When you "Duplicate as dependent view," the dependent view will appear as a node under the original view in the Project Browser.

- A dependent view can at any point be converted to an independent view. You can do that in two different ways:

    - Right-click on the dependent view and "Duplicate with Detailing." This will keep the dependent view *and* create a new independent view.

    - Right-click on the dependent view and select "Convert to independent view."

CHAPTER 10

Construction Documentation

No set of documents is complete without the annotations that describe the drawings. Even in a parametric model, it's good to supply dimensions, tags, and text to aid in communicating the design and construction intent.

In the previous chapter, you worked with title blocks and positioned views onto sheets. In this chapter, we'll go into more detail about preparing those views for a construction document set. Specifically, we'll talk about:

- Formatting your sheets

- Annotating your views

- Tags

- Dimensions

- Text and keynotes

- Schedules

- Drafting views

- Importing CAD details

- Drafting tools

Formatting Your Sheets

When you begin documenting your project, most of your modeling should be complete. That doesn't necessarily mean that you have all your views established or all your sections cut, but it's helpful if the majority of your building geometry is in place.

To illustrate, let's go back to the house you've been working on. By this point, the model's geometry should be established; to begin the documentation, let's create a series of views using that model. You've already established views in the model. Some were in the Revit template file, and you made others while creating the model. However, the views you currently have for the floor plans are set up as presentation-style views, not as construction documents. Therefore, you need to create new views, customize their appearance, and put them onto sheets.

Laying Out Sheets

The following exercise will help get you started documenting the house. We will begin making some views and placing them on construction document sheets.

1. Open Source_House.rvt in the Chapter 10 folder on the CD included with this book.

2. To start, you'll duplicate Level 1 and Level 2 using the Project Browser. To do this, right-click the view name, and choose Duplicate View → Duplicate. Doing so creates a new view called "Copy of (*ViewName*)."

3. Rename the view "Copy of Level 1" to First Floor Plan by right-clicking the view name and choosing Rename. Use the same process to rename the view "Copy of Level 2" to Second Floor Plan.

The First Floor Plan view has a graphical appearance that doesn't match the Second Floor Plan view. Both views need to have the same fundamental graphical appearance. To do this, you'll create a new view template using the Second Floor Plan view as a baseline. You can then apply this template to the first floor plan so the two views have a consistent appearance.

Before making the view template, you need to make some graphical adjustments to the view. First, turn on the Sections and Elevations annotations:

1. Open the view Second Floor and choose View → Visibility Graphics from the menu.

2. Select the Annotation categories tab. Make sure the Sections and Elevations check boxes are selected. Click OK.

Another way to make hidden categories visible is to use the Reveal Hidden Elements mode. Click the lightbulb icon in the view controls, and the hidden sections and elevations will show up as a deep red color in the view. Select the annotations, and click the Unhide Categories button on the option bar. Click the lightbulb icon again to exit the mode.

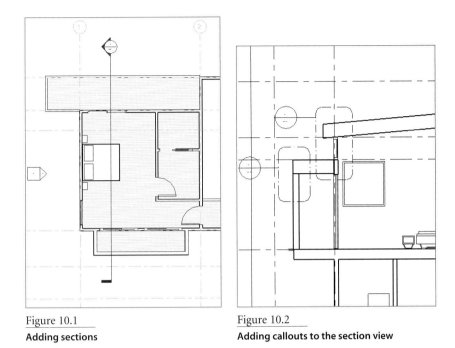

Figure 10.1

Adding sections

Figure 10.2

Adding callouts to the section view

3. In the Project Browser, right-click the Second Floor Plan view, and choose Create View Template from View.

4. Name the view template Floor Plan, and click OK. A dialog box appears; click OK again.

5. Right-click the First Floor Plan view, and choose Apply View Template. What you have just done is to unify the look of the First Floor and the Second Floor.

6. Choose Floor Plan from the list, and click OK.

Next, you need to create some additional views of the model: sections and callouts. Follow these steps:

1. Open the Second Floor Plan view, and cut a wall section through the west end of the house as shown in Figure 10.1. After creating this section, it will be pointed in the wrong direction. Using the Flip tool, flip the section cut to point in the other direction.

2. In the Section 3 view, create two callout views using the Callout tool on the View tab of the Design Bar. One callout should focus on the south clerestory condition, and the other should focus on the northern window in the stairwell. See Figure 10.2 for callout locations. Rename the details you have just created Detail 1 and Detail 2.

To reposition the callout Tag, select any of the callout lines and use the blue grips to reposition or resize the tag or the box.

Now that you have some views, you can begin laying them out on sheets. There is a sheet template on the CD that accompanied this book; let's use a few of these. You need one for plans; one for elevations; and one for details, sections, and 3D views. When you add sheets, they appear in the Project Browser under the Sheets node. Follow these steps:

1. Right-click mouse click on Sheets in the Project browser, and select New Sheet from the context menu. In the next dialog, choose Load and browse to the file named `Presentation.rfa` in the chapter 10 folder provided with the CD. Press OK.

2. The Sheet view will become your active view. Repeat this step three times, so that you have three sheets in the project.

Figure 10.3

Modifying the sheet name from in the view

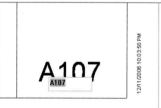

3. Rename the sheets as follows: A100 Floor Plans; A200 Elevations; and A300 Sections, and 3D views. A300–Section 1, Callout of Section 1, Callout (2) of Section 1, and 3D View (1). To do this, right-click the sheet name in the Project Browser, and choose Rename to bring up a renaming dialog. You can also rename the sheet interactively in the view when the sheet is opened. Click the blue text of the sheet name, and the text becomes active text field. Be sure to change the sheet name as well as the sheet number when you're editing from the sheet itself (see Figure 10.3).

With a sheet view opened, you can drag a view from the Project Browser into the view, and drop it onto the sheet:

1. Select the view name with the left mouse button, and then drag it into the sheet view. A preview graphic of the view extents appears to aid in placement.

2. When you get the view approximately where you want it, release the mouse button. The view drops into place.

Each view is assigned a unique number once it's placed on the sheet. This is referred to as the *detail number*, and it appears as a parameter of the view once it has been placed on a sheet.

For the next exercise, lay out the sheets with the following views on them:

• *A100*—First floor plan and second floor plan

• *A200*—North elevation and south elevation

• *A300*—A300–Section 1, Section 3, and 3D View (1)

Notice that on sheet A100, the two plans don't fit nicely on the sheet; they look something like Figure 10.4. Obviously, it's vital to be able to produce drawings that read clearly and easily. Revit provides control over the sizes of your views as they appear on the sheets, so it's easy to fix issues like this.

You can do this directly from the sheet, giving you real-time feedback about the view and its relation to the sheet:

1. Open Sheet A100. Mouse over one of the views on the sheet, and right-click.

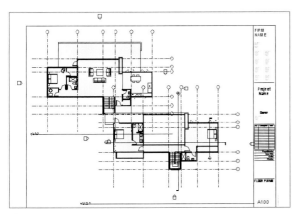

Figure 10.4

Plans initially don't fit on the sheet.

Figure 10.5

Floor plans arranged

2. Select Activate View.

3. Use the View Control bar to select Show Crop Region. The lightbulb in the icon turns yellow, indicating that the crop region is on.

> To make minor adjustments to a view location, select the view and use the arrows on the keyboard to nudge it around. The tighter you're zoomed in on a view, the smaller the increment of movement is.

4. Finish laying out the other two sheets. A200 and A300 should look like Figures 10.6 and 10.7, respectively.

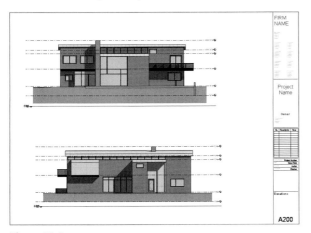

Figure 10.6

A200

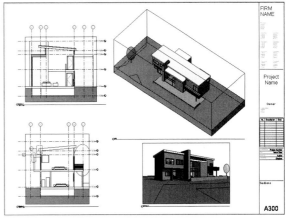

Figure 10.7

A300

In a typical, professional-looking sheet arrangement, especially when you have multiple views (plans or elevations) on a sheet, it's common to line up gridlines. Revit automatically aligns the grids between views on the sheet when you drag views. Select a view, and drag it—a snap-alignment line appears when grids are lined up with grids in the other views. On your elevation sheet, this alignment graphic doesn't appear because you're using opposite elevations, and the grids are opposite each other. Revit also provides snap alignments between levels from view to view. This comes in handy when you lay out a sheet with multiple wall sections, and you want the levels to all be lined up relative to one another on the sheet.

Annotating Your Views

In any set of documents, showing geometry alone isn't sufficient to communicate all the information a builder or fabricator needs to construct the building. Tags, keynotes, text, and dimensions all need to be added to the drawing in order to clearly and concisely guide construction. Revit provides tools for doing precisely that. They assist you in taking your model data and clearly documenting it for others to read and understand.

Starting where you left off, with some views placed on sheets, you'll continue to build out your set of drawings by adding annotations to the views.

> Annotations, dimensions, and tags are placed in the views themselves, not on the sheet. This allows you to annotate a view at any point in the process, before or after views have been placed on a sheet.

Tags

Tags are textual labels for doors, walls, windows, rooms, and a host of other objects that architects typically need to reference in a set of drawings. In Revit, tags are intelligent bidirectional symbols that report information stored in the properties of an element. A value can be directly edited from the tag; likewise, editing an element's properties affects the tag. Selecting a wall tag, for example (Figure 10.8), returns the wall type that is set in the properties of the wall itself; but it can show much more information than that, such as the wall's fire rating or manufacturer.

Figure 10.8

The default wall tag in Revit

Loading Tags

Revit comes with a variety of generic tags. All of these can be customized to meet your office's graphic requirements. The set of tags that is preloaded into the default template covers many common requirements but is by no means exhaustive.

Every category can be tagged, and you can load multiple types of tags for each category. Tags are loaded like any other family or component in Revit. Go to File → Load from Library → Load Family, and navigate to the tag you want to add to the project.

Placing Tags

You can insert tags from the Tag button on the Drafting tab. (See Figure 10.9.)

During tag placement, the Options bar lets you position a tag in several ways. Figure 10.10 shows how the Options bar appears in this circumstance. The Tag button allows you to load additional tags without having to cancel the command and go back to the Load Families tool. If you click this button but don't have a tag loaded, you're prompted to do so.

Tags can have a horizontal or vertical orientation and may or may not have a leader line. In the case of a wall tag, you typically have a leader coming from the wall, whereas you don't use a leader with a door or window tag.

Tags dynamically adjust to the scale of the drawing. If the text of a tag is set to read at ⅛″ (3mm), it appears in the view at such a size to always print at ⅛″ (3mm). (See Figure 10.11.)

The Tag button presents three options:

By Category This option allows you to tag elements in the model by category or type. Examples are doors, walls, windows, and other commonly tagged elements. After you choose By Category, the elements you can tag highlight as you mouse over them in your view. Revit also displays a ghost image of the tag you're inserting and the value in that tag, as shown in Figure 10.12.

Multi-Category Use the Multi-Category tag when you want to tag an element across different family types—for instance, when you're using a similar glazing type in your windows and exterior doors and you want to be able to tag the glazing consistently. The Multi-Category tag allows you to have the same tag and tag value for the glazing in both families. (Fire rating is another common application of this tag.)

Material The Material tag lets you tag the materials in a given family. For example, tagging a wall by material exposes materials used in the wall construction. This allows you to tag the gypsum board and studs separately.

Figure 10.9

The Drafting tab

Figure 10.10

The Options bar when a tag is inserted

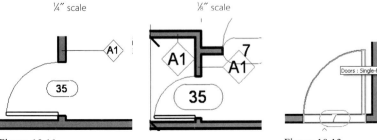

Figure 10.11

Tags change with the view scale.

Figure 10.12

Tagging by category

Figure 10.13

Changing the wall type

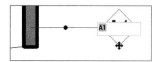

URL	
Description	
Assembly Description	Exterior Walls
Assembly Code	B2010
Type Mark	A1
Fire Rating	
Cost	

The Properties dialog box

Changing a Tag Value

There are two ways to modify text in a tag. Selecting the tag makes the text an active control and turns the text blue; just click the blue text and start typing. The second option is to go to the properties of the element being tagged. Using a wall example again, if you select the wall, go to its properties, and change the Type Mark field, the wall tag updates to reflect this. See Figure 10.13 for examples of each location.

Whichever way you choose, you change the symbol text for every instance of that tag type. Therefore, if you change a wall type from A1 to A2, you change every instance of that wall that was previously tagged A1. If 10 walls were tagged A1, all 10 are now A2.

Only if you use the first method to modify text—changing it directly in the tag—are you notified that you're making a global change (see Figure 10.14).

Figure 10.14

Changing all type parameters

Some tags only report instance values—values that are unique to the individual element. A room tag or door tag is a common example. The room-tag graphics are consistent, but the room name varies from room to room. Doors are often tagged like this, with a unique numeric value for each door. With these types of tags, Revit detects if you enter duplicate values and warns you when that happens.

> **Revit**
>
> **?** You are changing a type parameter. This could affect many elements. Continue?
>
> Yes   No

When you're creating elements that you plan to tag, you can add the tag text directly into the properties of the family or element. To do this, go to the Properties dialog box, and modify the Type Mark field. This field is identically named in every family.

Tag All Not Tagged

You can tag many elements at once using the Tag All Not Tagged tool on the Drafting tab (see Figure 10.9). This time-saving feature lets you tag all the elements in a view simultaneously. During early phases of design, you often aren't concerned with tags and annotations but are more focused on the model. Tags can become graphic clutter that obscures the design at times.

Later in the process, when you're happy with the design, you may want to annotate the drawing quickly. This is where the Tag All Not Tagged tool is helpful. When you select this tool, the dialog box shown in Figure 10.15 appears. You can orient your tag or add a leader to it before tagging all the listed elements in your current view.

If you have elements selected, you can choose to tag only the selected elements. Note that this option is grayed out in the sample dialog box in Figure 10.15 because nothing in the model is selected.

In the Source_House file you've been using, open the view called First Floor Plan. In this view, using the tools mentioned, let's add tags for the doors and walls:

1. Select Tag → By Category.

2. Mouse over the door, and click when it highlights. Make sure your leaders are turned off in the Options bar for door tags.

3. Highlight and select the interior walls. For wall tags, make sure to turn on your leaders, but adjust the leader size in the Options bar to ¼″ rather than ½″. The finished floor plan looks like Figure 10.16.

Figure 10.15

Tag All Not Tagged dialog

Dimensions

Dimensions are used to convey the distance between elements or parts of elements. In Revit, a dimension is a bidirectional annotation that essentially tags distance. You can edit the distance directly when elements are selected; likewise, the dimension updates automatically as the distance between elements changes. Dimensions are annotations, making them view-specific elements that appear only in the view where they're drawn.

Figure 10.16

Finished floor plan

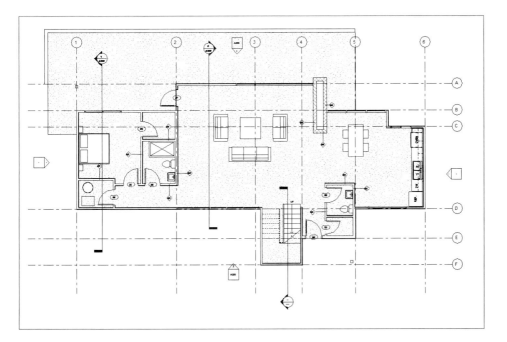

Figure 10.17

**Dimensions dynami-
cally change by
scale.**

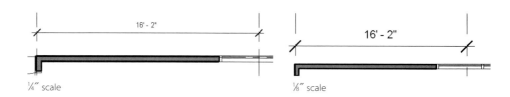

The parametric nature of dimensions in Revit means that dimensions can't be overridden as they can be in CAD. This preserves the integrity of the model and the design. If you hear that Revit won't let you "cheat," it's true.

Dimensions in Revit report the actual value of the distance they span. If the distance is 4′-0″ (120cm), the dimension reads 4′-0″ (120cm). You can't modify the text of the dimension to read anything other than its actual value. If, in this example, the distance was supposed to be 3′-6″ (106cm), you would need to modify the distance between the elements.

Dimensions adjust to the scale of the drawing. Like tags, dimensions always appear at the proper scale in the view. If you change the view scale, the dimensions automatically resize. In Figure 10.17, the first image shows the dimensions at ¼″ scale, and the second image shows the same dimension string after the scale was changed to ⅛″ in the View Control bar.

Figure 10.18

Enlarged door jamb

By default, a linear string of dimensions only dimensions parallel entities. Dimensions in Revit always read from the bottom or the right. This follows standard architectural sheet layout conventions. Dimensions auto-snap horizontally or vertically to align with another dimension string if they're close to being in line with each other.

To dimension non-coplanar entities, such as two walls, select the first element. Then, before selecting the second element, use the Tab key to cycle through the selection options until you highlight a point, as shown in the enlarged door jamb in Figure 10.18.

The finished dimension appears in Figure 10.19.

Figure 10.19

**The finished
dimension**

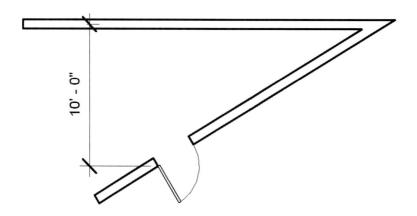

Adding Dimensions

You can find the Dimension tool () on both the Basics and Drafting tabs.

To create dimensions, select the Dimension tool, and begin picking references to dimension. Parallel references highlight as the mouse moves over them, indicating a valid dimension candidate. After two references are selected, a preview graphic of the dimension line appears and moves with the mouse. When you've finished selecting references, move the dimension string to the desired location, and click empty screen space to finish the string.

Figure 10.20
Dimensions Options bar

When you add dimensions in Revit, use the Tab key to cycle though the selection options.

Once the Dimension tool is activated, buttons on the Options bar (see Figure 10.20) let you choose the type of dimension to create; they preset some behaviors to aid in placement. Here are the buttons in the order in which they're listed (from left to right) on the Options bar:

Aligned This is the default dimension style. It places dimensions of elements parallel to the element itself. In the case of an angled wall, the dimension reads parallel to the angled wall. (See Figure 10.21.)

Linear Linear dimensions are parallel to the sheet edges. In the case of your angled wall, the dimension is parallel to the bottom of the sheet, as shown in Figure 10.21.

Angular This option dimensions the angle between two elements.

Radial This option dimensions the radius of an arc or circle.

Arc Length This option returns the length of an arc.

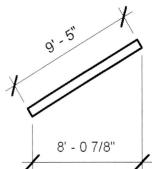

Figure 10.21
Aligned and linear dimensions

The other choices on the Options bar allow you to choose your preferred pick points:

Prefer This gives you the option to choose what references in walls you want the dimension to prefer during placement. You can change what a dimension prefers during placement by using the Tab key to cycle through nearby references. The options shown in Figure 10.22 are "Wall centerlines", "Wall faces", "Center of core", and "Face of core".

Pick This gives you the option to either choose individual references in sequence using the Individual References option or use the Entire Wall option, in which case you click walls and Revit automatically finds the ends of the walls and puts a dimension there. The Entire Wall option can be further refined so door and window openings are auto-dimensioned as well.

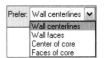

Figure 10.22
Prefer wall dimension locations

Modifying Dimension Appearance

By selecting a dimension and going to its properties, you uncover a host of options, shown in Figure 10.23. You can also access this dialog box and settings by choosing Settings → Annotations → Dimensions → Linear.

First, we'll discuss the parameters for which you can set values. These are listed in the upper pane of the dialog box:

Type Properties ✕

Family:	System Family: Linear Dimension Style ▾	Load...
Type:	Linear - 3/32" Arial ▾	Duplicate...
		Rename...

Type Parameters:

Parameter	Value
Tick Mark	Diagonal 1/8"
Line Weight	1
Tick Mark Line Weight	5
Dimension Line Extension	3/32"
Flipped Dimension Line Extension	3/32"
Witness Line Control	Gap to Element
Witness Line Length	3/32"
Witness Line Gap to Element	1/16"
Witness Line Extension	3/32"
Centerline Symbol	None
Centerline Pattern	Solid
Centerline Tick Mark	Default
Interior Tick Mark	Diagonal 3/64"
Color	■ Black
Dimension Line Snap Distance	1/4"
Text	
Text Size	3/32"
Text Offset	1/16"
Read Convention	Up, then Left
Text Font	Arial
Text Background	Opaque
Units Format	1' - 5 11/32" (Default)
Show Opening Height	☐

<< Preview	OK	Cancel	Apply

Tick Mark   This option allows you to select the style and size of the tick marks in Revit. The *tick mark* is the angled line crossing the intersection of the witness and dimension lines (shown in Figure 10.24).

Line Weight   This option controls the line thickness for the dimension string.

Tick Mark Line Weight   This option controls the line thickness for the tick mark only.

Dimension Line Extension   This option controls the length of the extension to the dimension line after the tick mark (shown in Figure 10.25). The *dimension line* is the line the dimension text sits on or over.

Flipped Dimension Line Extension   This option is available only if Tick Mark is set to Arrow. It controls the extent of the dimension line beyond the flipped arrow if the arrow flips on the ends of the dimension string.

Witness Line Control   A *witness line* is the line parallel to the elements dimensioned and perpendicular to the dimension line. This option toggles the setting to show or not show the second witness line. To have both witness lines show, use the "Gap to Element" setting.

Witness Line Length   This field becomes active only if the Witness Line Control is set to Fixed Dimension Line. You can set the length of all the witness lines in the dimensions.

Witness Line Gap to Element   This option controls the distance between the witness line and the element dimensioned.

Witness Line Extension   This option controls the length of the witness line after a tick mark.

Centerline Symbol   This option shows a symbol if you've dimensioned to the centerline of an element. (See Figure 10.26.)

Centerline Pattern   This field changes the line style of a centerline.

Center Tick Mark   This field by default is blank. This allows you the option to add a tick mark on the inside of the witness lines.

Interior Tick Mark This option is available only when Tick Mark is set to Arrow. It designates the tick-mark display for inner witness lines when adjacent segments of a dimension line are too small for arrows to fit.

Color This field changes the color of the dimension strings.

Dimension Line Snap Distance This option aids in the use of stacked dimension strings.

Next, let's look at the options in the Text pane, which occupies the lower half of the Type Properties dialog box:

Text Size This field changes the size of the dimension text.

Text Offset This option changes the distance the text is placed from the dimension line.

Read Convention This option shows you the default values of the dimension text position. In Up, then Left (the default value), the dimension text reads from the bottom of the sheet and then from the right of the sheet, appearing above the dimension string depending on whether it's horizontal or vertical.

Text Font This field controls the font of the dimension string. It's possible in Revit to have a font for dimensions that's separate from notes or other text.

Text Background The options for this value are Opaque and Transparent. It changes the appearance of the box surrounding the text.

Units Format This option controls the dimension string tolerance and unit displays.

Show Opening Height This option returns the height of an opening below the dimension string. In the dimensioned window shown in Figure 10.27, the width is shown as 3′-0″ and the height as 4′-0″.

Figure 10.26
Centerline symbol

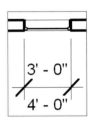

Figure 10.27
Show Opening Height

Dimensioning a Floor Plan

Now that we have covered the basics of dimensioning, let's try it on the First Floor Plan view you've been working on. Using the default dimension settings and the linear dimension style, you'll add dimension strings to the walls in the floor plan.

For interior walls, choose the Dimension tool. In the Options bar, select Wall Faces from the Prefer menu.

For the gridlines, use the Pick Entire Walls option. Before placing the dimensions, click the Options button, and then select Intersecting Gridlines. Pick parallel walls that are perpendicular to the grids, and you'll see the ease with which a string of dimensions can be generated (see Figure 10.28).

The finished floor plan should look similar to Figure 10.29.

Figure 10.28
Dimension Options bar

Figure 10.29

**The dimensioned
first-floor plan**

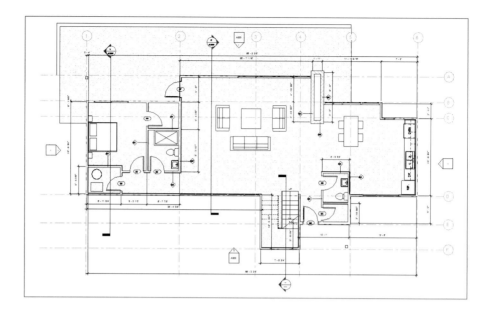

This shows you how to use Automated Dimensioning. Of course, if you don't change the Pick option to Entire Walls but to Individual References, you could make individual dimensions wherever needed.

Text and Keynotes

Notes are a critical part of communicating design and construction intent to contractors, subs, and owners. No drawing set would be complete without textual definitions and instructions on how to assemble the building. Revit has two primary ways of adding this information to the sheets. One way is through text. Text in Revit consists of words arranged in paragraphs with or without a leader. Text can be used for specialized annotations, sheet notes, legends, and similar applications. Keynotes, the other tool for annotating a drawing, are element-specific and can be scheduled and standardized in the Revit database. We'll explore the use and function of both tools in this section.

Text

Text is easy to add to your view. You can access the Text tool (| T Text) from both the Basics and Drafting tabs in Revit.

Text can be added to any view, including a 3D view. To begin adding text, click the Text button after you've opened the view of your choice, select where in the view you wish to place text, and begin typing. To edit text you've already placed, click the text to highlight it, and then click it again to activate the text box. To move text once you've located it, select it and drag it, or use the Move command.

When you use the Move command, you move both the text and the leader. When you move text by dragging the arrow icon, you move only the text box, leaving the leader anchored in its original position.

> To drag an entire textnote, select the note and drag it.

As with all the tools in Revit, there are ways to change the look and feel of your text during creation. Once you've selected the Text tool, the Type Selector and Options bar highlight, giving you some formatting choices. Figure 10.30 shows the options available with the Text command.

Figure 10.30

Text format tools

The Type Selector allows you to choose a style for the text you're using. Each text style is managed through the familiar Properties dialog box, where you can modify parameters such as font and size. To create a new text style from an existing one, click the Properties button in the Type Selector, and choose Edit/New in the properties. From there, choose Duplicate, give the style a new name, and make your adjustments to the properties. This process is identical to adding a new type to any existing Revit family.

Figure 10.31

Text tools

Justification options are displayed as icons, allowing for left-, center-, or right-justified textnotes.

After selecting a textnote, click the blue letters to edit the text. When you're editing the text, you're given additional formatting in the Options bar for Bold, Italic, and Underline. These apply to whatever text you've selected in the note (Figure 10.31).

Text Properties

Figure 10.32

Text Properties dialog box

Most text parameters are located in the Properties dialog box for text. It's here that you define font, style, and size. Figure 10.32 shows the Properties dialog box for text. The list below discusses the Text properties and how you can modify those values to customize your text within your project.

Color   This is where you can choose the font color.

Line Weight   This option allows you to choose the line weight for the font. Note that line weight options for the leader are found under Object Styles.

Background   This gives you the option to have a background for your text box that is either opaque or transparent. Opaque creates a white box (blotting out the model behind it, as shown in Figure 10.33). Transparent leaves the text box clear and lets you see the model data behind the text (Figure 10.34).

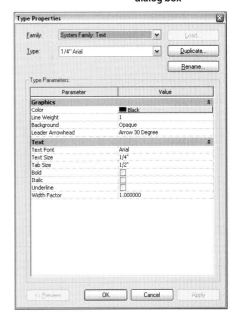

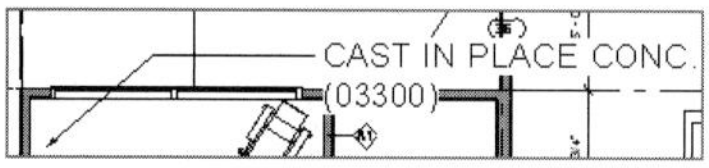

Figure 10.33

Opaque text box

Figure 10.34

Transparent text box

Leader Arrowhead This option allows you to choose the symbol that appears at the end of the leader lines. Leader arrows are customizable using Revit families.

Text Font This option lets you choose a font style from any of the fonts available in your `C:\WINDOWS\Fonts` folder.

Text Size This option allows you to control the size of the font. Note that the font size shown here is the printed size of the font. So, if you choose a ¼″ font size, when you print your drawing at 100% scale, the text will be ¼″ tall. As previously discussed with tags and dimensions, Revit dynamically scales the font depending on the scale of the view.

Tab Size This option sets the distance your cursor offsets when you use the Tab key in a text box.

Bold, Italic, Underline These options mirror the commands available on the Options bar, allowing you to bold, italicize, or underline your text.

Width Factor This value lets you control the width of your text boxes. A value less than 1 reduces the width of the text characters by a factor, and a value greater than 1 makes the text field wider.

After you've placed a text box in the drawing, you have the option to go back and change some of the parameters. When text is selected, check the Options bar: You can add and remove leaders and change the text justification (see Figure 10.35).

The leader buttons allow you to choose a leader style for your text before you add it to the view. From left to right in Figure 10.35, you can choose none, one segment, two segments, or an arc for a leader line. In Figure 10.35, a two-segment leader has been chosen.

You can add any number of additional leaders to the left or right of the text box. The first two leader options are for leaders with lines, whereas the second two are for leaders with arcs. (You can't have a text box with both linear and arc leaders.) You also have the option to remove leaders you've added. Note that leaders are removed in the opposite order in which they were added.

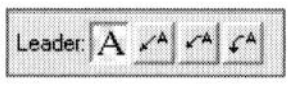

Figure 10.35

Adding leaders

Model Text

Model text (▌M Model Text... ▐) is 3D text that appears as a model element in your project. The properties of model text are similar to the properties of other model elements, rather than those of other text. Model text can have thickness, material, keynote, and other common model properties.

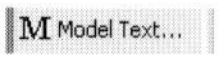

A classic use for model text is signage for a building entrance (Figure 10.36).

Model text's height dimensions are given relative to the model. If you want the text to be 3′ tall in the model, it stays 3′ tall but becomes larger or smaller in the view depending on the view scale.

The Model Text command is located on the Modeling tab. Choosing Modeling → Model Text also activates the Type Selector, allowing you to choose or add as many types of 3D text as you'd like.

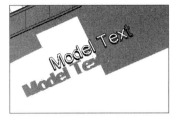

Figure 10.36
Model text

To add model text to your drawing, click the Model Text button. You'll see a dialog box asking you for your text entry. Type your text, and click OK when you're finished. At this point, you're asked to place the text in the view you currently have active. If you're in a 3D view, Revit chooses a work plane closest to the angle of your 3D view. After you've placed the text, you can highlight it and use the tools in the Options bar shown in Figure 10.37:

Edit Text This button lets you change the text you typed. You can also edit the work plane on which the text was created.

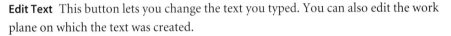

Figure 10.37
**Model text
Options bar**

Edit Work Plane This button opens another dialog box (Figure 10.38) where you can select a new work plane from an existing one or choose a plane of an existing Revit element.

Rehost This button allows you to move text from the element you've selected to another host element in the model. (We discussed this feature earlier, in the context of windows and doors.)

Keynotes

Keynotes are textual annotations that relate text strings to specific elements in the model to an external file (see Figure 10.39). You can format font style, size, and justification in the same manner as for standard text, but keynotes behave like a Revit family. This means you can insert different family types of text in Revit, just as you would door or window families. Changing one instance of the family type changes all the instances in the project. Because keynotes act as families in Revit, they can also be scheduled.

Figure 10.38
Selecting a work plane

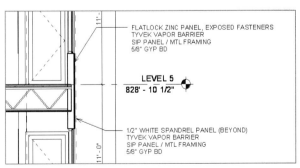

Figure 10.39
Keynotes

Figure 10.40

The Keynote tool

Keynote Types

The Keynote command is located on the Drafting tab. Adding keynotes in Revit gives you three options similar to those mentioned in our discussion of adding tags. When you select the Keynote command, you see a menu giving you the following options (see Figure 10.40):

Element This option allows you to note an element in the model, such as a wall or a floor. This type of note is typically used if you want to note an entire assembly, such as a wall assembly. You can find this value in the family properties of that element.

Material This note type allows you to note a specific material in Revit. It lets you add a note to concrete, gypsum board, or acoustical tile. This value can also be found at Settings → Materials. The Identity tab lets you add keynote values directly to your materials. (See Figure 10.41.)

User This option allows you to select any model-based component in Revit and define a custom keynote for it. Notes defined this way differ from those defined under Element or Material because they're unique to the particular object selected. They can be used in conjunction with Element and Material notes.

Keynote Behavior and Editing

A core concept in keynoting is how the notes react in the model. Keynotes are integrated into Revit just like any model element. Keynoting an object in Revit lets you associate a text value to that family's keynote parameter. This value is consistent for every identical element in the model.

You can't edit the text of a keynote. All the keynotes in Revit are tied to an external text file, which is the only place you can edit them. This file can be edited to add or remove values. A sample list is shown in Figure 10.42. This external .txt file is designed to keep annotations consistent by storing all of them in one repository. Every time you add or change the text of an annotation and reload the text file, it dynamically updates all the keynotes of that type inserted in the project.

Figure 10.41

Assigning a keynote to a material

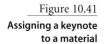

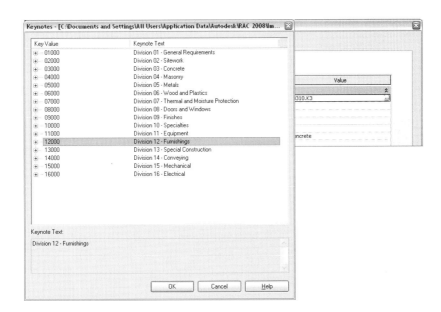

Figure 10.42
A keynote text file

You can edit a keynote text file or add one to a project at any time. You can have multiple .txt files for various projects, but you can have only one .txt file per project.

> A powerful way to ensure consistent use of notes throughout your office is to create a master .txt file for your various project types.

> If you send a project file to someone and don't send the keynote .txt file, they will be able to see all the keynotes without a problem. However, they can't edit or add keynotes without the .txt file.

Keynote File-Naming Conventions

The default .txt file in Revit out of the box, which is shown in Figure 10.42, is found at

```
C:\Documents and Settings\All Users\Application Data\Autodesk\RAC 2008\
Imperial Library
```

To edit this file, open it in Notepad or Excel, and follow the format already established in the file. Let's look at that format to get a better understanding of how to customize keynotes.

The first few rows designate the groupings. They consist of a label (in this case, a number) followed by a tab and then a description. An example is

```
03000        Division 03 - Concrete
```

Figure 10.43

**Keynoting Settings
dialog box**

Below that, with no empty lines in the file, are the contents of that grouping. These are shown with a minor heading, a tab, a description, a tab, and the original grouping. An example is

    03200   Concrete Reinforcement   03000

Here, 03200 is the subheading, Concrete Reinforcement is the description, and it all falls under the 03000 grouping from the previous example.

Keynote Settings

Once you change a keynote .txt file, you need to reload the file into Revit. This dialog box can be found at Settings → Keynoting Settings (Figure 10.43). The following list describes the settings within this dialog box.

Keynote Table This dialog box is fairly straightforward. The Browse button lets you load or reload a keynote .txt file.

Path type You can define where Revit looks for your .txt file:

Absolute This option follows the UNC naming conventions and searches across your network or workstation for a specified location.

Relative This option locates the .txt file relative to the project RVT file. If you move the RVT file and the .txt file, as long as they're moved in the same folder structure, Revit knows where to look for them.

At Library Locations This option lets you put the .txt file in the default library locations you've defined under Settings → Options → File Locations tab.

Numbering method You can also modify the numbering method of the keynotes:

By keynote This option allows you to number keynotes as they come from the associated .txt file.

By sheet This option numbers the keynotes sequentially as they're created in the model.

Creating Keynotes

To add keynotes to a Revit model, choose one of the three keynote types from the Drafting tab. In your view, mouse over the various model objects until you find the one you wish to note, and click to add the keynote. Once you've placed the note on the sheet, you'll see a dialog box (Figure 10.44) asking you to identify the element you're trying to note.

Expand the plus signs until you find your desired keynote, and double-click it. Doing so associates that particular note with the element or material in the model. As mentioned previously, you need to make this association only once. For example, if you keynote a material called Concrete, then every time you hover over that material anywhere else in the model with a keynote tag, you'll see the preview graphic of the tag showing Concrete (Figure 10.45). This way, you can define the materials and assemblies in the model and begin your documentation process.

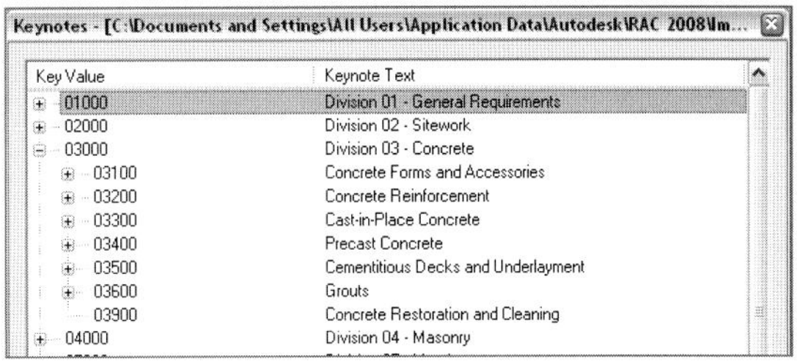

Figure 10.44

Selecting a keynote

> With the exception of detail components (covered later in this chapter), you can't keynote lines or other 2D information.

Keynote Legends

Depending on your workflow and style of annotation, you may want to create a legend for your keynotes that appears on each sheet. Creating a legend in Revit is simple: Choose **View → New → Keynote Legend**. You're prompted to name the legend; enter a name, and click OK.

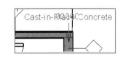

Figure 10.45

Adding a note

> Doing a schedule for keynotes is a great way to find rogue notes. In situations when you have more than one person working on a project, it's possible to incorrectly note an element in the model. Scheduling the notes allows you to find instances where you may have one or two of a type of note and determine if it's the proper description of that material.

Schedules

In Chapter 3, we explained that schedules are a live, textual view of the model. We also discussed the different types of schedules you can create and walked through a simple example. For your documentation, you need to know how to modify the graphical appearance of a schedule and filter out information you don't need to show.

Manipulating a Schedule

When you create a new schedule, you're presented with a number of format and selection choices. These let you set the font style and text alignment and decide how to organize and filter the data for display in the schedule. Let's explore the options in the New Schedule dialog box.

> Revit is essentially a database of model objects that are loaded with information, so many of the same functionalities available in database queries are available in Revit. If you're unfamiliar with database conventions, don't stress—you don't need to know about databases to run Revit successfully.

Choose Design Tab View → Schedules to create a new schedule. The New Schedule dialog box (Figure 10.46) first asks you which Revit category you want to schedule. You can provide a name for the schedule and choose which phase of construction the schedule represents. We've left the phase as New Construction, because that is what you're creating with the sample model.

Once you select the schedule you would like to create, you will be presented with another dialog box that contains the following tabs. These tabs are designed to help you format your data and its visual presentation.

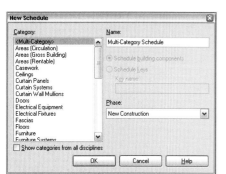

Figure 10.46

New Schedule dialog box

Fields This tab lets you select the data that will appear in your schedule. For the wall schedule, it shows all the properties available in the wall family.

Filter This tab allows you to filter out the data you don't wish to show. You'll use this tab to restrict displayed data so that only information about the concrete walls in the project appears in the schedule.

Sorting/Grouping This tab lets you control the order in which information is displayed. It also allows you decide whether you want to show every instance of an item or only the totals for a given family.

Formatting This tab controls the display heading for each field and whether the field is visible on the schedule. It's possible to add fields that are necessary for calculations or sorting but don't show on the printed copy of the schedule. Additionally, this tab can tell Revit to calculate the totals for any of the fields.

Appearance This tab controls the graphical aspects of the schedule, including the font size and type of text for each of the columns and headers in the schedule. It also allows you to turn the grids on and off or modify the line thickness for the grid and boundary lines.

The following example walks through the different options in the New Schedule dialog box while you create a new wall schedule. In this example, you'll create the schedule, filter out all but the concrete walls, and calculate the volume of recycled content in the walls based on the assumption that you're using 15% recycled content in all the concrete you pour on this project. When you're finished, the schedule should look like Figure 10.47.

Follow these steps:

1. Open the `Station.rvt` file found in the `Chapter 10` project folder on the CD.

2. Navigate to the View tab, and choose Schedule/Quantity.

3. Choose Walls from the category menu, and name the schedule **Concrete Walls** (see Figure 10.48).

4. Click OK.

5. Select the fields to be scheduled (see Figure 10.49). The fields are parameters used by the category, and they all appear in the properties of the element being scheduled. Add a field by double-clicking the name of the field in the left pane or by highlighting the field and clicking the Add button. Doing so moves the field from the left to the right column. Alternately, you can remove a field by highlighting it in the right column and clicking Remove.
6. Choose the following fields for the schedule:

   Area
   Description
   Family and Type
   Length
   Volume
   Width

7. With a field selected, use the Move Up and Move Down buttons in the lower-right corner of the dialog box to sort the fields in the order you want them to appear in the schedule table. For example:

   Family and Type
   Description
   Width
   Length
   Area
   Volume

Concrete Walls					
	Wall Properties				
Wall Type	Width	Length	Area	Volume	Recycled Volume
Basic Wall: N1 - CIP CONC	0' - 8"	20' - 2"	62 SF	41.00 CF	6.15 CF
Basic Wall: N1 - CIP CONC	0' - 8"	9' - 0 7/32"	81 SF	53.88 CF	8.08 CF
Basic Wall: N1 - CIP CONC	0' - 8"	4' - 10"	94 SF	62.74 CF	9.41 CF
Basic Wall: N1 - CIP CONC	0' - 8"	15' - 0 5/8"	143 SF	95.33 CF	14.30 CF
Basic Wall: N1 - CIP CONC	0' - 8"	18' - 0"	150 SF	100.00 CF	15.00 CF
Basic Wall: N1 - CIP CONC	0' - 8"	18' - 2 3/8"	167 SF	111.03 CF	16.65 CF
Basic Wall: N1 - CIP CONC	0' - 8"	18' - 2 3/8"	167 SF	111.03 CF	16.65 CF
Basic Wall: N1 - CIP CONC	0' - 8"	56' - 6"	168 SF	111.98 CF	16.80 CF
Basic Wall: N1 - CIP CONC	0' - 8"	18' - 0"	202 SF	134.33 CF	20.15 CF
Basic Wall: N1 - CIP CONC	0' - 8"	18' - 0"	202 SF	134.70 CF	20.20 CF
Basic Wall: N1 - CIP CONC	0' - 8"	78' - 10"	235 SF	156.49 CF	23.47 CF
Basic Wall: N1 - CIP CONC	0' - 8"	22' - 0"	269 SF	179.41 CF	26.91 CF
Basic Wall: N1 - CIP CONC	0' - 8"	93' - 8"	279 SF	186.00 CF	27.90 CF
Basic Wall: N1 - CIP CONC	0' - 8"	29' - 4 15/16"	327 SF	190.11 CF	28.52 CF
Basic Wall: N1 - CIP CONC	0' - 8"	22' - 4"	304 SF	202.95 CF	30.44 CF
Basic Wall: N1 - CIP CONC	0' - 8"	18' - 0"	323 SF	215.22 CF	32.28 CF
Basic Wall: N1 - CIP CONC	0' - 8"	40' - 4"	338 SF	225.56 CF	33.83 CF
Basic Wall: N1 - CIP CONC	0' - 8"	35' - 4 17/32"	480 SF	320.29 CF	48.04 CF
Basic Wall: N1 - CIP CONC	0' - 8"	17' - 6"	530 SF	353.17 CF	52.98 CF
Basic Wall: N1 - CIP CONC	0' - 8"	7' - 4"	553 SF	368.67 CF	55.30 CF
Basic Wall: N1 - CIP CONC	0' - 8"	22' - 4"	619 SF	389.81 CF	58.47 CF
Basic Wall: N1 - CIP CONC	0' - 8"	7' - 4"	617 SF	411.44 CF	61.72 CF
Basic Wall: N1 - CIP CONC	0' - 8"	77' - 10 1/8"	906 SF	546.71 CF	82.01 CF
Basic Wall: N1 - CIP CONC	0' - 8"	36' - 3"	855 SF	570.08 CF	85.51 CF
Basic Wall: N1 - CIP CONC	0' - 8"	100' - 5 1/8"	954 SF	636.23 CF	95.44 CF
Basic Wall: N1 - CIP CONC	0' - 8"	17' - 8 3/4"	1032 SF	678.81 CF	101.82 CF
Basic Wall: N1 - CIP CONC	0' - 8"	83' - 11 13/3	1039 SF	692.45 CF	103.87 CF
Basic Wall: N1 - CIP CONC	0' - 8"	73' - 4 3/4"	1179 SF	786.28 CF	117.94 CF
Basic Wall: N1 - CIP CONC	0' - 8"	17' - 8 3/4"	1401 SF	933.74 CF	140.06 CF
Basic Wall: N1 - CIP CONC	0' - 8"	124' - 0 19/3	1444 SF	962.36 CF	144.35 CF
Basic Wall: N1 - CIP CONC	0' - 8"	148' - 5 13/3	4419 SF	2803.17 CF	420.48 CF
31	20' - 8"	1270' - 2	19537 SF	12764.98 CF	1914.75 CF

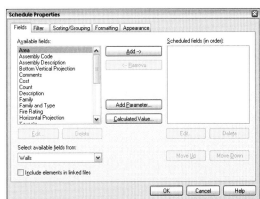

Figure 10.47
The completed schedule

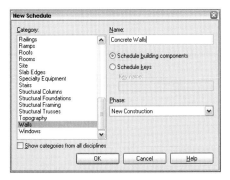

Figure 10.48
Starting a schedule

Figure 10.49
Fields tab

There is no predefined field in Revit for recycled content, but Revit lets you create custom fields and custom formulas.

8. To make a new field to display information about the recycled content of your walls, click the Calculated Value button (Calculated Value...).

9. The Calculated Value dialog box opens (Figure 10.50). In this dialog box, you can create new columns in your schedule based on relationships to other fields in the table. Name your new value **Recycled Volume**. For Type, choose Volume from the drop-down list; and in the Formula box, type **Volume*.15**.

10. When you're done, click OK.

Figure 10.50

Adding a calculated value

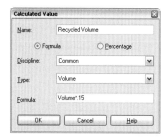

TIPS FOR CUSTOM FIELDS

There are a few things to note when you create custom fields:

- You can't mix field types. This means you can't select a field type of Area or Number and take a percentage of volume. You need to calculate apples-to-apples.

- The formula area is case sensitive. This is also true for custom family types and other calculated Revit fields.

- You can't calculate with fields that aren't included in the schedule.

Revit's Help menu lists valid formula syntaxes. You can enter integers, decimals, and fractional values in formulas using normal mathematical syntax, as shown in the following examples:

- Length = Height + Width + sqrt (Height*Width)

- Length = Wall 1 (11000mm) + Wall 2 (15000mm)

- Area = Length (500mm) * Width (300mm)

- Volume = Length (500mm) * Width (300mm) * Height (800 mm)

- Width = 100m * cos(angle)

- x = 2*abs(a) + abs(b/2)

- ArrayNum = Length/Spacing

11. Choose the Filter tab (Figure 10.51). Because you want to show only the concrete walls, you need to filter out all the other walls in this schedule.

12. From the upper-left "Filter by" drop-down menu, choose Description.

13. The right "Filter by" menu allows you to select from a standard list of database queries: equals, doesn't equal, contains, doesn't contain, and so on. For this schedule, use the default value, which is equals.

14. From the lower-left "Filter by" menu, choose Cast In Place Concrete. (This menu dynamically generates from the descriptions given in the properties for the element in question. In this example, wall properties are displayed.)

15. Select the Sorting/Grouping tab shown in Figure 10.52. Using this dialog box, sort the walls first by "Family and Type," and then by Volume.

> In this example, you don't have more than one type of concrete wall, but if you did, Revit would sort the walls by type and then by volume, smallest to largest. Additionally, you can choose to add a header and/or footer to each of the line items in the schedule. This tab also gives you the option to display the title, count, and total by each line. These aren't needed for this schedule, but they can be useful in other schedules.

16. Near the bottom of this tab, select the "Grand totals" check box. Choose "Counts and totals" from the drop-down menu at right.

> On this tab, choosing "Counts and totals" means you're telling Revit to autocalculate a few things. First, you're counting all the instances of a type family in the model. You also have the option to report totals for those counted types. For example, you may have two sizes of fixed windows in a project. The count tells you how many of each type you have. The total gives you a sum of all the fixed windows, regardless of size. This count and total relate only to family or type quantities.

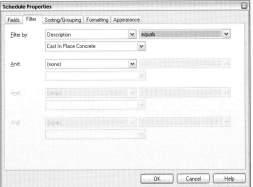

Figure 10.51
Filter tab

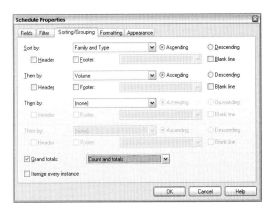

Figure 10.52
Sorting/Grouping tab

17. At the bottom of this tab is an "Itemize every instance" check box. Leave it deselected for now, which makes it a hidden field.

> If you select "Itemize every instance", a separate line will appear on the schedule for each instance of an object type in the model. This may be useful when you're listing every door or window, but it can make for a long schedule.

18. Select the Formatting tab shown in Figure 10.53. Change the Heading value of the "Family and Type" field to Wall Type. To do this, select "Family and Type" in the Fields list, and type **Wall Type** in the Heading box.

19. Select Description in the Fields list, and select the "Hidden field" check box.

20. Select each of the remaining fields (Width, Length, Area, Volume, and Recycled Volume), set their alignment to Right, and select the "Calculate totals" check box. This option tells Revit to add a list of other values together that aren't type related (like the calculation in step 15). This allows you the ability to calculate values between similar fields within Revit and return customized, but accurate data. So, in English, this means that you can customize your schedules in a variety of ways and know they are always reporting accurate and current information.

> You can select fields individually, or you can select them all by holding down the Ctrl key and left-clicking each field name.

21. Select the Appearance tab shown in Figure 10.54. In this dialog, you define gridlines, outlines, header text, and body text. Select the Bold check box to the right of "Header text". The rest of the settings are fine, unless you feel like experimenting with fonts and size.

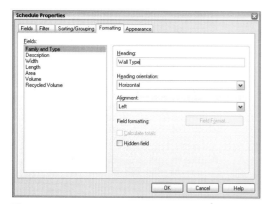

Figure 10.53
Formatting tab

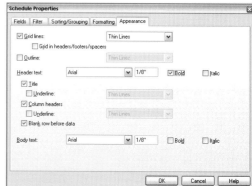

Figure 10.54
Appearance tab

22. Click OK. Revit will generate a schedule that shows all the information you asked for from the model. At the bottom of the schedule, the total for each of the fields is displayed. (See Figure 10.47.)

Additional Formatting

You can do some additional formatting after you create a schedule. By highlighting multiple headers, you can group them and add secondary tier headers. Let's combine Width, Length, Area, and Volume:

1. Click in the Width header. Holding down the left mouse button, drag your cursor to the left or right, selecting additional headers until you've selected all four (see Figure 10.55).

2. Click the Group button on the Options bar.

3. Revit groups all four headers together. Add a title for the new grouping: **Wall Properties** (Figure 10.56).

Finding Elements in the Model

Now that you have a schedule showing all the concrete walls, you can use the schedule to locate any of these walls in the model. To do this, select a wall from the schedule list. In the Options bar, you can choose to delete or show the element you've selected. Be aware that the Delete option removes that element from the model and every view in which it appears. This is the essence of Revit: You don't need to manually seek all views in which this wall appears, to delete it.

When you choose Show, Revit opens any view the element can be displayed in, zooms in on that element, and highlights it in red. This powerful tool lets you find the location of any model element in the project.

You also can add new rows to the schedule. This option is available for things like room schedules, where you may want to predefine room names before adding the tags to the model.

Not only do Revit schedules report information about elements in the project, but they also can be used to control elements. If you decide to exchange one wall type for another, you can do so by clicking in the schedule—under wall types, in this example. A menu appears, listing all available types currently in the model, and you can choose the type you want. Again, this automatically changes the instance of the wall to another wall type in all views in which the wall is present.

Figure 10.55
Grouping schedule headings

Figure 10.56
Adding headings to schedules

Coordinated documentation is a key value of Revit. After you create a schedule, it doesn't require manual updating. Any time you add or remove content from the model, the schedule dynamically updates itself, even if it's placed on a sheet.

Schedule View Templates

Revit allows you to save a schedule that you've carefully prepared as a view template and apply it to other schedules. When you have many schedules in a project, you typically want to provide visual continuity by using the same font and graphical conventions. You can predefine these things in a schedule template. Here's how to create a schedule view template:

1. Right-click the schedule in the Project Browser, and choose `Create Template from View`.

2. Give the template a name.

The Schedule View template allows you to standardize all the font types, styles, and any other settings found on the Appearance tab in your project. Maybe you've already created schedules using various graphical styles. It's never too late to apply a view template and tidy things up. To apply a schedule template to a previously created schedule, follow these steps:

1. Right-click the schedule in the Project Browser, and choose Select Apply View Template.

2. Select the template you wish to apply.

Placing and Handling Schedules on Sheets

To place a schedule on a sheet, follow the same steps you use to place a view on a sheet. Drag and drop, adjust and nudge, until you get the correct layout. Once you've placed your schedule on a sheet, you can start to take advantage of Revit's productivity tools.

Traditionally, schedules have been time-consuming and extensive exercises in data entry and table manipulation. Schedules are often long lists that are hard to manipulate and that need to be updated whenever new content is added to a project. Few applications have an intelligent way of doing all this. For example, splitting a schedule usually requires cutting, copying, and a lot of rework to achieve the needed appearance and coordinate the data. Revit makes this process easy by putting graphical controls directly onto a schedule once it's on a sheet. Click the Split icon, and the schedule splits in half. Drag the blue control at the bottom of the schedule to move rows back and forth across the split. If you need to unsplit the schedule, drag one of the split sections on top of the other one, and they merge back together. All graphic edits of the schedule, such as changes in column width, propagate to all split segments of the schedule.

Let's practice by placing a schedule on a sheet in the Station.rvt file where you created the Concrete Wall schedule:

1. Create a new sheet by right-clicking the Sheets group from the Project Browser and choosing New.

2. Select the Presentation : Presentation sheet.

3. Drag the Concrete Walls schedule from the Schedule list in the Project Browser onto the sheet in the view window.

4. When you drop the schedule onto the sheet, it appears too long for the sheet; the text in each cell is returned and wrapped in the cell, further adding to the schedule length (see Figure 10.57). This isn't the look you're aiming for. To modify it, grab the highlighted blue arrows at the top of the schedule header, and drag them to the right to enlarge the width of each column. Doing this makes the schedule wider and also shortens the column.

5. Unfortunately, even though the column has been shortened, it still doesn't fit on the 11 × 17 sheet you've placed it on. Fortunately, Revit lets you split a schedule into multiple segments. To do this, click the blue squiggle that appears in the center of the schedule on the left or right side (shown in Figure 10.58). This splits the schedule in the center and adds a new header to the new column.

> You can split a schedule as many times as needed to fit it onto a sheet.

6. To finally locate the schedules on the sheet, you can drag each set of columns independently by grabbing the blue cross in the center of the schedule. (These individual segments can't be placed on separate sheets.) The finished schedule on the sheet should look like Figure 10.59.

In addition to letting you split a schedule into separate segments, Revit lets you rejoin the segments into a single schedule. You can do this as follows:

1. Select the blue cross at the middle of the second segment.

2. Drag it over the first segment of the schedule. Your schedule is complete and displays in its original form.

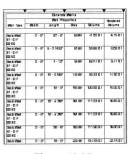

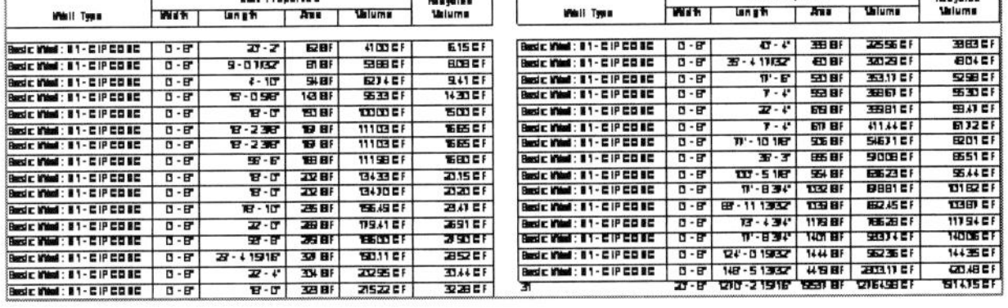

Figure 10.57

Adding a schedule to a sheet

Figure 10.58

Splitting a schedule

Figure 10.59

The schedule on a sheet

Drafting Views

Figure 10.60

New Drafting View dialog box

Because it isn't feasible, or even reasonable, to model every construction detail in 3D, Revit provides the means to draft 2D information. Revit's drafting views are strictly 2D views used for drawing details for a construction document set. When placed on a sheet, drafting views have the same intelligent referencing as other views. This lets you produce coordinated drawings. Even though drafting views present only 2D details, because they're in Revit, they can be tied parametrically to sheets so all the references are dynamic.

To create a new drafting view, follow these steps:

1. Go to the View tab, and choose the Drafting View tool (⚓ Drafting View...).

2. A dialog box appears, prompting you for a detail name and scale (Figure 10.60).

3. Using the Scale drop-down menu, choose from a list of standard and custom view scales.

4. Click OK. A new node, Drafting Views (Detail), is added to the Project Browser (see Figure 10.61). This new drafting view is primed for either drafting a new detail or importing existing CAD details.

Figure 10.61

Drafting Views node

If your office reuses standard details from project to project, you can save your drafting views as a separate external file once they have been created in Revit. To do this, right-click the Drafting View in the Project Browser, and choose Save to New File. This lets you save your file as a separate .rvt file that can be stored in a library folder on your office's server and linked into other new or existing projects.

Importing CAD details

In Chapter 7, we discussed how to import a CAD file into Revit. Existing libraries of CAD details or details you receive from a manufacturer can also be imported directly into a Revit project. If you're working with someone who only produces details using CAD, you can incorporate their work into your Revit model without disrupting workflow.

To prepare a CAD file for import, it's strongly recommended that you delete all the superfluous data in that file. If your import contains hatches or annotations that you don't intend to use in Revit, delete them first.

We also recommend that you import only one detail at a time so you can take better advantage of Revit's ability to manage sheet referencing. If you have a series of details organized in a single CAD file that you'd like to import into Revit, isolate each detail, save it as a separate file, and then import it.

> Every time you explode a CAD file in Revit, you add objects to the database. An inserted CAD file is one object. An exploded CAD file is many objects—maybe thousands of objects. For the best performance, explode CAD files as rarely as possible.

Drafting Tools

The drafting tools available in Revit are similar to what you might find in any CAD application. You can draw lines, arcs, and circles and create groups of 2D lines to use repeatedly. Lines can be drawn, extended, moved, copied, mirrored, arrayed, and trimmed—everything you'd expect to be able to do to lines.

Figure 10.62

Drafting tools

To demonstrate Revit's drafting tools, you'll work on the house model (from the *Introducing Revit* CD) for the remainder of this chapter. Open the file `Source_House_Begining Detailing.rvt`, and find the Detail 2 view that you created earlier. This is the detail through the window at the clerestory. For the time being, you'll ignore the flashing and focus on the linework.

Several different drafting tools are available in Revit. You access them from the bottom of the Drafting tab (see Figure 10.62). We'll explore them in the order in which they appear on the tab, from top to bottom, and you'll use them on the callout detail.

Detail Lines

Detail lines are the most common drafting tool (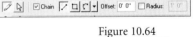).

These are view-specific lines that you can draw in any view and use to create 2D details. When you activate the Detail Lines tool, it lets you use the Type Selector to choose from existing line styles (Figure 10.63). Line styles are defined by line weight, color, and pattern.

Figure 10.63

Line styles in the Type Selector

If no existing line style conforms to your needs, or you want to edit the graphic properties of a line style, use the Line Styles dialog at Settings → Line Styles.

The detail lines Options bar shows all the drawing styles and line-shape choices available in Revit (see Figure 10.64).

The Draw and Pick Lines tools are similar to the tools used to create walls. The Draw tool (the default tool) allows you to choose any of the drawing options from the nearby button menus.

Figure 10.64

Detail lines Options bar

The Pick Line tool (also selected by default) is the most commonly used tool. It's illustrated in Figure 10.65. The second tool, shown as a rectangle in Figure 10.65, is dynamic and always appears as the tool most frequently used from the flyout menu represented by the third button shown in the Options bar in Figure 10.64.

Line This is a simple Line command. By default, when you choose the second point of your Line command, Revit automatically begins a new line from that point. You can disable this feature by deselecting the Chain button on the Options bar. The Flyout contains all the drawing shapes.

Rectangle This tool draws all four sides of a rectangle or square. It can only draw vertical and horizontal lines.

Figure 10.65

Pick Line options

Polygon This tool draws multisided shapes. When this tool is selected, a box on the Options bar lets you select the number of sides you want for your shape. If you want a rectangle that is non-orthogonal, use the Polygon tool and enter **4** for the number of sides.

Circle This tool draws circles by radius.

Arc passing through three points This tool draws an arc using the following sequence of points: first point, last point, midpoint.

Arc from center and end points This tool draws an arc using the following sequence of points: center point, start point, end point.

Tangent arc This tool draws an arc from a starting point. You must select a point in the view to begin the tangent arc.

Fillet arc Selecting this tool prompts you to choose two non-parallel lines and create a fillet arc between them.

Spline This tool draws a spline. The points of the spline can be edited after the line has been drawn, but you can't fillet or trim a spline.

Ellipse This tool draws ellipses by letting you locate the center and then the major and minor radii.

Partial ellipse This tool draws a half segment of an ellipse using the following sequence of points: start point, end point, radius.

In addition to these tools, a check box next to the Line button allows you to chain your lines together by pairing the end point of one line with the start point of another.

Lines

The Lines tool ([🖉 Lines])(not to be confused with the Detail Lines tool) is found on the Basics and Modeling tabs.

Lines are model elements (as opposed to detail/annotation elements) and appear in every view applicable. This means if you draw a line in an elevation view, it appears in every 3D view, elevation view, detail view, and so on, where that portion of the elevation is visible.

The lines use all the same draw commands as the Detail Lines tool; however, they're drawn on a 3D work plane in the model.

If the view you're in isn't an active work plane, then when you select the Lines tool, it will ask you to define or select a work plane by displaying the dialog box shown in Figure 10.66.

Figure 10.66

Choosing a work plane

Here, you can either use the Name option to choose a work plane that is already defined, use the "Pick a plane" option to choose a face (such as the face of a wall or floor) to draw on, or use the "Pick a line and use the work plane it was sketched in" option, which we hope is self-evident.

You may be wondering, "When do I use lines, and when do I use detail lines?" Use a detail line when you're drawing things in 2D that will appear only in the view they're created in. Use lines when you want the same line to appear in all views but you don't necessarily need a 3D modeled element to communicate the design intent. A good example for the use of lines is control joints or gaps between panels in a façade.

Detail Groups

Detail groups are similar to blocks in AutoCAD. They're collections of 2D graphics that you'll probably want to repeat again and again in the same or different views. A classic example is wood studs or blocking. You can easily and quickly set up a group and use that group over and over in the model. Doing so helps control consistency throughout the drawing.

To make a detail group, create the detail elements you'd like, and then group them using the Group command: **Edit → Group → Create Group**.

You can also use the keyboard shortcut GP, which prompts you for a group name. We suggest that you name the group rather than accepting the default name Revit wants to give it (Group 1, Group 2, and so on).

To place a detail group, use the Detail Group button (Detail Group) in the Drafting tab. Then, use the Type Selector to choose which group you want to place.

Detail Components

Detail components are parametric 2D families. They're similar to detail groups but are created in the Family Editor and can be designed with dimensional variation built right into the family. In other words, a single detail component can make a full range of shapes available in a single component. Being families, this also means they can be stored in your office library and shared across projects easily. To add a detail component to your drawing, select the Detail Component button (Detail Component) from the Drafting bar.

If you need to load a new component, click the Load button in the Options bar, and browse to the Detail Components folder. Revit has a wide range of common detail components in the default library.

To make a new Detail Component, use the Family Editor, and go to File → New Family → Detail Component.rft. Now you can begin drawing lines, as you did in the project, and then save the file as an independent family that can be loaded into any project. We'll go a bit deeper into how to make families in Chapter 12.

A detail component is an incredible feature, not to be underestimated. Not only can you insert detail components into a project, but you can also insert them into 2D and 3D families and set them to show only at fine levels of detail. One way to use a detail component is to insert it into a family and use it to demonstrate a higher level of detail when the family is cut in section. An example is the shims and silicone in a window head that you don't necessarily want to model, but that you do want to show in a wall section or detail.

Masking Regions

A masking region is similar to a filled region (which we'll discuss later in this chapter). A masking region is designed to hide portions of the model that you don't want to see in the view. Affectionately referred to as "white out," a masking region imposes a 2D shape on top of the model that masks elements behind it.

The masking region obscures only the model and other detail components. It can't mask annotations.

To add a masking region to your view, click the Masking Region button (☐ Masking Region) on the Drafting tab.

This takes you to sketch mode, where you can draw a closed loop of lines. When you draw a masking region, you can assign the boundary lines different line styles—check the Type Selector to make sure you're using the line style you want. One of the line styles that is particularly useful for the Masking Region tool is the invisible line style. It allows you to create a borderless region—ideal if you want to truly mask an element in the model.

Each line can be given its own linestyle, making it possible to create a shape with different boundary line representations. A masking region is shown in Figure 10.67.

To edit a masking region, highlight the region, and choose the Edit button from the Options bar. Doing so brings you back to the Sketch tool and lets you edit the region.

Adding to the Detail

Now that you have a better understanding of detail components and masking regions, let's add them to your detail:

1. You need to add a gutter to the roof. Select the Detail Component button, and choose the 4″ × 4″ Gutter that has been preloaded into this model.

2. Open the view Detail 2, select the Detail Component button from the Design tab and choose Gutter Bevel Section 4″ × 4″ (15cm × 15cm) from the Type Selector.

3. Use the mirror tool to flip the gutter. Be sure to uncheck Copy in the options bar. After mirroring the gutter, align it with the roof edge.

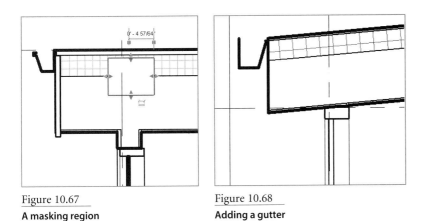

Figure 10.67

A masking region

Figure 10.68

Adding a gutter

You also need to add a fascia board, which is something you didn't model with the Roof family. But before you do that, you need to mask some of the rigid insulation in the roof in order to build the fascia board back in from the roof edge:

1. Use the Masking Region tool to draw a box at the roof edge. Make the box using four medium lines, and make it 1″ (2.5cm) wide. Bring it to the underside of the roof sheathing, and run it just past the bottom of the soffit, as shown in Figure 10.69.

2. Use the detail component Nominal Cut Lumber-Section 2x4 to build out the window heads. You can use the space bar to rotate the component during placement.

3. Although you could use a detail component to place blocking above the window head, let's use detail lines instead. Select the Detail Lines tool, and a medium line from the Type Selector.

4. Draw a box from the window head to the bottom of the rigid insulation.

5. Using a thin line, draw a line from corner to corner in the box. The finished detail looks like Figure 10.70.

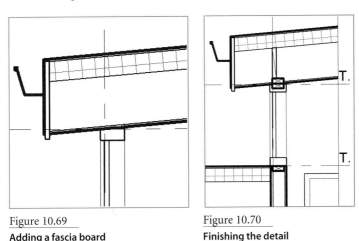

Figure 10.69

Adding a fascia board

Figure 10.70

Finishing the detail

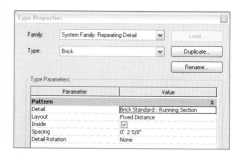

Figure 10.71

Grouping common elements

Figure 10.72

Repeating detail properties

If you decide to move or change those lines you've just drawn, you want them to all move together. This is a great use for groups. By selecting the window head and the blocking, you can use the GP keyboard shortcut to group those elements into one unit. Another way to group a selection of elements is using the Group Tool located in the toolbars at the top of the UI. This allows you to reuse them in other sections or detail in the project. Figure 10.71 shows the elements grouped together.

Creating a Repeating Detail

Repeating details are a common occurrence in architectural projects. Masonry walls, metal decking, and roof tiles all comprise a series of repeating elements. Most of these elements aren't modeled as 3D components in Revit but are represented with symbolic detail components.

You create repeating details in Revit by selecting the Repeating Detail button () on the Drafting tab.

This tool takes a single detail component and arrays it along a straight line at regular intervals. Let's open the properties of a repeating detail to get a feel for how it's laid out. Figure 10.72 shows the Type Properties dialog box for a brick repeating detail.

When you select a repeating detail, the Type Selector is activated so you can select any repeating detail you've already loaded in the project. Repeating details are similar to families; they have types and properties. If you don't have the repeating detail that you want loaded, it's easy enough to create one on the fly. All you need is a detail component that you wish to repeat.

Repeating-detail placement is similar to placement of a line—the repeating detail has a starting point, an end point, and repeating 2D geometry in between. Let's make one to demonstrate this feature:

1. Click the Repeating Detail tool on the Drafting bar.

2. Choose the Properties button next to the Type Selector.

3. Click Edit/New.

4. Click Duplicate.

5. Give your new repeating detail a name.

Now, you need to select a detail component from the Revit library or use one you created on your own with the Detail field in the Properties dialog box.

The default repeating detail in Revit is a running brick pattern. If you look at it in detail, it consists of a brick detail component and a mortar joint (see Figure 10.73).

When you create a repeating detail layout, measure the distance between the beginning of the brick and the end of the mortar joint to understand the module on which the detail will repeat. When the detail component is inserted, it acts like a Line tool and allows you to pull a line of brick, as shown in Figure 10.74. This line can be lengthened, shortened, or rotated like any other line.

> If you're making a repeating detail from a component that isn't loaded in your project, you won't find it listed under the Detail item in the Properties dialog box. You first need to load it in your project and then make it a repeating detail component.

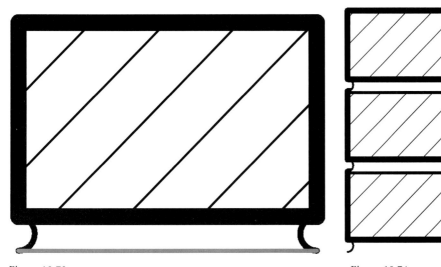

Figure 10.73

A repeating detail unit

Figure 10.74

A repeating detail

Let's take a closer look at the various options you can set in the Type Properties pane (Figure 10.75):

Detail Here you can select the detail component you wish to have repeated.

Layout This option offers four different modes:

> **Fixed Distance** The path drawn between the start and end point when drawing the repeating detail is the length at which your component repeats at a distance of the value set for spacing.

Figure 10.75

**Repeating Detail
Properties**

> **Fixed Number** Here you can set how many times a component repeats itself in the space between the start and end point (the length of the path).

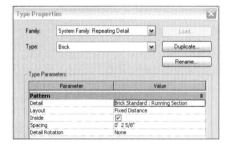

> **Fill Available Space** Regardless of the value you choose for Spacing, the detail component is repeated on the path using its actual width as the Spacing value.

> **Maximum Spacing** The detail component is repeated using the set spacing, and the number of repeated components is set so that only complete components are drawn. Revit creates as many as fit on the path.

Inside This check box adjusts the start point and end point of the detail components that make up the repeating detail.

Spacing This value is active only when Fixed Distance or Maximum Spacing is selected as the method of repetition. It represents the distance at which you want the repeating detail component to repeat. It doesn't have to be the actual width of the detail component.

Detail Rotation This allows you to rotate the detail component in the repeating detail.

Custom Line Types

You can use the Detail Component tool to create custom line types (lines with letters or numbers for various services such as fireproofing, rated walls, fencing, and so on). Note

Figure 10.76

**Making a custom
repeating detail**

that when you create a detail component, you can't use text for the letters but need to draw them using lines.

Figure 10.76 shows the creation of a detail component in the Family Editor and the final result used as a repeating detail in the project environment.

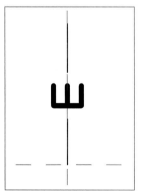

Insulation

The Insulation tool (⊞ Insulation) works just like any other line type.

It's specifically designed as a symbolic representation for batt insulation. When drawn, it has two blue grips that let you change its length later. The element properties of the insulation include only two changeable parameters:

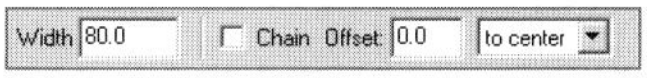

Figure 10.77

The insulation Options bar

Width This parameter is used to control the width of the insulation that is used. The Width parameter is also available in the Options bar when insulation is selected (see Figure 10.77).

Insulation Bulge to Width Ratio This parameter is used to control the density of the circles used in the insulation line.

In most cases, you'll have two lines representing the space in the wall where the insulation needs to fit. Revit allows you to place the insulation using the center line of the insulation as a location line.

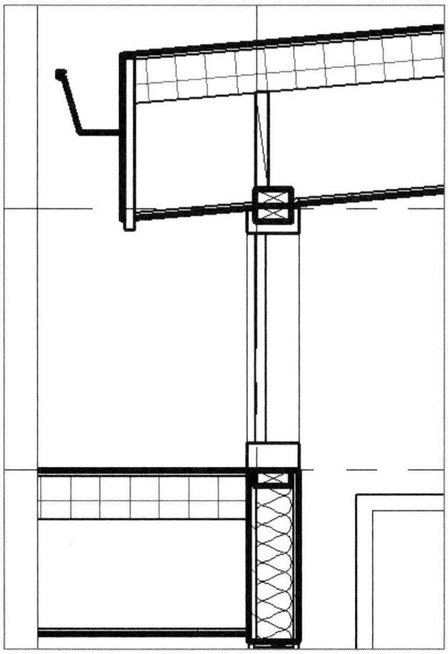

Figure 10.78

Adding insulation to the detail

Adding Insulation

Now, let's add some insulation to your detail:

1. Select the Insulation tool from the Drafting tab.

2. In the Options bar, set the width to 3 ½″ (10cm).

3. Draw in the insulation below the window sill. The finished detail will look like Figure 10.78.

Filled Region

The Filled Region tool (⊠ Filled Region) is a 2D drafting tool that can be applied for many different purposes.

It can help you color surfaces or areas for graphic representations during the conceptual or design-development phase. It also can be a useful tool to document details and show material texture. Figure 10.79 shows how filled regions are used to communicate different functional zones in section.

A filled region consists of a boundary, which can use any line type, and a fill pattern that fills the area defined in the boundary. Figure 10.80 shows a filled region used with a hatch pattern.

Filled regions can also be transparent or opaque to show or hide what is behind them. Figure 10.81 below shows two filled regions: The one at left is opaque, and the one at right is transparent.

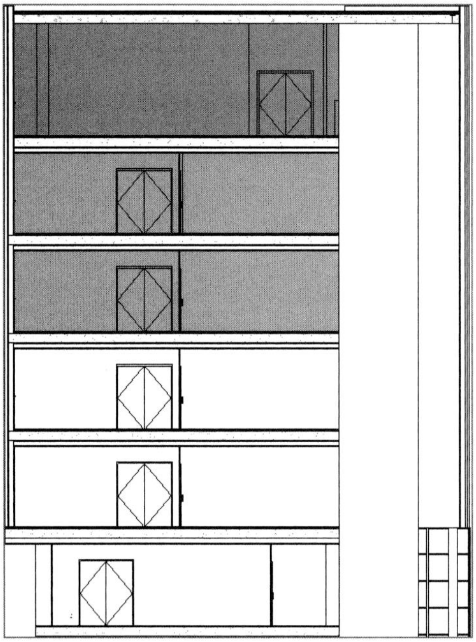

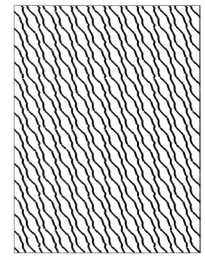

Figure 10.79

Filled regions

Figure 10.80

Filled region with a hatch pattern

Figure 10.81

Transparent and opaque filled regions

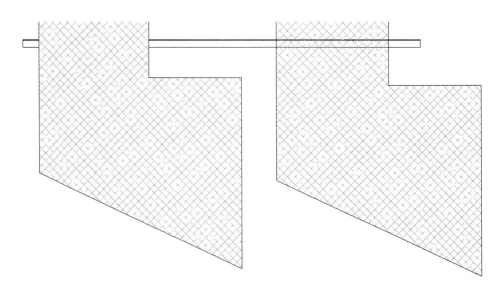

Filled-Region Type Properties

Filled-region type properties define how the fill appears. This includes pattern, pattern color, and transparency (see Figure 10.82).

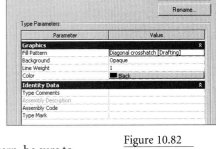

Should you want to change the line type of the region boundary, you need to edit the region and then change the line style in sketch mode. The Edit button appears in the Options bar when a filled region is selected.

For each filled region that has a different pattern, transparency, or other variation in appearance, you need to make a new filled-region type. Remember that type properties propagate to all instances of the type, so making a change to one type may affect many instances in many different views. If you want to make a filled region with a new pattern, be sure to duplicate an existing type before you start changing type parameters.

Revit lets you define different line styles for each boundary segment of a filled region. This can be handy depending on how you're using the filled region.

The effective use of fill regions depends on the fill patterns used in them. Let's review in more detail some basic aspects of fill patterns:

- Fill patterns can be drafting or model patterns.

- Drafting fill patterns are visible only in the view in which they're created; they aren't visible in 3D view.

- Model patterns represent the material characteristics of an element (brick, stone, and so on) and do appear in 3D view.

Figure 10.82

Filled region Type Properties dialog box

> Revit comes with a nice selection of both drafting and model pattern, but, as with any library, it's never enough. You'll often want to create patterns or reuse patterns from other projects or applications.

Show/Remove Hidden Lines

The Show Hidden Lines tool isn't on the Drafting tab. It's part of the Tools toolbar (see Figure 10.83).

In visual communications between architects and engineers, when one element obscures another, either partially or fully, the hidden element is usually graphically represented with dashed lines. Often, just a portion of an element is hidden. In the CAD world, it can take a lot of work to explode a block, split lines, and change many of the line styles to a hidden line type.

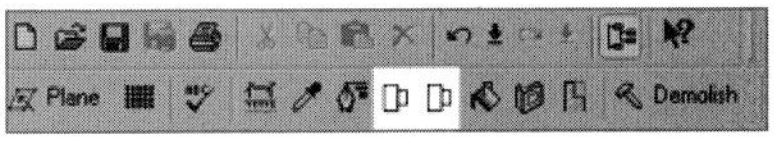

Figure 10.83

Show Hidden Lines tool

Revit has a special tool for recognizing obscured elements and representing the portion that is hidden with dashed lines while still maintaining the complete object. You select the Show Hidden Lines tool, click the element that obscures the object, and then click the element that is obscured. The hidden portion of the element becomes dashed. If an element is obscured with more than one element, keep repeating this operation until you get the desired look. Because Revit is a parametric engine, when you relocate or delete the obscuring element, the hidden element responds intelligently to those changes.

The first image in Figure 10.84 shows an I-beam hidden by another beam. The second image shows the results after the first iteration of the Show Hidden Lines tool, when the second beam is selected as an obscuring element and the I-beam is selected as an obscured element.

Figure 10.84

Using the Show Hidden Lines tool

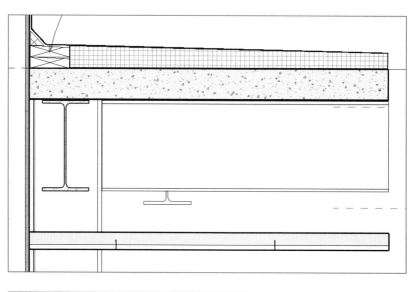

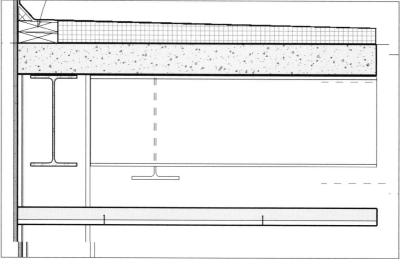

The Show Hidden Lines tool applies to 2D and 3D elements in all possible combinations (detail over detail, detail over model, model over detail, model over model).

Next to the Show Hidden Lines tool is the Remove Hidden Lines tool, which resets the graphic display of the elements so they look like they did before you applied the hidden line mode. This is the second button in Figure 10.83.

CHAPTER 11

Printing

We've reviewed how to create building elements, generate views, and get these views on to sheets. We also covered how to export the information you create in Revit so that it can be used by other downstream applications.

In this chapter, we'll review paper printing as well as some lightweight digital outputs (PDF, and DWF). We'll also look at how to take advantage of Autodesk Design Review in conjunction with Revit, as a way to exchange digital mark-ups. We then offer some best practice tips on printing. This chapter is divided into three sections:

- **Printing your documents**
- **Printing tips**
- **Publishing your BIM data**

Printing Your Documents

In this section, we'll discuss a few of the specific settings and commands that you'll use to print from Revit. If you've been working in the Windows environment, you'll find that printing from Revit is straightforward, because it isn't very different from printing in other Windows-based applications.

Print

Selecting **File → Print** brings you to the dialog box in Figure 11.1.

Print to File

Printing to a file allows you to create a printing/plot file (.prn or .plt) that can then be sent to a print house and can be printed independently of the software in which it was created. This means the recipient doesn't have to have a copy of Revit, Adobe Acrobat, or any other application to print the files. Creating a .plt or .prn file means you can print many copies of the drawing set, at any time, without having to interrupt your workflow while you print. To print to file, select the "Print to file" check box below the Properties button.

Selecting "Combine multiple selected views/sheets into a single file" lets you create one plot file that contains all selected views or sheets as shown in Figure 11.2.

Selecting "Create separate files. View/sheet names will be appended to the specified name" creates a separate file for each view or sheet in the selection. This option is sometimes more practical for printing large sets. If paper runs out or any interruption happens during the printing process, you don't lose any time and can continue printing the remainder of the sheets later. By contrast, if you're printing from a single file, you'll need to start the print job over.

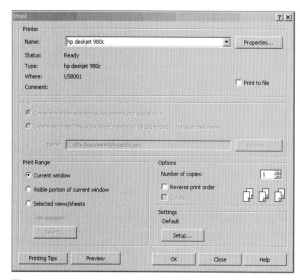

Figure 11.1

Print dialog box

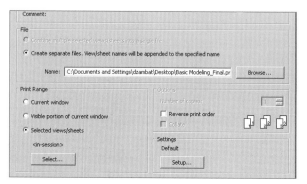

Figure 11.2

Print options when Selected views/sheets is active

Print Range

In this section of the Print dialog box, you can define what exactly you want to print. It includes these options:

Current window This option prints the full extent of the open view, regardless of what extents of that view are visible currently on your screen. For example, if Figure 11.3 is what you see in Revit, Figure 11.4 will be the output when "Current window" is selected.

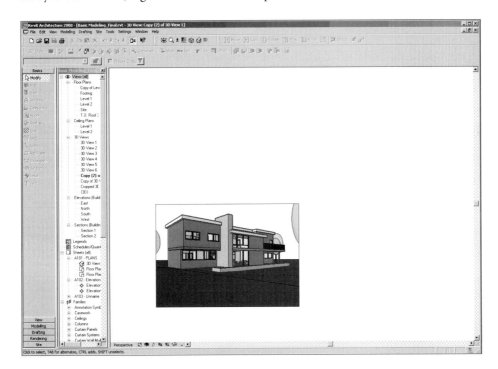

Figure 11.3

Revit view

Figure 11.4

Output: current window

Visible portion of current window This option prints only what you see in the frame of the open window. It's a substitute for Windows' **Print → Page Range → Selection** command, which Revit doesn't currently support.

Figure 11.5 shows a Revit screen (what you see), and Figure 11.6 shows what will print if you select "Visible portion of current window."

Figure 11.5

Revit view

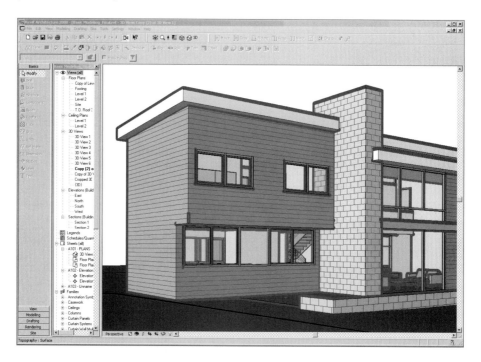

Figure 11.6

Output: visible portion of current window

Another way to print what you see on your screen is to use the Print Screen key, typically found at the upper right of a Windows keyboard. Pressing this key copies a full image of the screen to the Clipboard. From there, you can paste it into Paint or another image application.

Selected views/sheets This option allows you to define a re-usable list of views, sheets, or any combinations of views and sheets. This way, you can essentially batch print a job by sending large quantities of sheets to the printer in one shot. Figure 11.7 shows the View/Sheet Set dialog box.

The dialog box lets you pick any view or sheet to include in the View/Sheet Set. If you only want to include sheets in a set, use the Show option at the bottom of the dialog box to cull the list.

These check boxes only control what you see in the sheet/view list. They don't control what will or won't be printed.

Print Setup

The printing environment is set up using the Print Setup (Figure 11.8) dialog box. From here you set up a printer and settings for printing. You can save these settings with a name so that they can be re-used on later sessions of Revit. These settings can also be transferred to other Revit projects if need be, using the Transfer Project Standards tool. Let's take a look at some of the printing options available to you:

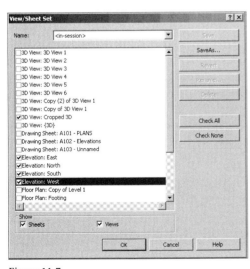

Figure 11.7

View/Sheet Set dialog box

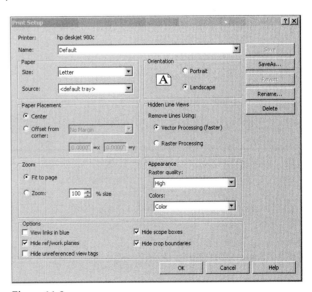

Figure 11.8

Print Setup dialog box

To transfer print settings from one project to another, open both in the same session of Revit, and choose **File → Transfer Project Standards**.

Hidden Lines Views

As mentioned previously, views in Revit can be displayed in four graphic modes: wireframe, hidden-line, shaded views, and shaded views with edges. The most commonly used type of view is hidden-line. You'll choose this type for floor plans, sections, and elevations, and sometimes even for 3D.

Revit lets you select whether you wish to print this type of view with vector processing or raster processing. Vector is faster; however, you need to be aware of some nuances when working with hidden-line views. For example, in Hidden Line mode, transparent glass material prints transparent with raster processing but opaque with vector processing.

Figure 11.9 shows a perspective in Hidden Line mode printed using raster processing. Figure 11.10 shows the same perspective printed with vector processing. Note that you can't see through the glass.

Raster processing offers a higher level of quality of the final image and more predictable results, but it can be slower than vector processing.

If you have many views on a sheet, even if only one of them is an image or a shaded view, Revit automatically changes the printing to raster processing.

Figure 11.9
**Vector print
example**

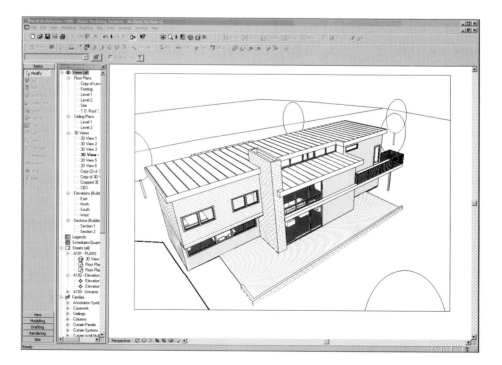

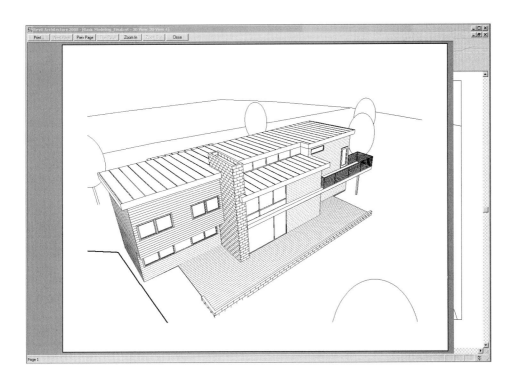

Figure 11.10

Raster print example

Options

The Options pane is at lower left in the Print Setup dialog box. It includes these options:

View links in blue View links are hyperlinked tags that lead you from one view to another or from a sheet to a view. They appear blue in Revit and print black by default, but you can specify to print them in blue, which is how they appear on the screen.

Hide ref/work planes; hide scope boxes; hide crop boundaries These three check boxes let you decide whether to print various datums, including reference planes, scope boxes, and crop boundaries.

Hide unreferenced view tags During the course of a project, you may create a lot of elevation tags, section flags, or detail callouts for working purposes that you don't wish to be printed in the final documents or placed on any sheet. Such view tags are referred to as *unreferenced*, and Revit gives you the option to not print them.

In Figure 11.11, note the section lines, callout views, and crop region in the floor plan.

Figure 11.12 shows that when you select "Hide crop boundaries" and "Hide unreferenced view tags," some features from the view don't appear on the print. These will not show up in the Print Preview either.

Figure 11.11

The view as it appears in Revit

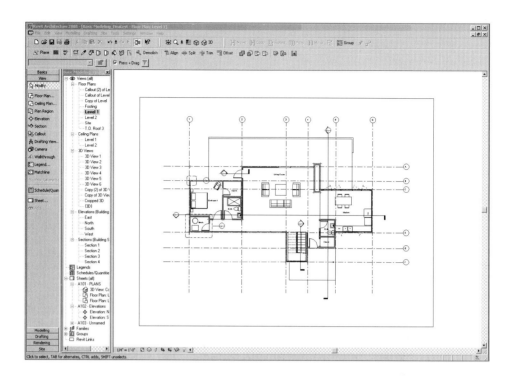

Figure 11.12

The printed view with Hide options selected

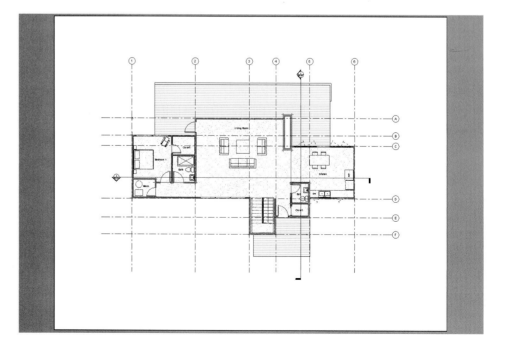

Revit Printing Tips

Here are some helpful, specific hints about printing from Revit:

- When you're plotting large-format sheet sizes to plotters such as the HP DesignJet, change the plotter's settings so the data is processed in the computer. (This will probably be handled through the printer's advanced settings menu. Each printer has its own command sequence.)

- Be sure the far clip plane is active for the view. (**View Properties → Far Clip Plane** should be on in each view.) Having a distant clip plane can significantly slow your printing process.

- Hatches and other types of fill patterns, when used extensively or in high density, can affect performance. (The Sand fill pattern is an example.) If possible, turn them off, or exchange them for less performance-intensive patterns.

- Level of detail can affect performance. If you don't need to print in Fine view, reduce it to Medium or Coarse.

- A DWG, when mistakenly inserted in all views, can affect printing speed. If you notice that your elevation or section prints slowly, the reason may be a DWG that is imported into that view but shows as a single line and thus is unnoticeable. You can check which DWGs are showing by going to the Visibility/Graphics dialog box, clicking the Imported Categories tab, and deselecting the "Show imported categories in this view" check box.

- For general performance improvements, including when you're printing, Revit has a 3GB switch functionality. You can learn about it by navigating to the Knowledge Base area of the Autodesk website. Go to `www.autodesk.com/support`, and choose Autodesk Revit Building. The 3GB switch document is linked on the resulting page.

- Most offices have a finite number of printers. Set up each of your plotters and printers in your Revit template. That way, you don't have to re-create them for each new project.

- Set up some standard sheet sizes. 11″ × 17″, ½ Size E1, and Full Size E1 are some standard architectural sheets. Put those into your template as well.

Publishing Your BIM Data

The construction process goes through many iterations and exchanges of information among different parties. Exchanging a full-blown data-rich Building Information Model is not always required, and not everyone on the project team will be using Revit. Many team members just need to see a drawing to approve or mark-up some changes and send it back to you. Some team members may be using dial-up Internet connections or older computers that can't handle big downloads effectively (or at all). You may not be ready to share your intellectual property with the world in the form of editable drawings. Finally, you may be concerned about unauthorized appropriation or editing of your documents by others. This is where utilizing light-weight digital output comes into play.

You need to be able to share drawings and documentation in a safe, non-editable, light-weight form that can be viewed by others outside the world of Revit. This is the problem that some new publishing technologies are trying to solve.

Design Web Format (DWF)

Design Web Format (DWF) is Autodesk's solution for publishing intelligent data in a light, easy, and secure way while preserving the power of the information embedded in the design documents. DWF files are highly compressed and thus are capable of transmitting big design models via email or other limited-transfer technologies.

DWF Publishing Options

You can publish a Revit project as a DWF file and send these to various stakeholders in the building process. With the latest version of Autodesk Design Review it is possible to view, and even mark up these files. Microsoft Vista has an embedded DWF viewer, so the receiver won't have to install a separate DWF viewer as required with machines running Windows XP or earlier. If you are running Windows XP, we suggest you and your design team install the latest version of Autodesk Design Review. If you want to leverage the full power of what DWF offers, you can suggest that the recipients of your DWFs download the Autodesk DWF viewer from www.Autodesk.com/DWF.

Revit has a built-in DWF publisher, so you don't need to install any additional drivers in order to create DWFs. There are two ways to publish a DWF from Revit:

- 2D DWF (good for sending out 2D sheets and individual drawings)

- 3D DWF (good for creating a lightweight 3D representation of your BIM model)

You'll find the Publish DWF functionality at **File → Publish DWF** (see Figure 11.13).

Figure 11.13
Publish to DWF options

DWF EXPORT OPTIONS

Revit is a BIM model with tons of information embedded in it. Much of this information is also published into the DWF format. You can send model and room data with the DWF, or choose not to. This option is available under **File → Publish → 2D or 3D DWF** and choose the Options button (Figure 11.14).

When you select the Model Elements option in the DWF Export Options dialog box, all the property information about the model elements in the view that is being exported are published to DWF. This allows anyone viewing the DWF to select an object in that view and see its properties. Some examples of these properties are area, length, family name, and so on.

Selecting the "Rooms and Areas" check box publishes additional information that isn't included in Model Elements, because in Revit, rooms and areas are objects rather than physical elements. Room area and perimeter are two examples. This information can be helpful, especially to facility managers to whom you may be sending your DWFs.

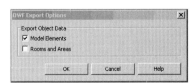

Figure 11.14

The Publish dialog and DWF Export-Options dialog

EXPORTING A VIEW OR SHEET AS A SINGLE FILE

When publishing to DWF, you can make separate DWF files for each view or publish all views into one DWF file. To do so, select the "Export each view or sheet as a single file" check box in the Export dialog box. Note that even though DWF is a lightweight format, depending on the size and complexity of the project you're dealing with, a DWF can be large; you may want to consider splitting it into a few separate DWFs.

Publishing to 2D DWF

When you publish to 2D DWF, the information is published in 2D flat drawings, regardless of the view type. This means that perspective and axonometric views are published as flat images. Figure 11.15 shows a 2D DWF. Note that although the drawing is technically in two dimensions, it retains its visibility settings and element properties.

Publishing to 3D DWF

Publishing a 3D DWF creates a full-blown 3D DWF model. When opened with a DWF viewer you can turn visibility of separate elements on and off, slice the model in sections, make elements transparent, and review the model in a variety of ways. Figure 11.16 shows some of this functionality.

Figure 11.15

A 2D DWF

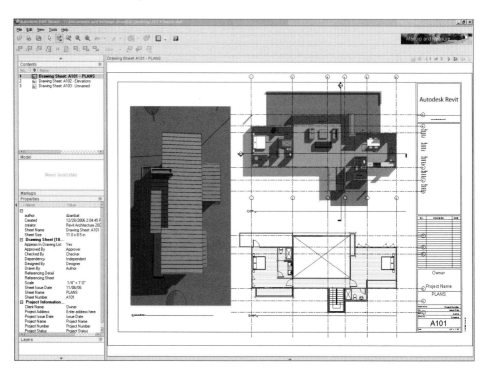

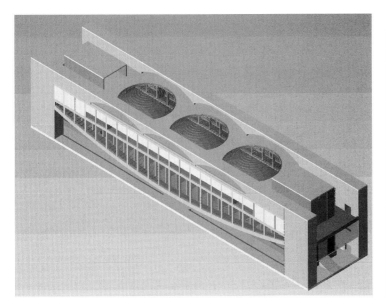

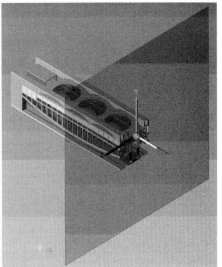

Figure 11.16

**A 3D DWF
Image courtesy of
Simone Cappochin**

The cross-section tool lets you slice the model in any direction and reveal the exterior. You not only see the 3D information and can easily move around and review parts of the building, but you can inspect the properties of any element available in the model.

Sharing digital models using 3D DWF has proven to be of special value for construction companies. It both facilitates design visualization in the field and allows builders to do a constructability review in the office before problems arise in the field. 3D DWFs are also useful to owners because they effectively convey the future look and feel of their building.

In the Design Review application, when you select a Revit wall in the 3D view (Figure 11.17) it displays all its properties in the left pane. Viewing models and querying element properties is just one advantage of this tool. The DWF environment opens up new, intelligent ways to share information, propose revisions, and discuss document changes to the BIM model.

Marking Up Drawings with Design Review

Autodesk Design Review allows you to mark up DWFs with annotations and redline clouds with questions and comments. These comments are stored in the DWF file, and even show up in your Revit file by linking in a DWF file.

Figure 11.17

**DWF element
properties**

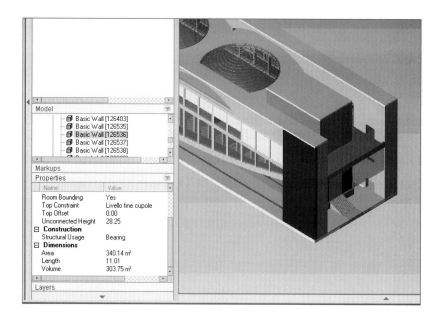

In a time-honored scenario, an architect sends a set of physical drawings to their engineer. The engineer reviews them, marks with a red pen the necessary changes, and sends the drawings back to the architect. The architect reviews the revised drawings and makes the changes in their digital files. This process is repeated throughout the life of the project. Not only is there a lot of room for error with all the transposing of information, but a lot of money is spent on printer paper, postage, and shipping. The transmission of black-and-white, smeared facsimiles often results in misinterpreted information. Using DWF reduces costly errors and omissions in your communications with team members and clients. Let's review how you can leverage these tools.

A WORKFLOW SCENARIO: MARKING UP A 2D DWF FROM A REVIT MODEL
In Revit, the architect opens the sheet that they wish to send to a consultant, then publishes it to 2D DWF, and sends it via email.

Mark-up functionality only works with Revit Sheets—make sure you are publishing Sheets, not views when working with the DWF mark-up features.

The consultant opens the DWF in Design Review, reviews the drawings, makes a markup with desired changes, and sends the DWF back to the architect (email again). Figure 11.18 shows a sample marked-up DWF.

The architect links the DWF markup (**File → Import/Link → Link DWF** markup set…) into the Revit file form which the DWF was originally generated. The red markup shows up on the correct sheet and in correct position, shown in Figure 11.19.

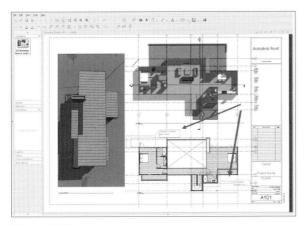

Figure 11.18
A marked-up DWF

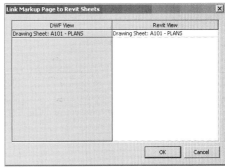

Figure 11.19
Link Markup Page to Revit Sheet

Each linked markup has a defined status (None, Question, For Review, or Done), which is shown in the Element Properties dialog box (Figure 11.20). When initially linked, the default status is None, but it can be changed to another status after an initial review. Thus, the architects in the team can track whether a certain change request has been executed or is still under review or discussion.

MARKING UP 3D DWFS

Collaborating through a digital publishing mechanism is of value for many participants in the building industry because if allows for shorter review cycles; faster decisions; better communication of information; better visualization of projects; and better tracking, archiving, and documenting of change orders.

Figure 11.20
Element Properties dialog box

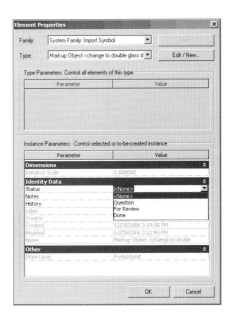

Publishing to PDF

Portable Document Format (PDF) is an Adobe product. The main uses of PDF in the past were securing documents the originator didn't wish to have edited, and putting content into a manageable file size for digital transfer. Today, PDF is also commonly used to transfer drawings among team members and reprographic companies.

Revit supports printing to PDF through the use of printer drivers. You need at least one PDF driver installed on your machine to be able to print to PDF.

Figure 11.21

With Design Review, mark-ups can even be added to 3D views

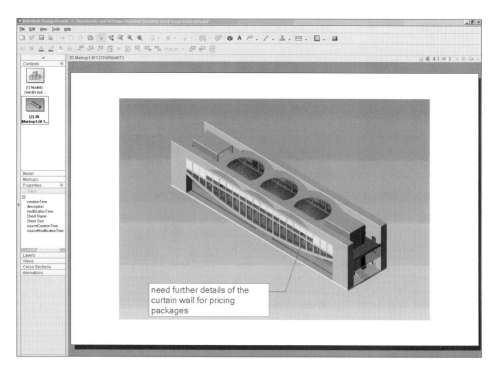

CHAPTER 12

Advanced Topics

This chapter touches on three topics in Revit that are beyond the basics. These topics are the fodder for an advanced book, but knowing the fundamentals about them can be useful for your projects.

In this chapter, we will review the basics of the Family Editor, using Design Options, and Worksharing. The Family Editor allows you to create and edit components in Revit. The Design Options tool allows you to make design iterations within Revit. And Worksharing lets you divide the model so more than one person can work on it at the same time. This chapter includes these sections:

- ■ **Families**

- ■ **Design Options**

- ■ **Worksharing**

Families

Within Revit, components and other content are referred to as *families*. Many of these elements can be created and edited outside of a project file. Revit comes with a built-in family-editing application that is tailored for making all types of content, from doors and windows, to annotation symbols, to stand-alone furniture. Creating families is a critical aspect of working with Revit, because families make up a vast amount of what goes into a model. Family editing is a more complex workflow involving geometry, constraints, and adding parametric variability into your components. That can't be covered completely in one chapter, but we will cover the basics so that you can at least get started.

All elements in Revit are considered families. When you open Revit, many architectural objects and annotation symbols are already created and ready to use. Families can be found or pointed to from several places in the UI:

- Under the Project Browser you can find all Loaded Families in the project.

- In the Type Selector when an element is selected.

- At **File → Load from Library → Load** Family. Here you'll find all the available default families that exist outside of the project, in an external library that you can load in the project. You can also browse from this location to any custom location where you have saved families that you've created.

- Via a link to a web library that's available when you're loading a family (**File → Load from Library → Load Family**. See the Web Library button), where you can also find additional content.

- At www.autodesk.com/revitarchitecture. Click "Data and Downloads," and then click "Templates and Libraries." You can download thousands of families created for different geographic regions.

As we mentioned earlier in this book, Revit uses three types of families:

- System families

- In-place families

- Component families

We'll discuss them next.

System Families

System families are created in the context of a Revit project, on the fly. You can create a new type of system family only by duplicating an existing family and then changing preset properties. Below is a list of the Families that fall into this category.

- Walls

- Roofs

- Stairs
- Floors
- Ceilings
- Ramps
- Mullions

To create a new system family, select one that is the most similar to the one you need, duplicate its type, rename it, and modify it. Let's use a wall as an example:

1. Activate the Wall tool. From the Type Selector, select a wall that has similar properties to the wall you need to create. If none are similar, it's easiest to use a Generic wall.

2. Click the Properties button, then click the Edit/New button, and click Duplicate.

3. You're prompted to give the new wall type a name. Rename the wall to reflect your design intent.

4. Start editing the wall by clicking the Edit button under Structure. Doing so opens another dialog box where you can add and modify layers of the wall structure. By clicking the fields for Function, Material, and Thickness, you can change the values (see Figure 12.1).

Using the Preview button at the bottom of this dialog box you can switch the Preview of the wall structure from Plan to Section.

Figure 12.1
Modifying wall types

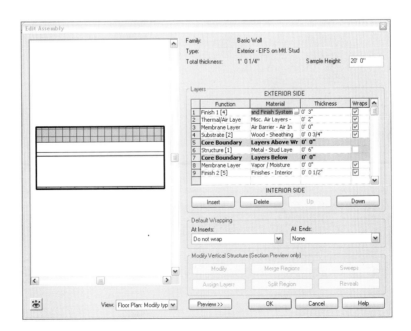

In-Place Families

In-place families are built in the context of your project using the Family Editor interface. This allows you to model geometry using your project as a reference point. These families are useful for one-off objects that are highly specific to your project and unlikely to be reused in other projects. Usually they are connected with some complex geometry or have complicated shapes.

Figure 12.2

Family Category and Parameters dialog box

You create in-place families by clicking Create on the Modeling tab of the Design bar (|| Create...) or from the Modeling Pulldown menu. Revit then lets you draw whatever you want and assign that to whatever category of element you wish. Having the elements belong to a correct category is important later in the process for scheduling and controlling visibility of those elements. The list of categories is a fixed list—if no category maps to what you intend to create, use the Generic Model category. Some of these fields are shown in the "Family Category and Parameters" dialog box that pops up the moment you click the Create button. See Figure 12.2.

The in-place family is good for creating nonstandard element types such as slanted and tapered walls, unusual roof shapes, and furniture or other building elements that must conform to specific geometry in your model (a bench along a curved wall for example). Figure 12.3 shows an in-place wall that follows the shape of a site and has a non-orthogonal profile.

Figure 12.3

Sample in-place wall

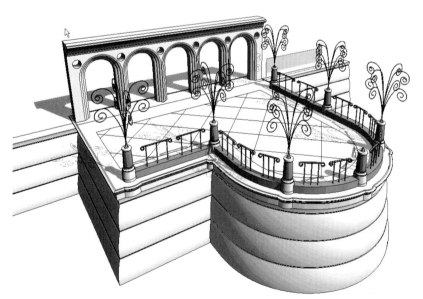

Courtesy of Emmanuel Di Giacommo

Component Families

Component families are created and can be modified in an environment outside the Revit project, called the Family Editor. The fact that these types of families aren't created directly within the project environment allows some diversification of the project workflow and can help to minimize the number of users directly in a project file on large projects.

Component families can include doors, windows, furniture, plumbing fixtures, light fixtures, entourage, columns, annotations, title blocks, massing families, structural elements, electrical equipment, site equipment, plants, profiles, and so on. Some examples are shown in Figure 12.4.

You will periodically need to open the Family Editor to create a new family. To do so, select **File → New → Family**. Often however, you are working within a project and need to change a family already inserted into that project. To edit a family that is being used in your project, select the family, and then click the Edit Family tool in the Options bar. You'll find yourself in the Family Editor environment.

Because this is an introductory book about Revit, we won't explain the Family Editor in detail (it deserves an entire, separate book), but we would like to explain its basic principles. The Family Editor is designed to do two primary tasks:

- Modify an existing element

- Create a new element

The Family Editor is a unique design environment (see Figure 12.5), but it isn't separate software that you have to install. It's an integral application that is automatically installed with Revit. The Family Editor resembles the Revit project environment but is tailored for specific modeling tasks. It has only one Design bar in which relevant tools are located. This is a task-oriented design environment.

Figure 12.4

Component family examples

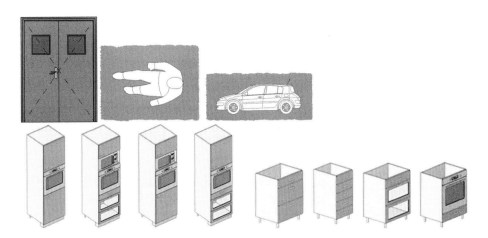

Figure 12.5

The Family Editor

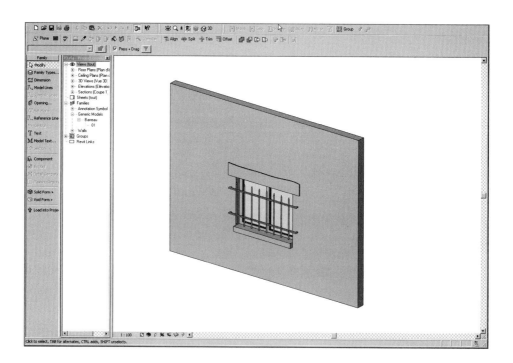

You can open the Family Editor several ways:

- Edit a family directly from within a project.

- Open a `.rfa` file from Windows Explorer.

- Choose **File → New → Family** (to create a new family).

When you create a new family, you're prompted to select a template. The templates are predefined files that are set up for the purpose of creating specific content that will behave according to the characteristics of the element to be created. For example, the window template looks different than the door template. The next section discusses templates in more detail.

Family Templates

If you're creating a table, you need to start with the furniture template. If you wish to create a sink, you start with a plumbing fixture template. To create a new door, open a door template. You get the idea. The available templates for modeling elements are listed in Figure 12.6 and can be found in your `Libraries` folder, located here:

```
C:\Documents and Settings\All Users\Application Data\Autodesk\RAC
2008\Imperial Library
```

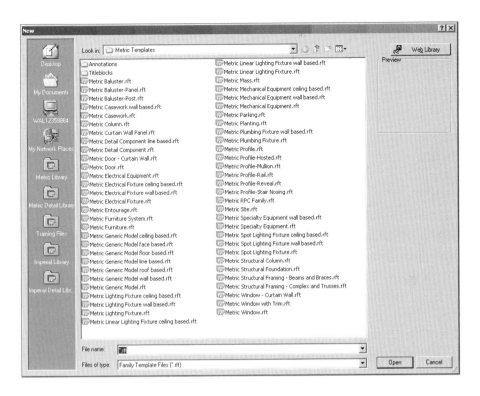

Figure 12.6
Family types

The family templates are different for Metric and Imperial content. Make sure you select the correct ones when you install Revit.

The family templates are grouped in three categories:

- Model templates (the one you see listed when you open this dialog box)
- Annotation family templates (tags, keynotes, and so on)
- Title block families (you can create custom title blocks per project or company)

Selecting a correct template before you create a family is essential. A correct template does the following:

- Categorizes the family you create. This ensures that your family is located in the Project Browser and has a graphic appearance that's consistent with other elements of the same category.
- Lists that family in the correct Type Selector when elements are selected.
- Schedules the family according to the type you selected.
- Enables content-specific parameters and behaviors.

If you want to create a window, but you choose the door template, your window won't have the parameters necessary to interact properly with the model. If you wish to create furniture, but you select a generic family, your furniture piece won't schedule when you schedule your furniture, and so on.

Rule number one: Select the correct template.

If none of the categories match what you're hoping to create, use the generic family template.

Templates are provided for each category; some additional family templates are also provided. Depending on the type of element, you'll notice that some templates are host-based. (Light fixtures can be wall-based, ceiling-based, floor-based, and so on.) Make sure you select the one that will make your element behave appropriately. Figure 12.7 shows some hosted families.

You CAN change the family type after the creation of the family. To do that, go to **Settings →
Family Categories** and change to the New category. This will categorize your element correctly for scheduling, however, most probably will not transform the element to behave
according to that category.

Figure 12.7

**Floor-based and
wall-based lighting
fixtures**

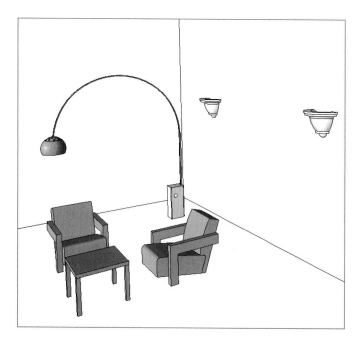

Parametric and Nonparametric Family Types

You can create 2D and 3D families in the Family Editor that can be either parametric or non-parametric.

Parametric families allow variation in size and material to be captured and edited as parameters. Many types of parametric variations can be stored in a single family as types. An example of a parametric object is a table that is produced in 4 different sizes and 2 different wood types, or a window that is manufactured in 20 different sizes. Figure 12.8 shows a parametric family in two different sizes: As the family is changed, the table size and chair count increase or decrease.

Nonparametric families do *not* provide changeable dimensions; they may provide variation in material, if anything. An example is a furniture family that is produced in only one size (a Le Corbusier chair or a designer lamp as an example). You can't buy it in other sizes, and thus there is no need for parametric properties. Note that you can make any family parametric at any time by adding a parametric dimension to it. Nothing in the family template limits a family to being nonparametric. Figure 12.9 shows a sample nonparametric family.

Figure 12.8
A parametric family

Figure 12.9
Nonparametric family

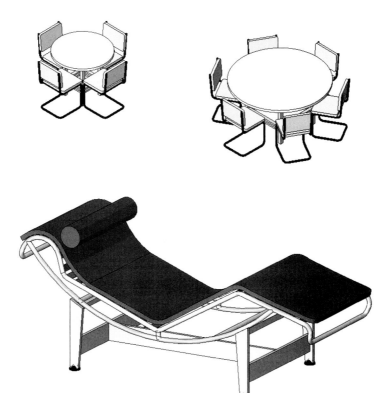

A possible scenario for nonparametric families can involve using content previously made with other and importing it into the Family Editor. Revit allows you to import 2D as well as 3D DWG or SKP files (SketchUp files). Revit reads these file types, and you can leverage them to extend your Revit library with elements you've created with other software packages.

Levels of Detail and View Visibility

Figure 12.10

Family Element Visibility Settings dialog box

Families in Revit let you control the visibility of their individual parts based on the view's detail level. (You can change the detail level in the model using the View Control bar.) When you're working in the Family Editor, you can select any element(s) and choose Visi-

bility from the Options bar. A dialog box allows you to change the element's visibility using three levels of detail: Coarse, Medium, and Fine. If all levels of detail are selected, then the element appears all the time, in each possible level of detail. The Family Element Visibility Settings dialog box is shown in Figure 12.10. You can also make elements appear or not in different types of views: plan, front/back, and left/right. Elements are always visible in 3D views, provided all levels of detail are selected.

If you make a simple table or a chair, you'll probably view the table as a rectangle in all three levels of detail. If you make a door family, however, you'll want to change the display at different scales. Figure 12.11 shows the three levels of detail. Note that the table doesn't change; the walls get two different representations, and the door has three.

Revit families are flexible: You can choose to display only certain elements of the family in one level of detail and a more complicated presentation in another.

Family Types

Figure 12.11

Left to right: Coarse, Medium, and Fine levels of detail

The Family Editor allows for the creation of *family types*. These are typically objects created by manufacturers: The fundamental geometry is the same, but it has a variety of standard sizes.

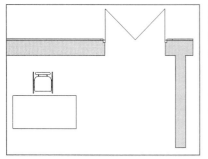
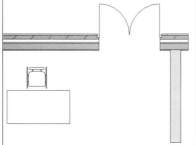
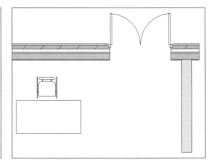

Instead of creating 60–70 families that are the same shape and material but have many dimensional variations, with Revit, you only need to model one family and create types for each variation. You can then add these types to a *type catalog* (a simple comma-delimited .txt file) that makes types of that family, as shown in Figure 12.12.

In the project environment, you can select all available types in the Project Browser or in the Type Selector.

You can design Revit families that use simple mathematical formulas to determine rules of behavior. For example, a shelving family can be set up so that when a shelf spans longer than 20″ (50 cm), it gets another support, as illustrated in Figure 12.13.

All the different family templates let you use custom fields and formulas, so there is no limit to what you can create.

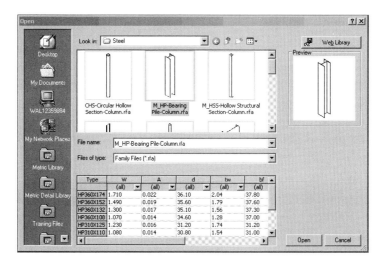

Figure 12.12

A family using a type catalog

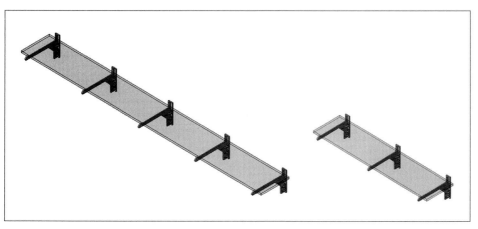

Figure 12.13

Formulas in families

Visual Control

Each family belongs to a category, but you can create additional subcategories in the Family Editor to provide a richer set of controls over the visual and graphic appearance of geometry in the family. A door family, for example, can have several meaningful subcategories: door leaf, handle, hardware, opening direction, frame, and so on. You can control visibility of each of those subcategories by selecting and deselecting them.

Nested Families

Revit lets you combine multiple families into one family. Imagine a door that incorporates a fixed transom window above it. These can be created as two separate families initially but combined into one to be inserted into the project. Nesting one family into the other, rather than using two, simplifies placement and design management in the final project. Revit also allows you to match the parameters so that when you change the width of a door, the transom window width changes, too. Figure 12.14 shows a door with a nested transom: rectangular and arched. Both are separate families combined into one family.

Figure 12.15 shows the dependency of the width of the door and the transom; any changes to one apply to the other automatically.

All these behaviors are defined by you, the user. No other software lets you do this without knowing some form of programming language. Similar to the previous example, Figure 12.16 shows a two-pick Brise Soleil family with exchangeable lamellas that are nested.

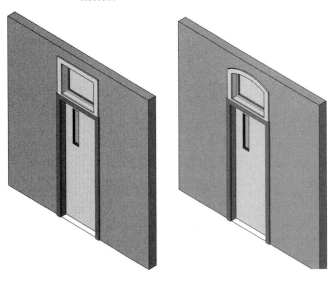

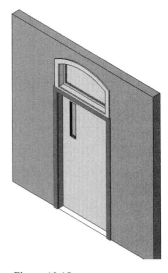

Figure 12.14
A nested family

Figure 12.15
Nested families change together.

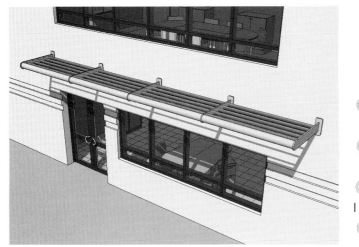

Figure 12.16
Another example of nested families

Courtesy of Philippe Drouant

The Family Editor supports shared families: You may have one family repeating as a nested family in many different families (a handle can be used on various types of doors, windows, and so on). These families can be shared so that when one changes, all others change, regardless of the host in which they're nested.

The Revit Family Editor allows for complex families, from both a geometrical and a behavioral aspect. Figure 12.17 shows some complex nested families that you can create in Revit.

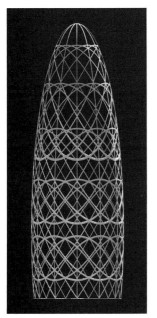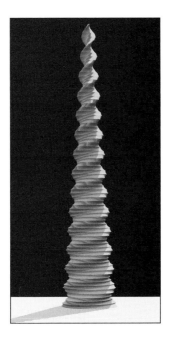

Figure 12.17
Complex nested families

Courtesy of Phil Read

Figure 12.18
Historical windows

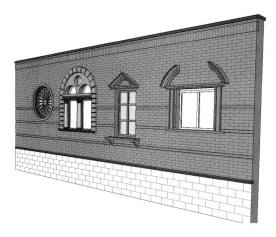

Historical architecture is no challenge for Revit; extremely complex content has been created using the Family Editor all around the world. Figure 12.18 shows an example of some historical windows.

Upgrading Families

Regardless of which version of Revit you use to create families, you can always open them in a version that is the same or higher. Revit automatically upgrades families from previous releases. Note that once a family has been upgraded and saved, you can't reopen that family in an older version of Revit.

> Revit families are part of the project where they're used. There's no need to send out archive packages or extra libraries when you share the project with someone else. The families are an integral part of the Revit project.

Design Options

Design iteration is an integral part of a design process, and as architects we're all familiar with the need for and importance of working through multiple solutions. Design alternatives, schemes, options, versions—whatever you may call them—happen throughout the life of a project. During initial feasibility studies, deciding how to best orient functional program elements relative to the site is common and often involves myriad schemes. Comparing and estimating cost becomes a key factor as well. For each proposal, what is the associated cost? For example, when you move into a more detailed design and want to iterate through a series of an entry-canopy options, countless sketches and ideas are processed, and the ability to visualize and analyze multiple solutions is essential to making decisions. Regardless of the stage in the process, you often need to create several design variations.

A typical method for making multiple design schemes, if you're working with a legacy CAD application, is to create one initial design and then make copies of it. Each copy becomes a separate file that is used to explore an alternate design solution independently. Although this approach can work well initially, the downstream effects can be difficult to manage. Integrating ideas from one file to another, maintaining a common set of references, and even something as mundane as file-naming schemes can be tedious and error prone.

Revit has a tool specifically designed to address this problem: Design Options. To examine Design Options, we'll use Figure 12.19, which shows variations of balcony solutions.

Figure 12.19

Design Options for balconies

The Design Options Interface

You won't see the Design Options tools the first time you open Revit. To display the Design Options tools, right-click above the Options bar, and choose Design Options from the flyout menu that appears. Figure 12.20 shows this option and the toolbar that appears as a result.

Because this book is an introduction to Revit, we won't go into the use of design options in depth, but we'll cover the principles behind this tool. Let's briefly explore a scenario for Design Options. Let's say you need to create various schemes for laying out interior partitions and desks in an office. You want to make two options, which are shown in Figure 12.21: an area with private offices and an open office plan.

Figure 12.20

Making the Design Options toolbar visible

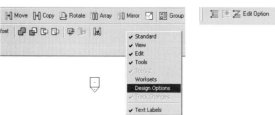

Figure 12.21

Two design options

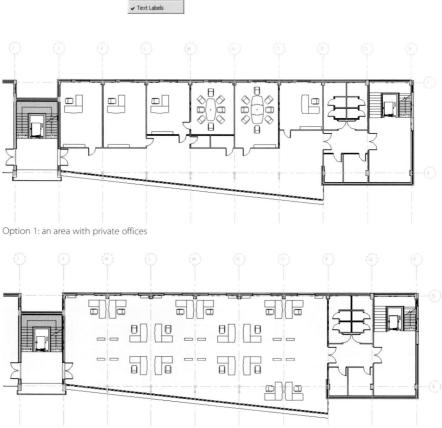

Option 1: an area with private offices

Option 2: an open office plan

It's possible to create both of these options in one Revit file. You can move elements from option to option on the fly. You can also generate views that show the two options, place these views on sheets, and then present them for review. Here are some steps describing a design options workflow in Revit:

Figure 12.22

Design Options dialog box

1. Open the Design Options dialog box by clicking the Design Options button on the toolbar ( ). It will be the only button active.

2. To create a new Option Set, click New in the Option Set section of the dialog box. Option Sets control subsets of options. For example, if you want two different entry canopies, the Option Set will be for entry canopies, and the options will be for canopy A and canopy B.

3. Create Option 1 and Option 2 within that option set by clicking New in the Option section of the dialog box. Your Option Set and options should look like Figure 12.22 when you're finished.

4. When you're finished, click Close to exit the dialog box.

You can make as many option sets with as many options in the same model as you need.

Setting Your Views

You can customize each view to show various design options. Note that only one option from each Option Set can be viewed at a time. Once design options have been created, a new Design Options tab shows up in the Visibility/Graphic Overrides dialog box. From here, you can specify which option you want to appear in the view. To have the same view type show two different options, you must duplicate the view and in that dialog box change the design option that you want to display. Figure 12.23 shows the option sets in the Visibility/Graphic Overrides dialog box.

By default, the first option you created will be set to Primary and that will remain so unless you specify otherwise. To change the primary option, select the option, and click the Make Primary button. So, if the first Option you created is Option 1, then that will be the Primary option and this option will be displayed by default automatically in each view (see the Automatic setting in Figure 12.23). To change the Option you want displayed by default in a view, click on Automatic—a list of all available options will be displayed and you can select the one you wish to display in that particular view.

Figure 12.23

Visibility/Graphic Overrides dialog box

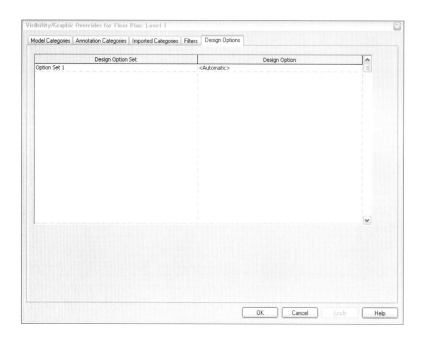

Creating the Elements in the Options

To add elements to an option, click the Edit Option button on the Design Options toolbar, and select the option you want to work in. Figure 12.24 shows these selections for the example we've set up.

Once you're in the proper view with the correct option set and visibility selected, you can start designing for that option. You can tell when an option is active for editing in two ways:

- You can't select elements outside the option set.
- The Edit Option button on the toolbar appears depressed.

In real practice, you'll probably start with one design and then realize you want to study some iterations of an element of that design. As an example, let's consider a canopy. If you've already modeled a canopy, but you want to study some design iterations on it, you need to create Design Options. When you do, make sure to move the current canopy design to one of those Option Sets. If you don't, you'll see multiple canopies overlaying each other in your views.

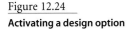

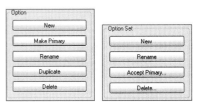

Figure 12.24
Activating a design option

Figure 12.25
Adding elements to a design option

Figure 12.26
Make Primary and Accept Primary

With no design options active, select all the elements for an option, and click the "Add to Design Option" button (⊞). Move the elements to one design option by selecting the appropriate check boxes shown in Figure 12.25. To remove an element from a design option, highlight the element, and click the third button (⊠).

Now, in your first view, open the Visibility/Graphic Overrides dialog box, and click the Design Options tab. Change the design option from Automatic to Option 1. In the duplicate view, do the same thing, but change the design option to Option 2. In each plan view, only one option is now shown.

You may want a quantity overview showing how much material one option uses versus the other. You can generate a schedule that reports information about elements in a specific option. To define what the schedule reports relative to what is visible in the model, edit the visibility. Click the Edit button to open the Visibility/Graphic Overrides dialog box.

Revit won't report double or triple entities of all options for quantity calculations. It reports quantities for only one design option at a time.

Once you've decided on a solution, make the option with which you want to continue the design the primary option (see Figure 12.26). You can do this by clicking the Make Primary button in the Design Options dialog box. Then, click Accept Primary. This eliminates all the other options and merges your chosen option back into the model.

Worksharing

Most projects involve more than one person working at any given time. Often, many people work in tandem to meet deadlines and produce construction documents. Keeping with the theme of an integrated single-file building model, Revit allows for this workflow without breaking apart the model. A complex model can be edited by many people at once using what is called *worksharing*.

There are various ways that you can share work across a team with Revit:

- File linking
- Borrowing elements
- Worksets

We covered the idea of linked file-sharing methodology in Chapter 7.
In this section, we'll focus on the other two methods of sharing.

Borrowing Elements

This methodology allows team members to work on the same file and take ownership of elements to work on. When elements aren't taken by anyone, they're free to be taken and then edited. When a team member needs to work on an element that belongs to someone else, that member gets a message that the element belongs to someone and can then send a notification to the current owner of the element requesting access. The owner of the element can then grant permission to take ownership—*relinquishing* elements, as it's called in Revit.

Worksharing Using the Worksets Methodology

A *workset* is a collection of building elements (floors, roofs, walls, windows, and so on) that can be edited by one team member at a time. You need to understand some core concepts about worksharing before you begin. By default, worksharing isn't enabled when you start a project.

> Once you enable worksharing in a model, you can't undo it. Remember that. We suggest that you make a copy of your file before you enable worksharing so you keep an unshared version as a backup.

You share your work by first creating a *central file*. Each user opens the central file and saves a local copy of it. All work is done from this copied—but still associated—copy. This enables every user to open their own file simultaneously. The elements in each separate file are still tied to an ownership rule tied to the central file, making it impossible for you to edit an element in your local file if that same element is owned by someone else. Revit is a database. In effect, you're taking permissions of one or more elements from the central database file and copying changes (and permissions) to the central file. If one user has ownership over an element, no other user can edit that element until its permissions and changes are reconciled with the central file.

Worksets also let you put collections of elements into a container, which is useful for turning off the visibility of elements that aren't being worked on. When you enable work-sharing, a new tab appears in the Visibility/Graphics Overrides dialog box for the worksets. You can turn on or off any workset in any view and make those settings part of your view templates.

Worksharing Basics

The other team members can view the elements of any workset but can only edit them using element borrowing.

Worksharing is designed to accommodate any division of labor you see fit. There are no inherent restrictions in how you use worksharing to accomplish work. For example, if you want to break up a team and have one group work on the exterior shell and one work on the interior core, this isn't a problem. At any point in a project, you can create or remove worksets.

By default, the Worksets toolbar isn't activated in Revit. To turn it on, right-click in a blank area of the toolbar, and select Worksets from the flyout menu.

You can start worksharing in two ways:

- Choose **File → Worksets** from the main menu.

- Click the Worksets button on the Worksets toolbar, shown in Figure 12.27.

Figure 12.27

The Worksets toolbar

Either of these actions opens a dialog box (Figure 12.28) telling you that you're about to enable worksharing and that what you're doing can't be undone. By default, Revit creates two worksets: One contains the levels and grids; the other contains every-thing else and is named Workset1.

Three other types of worksets are created automatically:

Views worksets Each view in a project has a dedicated view workset. It contains the view's definition and any view-specific elements (text, dimensions, and so on). View-specific ele-ments can't be moved to another workset.

Figure 12.28

Activating worksets with a project

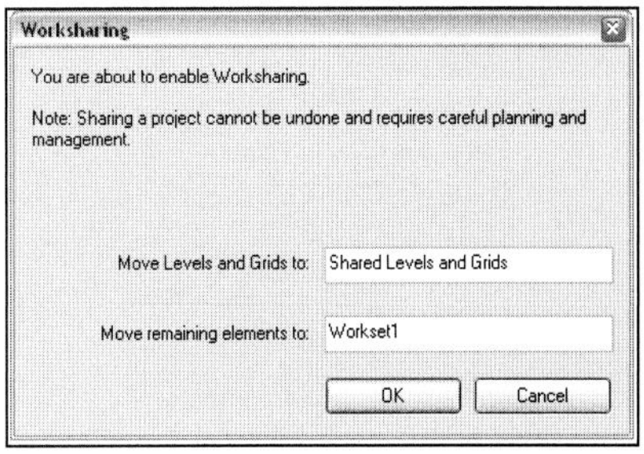

Family worksets For each loaded family in the project, an automatic workset is created.

Project standards worksets This automatic workset covers project set-tings like materials, line styles, and so on.

Once you've activated the worksets, you'll see the dialog box shown in Figure 12.29. Here, you can add and remove worksets.

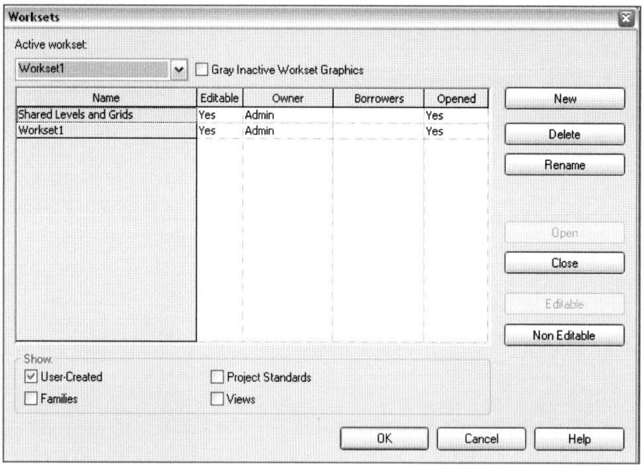

Figure 12.29
Worksets dialog box

Figure 12.29
Worksets dialog box

When you activate worksets, you're the owner of all of them. This is what the Yes value in the Editable column means.

> The activation of worksets is usually done by the team's project manager, who creates this first workset setup, creates user worksets, and assigns people to work on the project.

Workset Organization

It's important that you think of your project as a holistic building when dividing into worksets. Some good examples of worksets are "Shell and Core," Exterior Skin, First Floor Interior Partitions, and so on. Technically once you have activated worksharing, you do not need to add any more worksets than the ones Revit has generated. This is because Revit will automatically manage ownership of elements on a per-element basis and relinquish ownership automatically when you save to central. Worksets should be used to help define visibility and divisions of labor within the team.

Workflow

There is always one central file that spawns local files and manages element ownerships. This is the file that changes are saved into and from which you get updated versions of the model as you work. Work can be done directly in the central file, but that isn't a suggested workflow.

To begin using worksharing, follow these steps:

1. Activate worksets.

2. Draw the basic layout, exterior shell, and so on.

3. Create worksets.

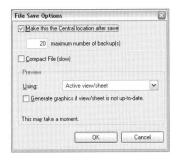

Figure 12.30

Saving a central file

Figure 12.31

Warning about creating a local file

4. Move elements into worksets (select the element, open the Element Properties and under Worksets change the workset to which it needs to belong).

5. Save the file as a central file. To do so, choose **File → Save As**, and click Options. In the resulting dialog box (Figure 12.30), select the "Make this the Central location after save" check box and finish by clicking OK.

6. Make local copies of the central file.

To use the central file, you go against everything any IT manager ever yelled at you for: You make a local copy of the central file and work directly off your C drive. Although this approach is a bad idea for most work, for the Revit database, it does a couple of good things:

- It allows more than one user to make changes to the file.

- It's more responsive as the file gets larger, because your access speed to your hard drive is faster than most networks.

You can make a local copy by dragging and dropping the central file to your desktop or anywhere on your C drive, or by opening the central file and 'Saving As' to your workstation. Open that file. You'll originally see the dialog box shown in Figure 12.31, alerting you to the fact that you have a local copy of a central file. Revit maintains the link between your local copy and the central file provided you don't move the central file from its location on your network.

Once you're in a worksharing environment, every element added to the file belongs to a workset. Try to keep model elements in a workset other than Shared Levels and Grids, because these worksets may be locked down at some point to avoid accidental movement of key datums. To make sure you're placing elements in the proper workset, check the Worksets toolbar (see Figure 12.32). The workset shown in this box is the workset your elements will be drawn on.

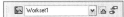

Figure 12.32

Workset field on the toolbar

A helpful toggle in the Worksets toolbar is the Gray Inactive Workset button (⬜). It grays out all elements that aren't in the active workset, helping you identify which elements are in the workset you're working on. This is a temporary view state and doesn't affect print output.

Saving Shared Work

There are two ways to save your work when you're using a workshared file.

Save The Save tool only saves the work you've done on your local copy; the work isn't shared. This is useful when you're in the design phase and trying different designs, and you aren't ready to share your work with others.

Save to Central Next to the Save tool is the Save to Central button (⬛). Use it to commit your work the central file. When you do so, your work appears in the central file and becomes available to the entire team. Saving to central also acquires the changes that others have made and loads them into your model. You can also do this using **File → Save to Central**.

Loading Work from Other Team Members

It's possible to update your model from the central file without committing your changes to central. Think of this process as getting an update of the model. To do so, choose **File → Reload Latest**. Your file gets the latest changes saved from the central file and brings them into your local file.

CHAPTER 13

Troubleshooting and File Maintenance

This chapter is designed to give you some tips and tricks about how to keep your file running quickly and smoothly. Listed here are some pointers to keep you from getting into trouble and some solutions if you do. We'll discuss the following topics:

- Performance
- File corruption

Performance

It should make sense that a small file on a good network runs the quickest. Depending on your hardware configuration, typical file sizes can run a large gambit. File sizes can range from as little as 10MB to 200MB and beyond. Much of that variation depends on how you've modeled your content (level of detail) and the complexity of your model. However, there are a number of things you can do to be proactive about keeping your model performance optimized. Here are a few we recommend:

Workshared files: Make a new local copy Sometimes your local copy can begin to have issues or perform poorly, but others on your team don't have the same problem. If this is the case, we recommend that you make a new local file once a week if you're working in a file that has worksharing activated.

Don't explode imported CAD files A CAD file is a collection of objects, but when you first bring an import into Revit, it's managed as one element. If you explode it, the single object immediately becomes many—and becomes that much more data to track. If you're unfortunate enough to explode a hatch pattern, your one object becomes many thousands. If you're importing CAD files, leave them condensed as much as possible; use the Visibility/Graphic Overrides dialog box to turn layers on and off. Explode *only* when you need to change the imported geometry, and start with a partial explode.

Delete or unload unused imported and linked files Often, you import a DWG as a reference, but then you don't need it later in the process. Users usually forget them, and they can be performance intensive. If you have DWGs or other CAD files in your Revit model and you no longer need them, remove them either by unlinking or deleting. This goes for unused linked or imported images as well.

Figure 13.1

Linking in the current view only

Import/Link DWGs in one view only Importing in all views can seriously affect performance. Figure 13.1 shows the "Link (instead of import)" check box in the "Import or Link" dialog box. Linking is even better than importing if you don't need to edit the geometry.

Watch out for imported geometry Although Revit has the ability to import files from a number of other sources, you should exercise caution when doing so. If you're importing a 60MB NURBS-based Rhino file into your model, expect your Revit model to grow accordingly.

Purge unused elements Revit has a built-in tool that allows you to purge unused families. This is a good way to reduce file size and thereby improve performance. Loaded but unused families can make your file grow quickly. To purge, choose **File → Purge Unused**. If your file is very large, it may take a few minutes to run this command before you see the dialog box shown in Figure 13.2. Here, you can opt to keep or purge families individually.

This is typically *not* a good idea at the beginning of a project, because your template may contain families that you intend to use but haven't as yet (such as wall types).

Manage your views Learn to manage your views. Don't show more than you need to show in a view, either in depth or in your level of detail. Here are a few easy ways to keep your views opening and printing smoothly:

Use the appropriate Detail Level Set your Detail Level (in the View Control bar) relative to the scale you're viewing. For example, if you're working on a ½″ plan, you probably don't need Detail Level set to Fine—it will cause your view performance to suffer needlessly.

Minimize view detail This goes along with the level of detail, but this tip is more user-based than tool-based. If you're printing a ½″ drawing, make sure you're showing the proper level of detail in the view. Even if Detail Level is set to Coarse, do you really need to show balusters in an elevation on your railing at that scale? They will print as a thick, black line. Remember to show the appropriate level of detail for the view.

Figure 13.2

"Purge unused" dialog box

Minimize View Depth View Depth is a great tool to enhance performance. It's especially valuable in section views. By default, Revit draws sections the full depth of the building. A typical wall section is shown in Figure 13.3: The default behavior causes Revit to regenerate all of the model geometry the full depth of that view every time you open the view. To reduce the amount of geometry that needs to be redrawn, drag the section's far clip plane in close to the front clip plane.

Figure 13.3

A typical wall section

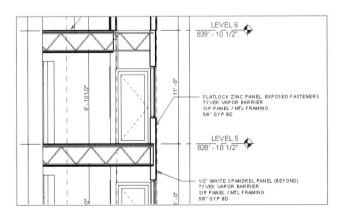

Figure 13.4

Close hidden windows when they aren't in use.

Close unused views Keeping the number of open views to a minimum helps the model's performance. Choose **Window → Close Hidden Windows** often (Figure 13.4), because it's easy to have many views open at once, even if you're concentrating on only a few views. Once you reduce your open views to just two or three, you can take advantage of the view switch toggle: Press Ctrl+Tab, and you'll cycle through your open views.

Open only what you need One of the benefits of having worksets is that you don't have to turn them all on at once. When you open the project, go to the Workset dialog box. There, you can highlight a workset and click the Close button (see Figure 13.5). Doing so drops that workset from active memory and gives you better performance. Remember, if worksets are closed, you can't do anything with them. If a workset isn't visible, it won't print. To print a current copy of the whole model, you'll need to turn the worksets back on.

Calculate volumes only when necessary You can turn on volume calculation by choosing **Settings → Room and Area Settings**. Check the volume only if you need room tags to display volumetric information. Don't forget to switch off this option after you print or view the information. Otherwise, the volumes will recalculate each time you edit something in the model, and this can affect the overall performance of your file dramatically.

Break up your model For larger projects, or campus-style projects, you can break up your model into smaller submodels that are referenced together. You can also do this on a single building. If you decide to divide your project, make your cuts along lines that make sense from a whole building standpoint. Don't cut between floors 2 and 3 on a multistory building unless you have a significant change in building form or program. Here's a list of some good places to split a model:

- At a significant change in building form or massing
- At a significant change in building program
- Between separate buildings on site
- At the building site

Turn off shadows Shadows can help you make beautiful presentations, give a sense of depth in façades, and show the effect of shadows in a site-plan view; however, shadows are performance intense. Make sure you turn them off whenever you don't need them.

Figure 13.5

Closing selected worksets

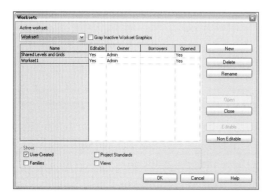

Printing paper, DWFs, or PDFs Printing big Revit files can sometimes take a long time. Enabling raster printing speeds up printing, although there is a trade-off compared to the quality that vector printing offers. Depending on the printer, you may get better line quality by going to a DWF or PDF first. It's best to experiment on a few sheets to see what your printer responds to best before sending your entire set.

Use the 3 GB switch Revit now supports Microsoft's 3GB switch. Windows XP allows any given application access to only 2GB of RAM at a given time; the rest goes to virtual memory. Microsoft's switch (which is available in XP Service Pack 2) allows you to change that 2GB limit to 3GB. To find out how to do this, visit www.autodesk.com/support, choose Revit Building from the menu, and read the support article on enabling the 3GB switch. Of course, you need more than 2GB of RAM in your workstation for this switch to do you any good.

Model just what you need Don't fall into the trap of over-modeling. Just because you can doesn't mean you need to. Be smart about the level of detail you choose to model based on the complexity and size of your project.

Don't over-constrain User-defined relationships are important to embed in the design. However, if you don't need to lock a relationship, don't. Even though the option to lock all alignments is available, it's often not necessary to do so.

Launch Revit without the default template Each time you launch Revit, it opens the default template. This template is often rich with data, and your computer will need a minute or two to open it. However, once a project is under way, the need to open a default template is removed—you most likely just need to open the file you're working on. Instead of opening Revit and then opening your project file, drag the project file over the Revit icon or double-click the file from Windows Explorer. Doing so launches Revit without first opening a template file.

Close Revit with an empty view To avoid long opening times for really large files, establish an office standard that you always close your last view as a drafting or legend view that is totally empty—or that maybe contains only some text with the project name. This way, when Revit opens, it will need much less processing time, because it always opens with the last view from when the project was last saved.

Manage major changes If you are making significant changes to your project by making major geometry changes, do it when there aren't any other users in the file. This will ensure there are no permissions issues constraining the changes and allow you to complete them quickly. Once you've saved your changes back to the central file, have all your other uses make new local copies.

Remove unused Design Options and Area Plans Both of these are excellent features in Revit, but do come at a cost. As Revit will continually keep changes up to date in all of your views, it will also continually recalculate areas and adjustments within design options. Remove unwanted or unused Area Plans and Design Options to keep things running smoother and reduce the number of concurrent calculations.

File Corruption

On the off chance your file becomes corrupted and begins to crash frequently, there are a few things you can do to help fix the problem before you call Revit Support in a panic. To proactively avoid this issue, focus on the tips above before you begin having problems: Otherwise, here are some suggestions on what to do when you begin to have trouble.

Audit the file Auditing the file will review the data structures and correct problems that are found with in the model. An audited file won't look any different when the audit is completed, however, it should (ideally) not crash. This is not a cure-all, by any means, however it can help you get out of a tight spot when necessary.

Get everyone out of any worksets and local files, and have them relinquish their permissions. Open the file using **File → Open**. The resulting Open dialog box lets you browse to a project location. Select your project, select the Audit check box in the lower-right corner (shown in Figure 13.6), and then click OK. Revit will perform an audit on your file (it can take some time). When this process is completed, save the project with a new name or in a new file location; don't save this file over the old Revit file. When you're finished, have everyone make a new local file, and you can get back to work.

Review warnings Each time you make something that Revit considers a problem, a warning is issued. If you ignore warnings, leaving them unresolved, then over time they stack up. Revit provides an interface where you can review all the warnings in the project and fix problems.

Try to read and react to the warning that Revit sends. You don't have to do it when you're under a tight deadline or when doing so will interrupt your work. But once a week, you should spend 30 minutes reviewing the warnings; this can improve your model's overall performance. You can find the list of warnings in your file under **Tools → Review Warnings** (Figure 13.7).

Figure 13.6

Auditing a file

Figure 13.7

Reviewing warnings and errors

Inspirational Revit Projects

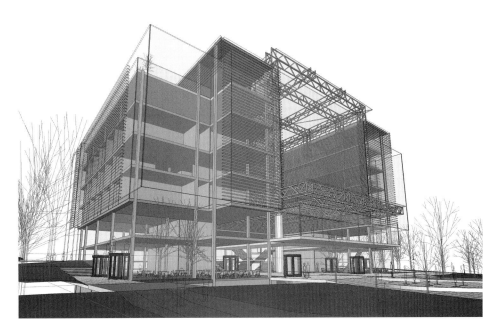

KUBIK AND NEMETH ARCHITECTS

The following projects, submitted to us by top-notch architects from around the world, show Revit's power and capabilities. The examples range from classical reconstructions to modern houses.

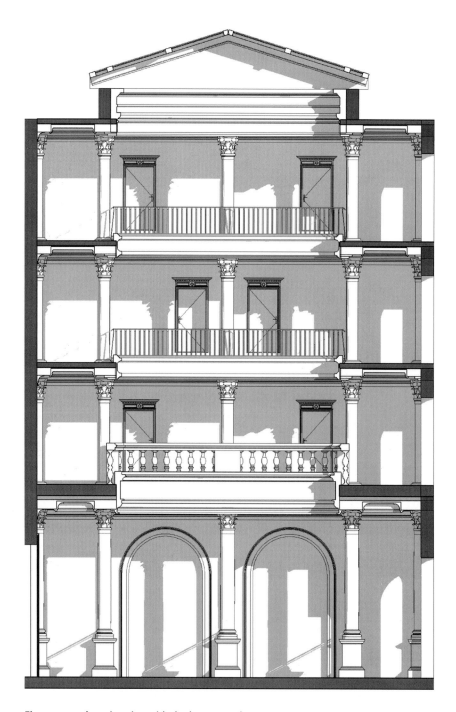

Figure ground: section view with shadows turned on

KUBIK AND NEMETH ARCHITECTS
SLOVAKIA

Formal expression: a dynamic perspective; inspired geometry

ARCHITECT KAMAL MALIK
INDIA

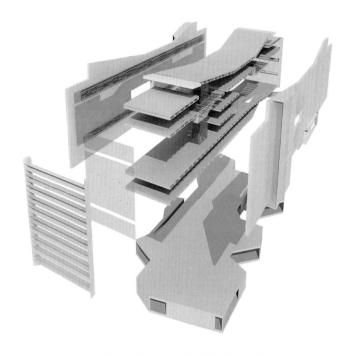

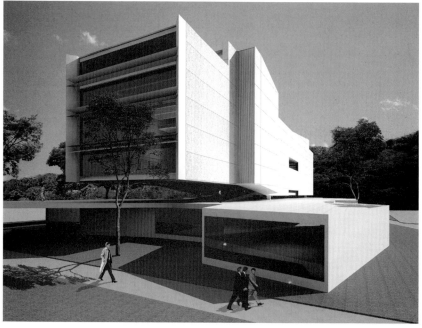

Mixed format: exploded components; photo-realistic expression

SPBR
BRAZIL

Superimposition: perspective view and plan

BNIM ARCHITECTS
USA

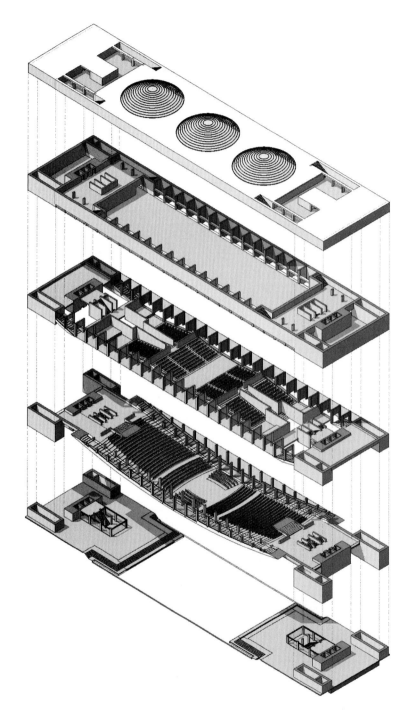

Diagrammatic expression: level-by-level axons showing plans in 3D

A.U.S. Simone Capocchin
Model of unbuilt Louis Kahn project: Congress Palace in Venice

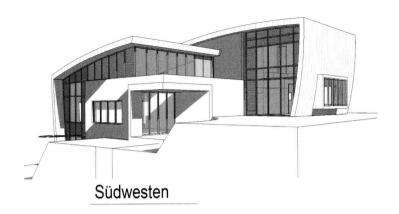

Südwesten

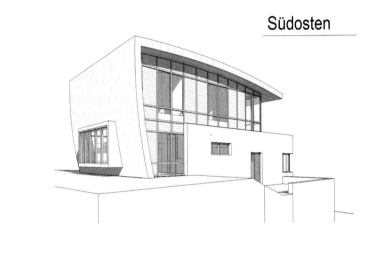

Südosten

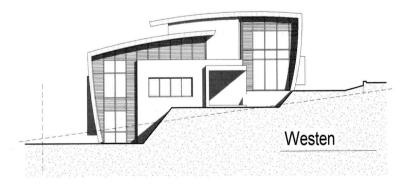

Westen

One model, multiple views: perspectives and elevation with shadows

ARCHITECT MARIO KIRCHMAIR
AUSTRIA

Articulation: perspectives; complex geometry

Simone Capocchin
A Loggia Del Capitaniao di Andrea Palladio

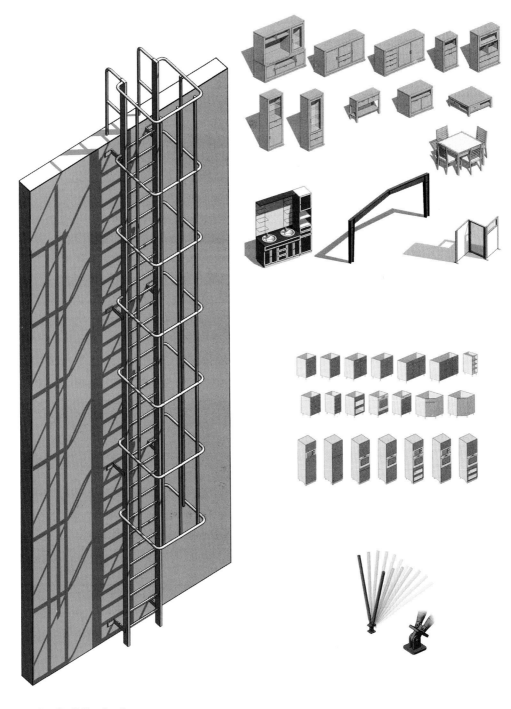

Design flexibility: family components

PHILIPPE DROUANT
FRANCE

Index

Note to the Reader: Throughout this index **boldfaced** page numbers indicate primary discussions of a topic. *Italicized* page numbers indicate illustrations and tables.

Wiley Publishing, Inc., End-User License Agreement

READ THIS. You should carefully read these terms and conditions before opening the software packet(s) included with this book "Book". This is a license agreement "Agreement" between you and Wiley Publishing, Inc. "WPI". By opening the accompanying software packet(s), you acknowledge that you have read and accept the following terms and conditions. If you do not agree and do not want to be bound by such terms and conditions, promptly return the Book and the unopened software packet(s) to the place you obtained them for a full refund.

1. License Grant. WPI grants to you (either an individual or entity) a nonexclusive license to use one copy of the enclosed software program(s) (collectively, the "Software," solely for your own personal or business purposes on a single computer (whether a standard computer or a workstation component of a multi-user network). The Software is in use on a computer when it is loaded into temporary memory (RAM) or installed into permanent memory (hard disk, CD-ROM, or other storage device). WPI reserves all rights not expressly granted herein.

2. Ownership. WPI is the owner of all right, title, and interest, including copyright, in and to the compilation of the Software recorded on the disk(s), CD-ROM or DVD "Software Media". Copyright to the individual programs recorded on the Software Media is owned by the author or other authorized copyright owner of each program. Ownership of the Software and all proprietary rights relating thereto remain with WPI and its licensers.

3. Restrictions On Use and Transfer. (a)You may only (i) make one copy of the Software for backup or archival purposes, or (ii) transfer the Software to a single hard disk, provided that you keep the original for backup or archival purposes. You may not (i) rent or lease the Software, (ii) copy or reproduce the Software through a LAN or other network system or through any computer subscriber system or bulletin-board system, or (iii) modify, adapt, or create derivative works based on the Software. (b) You may not reverse engineer, decompile, or disassemble the Software. You may transfer the Software and user documentation on a permanent basis, provided that the transferee agrees to accept the terms and conditions of this Agreement and you retain no copies. If the Software is an update or has been updated, any transfer must include the most recent update and all prior versions.

4. Restrictions on Use of Individual Programs. You must follow the individual requirements and restrictions detailed for each individual program in the About the CD-ROM appendix of this Book. These limitations are also contained in the individual license agreements recorded on the Software Media. These limitations may include a requirement that after using the program for a specified period of time, the user must pay a registration fee or discontinue use. By opening the Software packet(s), you will be agreeing to abide by the licenses and restrictions for these individual programs that are detailed in the About the CD-ROM appendix and on the Software Media. None of the material on this Software Media or listed in this Book may ever be redistributed, in original or modified form, for commercial purposes.

5. Limited Warranty. (a) WPI warrants that the Software and Software Media are free from defects in materials and workmanship under normal use for a period of sixty (60) days from the date of purchase of this Book. If WPI receives notification within the warranty period of defects in materials or workmanship, WPI will replace the defective Software Media. (b) WPI AND THE AUTHOR(S) OF THE BOOK DISCLAIM ALL OTHER WARRANTIES, EXPRESS OR IMPLIED, INCLUDING WITHOUT LIMITATION IMPLIED WARRANTIES OF MERCHANTABILITY AND FITNESS FOR A PARTICULAR PURPOSE, WITH RESPECT TO THE SOFTWARE, THE PROGRAMS, THE SOURCE CODE CONTAINED THEREIN, AND/OR THE TECHNIQUES DESCRIBED IN THIS BOOK. WPI DOES NOT WARRANT THAT THE FUNCTIONS CONTAINED IN THE SOFTWARE WILL MEET YOUR REQUIREMENTS OR THAT THE OPERATION OF THE SOFTWARE WILL BE ERROR FREE. (c) This limited warranty gives you specific legal rights, and you may have other rights that vary from jurisdiction to jurisdiction.

6. Remedies. (a) WPI's entire liability and your exclusive remedy for defects in materials and workmanship shall be limited to replacement of the Software Media, which may be returned to WPI with a copy of your receipt at the following address: Software Media Fulfillment Department, Attn.: Introducing Revit Achitecture 2008, Wiley Publishing, Inc., 10475 Crosspoint Blvd., Indianapolis, IN 46256, or call 1-800-762-2974. Please allow four to six weeks for delivery. This Limited Warranty is void if failure of the Software Media has resulted from accident, abuse, or misapplication. Any replacement Software Media will be warranted for the remainder of the original warranty period or thirty (30) days, whichever is longer. (b) In no event shall WPI or the author be liable for any damages whatsoever (including without limitation damages for loss of business profits, business interruption, loss of business information, or any other pecuniary loss) arising from the use of or inability to use the Book or the Software, even if WPI has been advised of the possibility of such damages. (c) Because some jurisdictions do not allow the exclusion or limitation of liability for consequential or incidental damages, the above limitation or exclusion may not apply to you.

7. U.S. Government Restricted Rights. Use, duplication, or disclosure of the Software for or on behalf of the United States of America, its agencies and/or instrumentalities "U.S. Government" is subject to restrictions as stated in paragraph (c)(1)(ii) of the Rights in Technical Data and Computer Software clause of DFARS 252.227-7013, or subparagraphs (c) (1) and (2) of the Commercial Computer Software - Restricted Rights clause at FAR 52.227-19, and in similar clauses in the NASA FAR supplement, as applicable.

8. General. This Agreement constitutes the entire understanding of the parties and revokes and supersedes all prior agreements, oral or written, between them and may not be modified or amended except in a writing signed by both parties hereto that specifically refers to this Agreement. This Agreement shall take precedence over any other documents that may be in conflict herewith. If any one or more provisions contained in this Agreement are held by any court or tribunal to be invalid, illegal, or otherwise unenforceable, each and every other provision shall remain in full force and effect.